The following guides by Dawn Apgar are available from Springer Publishing to assist social workers with studying for and passing the ASWB® examinations necessary for licensure.

Bachelors

The Social Work ASWB® Bachelors Exam Guide: A Comprehensive Guide for Success, Second Edition

Test focuses on knowledge acquired while obtaining a Baccalaureate degree in Social Work (BSW). A small number of jurisdictions license social workers at an Associate level and require the ASWB Associate examination. The Associate examination is identical to the ASWB Bachelors examination, but the Associate examination requires a lower score in order to pass.

Masters

The Social Work ASWB® Masters Exam Guide: A Comprehensive Guide for Success, Second Edition

Test focuses on knowledge acquired while obtaining a Master's degree in Social Work (MSW). There is no postgraduate supervision needed.

Clinical

The Social Work ASWB® Clinical Exam Guide: A Comprehensive Guide for Success, Second Edition

Test focuses on knowledge acquired while obtaining a Master's degree in Social Work (MSW). It is usually taken by those with postgraduate supervised experience.

Advanced Generalist

The Social Work ASWB® Advanced Generalist Exam Guide: A Comprehensive Guide for Success, Second Edition

Test focuses on knowledge acquired while obtaining a Master's degree in Social Work (MSW). It is usually taken by those with postgraduate supervised nonclinical experience.

Dawn Apgar, PhD, LSW, ACSW, has helped thousands of social workers across the country pass the ASWB® examinations associated with all levels of licensure. In recent years, she has consulted in numerous states to assist with establishing licensure test preparation programs.

Dr. Apgar has done research on licensure funded by the American Foundation for Research and Consumer Education in Social Work Regulation and has served as chairperson of her state's social work licensing board. She is a past President of the New Jersey Chapter of NASW and has been on its National Board of Directors. In 2014, the Chapter presented her with a Lifetime Achievement Award. Dr. Apgar has taught in both undergraduate and graduate social work programs and has extensive direct practice, policy, and management experience in the social work field.

Social Work ASWB® Bachelors Exam Guide

A Comprehensive Study Guide for Success

Second Edition

Dawn Apgar, PhD, LSW, ACSW

SPRINGER PUBLISHING COMPANY

Springer Publishing Company, LLC

11 West 42nd Street
New York, NY 10036
www.springerpub.com

Acquisitions Editor: Debra Riegert
Compositor: diacriTech, Chennai

ISBN: 978-0-8261-4715-8
ebook ISBN: 978-0-8261-4716-5

18 19 20 21 22 / 5 4 3 2

The author and the publisher of this Work have made every effort to use sources believed to be reliable to provide information that is accurate and compatible with the standards generally accepted at the time of publication. The author and publisher shall not be liable for any special, consequential, or exemplary damages resulting, in whole or in part, from the readers' use of, or reliance on, the information contained in this book. The publisher has no responsibility for the persistence or accuracy of URLs for external or third-party Internet websites referred to in this publication and does not guarantee that any content on such websites is, or will remain, accurate or appropriate.

Library of Congress Cataloging-in-Publication Data
Names: Apgar, Dawn, author. | Association of Social Work Boards.
Title: Social work ASWB bachelors exam guide : a comprehensive study guide
    for success / Dawn Apgar, PhD, LSW, ACSW.
Description: Second edition. | New York, NY : Springer Publishing Company,
    LLC, [2018] | Includes index.
Identifiers: LCCN 2017044812 | ISBN 9780826147158 | ISBN 9780826147165 (ebook)
Subjects: LCSH: Social workers—Certification—United States. | Social
    service—United States—Examinations—Study guides. | Social
    service—United States—Examinations, questions, etc.
Classification: LCC HV40.52 .A735 2018 | DDC 361.3076—dc23 LC record available at
https://lccn.loc.gov/2017044812

Contact us to receive discount rates on bulk purchases.
We can also customize our books to meet your needs.
For more information please contact: sales@springerpub.com

Printed in the United States of America by Gasch Printing.

To Bill, Ryan, and Alex

You remind me what is important, support me so I can do it all, and always inspire me to be a better person

Contents

Unit IV: Professional Relationships, Values, and Ethics (20%)

Preface

Congratulations on getting to this point in your social work career. The decision to become licensed is significant, and passing the licensing examination demonstrates that you have the basic knowledge necessary to safely practice. Social workers are employed in all kinds of settings including hospitals, correctional facilities, mental health and addictions agencies, government offices, and private practices. It is essential that those served have some assurance that these practitioners are competent to provide the services that they are charged with delivering.

Regulation through certification and licensure helps to assure that social workers will interact in an ethical and safe manner, and there is oversight to address actions that are not consistent with this standard.

Passing the licensing exam is only one step in becoming certified or licensed, but it is usually the most difficult challenge faced after graduating with your degree.

This guide aims to assist in helping you through this process in several important ways. It will:

1. Increase your knowledge of the Association of Social Work Boards (ASWB®) examination, **including the new blueprints used for all tests taken on or after January 2, 2018**

2. Provide valuable test-taking strategies that will assist in developing a good study plan and in analyzing question wording in order to select the correct answer

3. Summarize content areas that may be included on the examination as per the Knowledge, Skills, and Abilities (KSA) statements published by ASWB, which are used by test developers to formulate actual questions

4. Supply sample questions that can be used to simulate an actual examination experience

Although there are other test preparation materials produced, this guide provides all these essential elements in a single, manageable, easy-to-use guide.

Individuals who are studying for the social work licensing examination have a primary concern and request. They are worried that they do not know important information about the tests that will prove to be a barrier to passing, and they want a "place" to go that will have all the necessary materials in a single location. They want to focus their efforts on studying for the exam—not hunting around for what needs to be studied!

This guide was created based on this important information, and it has been gathered from thousands of social workers just like you. Although it is not produced by or affiliated with ASWB in any way, and does not guarantee a passing score on the examinations, the test-taking techniques have been developed and used successfully by others who were faced with the same challenge that you are—others who are now certified and licensed social workers! They found this information so helpful in passing because the skills that it takes to be a good social worker in practice can be very different than the skills that it takes to pass the examination.

Best wishes as you study for the examination. And remember that there is never only one way to achieve a goal, so use this guide in a way that works for you as you prepare. In choosing this guide as your roadmap, you have taken an important first step on the journey of passing the examination for certification and licensure.

New in the Second Edition

The new edition of this popular guide reflects the new blueprint for the ASWB Bachelors examination for those taking the exam on or after January 2, 2018. Revisions include new and enhanced material on the Knowledge Skills and Abilities (KSAs) statements added by ASWB in the four content areas and incorporates the information from the *Diagnostic and Statistical Manual of Mental Disorders* (5th ed., *DSM-5*), which was added to the exam in July 2015. Lastly, this new edition links questions in the practice examination to material being tested within the four content areas, making it possible to diagnose areas which require further study.

Many new knowledge areas which have been incorporated into the revised blueprint are found in this new edition including those listed as follows.

Unit I: Human Development, Diversity, and Behavior in the Environment

1. HUMAN GROWTH AND DEVELOPMENT
- Theories of human development throughout the lifespan (e.g., physical, social, emotional, cognitive, behavioral)—new material on Kohlberg's stages of moral development
- The effect of aging on biopsychosocial functioning
- Personality theories
- Theories of conflict
- Factors influencing self-image (e.g., culture, race, religion/spirituality, age, disability, trauma)
- Body image and its impact (e.g., identity, self-esteem, relationships, habits)
- Parenting skills and capacities

2. HUMAN BEHAVIOR IN THE SOCIAL ENVIRONMENT
- The family life cycle
- Family dynamics and functioning and the effects on individuals, families, groups, organizations, and communities

- Theories of couples development
- The impact of physical and mental illness on family dynamics—new material on effects of mental illness
- Role theories
- Models of family life education in social work practice

3. DIVERSITY, SOCIAL/ECONOMIC JUSTICE, AND OPPRESSION
   - Feminist theory
   - The effect of disability on biopsychosocial functioning throughout the lifespan
   - The influence of sexual orientation on behaviors, attitudes, and identity
   - The impact of transgender and transitioning process on behaviors, attitudes, identity, and relationships
   - Systemic (institutionalized) discrimination (e.g., racism, sexism, ageism)
   - The principles of culturally competent social work practice
   - Sexual orientation concepts
   - Gender and gender identity concepts—new material in gender identity
   - The impact of social institutions on society
   - The effect of poverty on individuals, families, groups, organizations, and communities—new material on wealth distribution
   - Person-in-environment (PIE) theory
   - Social and economic justice
   - Criminal justice systems

Unit II: Assessment

4. BIOPSYCHOSOCIAL HISTORY AND COLLATERAL DATA
   - The components and function of the mental status examination
   - Biopsychosocial responses to illness and disability
   - Biopsychosocial factors related to mental health
   - The indicators of psychosocial stress
   - The indicators of mental and emotional illness throughout the lifespan—new material on assessment

5. ASSESSMENT METHODS AND TECHNIQUES
   - Methods to incorporate the results of psychological and educational tests into assessment
   - Communication theories and styles—new material on communication theory and key terms
   - The concept of congruence in communication
   - Risk assessment methods
   - Methods to assess the client's/client system's strengths, resources, and challenges (e.g., individual, family, group, organization, community)—new material on individual assets and methods to identify them

- Methods to assess the client's/client system's coping abilities
- The indicators of the client's/client system's strengths and challenges—new material on methods to assess ego strength
- Methods used to assess trauma
- The indicators of addiction and substance abuse
- The Diagnostic and Statistical Manual of the American Psychiatric Association—new material listing types of disorders
- The indicators of somatization
- The indicators of feigning illness
- Common psychotropic and non-psychotropic prescriptions and over-the-counter medications and their side effects—new material on psychotropic medications and additional commonly prescribed drugs

6. CONCEPTS OF ABUSE AND NEGLECT

- The effects of physical, sexual, and psychological abuse on individuals, families, groups, organizations, and communities
- The characteristics of perpetrators of abuse, neglect, and exploitation

Unit III: Interventions With Clients/Client Systems

7. INDICATORS AND EFFECTS OF CRISIS AND CHANGE

- The impact of out-of-home placement (e.g., hospitalization, foster care, residential care, criminal justice system) on clients/client systems
- Theories of trauma-informed care
- Crisis intervention theories
- The indicators of traumatic stress and violence
- The impact of out-of-home displacement (e.g., natural disaster, homelessness, immigration) on clients/client systems
- Methods and approaches to trauma-informed care

8. INTERVENTION PROCESSES AND TECHNIQUES

- The components of intervention, treatment, and service plans
- Psychotherapies
- The impact of immigration, refugee, or undocumented status on service delivery
- The phases of intervention and treatment
- The principles and techniques for building and maintaining a helping relationship—new material on the process of engagement in social work practice
- Problem-solving models and approaches (e.g., brief, solution-focused methods or techniques)—new material on short-term interventions
- Methods to engage and motivate clients/client systems
- Methods to obtain and provide feedback
- Limit setting techniques
- Techniques for harm reduction for self and others
- Client/client system self-monitoring techniques
- Methods to develop, review, and implement crisis plans

- Cognitive and behavioral interventions—additional material on cognitive restructuring
- Client/client system contracting and goal-setting techniques
- Partializing techniques
- Task-centered approaches
- Group work techniques and approaches (e.g., developing and managing group processes and cohesion)—additional material on group work and types of groups
- Family therapy models, interventions, and approaches—new material on family therapy in general, strategic family therapy, structural family therapy, and Bowenian family therapy
- Mindfulness and complementary therapeutic approaches
- Techniques used for follow-up
- The elements of a case presentation
- Methods of service delivery
- Theories and methods of advocacy for policies, services, and resources to meet clients'/client systems' needs
- Community organizing and social planning methods
- Techniques used to evaluate a client's/client system's progress
- Primary, secondary, and tertiary prevention strategies
- Methods to create, implement, and evaluate policies and procedures that minimize risk for individuals, families, groups, organizations, and communities
- The indicators of client/client system readiness for termination
- Evidence-based practice—new material on its use and selection of interventions

9. USE OF COLLABORATIVE RELATIONSHIPS

- The basic terminology of professions other than social work (e.g., legal, educational)—new material on case consultation
- The effect of the client's developmental level on the social worker–client relationship
- Methods to clarify the roles and responsibilities of the social worker and client/client system in the intervention process
- Methods of networking
- Methods to assess the availability of community resources—new material on clients' use of services
- Methods to establish service networks or community resources
- The relationship between formal and informal power structures in the decision-making process

10. DOCUMENTATION

- The principles and processes for developing formal documents (e.g., proposals, letters, brochures, pamphlets, reports, evaluations)
- The principles and features of objective and subjective data—new material on use throughout the problem-solving process

Unit IV: Professional Relationships, Values, and Ethics

11. PROFESSIONAL VALUES AND ETHICAL ISSUES

- Legal and/or ethical issues related to the practice of social work, including responsibility to clients/client systems, colleagues, the profession, and society
- Professional values and principles (e.g., competence, social justice, integrity, dignity and worth of the person)—new material added
- The dynamics of diversity in the social worker–client/client system relationship
- The dynamics of power and transparency in the social worker–client/ client system relationship
- Legal and/or ethical issues regarding mandatory reporting (e.g., abuse, threat of harm, impaired professionals, etc.)—new material on professional impairment
- Legal and/or ethical issues regarding documentation
- Legal and/or ethical issues regarding termination
- Legal and/or ethical issues related to death and dying
- Research ethics (e.g., institutional review boards, use of human subjects, informed consent)
- Ethical issues in supervision and management
- Methods to create, implement, and evaluate policies and procedures for social worker safety

12. CONFIDENTIALITY

- The principles and processes of obtaining informed consent
- The use of client/client system records
- Legal and/or ethical issues regarding confidentiality, including electronic information security

13. PROFESSIONAL DEVELOPMENT AND USE OF SELF

- Methods to create, implement, and evaluate policies and procedures for social worker safety
- The social worker's role in the problem-solving process
- Social worker self-care principles and techniques
- The components of a safe and positive work environment
- The influence of the social worker's own values and beliefs on interdisciplinary collaboration
- Governance structures
- Accreditation and/or licensing requirements
- Time management approaches
- Models of supervision and consultation (e.g., individual, peer, group)
- Professional development activities to improve practice and maintain current professional knowledge (e.g., in-service training, licensing requirements, reviews of literature, workshops)—new material on stages of professional development

Introduction

About the Examination

Generally, when social workers are getting ready to take the Association of Social Work Boards (ASWB®) tests, they are anxious not only about knowing the content, but also about the examinations themselves. They have many questions about the number of questions that will be asked and the number of correct answers required to pass. Becoming familiar with the examination basics will assist in making you more comfortable with the examination conditions and structure, thereby reducing your anxiety about the unknown.

In order to ensure that the examinations are based on necessary knowledge and skills, ASWB conducts a practice analysis every 5 to 7 years. The first analysis was completed in 1981 and the most current collected data between 2015 and 2016 to construct the blueprint for all examinations taken after January 2, 2018. The structure of this guide and the material contained in it are based on this new blueprint.

10 THINGS THAT YOU SHOULD KNOW ABOUT THE ASWB EXAMINATIONS

1. All of the ASWB examinations have the same format, meaning that each has the same number of questions that each test-taker is given the same amount of time to complete. There are **170 multiple-choice questions** and you will have **4 hours** from the time that you start answering the questions. You can take a brief restroom break or stand to stretch, but the clock does not stop and these activities will be included in your 4-hour limit, so you want to be judicious with your time.

2. Although you will be answering a total of 170 questions, **20 of these questions are nonscored items** that are being piloted for possible inclusion as scored questions on future ASWB examinations. Thus, only 150 questions will determine whether you pass or not. However, you will never know which 20 are pilot items because they are mixed in with scored items, so you will need to try to select the right answers on all 170 questions.

3. You **do not want to leave any questions blank**; answer all 170 questions in the 4 hours.

4. The examination is **computerized**, but requires no specialized computer knowledge. There is a brief computer tutorial that will assist you when you first sit down and look at the screen, and spending time getting to feel comfortable with the device at that time is a good idea, since it will not count toward your 4-hour time limit.

5. You will be taking your examination at a **testing center with others who are being tested in different disciplines** and may be taking shorter or longer examinations, so do not be concerned if they finish before or after you.

6. Testing center activities are **closely monitored**, and you will need to leave all of your belongings, including your watch, in a provided locker. You can ask for earplugs, scrap paper, or a pencil, but will not be able to bring anything into the room with you. The room may be hot or cold, so you should dress in comfortable layers. All testing accommodations related to documented disabilities must be approved by your state licensing board and arranged in advance with ASWB. Some states allow for extra time or foreign language dictionaries as accommodations for those who do not have English as a first language.

7. You will leave the testing center with an unofficial copy of your examination results. It will tell you how many questions you were asked and how many you got correct in each of the four areas or domains. You will never know which specific answers were correct and incorrect. You will also not find out the correct answers for those that you answered incorrectly. **The exam is pass/fail**, and a passing score can be used for certification or licensure in any state.

8. Although the Knowledge, Skills, and Abilities (KSAs) are in four content areas and you may structure your studying to learn all the related material in a given domain before moving on to the next, **the questions on the examination are in random order** and skip across topics. There is not a separate section of questions labeled Human Development, Diversity, and Behavior in the Environment, or so on. You may have a human behavior question followed by one on ethics, so you really need to clear your head between

questions and avoid trying to relate them to one another in any way. Each question stands alone as a way to assess knowledge related to a distinct KSA.

9. Social workers always want to know how many questions of the 150 scored items they will need to answer correctly to pass the exam. Although this sounds like an easy question, it is not! Not all questions on the ASWB examinations are the same level of difficulty as determined by the pilot process, so individuals who were randomly assigned harder versions of the exams will need to answer fewer questions correctly than those who were lucky enough to have easier questions. This method ensures that the examination is fair for all those who are taking it, regardless of which questions were chosen. **The number of questions that you have to get correct generally varies from 93 to 106 of the 150 scored items**. You will find out how many needed to be answered correctly only after you are finished with your examination and it is immediately scored electronically. When you examine your unofficial test results, which are provided in a printout prior to leaving the testing center, you will be able to gauge the difficulty of your examination. If you needed to get closer to 93 correct, you had harder questions, and if you needed to get 106 or above correct, you had easier ones.

10. **If you do not pass the examination, you will not have the same questions repeated on any of your examinations in the future**. Other questions in the four areas will be selected. As the four domains are so broad, you may find that the topics of the questions may be quite different than those on a previous examination. To be adequately prepared, it is best to go back and study all the KSAs listed for a content area and not just those that may have caused you problems. If you do not pass, you will have to wait 90 days before taking the examination again.

If you have questions about the examination or scoring, such as the process for sending your passing exam score to another state in which you want to be licensed, visit the ASWB website at www.aswb.org for additional information and necessary forms. The *ASWB Examination Candidate Handbook*, which is free and located on this website, provides additional information about registering for the examination that may be useful.

Test-Taking Strategies and Tips

Social workers studying for the ASWB examinations always want to know techniques that will assist them in studying wisely and answering questions correctly. Remember that there are no replacements for good old-fashioned work, and test-taking strategies are not enough on their own to eliminate all of the incorrect answers. Usually, applying test-taking strategies can help you dismiss two of four possible multiple-choice responses and it is your knowledge of the content area that will be needed to select the correct answer from the two that are remaining. Thus, you will need to make sure that you are well versed in the examination content in order to pass the examination.

However, there are two types of strategies that may assist. The first concerns things to remember when developing your study plan. These are important pieces of information that may help when you are trying to decide what to learn and how to learn it. The second includes those tips that can assist you when actually answering the questions. These tips are important to remember after you have learned all the needed content and are tasked with applying it in the proper way to select the correct answer.

As both of these strategy types are keys to success on the examinations, they are outlined here.

10 ESSENTIAL STRATEGIES FOR STUDY SUCCESS

Strategy 1

This is an examination to assess knowledge of social work content, so you will need to make sure that you can describe an overview of the key concepts and terms related to each of the KSAs. You will know if you are ready to take the examinations when you are able to briefly explain these areas to someone who does not have any prior knowledge of them. The difference between passing and not passing the examinations almost always is a result of gaps in knowledge, not application of test-taking strategies, so you need to make sure that the bulk of your studying is aimed at filling in knowledge gaps or refreshing information already learned.

Strategy 2

You will never be "ready" to take the ASWB examination. Not unlike other standardized examinations, such as the Scholastic Aptitude Test (SAT) or Graduate Record Examination (GRE), you cannot judge readiness as knowing everything about the content areas. The ASWB examinations are not designed for test takers to "know it all" in order to pass. Often, picking a test date is the hardest task; as with the SAT or GRE, a deadline for admission to college or graduate school forces individuals to select a date even when they do not feel ready. For the ASWB examination, you will need to select a date in the next few weeks or months, perhaps dictated by job opportunities or promotions predicated on being licensed. You will walk into the examination without feeling totally ready, but this is typical of others who have passed.

Strategy 3

You need to limit your study materials to this guide or other key resources that summarize material. This is not the time to go back and read your textbooks! There are so many topics that you are asked to know about under each KSA that you cannot and are not expected to know everything related to the topic. This guide is geared to provide important information on these areas "under one roof." It will be hard enough to read through all this material. You should only use outside materials if something in this guide is unclear or you feel that you need more than the information included, perhaps because you never learned this area in the first place. In these instances, you can use free resources on the Internet or any other documents that have no more than a paragraph summarizing key points. Remember, you do not need to read a book on Freud to understand his work and its importance in explaining human development.

Strategy 4

Although individuals like to study from sample questions, this is not advisable. There are many reasons why using this technique will hurt you on the examinations, but here are just a few:

1. Although it makes individuals feel better when they get an answer correct on a sample test, getting an answer correct is not a valid

indicator of really knowing the content in the KSA for which the question was developed. Studying from the KSAs and the topics within them will ensure that you are able to answer any question, not just the one that is in a sample test.

2. Your answers to sample questions inappropriately influence your decisions on the actual examinations when asked about similar topics. For example, you may see an answer that is similar to one that was correct or incorrect in a practice test and you will be more apt or less apt to select it based upon this prior experience. However, the question in the "real" examination will not be exactly the same as the one on the practice test, and you must evaluate all four answers independently without any undue bias that may be caused by your practice question experience.

3. The sample questions that you study are not going to be on your examination and probably are not even written by those who developed items for your test. Thus, the idea that many social workers have of wanting to "get into the head" of the individuals writing the exam or understand their logic is not valid—though it might make them good clinicians in real life!

Strategy 5

If you have access to sample questions, such as those in the last section of this guide, you should use them to create a "mock" examination. Most people have trouble resisting the urge to look at the answer key to see if they were correct immediately after selecting a response. However, a far better way to use these questions is to pretend that they are an actual examination.

1. After you are done studying the content and think you are ready to take the ASWB examination, select a 4-hour period where you can create a quiet environment without interruptions.

2. Answer the questions as you would on the actual examination— using the strategies and having to pick one answer—even if you are not completely sure that it is correct.

3. If you do not take unnecessary breaks, you will see that you can easily get through 170 questions in the 4 hours allotted. This experience should relieve some of your anxiety about the timed nature of the examination.

4. See which answers you got correct and incorrect. The "mock" examination is not to be used to determine whether you are ready to take the actual test—even if getting 93 to 106 puts you in the range of having the knowledge to pass the actual examination. Instead, it gives you some idea of the length of the examination and how long you will need to focus, while giving you the confidence that you can get most of the answers correct within the time period allotted.

Strategy 6

It probably has been a long time since you had to sit for a 4-hour examination—if ever! Our lives are hectic, and we rarely get a chance to really focus on a single task or have the luxury of thinking about a single topic in a way that allows us to really understand it. Thus, many people find it helpful to study in 4-hour blocks of time rather than for a few minutes here and there. This may be difficult, but it will be beneficial because it will get you prepared to not lose your concentration or focus during such a long period. Remember, runners do not start with marathons, they need to build their strength and endurance over time before they can tackle 26.2 miles. Your preparation is similar: You do not want the first time that you have to sit and engage in critical thinking to be your actual examination.

Strategy 7

There is always a time lag between the generation of new social work content and when it appears on the ASWB examinations. It takes time to write and pretest questions on new material. For example, when the Health Insurance Portability and Accountability Act (HIPAA) of 1996 was passed, there were several years before questions related to this law were asked. Although the *Diagnostic and Statistical Manual of Mental Disorders* (*DSM-5*) was published in 2013, ASWB announced that it would not be included on examinations until July 2015. This lag is good and bad. The good news is that you do not have to know the "latest and greatest" in all content areas. It is hard to keep completely up to date in a profession that is changing so rapidly. Now for the bad news! For many, especially if they are working in a particular specialty area, some of the content or answers may appear to be dated. This is often the case in the area of psychopharmacology, because new medications are being approved and used rapidly. Remember the time lapse in your studying, and do not rely on breaking news or even practices in your own agency as information sources.

Strategy 8

As you think about what is important to learn or remember when you are reviewing this guide, you should recognize that social workers who have attended social work programs at different schools, as well as courses within a program taught by various instructors, have passed the examinations. Thus, although there is always information to add to a KSA related to experience or depth of knowledge, there are "core" elements included in any overview or lecture on the topic, regardless of school or professor. These elements are the ones that have to be learned and remembered because they are the basis of the knowledge being tested. In addition, there are also "core" or essential areas that contain information that is seen as critical to competent practice. Can you imagine a social worker leaving an undergraduate or graduate program without reviewing the signs of child abuse and neglect and his or her duty as a mandatory reporter? Of course not! This is a "core" topic that often is the basis of examination questions. The list of these areas is not fixed, but includes confidentiality, assessment of danger to self and others, cultural competence, and so on. You should ask yourself when studying, "Is this something that every social worker needs to know, regardless of setting or specialization?" If so, it may be essential to include it in your review of a topic because it is likely to be included on the examination.

Strategy 9

When studying, it is not necessary to memorize the content because you will not have to recall a term or definition from memory. The ASWB examinations are not tests geared to test your memory. Instead, they require you to be able to pick the one of several answers that most directly relates to the topic or is the best based on your knowledge of the content area. Thus, it is much more important that you understand each of the KSAs and are not focused on memorizing fancy terms or facts. If you stumble when asked a question about something that you are saying about a KSA, or cannot go off script when discussing these areas, you may be just memorizing the material instead of really understanding it.

Strategy 10

Often, social workers are focused on using the clinical and other jargon that they learned in their Bachelor of Social Work (BSW) programs; however, they may be unable to explain what these concepts mean in plain and understandable terms. For example, when asked what should happen when meeting with a client for the first time, social workers often use phrases such as "You need to build rapport," "It is essential that you start where a client is," or "Social workers should show empathy as to what a client is going through." Though all true, these statements give little insight into any real actions that a social worker should take in this first meeting. What should a social worker do to "build rapport"? How would a client know if a social worker was being "empathetic"? What would a social worker be doing or saying? Having to explain the KSAs to someone who knows little about social work practice and will ask you lots of questions about the content area can be a far better strategy than studying with a social work colleague who will not challenge you when you use jargon or technical terms without having to explain the basics.

20 TIPS YOU NEED TO USE TO ANSWER QUESTIONS CORRECTLY

Tip 1

This is an examination of your knowledge of social work content. Often, what we learn in the classroom and how we might act in practice based upon practice wisdom and clinical judgments are different. **When selecting an answer, you should base it upon the content that you studied from this guide and what you learned in the classroom.** Each question is written to make sure that you know requisite information about the KSAs. Thus, ask yourself— "What did I study in the guide that relates to this question?" or "Which KSA is being tested and what do I know about this content area?" If you are inappropriately asking, "What would I do in this case vignette?" or "How should I handle this situation?" you will be drawing upon your practice experience rather than the existing knowledge in a domain that is the basis for selecting the correct answer.

Remember, there is only one correct answer for each question. Since everyone has different practice experience, basing your answers on what you see or do in the field may lead you to a different response than someone else taking the examination. However, the textbook or existing body of knowledge on the KSAs is universal, regardless of setting or practice experience. Basing your responses on the information that is taught in the classroom and in social work textbooks, as outlined in this guide, will ensure that you get to the same correct response as others.

Tip 2

You may have a negative opinion about the need to take a standardized 4-hour examination after having successfully graduated from your social work program and even gotten the requisite clinical experience. However, it is a requirement for licensure and seen as a way of determining whether social workers possess the knowledge needed to practice safely. Just as the SAT and GRE are viewed as ways of determining the ability to perform in college or graduate school, the ASWB examinations are seen as indicators of proper social work preparation to successfully practice at various levels. You probably know individuals who have done well on the SAT and GRE and did not do well in postsecondary education and vice versa.

The use of standardized tests in social work and other life areas "is what it is" and **it will hurt your performance if you "fight" the use of such examinations**—in other words, do not approach the test with negative attitudes and resentment about having to take it.

It is important to approach the examination with a positive attitude and realize that your performance on this examination will not define your social work career. Passing it should not be viewed as an end in itself, but rather a step in the licensure process—just as the SAT is a step in the college acceptance process. Being resentful about the use of standardized testing as an indicator of competence or future performance will only get in your way.

Tip 3

Although there may be some questions that require you to simply "recall" content in a content area, many of them will be focused on you "applying" information to a particular situation or scenario. These questions come in the form of case vignettes and are often the ones in which social workers make mistakes. In practice, social workers often alter their actions based on many contextual variables. However, remember that the questions on the examination are about the application of social work knowledge within the KSAs, and this knowledge does not change regardless of the setting in the vignette. **You should not get "lost" in the scenario**. For example, the core components of a discharge plan are the same if it is prepared for a client leaving the hospital, a drug treatment facility, or an inpatient psychiatric treatment setting. The content within the components (i.e., history/assessment, treatment provided, follow-up needed) may be different, but each discharge plan has to contain information in these critical areas.

Thus, you need to stay focused on the content being tested and remember that it is not necessary to have worked in all the settings mentioned in the vignettes (schools, hospitals, drug treatment centers, nursing homes, etc.) to pass the examination; the KSAs or core social work content being tested is universal, regardless of venue.

Tip 4

The ASWB examination that you are taking is used for licensure in virtually every state. The correct answer to a question is the same for all social workers taking the examination. However, the systems of care and laws in each state differ; thus, responses to situations may be varied in real-life, everyday work. This is not the case on the examination, as **there is only one correct answer to each question**. Thus, if you are thinking about "rules" or laws that apply in your state, or resources that may be available, you are likely to get yourself in trouble on the examination because these vary between states and cannot influence your answer selection.

A simple way to avoid unconsciously using state-specific information when answering questions is to think of a state that you envision is very different than your own and ask yourself, "What answer would a social worker living in [insert name of state here] pick as the correct answer?" If your response is, "I don't know because I am not sure how things are done there," you are mistakenly drawing upon practice systems and rules that may differ between states and should not be considered. However, if your response is, "It would be the same as mine," you have considered the core social work content that applies to practice in all states.

Tip 5

Standardized examinations are often difficult and test-takers often find themselves struggling to identify the correct answer from several listed. In these instances, social workers can make a common mistake such as selecting the answer that has catchy social work phrases, such as "from a client's perspective" or "focus on a client's strengths and skills." Although these are important social work concepts, you need to make sure that these answers fit the scenario or question asked. **The "best" answer is not always the correct answer.** If you are judging answers solely based on the inclusion of important social work terms—independent of what the question is really asking—you will often be drawn to the "best" answers (judged to be so solely based on the inclusion of important social work terms or concepts), but they may not be correct. Remember, you always want to ask yourself, "What is the right answer to this question on the examination?"

Tip 6

If you are asked to select between four listed terms, diagnoses, or theories, and you do not know with certainty what all the terms listed mean or the criteria for all of the named diagnoses, you should only choose between those that you know. When they are uncertain about the answer to a question, social workers often mistakenly think that it must be the term, diagnosis, or theory listed that they do not know and will gravitate toward selecting this answer. It seems to make logical sense in their minds—"I am uncertain of the answer to the question and I am uncertain as to what this answer means, so they must go together." Although common, this logic is problematic.

Instead, you should concentrate on choosing between the answers that you know. **Only in instances in which you are able to eliminate with 100% certainty the three choices that you know—which is almost never the case—should you choose the "mystery" term, diagnosis, or theory.**

Tip 7

You will have plenty of time to answer the questions. Although the examination is timed, most people finish with a half-hour or more left in the 4 hours. However, you may be nervous about the time and feel rushed due to your anxiety. Use your time wisely, reading carefully and applying the tips described. You should answer the questions in the order in which they are listed. Skipping around will waste time. The most time that you will spend on a question is determining what the question is asking, so not answering a question after you have done this analysis serves no purpose because you will not have an epiphany or any more information that will be helpful to you later in the examination than you do at that moment. You need to select an answer and move on. You also will need to commit to an answer after having read the question no more than two to three times and applying the strategies. Individuals who run out of time are "stuck" because they are waiting for the feeling of certainty in their answers that does not come in these types of standardized examinations.

Tip 8

Look for qualifying words in examination questions. These words are often capitalized, but not always. Examples of qualifying words are "best," "next," "least," "most," "first," and "not." Whenever you see a qualifying word, it is the key to selecting the correct answer from the others and is directly related to the answer. Thus, when you read each of the response choices or answers, you should put the qualifying word in front of it to ensure that you are focusing on what, in this question, is important. You will repeat the qualifying word before reading each answer. By repeating the word before each response choice, you are making sure that you are focusing on what is important when selecting between the answers.

Tip 9

The examinations require you to have basic knowledge about many theories, practice models, and perspectives related to social work practice. A theory is a set of interrelated concepts that are organized in a way that explain aspects of everyday life. A practice model is a way in which a theory is operationalized. And a perspective is a point of view that is usually broader and at a higher level of abstraction (i.e., strengths perspective). Having a basic understanding of various theories, practice models, and perspectives, as well as the terms that are rooted in them, is necessary. Sometimes there are recall questions about theories, practice models, or perspectives, but knowledge in these areas is often tested through questions related to case vignettes. For example, the last sentence before the response choices or answers may state, "Using a systems approach, a social worker can expect this recent medical diagnosis to…." Examining the response choices or answers through the "lens" of systems theory is essential to selecting the correct answer. Systems theory states that individuals are in continual interaction with their environment and that parts within a system are interrelated. Thus, when one subsystem is affected, they are all affected. In this example, you would need to have this knowledge in order to select the correct answer, and you would be looking for the response choice that reflects the medical diagnosis affecting others in the family or other aspects of a client's life beyond health.

You do not have to be an expert in all theories, practice models, or perspectives. Instead, your knowledge base needs to be "an inch deep, but a mile wide." You do not need to know the material in great depth, but you do need to have basic knowledge about a lot of paradigms.

Remember to always make sure that you are determining whether a question asks you to use a particular theory, practice model, or perspective when selecting the correct answer. If so, it is not about what might be best to address the problem; instead, identify which answer most closely relates to the paradigm identified.

When studying the theories, practice models, and perspectives, make sure to also focus on their related terms. Sometimes questions do not specify paradigms, but use related terms that you would only know if you studied them.

Tip 10

Perhaps the biggest mistake that social workers make when taking the examinations is adding material to the questions. This is done unconsciously when social workers mistakenly think of a client or situation in their own lives that is similar to what is described in a question. Unfortunately, when this occurs, information related to this real-life client or situation is added to the information that you are considering when selecting the correct response choice or answer, even when it is not actually included in the question. For example, if a man is described as psychotic, you may inappropriately think that he is a danger to himself or others because you recently worked with someone who was psychotic and was exhibiting harm to self or others. However, being psychotic does not necessarily mean that you are posing any danger. This added information may cause you to choose the incorrect information.

In order to determine whether you are adding material to a question, ask yourself what a non–social worker might answer. If the non–social worker's answer would be different from your answer, you may be adding material based on practice experience, not what is stated in the question. Remember, the question has all the information needed to select the correct answer. **You should stay with the material in the question and not add information based upon practice experience.**

Tip 11

Look for quotation marks throughout the question or clues in the last sentence before the response choices, because both are often the keys to selecting the correct answers. For example, a case vignette may describe a client who walks into the first therapy session and states, "I don't have to tell you anything and I don't want to be here," followed by a question for a social worker's best actions. Although this question does not explicitly state that it is asking how to best address resistance, it is implied by the client's verbal statement as described in the quoted statement. These words are there for a reason and are usually important clues to the KSA being tested or the critical information needed to select between correct and incorrect answers.

In addition, a case vignette may ask you to use a particular practice modality or theoretical approach to select the correct response choice. The "lens" that you should use is often mentioned in the last sentence before the answers are listed. For example, a case vignette that ends with "using a task-centered treatment approach, a social worker should ..." requires you to look at the response choices to see which relates to an intervention that is brief, highly structured, and focused on quick results in which a client can take a very active role. The correct answer would be very different if a social worker, responding to the same case vignette, was asked to use a "psychodynamic model."

Tip 12

Many of the response choices to questions on the examination often begin with verbs. **If you are debating between multiple answers, the verb choices can often provide some clues**. For example, some answers describe a social worker doing something for a client that he or she should be doing or for which he or she should be taking responsibility. These response choices often begin with the word "provide" when the question asks what a social worker should do in a particular situation.

In addition, some verbs may denote less of an empowerment approach, which may help rule them out. "Explore" and "engage" are active verbs that usually indicate that a social worker is relying on a client to come up with the answer or be responsible for the treatment process. "Ignore" or "wait" may indicate that a social worker is not taking critical information into account or acting when needed.

Although examining the verb used in the response choices is only one piece of information that should be used when selecting the correct response choice, and may not be as critical in some instances as other selection criteria, it is a vital tool to consider when two response choices appear equally viable.

Tip 13

Often, questions on the examinations require social workers to identify what they would do "first" or "next" or to pick out the issue or problem that is "most" important in a case scenario. In practice, such decisions are often somewhat subjective and driven by practice wisdom that takes into account many clinical and contextual factors. However, for the examination, all social workers must select the same correct answer. **A useful framework for prioritizing client needs and addressing them sequentially is Maslow's hierarchy of needs.**

Although it is unlikely that Maslow's hierarchy of needs would ever be explicitly asked about on the examination, it is a tool that will be used repeatedly in questions that want the social worker to prioritize problems or order actions based on client need.

A social worker should always address health and safety issues before moving on to issues that relate to self-esteem and relationships. Thus, when the question includes the qualifying word "first," the answers should be considered in light of the health and safety needs of a client. Social workers should also provide concrete services to meet basic needs, such as housing, employment, and transportation, before moving up the hierarchy. Maslow's framework indicates that without health, safety, and basic needs being met first, a client cannot meet his or her higher level needs.

Tip 14

Another critical tool available to select the correct answer is the problem-solving process (i.e., engagement, assessment, planning, intervention, evaluation, and termination). Understanding the goal of each phase and the tasks to be completed therein is critical because many questions on the examination focus on making sure that things are happening in the correct order. For example, if the question is about the first session or meeting with a client, the activities of a social worker should be focused on engagement. Engagement includes finding out why a client is there and why he or she is seeking services now, explaining the role of a social worker and what to expect in treatment, listening to a client as he or she explains his or her situation, and explaining the limits of confidentiality. Including a reference to a specific session in the question is a clue for a social worker in determining what stage of the problem-solving process a social worker and client are in and what activities are appropriate for this stage.

When a question asks what actions a social worker should take when interacting with a client, attention should be paid to what part of the problem-solving process a social worker and client are theoretically engaged in. A social worker's response may be quite different if it is the beginning of the process versus the end. Although questions will rarely explicitly state the phase, it can be identified by what has occurred, such as "when gathering information on the problem" to indicate assessment or "when developing the contract" to indicate planning. Also, it may be useful to classify response choices into these stages in order to select what comes "first" or "next."

Tip 15

If the age of a client or others is included in a case vignette, it is usually relevant to selecting the correct response choice. For example, having an imaginary friend at age 4 is very different than having one at age 34. Imaginary friends in childhood are an extension of pretend play and part of Piaget's preoperational stage. However, having one in later life might be an indicator of psychosis resulting from a hallucination or delusion. Thus, in the former instance, a social worker would view this behavior as typical, which would require no special intervention, whereas in the latter, a social worker may need to do a mental status examination or refer for a psychiatric evaluation.

When studying, a social worker does not need to memorize the exact age at which an individual leaves one stage of development or reaches a milestone. However, when mentioned in a question, the age can be a useful hint as to where a client is in the life course and what may be expected.

Tip 16

Often, questions on the examinations aim to assess whether a social worker is appropriately placing a client as the priority and respecting his or her right to self-determination. Questions may focus on conflicts between meeting a client's needs versus adhering to practices or policies created by an agency. When there is a barrier to meeting a client's needs, a social worker should always take responsibility for trying to remove the barrier.

Answers indicating that a social worker should provide advice to a client because he or she has better solutions to a client's problems are never correct.

In practice, a social worker may often encounter practices or policies that limit a client's alternatives or rights to self-determination, and fighting to change these "rules" may seem unrealistic and futile. However, whether or not a social worker will be successful does not change the mandate to challenge them. Do not dismiss an answer just because it seems difficult to achieve.

A client is the expert on his or her situation and should be regarded as such. The supervisor in case vignettes is there to ensure that a client receives the most effective and efficient services possible—not to make things easier for a social worker or enforce agency mandates.

Always look at the answers through the lens of what is best for a client. The self-determination of a client is only limited in situations that would cause harm to a client or others. The correct response choice is always the one that puts a client first.

Tip 17

It is essential that the question is thoroughly understood before looking at the answers. The most difficult part of selecting the correct answer is understanding the knowledge area or concept that is being tested. In order to ensure that proper attention is given to understanding the question, a multistep process should be undertaken.

1. Read the question exactly as it is written, paying attention to qualifying words and those in quotes. Do not look at the response choices yet!

2. Ask "What is this question about?" to determine which of the KSAs is being tested.

3. Think about the important concepts related to the KSA; they will be essential in selecting the correct answers from the incorrect ones.

4. Examine the question again to confirm that your assumption about which KSA is being tested is correct and to determine how the important concepts related to the KSA are relevant to the question.

5. Now look at the response choices for the first time! Read each carefully.

6. Eliminate any that do not appear to be correct. If more than one response choice appears to be viable, go back and read the question again—looking only at the remaining viable responses. It is difficult to eliminate three of four possible answers immediately, so this process may involve multiple iterations. Each time a response choice is eliminated, read the question and the answers that are left. Going back to the question each time you are unable to dismiss all but one

response choice will assist in selecting the correct answer for that particular question.

Tip 18

It is critical not to be influenced to select a response choice simply because it has social work "buzz words" such as "rapport," "empathy," "support system," "joining with a client," "strengths perspective," "from a client's perspective," and so on. Often, social workers have a hard time eliminating response choices that contain terms that are important to effective service delivery. These are key concepts that are the cornerstone of competent social work services. However, a word or catch phrase does not make a response choice correct. An answer may not be correct because the other parts of it are inadequate, false, or simply do not address what the question is asking. When you see these social work "buzz words" in a response choice, it is essential to read the rest of the answer critically. You might want to ask yourself whether the answer would still be as appealing if a synonym was used in place of the "buzz word." The entire answer has to stand on its merits as correct, even when the actual term that is making it so appealing is omitted.

Tip 19

Often, social workers view the examinations as a vehicle by which to demonstrate their clinical knowledge and skills. They view all client behaviors through a psychotherapeutic lens and are inappropriately quick to attribute actions to symptomology of disorders or dysfunction. Social workers also are more apt on the ASWB examinations to wrongly view clinical attributes as the focus of treatment or intervention.

For example, if a client has just experienced unsuccessful infertility treatments, she may be likely to feel depressed, frustrated, and hopeless. These are typical reactions to her inability to get pregnant as a result of this medical intervention. The presence of these feelings does not mean that they must be the focus of social work treatment or clinically analyzed and diagnosed. Perhaps the client simply needs support for pursuing alternative methods for becoming a mother, such as through adoption or surrogacy.

You should not be quick to diagnose a client with a disorder on the examinations unless ALL the required clinical criteria are present. You should

also not make all client feelings or behaviors clinical issues to be addressed as part of an intervention or treatment.

The ASWB examinations, including the Clinical Examination, are taken by social workers employed in all types of settings and roles. Clinical work does not always imply the need for psychotherapy. Unless the setting or type of intervention to be employed is explicitly stated in a case vignette, you should use a more generalist approach to selecting the correct answer.

Tip 20

Most questions do not ask a social worker to "solve the problem" or even take action that will directly lead to resolving the issue or situation. For example, a question may ask what a social worker should do FIRST when having an issue with his or her supervisor or not getting a verbal response from a colleague. Although speaking directly to a supervisor or putting the request to a colleague in writing may likely not result in an acceptable outcome, such as getting a client a service, they are required steps in ensuring adherence to chain of command or appropriate documentation procedures. It is also important to remember that it is possible to speak to your supervisor first, even if it won't achieve the desired outcome, and then go to an agency directly immediately after—perhaps even the same day—in order to follow the proper chain of command.

Social workers like to get results, and this desire can cause them to choose answers that will make a difference even when questions are not asking for resolution.

There are not long waiting lists, scarce resources, or delays in referrals in examination case vignettes unless they are explicitly stated. In actual practice, social workers encounter these realities daily and often base their decisions and actions to ensure results despite these constraints. These factors should not influence selecting a response choice unless they are explicitly stated in the question.

Assessing Examination Difficulties

If you are having difficulty answering practice questions or even passing the examinations, it is useful to try to diagnose what is causing your problem. You should reexamine the tips outlined in this guide to see what strategies may be helpful in preparing for the examinations and/or answering questions. You also might want to relook at the self-assessment to determine which content areas require more studying.

Although strategies are important, failing the examinations is almost always a result of gaps in knowledge of social work content.

The ASWB examinations are very reliable. Thus, if you study using the same strategy or methods, you are likely to get the same results.

Just like in social work practice, a thorough assessment is critical to ensuring a strategy or intervention is created to address the targeted problem(s). A social worker should spend time analyzing what is causing the difficulties before taking an examination again. For example, difficulties with anxiety will not be addressed by "hitting the books." In addition, knowledge gaps cannot be filled by simply reviewing the test-taking strategies.

Although social workers who have failed the examinations may be anxious to start studying so that they can take the tests again in 90 days, it is worth spending time critically reflecting on the strategies used to study and answer questions so that corrections can be made before trying again.

Dealing With Test Anxiety

Perhaps one of the biggest issues that social workers have to address when preparing for and actually taking the examinations is anxiety. Although not designed to be an exhaustive resource on how to address test anxiety, this guide would be incomplete if it did not provide some guidance to social workers to assist with anxiety during this stressful time in their professional development.

It is important to acknowledge that anxiety can be useful during this process because it helps you prioritize studying and preparing above other demands placed upon you in everyday life. There are no magic ways to instill the necessary knowledge in your brain besides good old-fashioned studying. Anxiety can be a motivator to keep going over the material even when there are more interesting things you could be doing!

Remember, everyone who is studying for the examinations is feeling the same way. This stress is typical, and you are not alone in feeling anxious.

However, it is essential to manage this anxiety, and there are several strategies that can help.

1. *Make a Study Plan and Work the Plan*
   A great way to instill confidence is being able to walk into the testing center having prepared the way that you set out to do. A study plan will help you break the material into smaller manageable segments and avoid last-minute cramming.

2. *Don't Forget the Basics*
   You need to make sure that you don't neglect your biological, emotional, and social needs leading up to and on the day of the examination. Get plenty of rest, build in relaxation time to your study plan, and eat well to give you energy during this exhausting process.

3. *Familiarize Yourself With the Test Environment*
   Before the day of the examination, drive to the testing center so you know how to get there. Arrive early so you are not rushed. Take your time reviewing the tutorial on the computer before you start the examination.

4. *Use Relaxation Techniques*
   Breathe and give yourself permission to relax during the examination. You may need to shut your eyes and stretch your neck or stand up several times during the 4-hour exam to help you to refocus.

5. *Put the Examination Into Perspective*
   Rarely do people get the score that they want the first time taking any standardized test. Taking the SATs or GREs more than once is the rule rather than the exception. Social workers often attach too much meaning to whether or not they pass the examination the first or second time. They walk into the testing center feeling their entire career rests on the results. This is not true. There are many outstanding social workers who have had to take the test multiple times. Remember that you will be able to retake the examination if you do not pass—this is not your only chance. Not passing is not in any way reflective of your ability to practice social work. You will eventually pass, whether it is this time or another, so don't let the test define you. Avoid thinking in "all or nothing" terms.

6. *Expect Setbacks*
   The road to licensure is not different than other journeys in life and not usually without unexpected delays or even disappointments. It is important to see these as typical parts of the process and not ends in themselves. Try to figure out why these setbacks in studying or passing are occurring and how you can use this information as feedback for making improvements. You did not get a social work degree without some disappointments and challenges. Studying for and passing the examination will also not be easy, but you will be successful if you keep focused and learn from challenges encountered.

7. *Reward Yourself*
   You don't have to wait until you pass in order to celebrate. Build some enjoyment into the test-taking experience by creating little incentives or rewards along the way. Go out to dinner after having studied for 4 hours on a Saturday afternoon. Get up early and study before work so you can enjoy a movie when you get home. Improving your attitude about the test-taking experience can actually help you study more and improve your performance on the examination.

8. *Acknowledge and Address the Anxiety*

   Ignoring the anxiety that accompanies this process will not help. It is impossible to completely eliminate it through any of the techniques mentioned. However, you do need to assess whether it is manageable and can be addressed by some of these suggestions or if it is interfering so significantly with the learning process that you are "blanking out" or having problems in other areas of your life because of its presence. If this is the case, you may need more intensive anxiety reduction interventions. Repeatedly studying the content over and over will not reduce your anxiety. Although most people can develop their own strategies for anxiety management, others need outside help. Usually, individuals who need the assistance of others are those who have experienced debilitating anxiety in other areas of life prior to taking the examinations. No matter what the severity—anxiety management is a critical part of every study plan!

The following how If your workbook has a
translated ... ... in ... ... the process
will ... ... in ... ...

Examination Content

Although it is impossible to identify the information that will be tested in your examination, ASWB provides a listing of all content areas that are used as the basis for all question construction. These areas are identified by social workers in the field via a practice analysis conducted by ASWB. Through this process, a listing of topics that describe the KSAs that are important to the job of a social worker are used to make sure that questions focus on the areas of critical importance to social workers.

Although there is a separate set of KSAs for each of the four ASWB examinations (Bachelors, Masters, Advanced Generalist, and Clinical), there is tremendous overlap across these tests. Sometimes a KSA is not listed in the same content area or is described slightly differently (e.g., "theories of human development" versus "developmental theories"). However, upon review, you will see a tremendous overlap across the examinations.

This is good news, because doing well on one ASWB examination often means that you will do well on another. It is always easier to refresh your memory about a topic area than to learn it for the first time!

You do not have to be an expert in each of the KSAs, but you will need to recall critical content, as well as key concepts and terms that may be related to the area. Many people question whether they know enough or are ready to take the examination. With regard to content, it is challenging because individuals often define readiness by being an expert or highly skilled in each area.

For the examinations, you can use the following as a guide to assessing your readiness in having the requisite knowledge.

1. Would you be able to summarize the most relevant points related to the content area in a 5-minute "lecture" on the topic?

2. Do you understand the relevancy to social work practice and how social workers use this information to make decisions when interacting with clients?

3. Do you know how this content area relates to the assessment and treatment of clients? Does it in any way impact problems or issues that they may be experiencing?

In order to get the right answers, your exam questions may require you to broadly apply the overall key theme related to a theory or area (e.g., the understanding that what happens to a client early in life can influence later functioning) or specific terms associated with the area, even if the construct is not mentioned (e.g., picking a response that best represents "family homeostasis"). In order to help you to determine the areas in which you need to concentrate in your preparation for the examination, you should review KSAs, listed in the Self-Assessment in this guide. They are the basis for individual test questions.

If you feel that you have the requisite knowledge, you may only need to quickly review by reading through the content outlined in the subsequent pages of this guide. If you have gaps in content, you should mark the sections in this guide that relate to the topic and go over them in detail so you can get to the point that you have enough knowledge to recall the key concepts and terms. If you have never heard of the concept or recall little about its relevance to social work practice, do not worry—everyone has gaps in knowledge, but this just means that you will have to spend some extra time learning about the topic.

There are different learning styles and you will need to determine which one best fits you because researchers have shown that individuals perform better on examinations if they use study techniques that are consistent with their styles of learning.

The following are some suggested techniques for each learning style that can help fill in content gaps that may exist.

VISUAL LEARNERS

Visual learners learn best through what they see. Although lectures can be boring for visual learners, they benefit from the use of diagrams, PowerPoint slides, and charts.

- Use colored highlighters in this guide to draw attention to key terms.
- Develop outlines or take notes on the concepts in the guide.
- Write talking points for each of the KSAs on separate white index cards.

- Create a coding schema of symbols and write them in this guide next to material and terms that require further study.
- Study in an environment that is away from visual distractions such as television, people moving around, or clutter.

AUDITORY LEARNERS

Auditory learners learn best through what they hear. They may have difficulty remembering material that they read in this guide, but can easily recall it if it is read to them.

- Tape record yourself summarizing the material as you are studying it—listen to your notes as a way to reinforce what you read.
- Have a study partner explain the relevant concepts and terms related to the KSAs.
- Read the text from this guide aloud if you are having trouble remembering it.
- Find free podcasts or YouTube videos on the Internet on the content areas that are short and easy to understand to assist with learning.
- Talk to yourself about the content as you study—emphasizing what is important to remember related to each KSA.

KINESTHETIC OR HANDS-ON LEARNERS

Kinesthetic learners learn through tactile approaches aimed at experiencing or doing. They need activities and physical activities as a foundation for instruction.

- Make flashcards on material because writing it down will assist with remembering the content.
- Use as many different senses as possible when studying—read material when you are on your treadmill, use highlighters, talk aloud about content, and/or listen to a study partner.
- Develop mnemonic devices to aid in information retention (e.g., EAPIET or *EAt PIE* Today is a great way to remember the social work problem-solving process—Engaging, Assessing, Planning, Intervening, Evaluating, and Terminating).
- Write notes and important terms in your guide margins.
- Ask a study partner to quiz you on material—turn it into a game and see how many KSAs you can discuss or how long you can talk about a content area before running out of material.

One important thing to remember is that success on the examination does not require a lot of memorization of material, but rather the ability to recall terms when you see them and to draw upon your knowledge of multiple concepts to select the correct course of action in hypothetical vignettes or scenarios. Thus, spend your time really understanding the KSAs and not just being able to recite definitions.

Self-Assessment

In order to help you determine the areas in which you need to concentrate in your preparation for the examination, please review the KSAs that describe the discrete knowledge components that may be tested as part of the examination and are the basis for individual test questions.

If you are not able to recall basic content and/or key terms, indicate the need to study this area thoroughly by circling "1." If you have some basic information about the content and/or key terms, indicate the need to fill in knowledge gaps by circling "2." If you are able to summarize the key concepts and terms, as well as answer questions about its applicability to social work practice and impacts on client functioning, you may be well prepared and can circle "3." Adequate preparation should not be indicated until you can synthesize material from multiple content areas and can discuss all aspects of the KSAs easily and fluidly.

Association of Social Work Boards'
Content Outline for Bachelors Examination

3	2	1
Well Prepared	Somewhat Prepared	Not Prepared

I. Human Development, Diversity, and Behavior in the
Environment (25%)

Human Growth and Development

Theories of human development throughout the lifespan (e.g.,   3 2 1
physical, social, emotional, cognitive, behavioral)

(*continued*)

The indicators of normal and abnormal physical, cognitive, emotional, and sexual development throughout the lifespan	3	2	1
Theories of sexual development throughout the lifespan	3	2	1
Theories of spiritual development throughout the lifespan	3	2	1
Theories of racial, ethnic, and cultural development throughout the lifespan	3	2	1
The effects of physical, mental, and cognitive disabilities throughout the lifespan	3	2	1
The interplay of biological, psychological, social, and spiritual factors	3	2	1
Basic human needs	3	2	1
The principles of attachment and bonding	3	2	1
The effect of aging on biopsychosocial functioning	3	2	1
The impact of aging parents on adult children	3	2	1
Gerontology	3	2	1
Personality theories	3	2	1
Theories of conflict	3	2	1
Factors influencing self-image (e.g., culture, race, religion/ spirituality, age, disability, trauma)	3	2	1
Body image and its impact (e.g., identity, self-esteem, relationships, habits)	3	2	1
Parenting skills and capacities	3	2	1

Human Behavior in the Social Environment

The family life cycle	3	2	1
Family dynamics and functioning and the effects on individuals, families, groups, organizations, and communities	3	2	1
Theories of couples development	3	2	1
The impact of physical and mental illness on family dynamics	3	2	1
Psychological defense mechanisms and their effects on behavior and relationships	3	2	1
Addiction theories and concepts	3	2	1
Systems and ecological perspectives and theories	3	2	1
Role theories	3	2	1
Theories of group development and functioning	3	2	1
Theories of social change and community development	3	2	1
The dynamics of interpersonal relationships	3	2	1
Models of family life education in social work practice	3	2	1
Strengths-based and resilience theories	3	2	1

Diversity, Social/Economic Justice, and Oppression

Feminist theory	3	2	1
The effect of disability on biopsychosocial functioning throughout the lifespan	3	2	1
The effect of culture, race, and ethnicity on behaviors, attitudes, and identity	3	2	1
The effects of discrimination and stereotypes on behaviors, attitudes, and identity	3	2	1
The influence of sexual orientation on behaviors, attitudes, and identity	3	2	1
The impact of transgender and transitioning process on behaviors, attitudes, identity, and relationships	3	2	1
Systemic (institutionalized) discrimination (e.g., racism, sexism, ageism)	3	2	1
The principles of culturally competent social work practice	3	2	1
Sexual orientation concepts	3	2	1
Gender and gender identity concepts	3	2	1
The impact of social institutions on society	3	2	1
The effect of poverty on individuals, families, groups, organizations, and communities	3	2	1
The impact of the environment (e.g., social, physical, cultural, political, economic) on individuals, families, groups, organizations, and communities	3	2	1
Person-in-environment (PIE) theory	3	2	1
Social and economic justice	3	2	1
Criminal justice systems	3	2	1
The effects of life events, stressors, and crises on individuals, families, groups, organizations, and communities	3	2	1
The impact of the political environment on policy-making	3	2	1

II. Assessment (29%)

Biopsychosocial History and Collateral Data

The components of a biopsychosocial assessment	3	2	1
The components and function of the mental status examination	3	2	1
Biopsychosocial responses to illness and disability	3	2	1
Biopsychosocial factors related to mental health	3	2	1
The indicators of psychosocial stress	3	2	1
Basic medical terminology	3	2	1
The indicators of mental and emotional illness throughout the lifespan	3	2	1

(continued)

The types of information available from other sources (e.g., agency, employment, medical, psychological, legal, or school records)   3 2 1

Assessment Methods and Techniques

The factors and processes used in problem formulation   3 2 1

Methods of involving clients/client systems in problem identification (e.g., gathering collateral information)   3 2 1

Techniques and instruments used to assess clients/client systems   3 2 1

Methods to incorporate the results of psychological and educational tests into assessment   3 2 1

Communication theories and styles   3 2 1

The concept of congruence in communication   3 2 1

Risk assessment methods   3 2 1

Methods to assess the client's/client system's strengths, resources, and challenges (e.g., individual, family, group, organization, community)   3 2 1

The indicators of motivation, resistance, and readiness to change   3 2 1

Methods to assess motivation, resistance, and readiness to change   3 2 1

Methods to assess the client's/client system's communication skills   3 2 1

Methods to assess the client's/client system's coping abilities   3 2 1

The indicators of client's/client system's strengths and challenges   3 2 1

Methods used to assess trauma   3 2 1

Placement options based on assessed level of care   3 2 1

The effects of addiction and substance abuse on individuals, families, groups, organizations, and communities   3 2 1

The indicators of addiction and substance abuse   3 2 1

Co-occurring disorders and conditions   3 2 1

The Diagnostic and Statistical Manual of the American Psychiatric Association   3 2 1

The indicators of behavioral dysfunction   3 2 1

The indicators of somatization   3 2 1

The indicators of feigning illness   3 2 1

Common psychotropic and non-psychotropic prescriptions and over-the-counter medications and their side effects   3 2 1

Concepts of Abuse and Neglect

Indicators and dynamics of abuse and neglect throughout the lifespan   3 2 1

The effects of physical, sexual, and psychological abuse on individuals, families, groups, organizations, and communities	3 2 1
The indicators, dynamics, and impact of exploitation across the lifespan (e.g., financial, immigration status, sexual trafficking)	3 2 1
The characteristics of perpetrators of abuse, neglect, and exploitation	3 2 1

III. Interventions with Clients/Client Systems (26%)

Indicators and Effects of Crisis and Change

The impact of out-of-home placement (e.g., hospitalization, foster care, residential care, criminal justice system) on clients/client systems	3 2 1
The impact of stress, trauma, and violence	3 2 1
Theories of trauma-informed care	3 2 1
Crisis intervention theories	3 2 1
The indicators of traumatic stress and violence	3 2 1
The impact of out-of-home displacement (e.g., natural disaster, homelessness, immigration) on clients/client systems	3 2 1
The indicators and risk factors of the client's/client system's danger to self and others	3 2 1
Methods and approaches to trauma-informed care	3 2 1
The impact of caregiving on families	3 2 1
The dynamics and effects of loss, separation, and grief	3 2 1

Intervention Processes and Techniques

The principles and techniques of interviewing (e.g., supporting, clarifying, focusing, confronting, validating, feedback, reflecting, language differences, use of interpreters, redirecting)	3 2 1
Methods to involve clients/client systems in intervention planning	3 2 1
Cultural considerations in the creation of an intervention plan	3 2 1
The criteria used in the selection of intervention/treatment modalities (e.g., client/client system abilities, culture, life stage)	3 2 1
The components of intervention, treatment, and service plans	3 2 1
Psychotherapies	3 2 1
The impact of immigration, refugee, or undocumented status on service delivery	3 2 1

(continued)

Discharge, aftercare, and follow-up planning	3	2	1
The phases of intervention and treatment	3	2	1
The principles and techniques for building and maintaining a helping relationship	3	2	1
The client's/client system's role in the problem-solving process	3	2	1
Problem-solving models and approaches (e.g., brief, solution-focused methods or techniques)	3	2	1
Methods to engage and motivate clients/client systems	3	2	1
Methods to engage and work with involuntary clients/client systems	3	2	1
Methods to obtain and provide feedback	3	2	1
The principles of active listening and observation	3	2	1
Verbal and nonverbal communication techniques	3	2	1
Limit setting techniques	3	2	1
The technique of role play	3	2	1
Role modeling techniques	3	2	1
Methods to obtain sensitive information (e.g., substance abuse, sexual abuse)	3	2	1
Techniques for harm reduction for self and others	3	2	1
Methods to teach coping and other self-care skills to clients/client systems	3	2	1
Client/client system self-monitoring techniques	3	2	1
Methods to develop, review, and implement crisis plans	3	2	1
Methods of conflict resolution	3	2	1
Crisis intervention and treatment approaches	3	2	1
Anger management techniques	3	2	1
Stress management techniques	3	2	1
Cognitive and behavioral interventions	3	2	1
Strengths-based and empowerment strategies and interventions	3	2	1
Client/client system contracting and goal-setting techniques	3	2	1
Partializing techniques	3	2	1
Assertiveness training	3	2	1
Task-centered approaches	3	2	1
Psychoeducation methods (e.g., acknowledging, supporting, normalizing)	3	2	1
Group work techniques and approaches (e.g., developing and managing group processes and cohesion)	3	2	1
Family therapy models, interventions, and approaches	3	2	1
Permanency planning	3	2	1

Mindfulness and complementary therapeutic approaches	3	2	1
The components of case management	3	2	1
Techniques used for follow-up	3	2	1
The elements of a case presentation	3	2	1
Methods of service delivery	3	2	1
Concepts of social policy development and analysis	3	2	1
Theories and methods of advocacy for policies, services, and resources to meet clients'/client systems' needs	3	2	1
Community organizing and social planning methods	3	2	1
Techniques for mobilizing community participation	3	2	1
Methods to develop and evaluate measurable objectives for client/client system intervention, treatment, and/or service plans	3	2	1
Techniques used to evaluate a client's/client system's progress	3	2	1
Primary, secondary, and tertiary prevention strategies	3	2	1
Methods to create, implement, and evaluate policies and procedures that minimize risk for individuals, families, groups, organizations, and communities	3	2	1
The impact of domestic, intimate partner, and other violence on the helping relationship	3	2	1
The indicators of client/client system readiness for termination	3	2	1
Methods, techniques, and instruments used to evaluate social work practice	3	2	1
Evidence-based practice	3	2	1

Use of Collaborative Relationships

The basic terminology of professions other than social work (e.g., legal, educational)	3	2	1
The effect of the client's developmental level on the social worker–client relationship	3	2	1
Methods to clarify the roles and responsibilities of the social worker and client/client system in the intervention process	3	2	1
Consultation approaches (e.g., referrals to specialists)	3	2	1
Methods of networking	3	2	1
The process of interdisciplinary and intradisciplinary team collaboration	3	2	1
Methods to assess the availability of community resources	3	2	1
Methods to establish service networks or community resources	3	2	1

(continued)

The effects of policies, procedures, regulations, and legislation on social work practice and service delivery	3 2 1
The relationship between formal and informal power structures in the decision-making process	3 2 1

Documentation

The principles of case recording, documentation, and management of practice records	3 2 1
The elements of client/client system reports	3 2 1
The principles and processes for developing formal documents (e.g., proposals, letters, brochures, pamphlets, reports, evaluations)	3 2 1
The principles and features of objective and subjective data	3 2 1

IV.   Professional Relationships, Values, and Ethics (20%)

Professional Values and Ethical Issues

Legal and/or ethical issues related to the practice of social work, including responsibility to clients/client systems, colleagues, the profession, and society	3 2 1
Professional values and principles (e.g., competence, social justice, integrity, and dignity and worth of the person)	3 2 1
The influence of the social worker's own values and beliefs on the social worker–client/client system relationship	3 2 1
The dynamics of diversity in the social worker–client/client system relationship	3 2 1
Techniques to identify and resolve ethical dilemmas	3 2 1
Client/client system competence and self-determination (e.g., financial decisions, treatment decisions, emancipation, age of consent, permanency planning)	3 2 1
Techniques for protecting and enhancing client/client system self-determination	3 2 1
The client's/client system's right to refuse services (e.g., medication, medical treatment, counseling, placement, etc.)	3 2 1
The dynamics of power and transparency in the social worker–client/client system relationship	3 2 1
Professional boundaries in the social worker–client/client system relationship (e.g., power differences, conflicts of interest, etc.)	3 2 1
Ethical issues related to dual relationships	3 2 1
Legal and/or ethical issues regarding mandatory reporting (e.g., abuse, threat of harm, impaired professionals, etc.)	3 2 1
Legal and/or ethical issues regarding documentation	3 2 1

Legal and/or ethical issues regarding termination	3 2 1
Legal and/or ethical issues related to death and dying	3 2 1
Research ethics (e.g., institutional review boards, use of human subjects, informed consent)	3 2 1
Ethical issues in supervision and management	3 2 1
Methods to create, implement, and evaluate policies and procedures for social worker safety	3 2 1

Confidentiality

The principles and processes of obtaining informed consent	3 2 1
The use of client/client system records	3 2 1
Legal and/or ethical issues regarding confidentiality, including electronic information security	3 2 1

Professional Development and Use of Self

The components of the social worker–client/client system relationship	3 2 1
The social worker's role in the problem-solving process	3 2 1
The concept of acceptance and empathy in the social worker–client/client system relationship	3 2 1
The impact of transference and countertransference in the social worker–client/client system relationship	3 2 1
Social worker self-care principles and techniques	3 2 1
Burnout, secondary trauma, and compassion fatigue	3 2 1
The components of a safe and positive work environment	3 2 1
Professional objectivity in the social worker–client/client system relationship	3 2 1
Self-disclosure principles and applications	3 2 1
The influence of the social worker's own values and beliefs on interdisciplinary collaboration	3 2 1
Governance structures	3 2 1
Accreditation and/or licensing requirements	3 2 1
Time management approaches	3 2 1
Models of supervision and consultation (e.g., individual, peer, group)	3 2 1
The supervisee's role in supervision (e.g., identifying learning needs, self-assessment, prioritizing, etc.)	3 2 1
The impact of transference and countertransference within supervisory relationships	3 2 1
Professional development activities to improve practice and maintain current professional knowledge (e.g., in-service training, licensing requirements, reviews of literature, workshops)	3 2 1

Human Development, Diversity, and Behavior in the Environment (25%)

Human Growth and Development

THEORIES OF HUMAN DEVELOPMENT THROUGHOUT THE LIFESPAN (E.G., PHYSICAL, SOCIAL, EMOTIONAL, COGNITIVE, BEHAVIORAL)

Social work theories are general explanations that are supported by evidence obtained through the scientific method. A theory may explain human behavior by describing how humans interact with each other or react to certain stimuli. Because human behavior is so complex, numerous theories are utilized to guide practice.

Often, the name of the theory will not be used in a question, but understanding it will be essential to selecting the correct answer.

Study the theories broadly to understand their general theme or focus, and deeply enough to know the meaning of terms originating from them that may be mentioned in exam questions.

Social Development

Human beings are inherently social. Developing competencies in this domain enhances a person's mental health, success in work, and ability to achieve in life tasks.

Erik Erikson was interested in how children socialize and how this affects their sense of self. He saw personality as developing throughout the life course and looked at identity crises as the focal point for each stage of human development.

According to Erikson, there are eight distinct stages, with two possible outcomes. Successful completion of each stage results in a healthy personality and successful interactions with others. Failure to successfully complete a stage can result in a reduced ability to complete further stages and, therefore, a more unhealthy personality and sense of self. These stages, however, can be resolved successfully at a later time.

Trust Versus Mistrust

From birth to 1 year of age, children begin to learn the ability to trust others based upon the consistency of their caregiver(s). If trust develops successfully, the child gains confidence and security in the world around him or her and is able to feel secure even when threatened. Unsuccessful completion of this stage can result in an inability to trust, and therefore a sense of fear about the inconsistent world. It may result in anxiety, heightened insecurities, and feelings of mistrust in the world around them.

Autonomy Versus Shame and Doubt

Between the ages of 1 and 3, children begin to assert their independence by walking away from their mother, picking which toy to play with, and making choices about what they like to wear, to eat, and so on. If children in this stage are encouraged and supported in their increased independence, they become more confident and secure in their own ability to survive in the world. If children are criticized, overly controlled, or not given the opportunity to assert themselves, they begin to feel inadequate in their ability to survive, and may then become overly dependent upon others while lacking self-esteem and feeling a sense of shame or doubt in their own abilities.

Initiative Versus Guilt

Around age 3 and continuing to age 6, children assert themselves more frequently. They begin to plan activities, make up games, and initiate activities with others. If given this opportunity, children develop a sense of initiative, and feel secure in their ability to lead others and make decisions. Conversely, if this tendency is squelched, either through criticism or control, children develop a sense of guilt. They may feel like nuisances to others and will therefore remain followers, lacking self-initiative.

Industry Versus Inferiority

From age 6 to puberty, children begin to develop a sense of pride in their accomplishments. They initiate projects, see them through to completion, and feel good about what they have achieved. If children are encouraged and reinforced for their initiative, they begin to feel industrious and feel confident in their ability to achieve goals. If this initiative is not encouraged but instead restricted, children begin to feel inferior, doubting their abilities and failing to reach their potential.

Identity Versus Role Confusion

During adolescence, the transition from childhood to adulthood is most important. Children are becoming more independent, and begin to look at the future in terms of career, relationships, families, housing, and so on. During this period, they explore possibilities and begin to form their own identities based upon the outcome of their explorations. This sense of who they are can be hindered, which results in a sense of confusion ("I don't know what I want to be when I grow up") about themselves and their role in the world.

Intimacy Versus Isolation

In young adulthood, individuals begin to share themselves more intimately with others and explore relationships leading toward longer term commitments with others outside the family. Successful completion can lead to comfortable relationships and a sense of commitment, safety, and care within a relationship. Avoiding intimacy and fearing commitment and relationships can lead to isolation, loneliness, and sometimes depression.

Generativity Versus Stagnation

During middle adulthood, individuals establish careers, settle down within relationships, begin families, and develop a sense of being a part of the bigger picture. They give back to society through raising children, being productive at work, and becoming involved in community activities and organizations. By failing to achieve these objectives, individuals become stagnant and feel unproductive.

Ego Integrity Versus Despair

As individuals grow older and become senior citizens, they tend to slow down and explore life as retired people. It is during this time that they contemplate accomplishments and are able to develop a sense of integrity if they are satisfied with the progression of their lives. If they see their lives as being unproductive and failing to accomplish life goals, they become dissatisfied with life and develop despair, often leading to depression and hopelessness.

On a micro level, social development is learning how to behave and interact well with others. Social development relies on emotional development or learning how to manage feelings so they are productive and not counterproductive.

On a macro level, social development is about a commitment that development processes need to benefit people, particularly, but not only, the poor. It also recognizes the way people interact in groups and society, and the norms that facilitate such interaction.

Social development implies a change in social institutions. Progress toward an inclusive society, for example, implies that individuals treat each other fairly in their daily lives, whether in the family, workplace, or public office. Social cohesion is enhanced when peaceful and safe environments within neighborhoods and communities are created. Social accountability exists to the extent that individuals' voices are expressed and heard. Reforms aimed at improving rights and more participatory governance are part of the process by which institutional change is achieved.

Emotional Development

Emotional milestones are often harder to pinpoint than signs of physical development. This area emphasizes many skills that increase self-awareness and self-regulation. Social skills and emotional development are reflected in the ability to pay attention, make transitions from one activity to another, and cooperate with others.

During childhood, there is a lot happening during playtime. Children are lifting, dropping, looking, pouring, bouncing, hiding, building, knocking down, and more. Children are busy learning when they are playing. Play is the true work of childhood.

During play, children are also learning that they are liked and fun to be around. These experiences give them the self-confidence they need to build loving and supportive relationships all their lives.

Cognitive Development

Cognitive development focuses on development in terms of information processing, conceptual resources, perceptual skill, language learning, and other aspects of brain development. It is the emergence of the ability to think and understand.

A major controversy in cognitive development has been "nature and nurture," that is, the question of whether cognitive development is mainly determined by a client's innate qualities ("nature"), or by his or her personal experiences ("nurture"). However, it is now recognized by most experts that this is a false dichotomy: There is overwhelming evidence from biological and behavioral sciences that, from the earliest points in development, gene activity interacts with events and experiences in the environment.

There are six levels of cognition:

1. *Knowledge*: rote memorization, recognition, or recall of facts

2. *Comprehension*: understanding what the facts mean

3. *Application*: correct use of the facts, rules, or ideas

4. *Analysis*: breaking down information into component parts

5. *Synthesis*: combination of facts, ideas, or information to ma

6. *Evaluation*: judging or forming an opinion about the inf
   or situation

Ideally, in order for a client to learn, there should be objectives at each of these levels. Clients may have goals to learn in any of three domains of development:

1. *Cognitive*: mental skills (knowledge)

2. *Affective*: growth in feelings or emotional areas (attitude or self)

3. *Psychomotor*: manual or physical skills (skills)

Jean Piaget was a developmental psychologist best known for his theory of cognitive development. His stages address the acquisition of knowledge and how humans come to gradually acquire it. Piaget's theory holds that children learn though interaction with the environment and others.

Piaget also developed a theory of moral development, but the work by Lawrence Kohlberg is best known in this area. He agreed with Piaget's theory of moral development in principle, but wanted to develop the ideas further.

Stage	Age	Characteristics
1. Sensorimotor	0–2 years	a. Retains image of objects b. Develops primitive logic in manipulating objects c. Begins intentional actions d. Play is imitative e. Signals meaning—infant invests meaning in event (i.e., babysitter arriving means mother is leaving) f. Symbol meaning (language) begins in last part of stage
2. Preoperational	2–7 years	a. Progress from concrete to abstract thinking b. Can comprehend past, present, future c. Night terrors d. Acquires words and symbols e. Magical thinking f. Thinking is not generalized g. Thinking is concrete, irreversible, egocentric h. Cannot see another point of view i. Thinking is centered on one detail or event

(continued)

Stage	Age	Characteristics
		Imaginary friends often emerge during this stage and may last into elementary school. Although children do interact with them, most know that their friends are not real and only pretend they are real. Thus, having an imaginary friend in childhood does not indicate the presence of a disorder. It is a normal part of development and social workers should normalize behavior with parents who are distressed about this activity during this developmental stage.
3. Concrete Operations	7–11 years	a. Beginnings of abstract thought b. Plays games with rules c. Cause and effect relationship understood d. Logical implications are understood e. Thinking is independent of experience f. Thinking is reversible g. Rules of logic are developed
4. Formal Operations	11 through maturity	a. Higher level of abstraction b. Planning for future c. Thinks hypothetically d. Assumes adult roles and responsibilities

Kohlberg believed that moral development parallels cognitive development. Kohlberg's theory holds that moral reasoning, which is the basis for ethical behavior, has six identifiable developmental constructive stages—each more adequate at responding to moral dilemmas than the last. Kohlberg suggested that the higher stages of moral development provide the person with greater capacities or abilities in terms of decision making and that these stages allow people to handle increasingly complex dilemmas. He grouped his six stages of moral reasoning into three major levels. A person must pass through each successive stage of moral development without skipping a stage.

Level	Age	Stage	Orientation
Preconventional	Elementary school level (before age 9)	1	Child obeys an authority figure out of fear of punishment. Obedience/punishment.
		2	Child acts acceptably as it is in her or his best interests. Conforms to rules to receive rewards.

(continued)

Level	Age	Stage	Orientation
Conventional (follow stereotypic norms of morality)	Early adolescence	3	Person acts to gain approval from others. "Good boy/good girl" orientation.
		4	Obeys laws and fulfills obligations and duties to maintain social system. Rules are rules. Avoids censure and guilt.
Postconventional (this level is not reached by most adults)	Adult	5	Genuine interest in welfare of others; concerned with individual rights and being morally right.
		6	Guided by individual principles based on broad, universal ethical principles. Concern for larger universal issues of morality.

Learning theory is a conceptual framework describing how information is absorbed, processed, and retained during learning. Cognitive, emotional, and environmental influences, as well as prior experience, all play a part in how understanding, or a worldview, is acquired or changed, as well as how knowledge and skills are retained.

There are many learning theories but all can be conceptualized as fitting into four distinct orientations:

1. Behaviorist (Pavlov, Skinner)—learning is viewed through change in behavior and the stimuli in the external environment are the locus of learning. Social workers aim to change the external environment in order to bring about desired change.

2. Cognitive (Piaget)—learning is viewed through internal mental processes (including insight, information processing, memory, and perception) and the locus of learning is internal cognitive structures. Social workers aim to develop opportunities to foster capacity and skills to improve learning.

3. Humanistic (Maslow)—learning is viewed as a person's activities aimed at reaching his or her full potential, and the locus of learning is in meeting cognitive and other needs. Social workers aim to develop the whole person.

4. Social/Situational (Bandura)—learning is obtained between people and their environment and their interactions and observations in social contexts. Social workers establish opportunities for conversation and participation to occur.

Behavioral Development

Behavioral theories suggest that personality is a result of interaction between the individual and the environment. Behavioral theorists study observable and measurable behaviors, rejecting theories that take internal thoughts and feelings into account.

These theories represent the systematic application of principles of learning to the analysis and treatment of behaviors. Behaviors determine feelings. Thus, changing behaviors will also change or eliminate undesired feelings. The goal is to modify behavior.

The focus is on observable behavior—a target symptom, a problem behavior, or an environmental condition, rather than on the personality of a client.

There are two fundamental classes of behavior: respondent and operant.

1. Respondent: involuntary behavior (anxiety, sexual response) that is automatically elicited by certain behavior. A stimulus elicits a response.

2. Operant: voluntary behavior (walking, talking) that is controlled by its consequences in the environment.

Best known applications of behavior modification are Sexual Dysfunction, phobic disorders, compulsive behaviors (i.e., overeating, smoking), and training of persons with Intellectual Disabilities and/or Autism Spectrum Disorder.

It is impractical for those using behavior modification to observe behavior when clients are not in residential inpatient settings offering 24-hour care. Thus, social workers train clients to observe and monitor their own behaviors. For example, clients can monitor their food intake or how many cigarettes they smoke. Client self-monitoring has advantages (i.e., inexpensive, practical, and therapeutic) and disadvantages (i.e., clients can collect inadequate and inaccurate information or can resist collecting any at all).

There are several behavioral paradigms.

A. RESPONDENT OR CLASSICAL CONDITIONING (Pavlov): Learning occurs as a result of pairing previously neutral (conditioned) stimulus with an unconditioned (involuntary) stimulus so that the conditioned stimulus eventually elicits the response normally elicited by the unconditioned stimulus.

Unconditioned Stimulus ⟶ Unconditioned Response
Unconditioned Stimulus + Conditioned Stimulus ⟶ Unconditioned Response
Conditioned Stimulus ⟶ Conditioned Response

B. OPERANT CONDITIONING (B. F. Skinner): Antecedent events or stimuli precede behaviors, which, in turn, are followed by consequences. Consequences that increase the occurrence of the behavior are referred to as reinforcing consequences; consequences that decrease the occurrence of the behavior are referred to as punishing consequences. Reinforcement aims to increase behavior frequency, whereas punishment aims to decrease it.

Antecedent ⟶ Response/Behavior ⟶ Consequence

Operant Techniques:

1. **Positive reinforcement:** Increases probability that behavior will occur—praising, giving tokens, or otherwise rewarding positive behavior.

2. **Negative reinforcement:** Behavior increases because a negative (aversive) stimulus is removed (i.e., remove shock).

3. **Positive punishment:** Presentation of undesirable stimulus following a behavior for the purpose of decreasing or eliminating that behavior (i.e., hitting, shocking).

4. **Negative punishment:** Removal of a desirable stimulus following a behavior for the purpose of decreasing or eliminating that behavior (i.e., removing something positive, such as a token or dessert).

Specific Behavioral Terms:

1. **Aversion therapy:** Any treatment aimed at reducing the attractiveness of a stimulus or a behavior by repeated pairing of it with an aversive stimulus. **An example of this is treating alcoholism with Antabuse.**

2. **Biofeedback:** Behavior training program that teaches a person how to control certain functions such as heart rate, blood pressure, temperature, and muscular tension. Biofeedback is often used for Attention-Deficit/Hyperactivity Disorder (ADHD) and Anxiety Disorders.

3. **Extinction:** Withholding a reinforcer that normally follows a behavior. Behavior that fails to produce reinforcement will eventually cease.

4. **Flooding:** A treatment procedure in which a client's anxiety is extinguished by prolonged real or imagined exposure to high-intensity feared stimuli.

5. **In vivo desensitization:** Pairing and movement through a hierarchy of anxiety, from least to most anxiety-provoking situations; takes place in "real" setting.

6. **Modeling:** Method of instruction that involves an individual (the model) demonstrating the behavior to be acquired by a client.

7. **Rational emotive therapy (RET):** A cognitively oriented therapy in which a social worker seeks to change a client's irrational beliefs by argument, persuasion, and rational reevaluation and by teaching a

client to counter self-defeating thinking with new, nondistressing self-statements.

8. **Shaping:** Method used to train a new behavior by prompting and reinforcing successive approximations of the desired behavior.

9. **Systematic desensitization:** An anxiety-inhibiting response cannot occur at the same time as the anxiety response. Anxiety producing stimulus is paired with relaxation producing response so that eventually an anxiety-producing stimulus produces a relaxation response. At each step a client's reaction of fear or dread is overcome by pleasant feelings engendered as the new behavior is reinforced by receiving a reward. The reward could be a compliment, a gift, or relaxation.

10. **Time out:** Removal of something desirable—negative punishment technique.

11. **Token economy:** A client receives tokens as reinforcement for performing specified behaviors. The tokens function as currency within the environment and can be exchanged for desired goods, services, or privileges.

THE INDICATORS OF NORMAL AND ABNORMAL PHYSICAL, COGNITIVE, EMOTIONAL, AND SEXUAL DEVELOPMENT THROUGHOUT THE LIFESPAN

Human growth, development, and learning become progressively complex over time and are influenced through a variety of experiences and interactions. Growth, development, and learning proceed in predictable patterns reflecting increasingly complex levels of organization across the life course. Each developmental stage has distinctive characteristics; however, each builds from the experiences of earlier stages. The domains of development are integrated within the child, so when one area is affected, other areas are also affected. Development proceeds at varying rates from child to child, as well as across developmental domains for individual children, reflecting the unique nature of each. Because growth and development are generally predictable, social workers should know the milestones of healthy development and the signs of potential delay or disability.

Child Development

Child development refers to the physical, mental, and socioemotional changes that occur between birth and the end of adolescence, as a child progresses from dependency to increasing autonomy. It is a continuous process with a predictable sequence, yet having a unique course. Individuals do not progress at the same rate, and each stage is affected by the preceding types of development. Because these developmental changes may be strongly influenced by genetic factors and events during prenatal life, genetics and prenatal development are usually included as part of the study of child development.

Infants and Toddlers (Age 0–3)

Healthy Growth and Development

- Physical—grows at a rapid rate, especially brain size
- Mental—learns through senses, exploring, playing, communicates by crying, babbling, then "baby talk," simple sentences
- Social–Emotional—seeks to build trust in others, dependent, beginning to develop a sense of self

Key Health Care Issues

- Communication—provide security, physical closeness; promote healthy parent–child bonds
- Health—keep immunizations/checkups on schedule; provide proper nutrition, sleep, skin care, oral health, routine screenings
- Safety—ensure a safe environment for exploring, playing, sleeping

Examples of age-specific care for infants and toddlers:

- Involve child and parent(s) in care during feeding, diapering, and bathing
- Provide safe toys and opportunities for play
- Encourage child to communicate—smile, talk softly to him or her
- Help parent(s) learn about proper child care

Young Children (Age 4–6)

Healthy Growth and Development

- Physical—grows at a slower rate; improving motor skills; dresses self, toilet trained
- Mental—begins to use symbols; improving memory; vivid imagination, fears; likes stories
- Social–Emotional—identifies with parent(s); becomes more independent; sensitive to others' feelings

Key Health Care Issues

- Communication—give praise, rewards, clear rules
- Health—keep immunizations/checkups on schedule; promote healthy habits (good nutrition, personal hygiene, etc.)
- Safety—promote safety habits (use bike helmets, safety belts, etc.)

Examples of age-specific care for young children:

- Involve parent(s) and child in care—let child make some food choices
- Use toys and games to teach child and reduce fear
- Encourage child to ask questions, play with others, and talk about feelings
- Help parent(s) teach child safety rules

Older Children (Age 7–12)

Healthy Growth and Development

- Physical—grows slowly until a "spurt" at puberty
- Mental—understands cause and effect, can read, write, do math; active, eager learner
- Social–Emotional—develops greater sense of self; focuses on school activities, negotiates for greater independence

Key Health Care Issues

- Communication—help child to feel competent, useful
- Health—keep immunizations/checkups on schedule; give information on alcohol, tobacco, other drugs, sexuality
- Safety—promote safety habits (playground safety, resolving conflicts peacefully, etc.)

Examples of age-specific care for older children:

- Allow child to make some care decisions (in which arm do you want vaccination?)
- Build self-esteem—ask child to help you do a task, recognize his or her achievements, and so on
- Guide child in making healthy, safe, lifestyle choices
- Help parent(s) talk with child about peer pressure, sexuality, alcohol, tobacco, and other drugs

Adolescent Development

The development of children ages 13 to 18 years old is a critical time as children develop the ability to understand abstract ideas, such as higher math concepts, and develop moral philosophies, including rights and privileges, and move toward a more mature sense of themselves and their purpose.

Healthy Growth and Development

- Physical—grows in spurts; matures physically; able to reproduce
- Mental—becomes an abstract thinker (goes beyond simple solutions, can consider many options, etc.); chooses own values
- Social–Emotional—develops own identity; builds close relationships; tries to balance peer group with family interests; concerned about appearances, challenges authority

Key Health Care Issues

- Communication—provide acceptance, privacy; build teamwork, respect
- Health—encourage regular checkups; promote sexual responsibility; advise against substance abuse; update immunizations
- Safety—discourage risk-taking (promote safe driving, violence prevention, etc.)

Examples of age-specific care for adolescents:

- Treat more as an adult than child—avoid authoritarian approaches
- Show respect—be considerate of how treatment may affect relationships
- Guide teen in making positive lifestyle choices (i.e., correct misinformation from teen's peers)
- Encourage open communication between parent(s), teen, and peers

Adult Development

Adult development refers to the changes that occur in biological, psychological, and interpersonal domains of human life from the end of adolescence until the end of life. These changes may be gradual or rapid, and can reflect positive, negative, or no change from previous levels of functioning.

Young Adults (Age 18–35)

Healthy Growth and Development

- Physical—reaches physical and sexual maturity, nutritional needs are for maintenance, not growth
- Mental—acquires new skills, information; uses these to solve problems
- Social–Emotional—seeks closeness with others; sets career goals; chooses lifestyle, community; starts own family

Key Health Care Issues

- Communication—be supportive and honest; respect personal values
- Health—encourage regular checkups; promote healthy lifestyle (proper nutrition, exercise, weight, etc.); inform about health risks (heart disease, cancer, etc.); update immunizations
- Safety—provide information on hazards at home, work

Examples of age-specific care for young adults:

- Support the person in making health care decisions
- Encourage healthy and safe habits at work and home
- Recognize commitments to family, career, community (time, money, etc.)

Middle Age Adults (Age 36–64)

Healthy Growth and Development

- Physical—begins to age; experiences menopause (women); may develop chronic health problems
- Mental—uses life experiences to learn, create, solve problems
- Social–Emotional—hopes to contribute to future generations; stays productive, avoids feeling "stuck" in life; balances dreams with reality; plans retirement; may care for children and parents

Key Health Care Issues

- Communication—keep a hopeful attitude; focus on strengths, not limitations
- Health—encourage regular checkups and preventive exams; address age-related changes; monitor health risks; update immunizations
- Safety—address age-related changes (effects on sense, reflexes, etc.)

Examples of age-specific care for middle adults:

- Address worries about future—encourage talking about feelings, plans, and so on
- Recognize the person's physical, mental, and social abilities/ contributions
- Help with plans for a healthy active retirement

Older Adults (Age 65–79)

Healthy Growth and Development

- Physical—ages gradually; natural decline in some physical abilities, senses
- Mental—continues to be an active learner, thinker; memory skills may start to decline
- Social–Emotional—takes on new roles (grandparent, widow or widower, etc.); balances independence, dependence; reviews life

Key Health Care Issues

- Communication—give respect, prevent isolation, encourage acceptance of aging
- Health—monitor health closely; promote physical, mental, social activity; guard against depression, apathy; update immunizations
- Safety—promote home safety; especially preventing falls

Examples of age-specific care for older adults:

- Encourage the person to talk about feelings of loss, grief, and achievements
- Provide information, materials, and so on, to make medication use and home safe
- Provide support for coping with any impairments (avoid making assumptions about loss of abilities)
- Encourage social activity with peers, as a volunteer, and so on

Elders (Age 80 and Older)

Healthy Growth and Development

- Physical—continues to decline in physical abilities; at increasing risk for chronic illness, major health problems

■ Mental—continues to learn; memory skills and/or speed of learning may decline; confusion often signals illness or medication problem

■ Social–Emotional—accepts end of life and personal losses; lives as independently as possible

Key Health Care Issues

■ Communication—encourage the person to express feelings, thoughts, avoid despair; use humor, stay positive

■ Health—monitor health closely, promote self-care; ensure proper nutrition, activity level, rest; reduce stress, update immunizations

■ Safety—prevent injury, ensure safe living environment

Examples of age-specific care for adults ages 80 and older:

■ Encourage independence—provide physical, mental, and social activities

■ Support end-of-life decisions—provide information, resources, and so on

■ Assist the person in self-care—promote medication safety; provide safety grips, ramps, and so on

THEORIES OF SEXUAL DEVELOPMENT THROUGHOUT THE LIFESPAN

Many people cannot imagine that everyone—babies, children, teens, adults, and older adults—are sexual beings. Some inappropriately believe that sexual activity is reserved for early and middle adulthood. Teens often feel that adults are too old for sexual intercourse. Sexuality, though, is much more than sexual intercourse. Humans are sexual beings throughout life.

Sexuality in infants and toddlers—Children are sexual even before birth. Males can have erections while still in the uterus, and some boys are born with an erection. Infants touch and rub their genitals because it provides pleasure. Little boys and girls can experience orgasm from masturbation, although boys will not ejaculate until puberty. By about age 2, children know their own gender. They are aware of differences in the genitals of males and females and in how males and females urinate.

Sexuality in children (age 3–7)—Preschool children are interested in everything about their world, including sexuality. They may practice urinating in different positions. They are highly affectionate and enjoy hugging other children and adults. They begin to be more social and may imitate adult social and sexual behaviors, such as holding hands and kissing. Many young children play "doctor" during this stage, looking at other children's genitals and showing theirs. This is normal curiosity. By age 5 or 6, most children become more modest and private about dressing and bathing.

Children of this age are aware of marriage and understand living together, based on their family experience. They may role play about being married or having a partner while they "play house." Most young children talk about marrying and/or living with a person they love when they get older. Most sex play at this age happens because of curiosity.

Sexuality in preadolescent youth (age 8–12)—Puberty, the time when the body matures, begins between the ages of 9 and 12 for most children. Girls begin to grow breast buds and pubic hair as early as 9 or 10. Boys' development of the penis and testicles usually begins between 10 and 11. Children become more self-conscious about their bodies at this age and often feel uncomfortable undressing in front of others, even a same-sex parent.

Masturbation increases during these years. Preadolescent boys and girls do not usually have much sexual experience, but they often have many questions. They usually have heard about sexual intercourse, homosexuality, rape, and incest, and they want to know more about all these things. The idea of actually having sexual intercourse, however, is unpleasant to most preadolescent boys and girls.

Same-gender sexual behavior can occur at this age. Boys and girls tend to play with friends of the same gender and are likely to explore sexuality with them. Same-gender sexual behavior is unrelated to a child's sexual orientation.

Some group dating occurs at this age. Preadolescents may attend parties that have guests of both genders, and they may dance and play kissing games. By age 12 or 13, some young adolescents may pair off and begin dating and/or "making out." Young women are usually older when they begin voluntary sexual intercourse. However, many very young teens do practice sexual behaviors other than vaginal intercourse, such as petting to orgasm and oral sex.

Sexuality in adolescent youth (age 13–19)—Once youth have reached puberty and beyond, they experience increased interest in romantic and sexual relationships and in genital sex behaviors. As youth mature, they experience strong emotional attachments to romantic partners and find it natural to express their feelings within sexual relationships. There is no way to predict how a particular teenager will act sexually. Overall, most adolescents explore relationships with one another, fall in and out of love, and participate in sexual intercourse before the age of 20.

Adult sexuality—Adult sexual behaviors are extremely varied and, in most cases, remain part of an adult's life until death. At around age 50, women experience menopause, which affects their sexuality in that their ovaries no longer release eggs and their bodies no longer produce estrogen. They may experience several physical changes. Vaginal walls become thinner and vaginal intercourse may be painful because there is less vaginal lubrication and the entrance to the vagina becomes smaller. Many women use estrogen replacement therapy to relieve physical and emotional side effects of menopause. Use of vaginal lubricants can also make vaginal intercourse easier. Most women are able to have pleasurable sexual intercourse and to experience orgasm for their entire lives.

Adult men also experience some changes in their sexuality, but not at such a predictable time as with menopause in women. Men's testicles slow testosterone production after age 25 or so. Erections may occur more slowly once testosterone production slows. Men also become less able to have another erection after an orgasm and may take up to 24 hours to achieve and sustain another erection. The amount of semen released during ejaculation also decreases, but men are capable of fathering a baby even when they are in their 80s and 90s. Some older men develop an enlarged or cancerous prostate gland. If the doctors deem it necessary to remove the prostate gland, a man's ability to have an erection or an orgasm is normally unaffected.

Although adult men and women go through some sexual changes as they age, they do not lose their desire or their ability for sexual expression. Even among the very old, the need for touch and intimacy remains, although the desire and ability to have sexual intercourse may lessen.

THEORIES OF SPIRITUAL DEVELOPMENT THROUGHOUT THE LIFESPAN

Many models attempt to explain the impact of spirituality and/or religious beliefs on behavior. Many of them describe this impact along a continuum as follows, with some individuals changing during their life course and others remaining at the same point.

Individuals are unwilling to accept a will greater than their own.

Behavior is chaotic, disordered, and reckless. Individuals tend to defy and disobey, and are extremely egoistic. They lack empathy for others. Very young children can be at this stage. Adults who do not move beyond this point in the continuum may engage in criminal activity because they cannot obey rules.

Individuals have blind faith in authority figures and see the world as divided simply into good and evil and right and wrong.

Children who learn to obey their parents and other authority figures move to this point in the continuum. Many "religious" people who have blind faith in a spiritual being and do not question its existence may also be at this point. Individuals who are good, law-abiding citizens may never move further in the continuum.

Scientific skepticism and questioning are critical, because an individual does not accept things on faith, but only if convinced logically.

Many people working in a scientific and technical field may question spiritual or supernatural forces because they are difficult to measure or prove scientifically. Those who do engage in this skepticism move away from the simple, official doctrines.

The individual starts enjoying the mystery and beauty of nature and existence.

The individual develops a deeper understanding of good and evil, forgiveness and mercy, compassion and love. Religiousness and spirituality differ significantly from other points in the continuum and things are not accepted on blind faith or out of fear. The individual does not judge people harshly or seek to inflict punishment on them for their transgressions. This is the stage of loving others as one loves oneself, losing attachment to ego, and forgiving enemies.

Basic principles of all models move from the "egocentric," which are associated particularly with childhood, to "conformist," and eventually to "integration" or "universal."

THEORIES OF RACIAL, ETHNIC, AND CULTURAL DEVELOPMENT THROUGHOUT THE LIFESPAN

Ethnicity refers to the idea that one is a member of a particular cultural, national, or racial group that may share culture, religion, race, language, or place of origin. Two people can share the same race but have different ethnicities.

The meaning of **race** is not fixed; it is related to a particular social, historical, and geographic context. The way races are classified has changed in the public mind over time; for example, at one time racial classifications were based on ethnicity or nationality, religion, or minority language groups. Today, society classifies people into different races primarily based on skin color.

Cultural identity is often defined as the identity of a group or culture of an individual who is influenced by his or her self-identification with that group or culture. Certain ethnic and racial identities may also bestow privilege.

Cultural, racial, and ethnic identities are important. They may instill feelings of shared commitment and values and a sense of belonging that may otherwise be missing.

Cultural, racial, and ethnic identities are passed from one generation to the next through customs, traditions, language, religious practice, and cultural values. Current events, mainstream media, and popular literature also influence cultural, racial, and ethnic identities.

Cultural, racial, and ethnic identities play a particularly large role among minority youth because they experience the contrasting and dominant culture of the majority ethnic group. Youth who belong to the majority ethnic culture may not even recognize or acknowledge their cultural, racial, and ethnic identities.

Following is a three-stage model for adolescent cultural and ethnic identity development. These stages do not correspond to specific ages, but can occur at any time. Individuals may spend their entire lives at a particular stage.

- The first stage, **unexamined cultural, racial, and ethnic identity**, is characterized by a lack of exploration of culture, race, and ethnicity and cultural, racial, and ethnic differences—they are rather taken for granted without much critical thinking. This is usually the stage reserved for childhood when cultural, racial, and ethnic ideas provided by parents, the community, or the media are easily accepted. Children at this stage tend not to be interested in culture, race, or ethnicity and are generally ready to take on the opinions of others.

- The second stage of the model is referred to as the **cultural, racial, and ethnic identity search** and is characterized by the exploration and questioning of culture, race, and ethnicity in order to learn more about them and to understand the implications of belonging. During this stage, there is questioning of where beliefs come from and why they are held. For some, this stage may arise from a turning point in their lives or from a growing awareness of other cultures, races, and ethnicities. It can also be a very emotional time.

- Finally, the third stage of the model is **cultural, racial, and ethnic identity achievement**. Ideally, people at this stage have a clear sense of their cultural, racial, and ethnic identity and are able to successfully navigate it in the contemporary world, which is undoubtedly very interconnected and intercultural. The acceptance of cultural, racial, and ethnic identity may play a significant role in important life decisions and choices, influencing attitudes and behavior. This usually leads to an increase in self-confidence and positive psychological development.

The classic model of cultural, racial, and ethnic identity development refers to identity statuses rather than stages, because stages imply a linear progression of steps that may not occur for all.

- **Preencounter:** At this point, the client may not be consciously aware of his or her culture, race, or ethnicity and how it may affect his or her life.

- **Encounter:** A client has an encounter that provokes thought about the role of cultural, racial, and ethnic identification in his or her life. This may be a negative or positive experience related to culture, race, and ethnicity. For minorities, this experience is often a negative one in which they experience discrimination for the first time.

- ■ **Immersion–Emersion:** After an encounter that forces a client to confront cultural, racial, and ethnic identity, a period of exploration follows. A client may search for information and will also learn through interaction with others from the same cultural, racial, or ethnic groups.
- ■ **Internalization and Commitment:** At this point, a client has developed a secure sense of identity and is comfortable socializing both within and outside the group with which he or she identifies.

THE EFFECTS OF PHYSICAL, MENTAL, AND COGNITIVE DISABILITIES THROUGHOUT THE LIFESPAN

The impacts of disabilities on human development are extremely varied depending upon the manifestations of the disability and when it occurs during the life course. Some disabilities are short-term, whereas others are lifelong. Critical to mitigating the negative impacts is the development of coping skills that strengthen a client's ability to deal with his or her limitations. Support (formal and informal) is also critical.

There may also be positive effects of disabilities because familial bonds may be stronger or individuals may develop skills to compensate for other tasks that cannot be performed.

Disability is a normal phenomenon in the sense that it exists in all societies. Although medical explanations remain primary in defining disability, the history of disability took an important turn in the latter half of the 20th century that has significantly influenced responses to it. Disability rights scholars and activists rejected the medical explanation for disability, since such explanations of permanent deficit did not advance social justice, equality of opportunity, and rights as citizens. Rather, these leaders proposed the intolerance and rigidity of social institutions, rather than medical conditions, as the explanation for disability. Words such as "inclusion," "participation," and "nondiscrimination" were introduced into the disability literature and reflected the notions that people who did not fit within the majority were disabled by stigma, prejudice, marginalization, segregation, and exclusion. This notion of disability requires the modification of societal structures to include all, rather than "fixing" individuals with varying abilities.

THE INTERPLAY OF BIOLOGICAL, PSYCHOLOGICAL, SOCIAL, AND SPIRITUAL FACTORS

Human development is a lifelong process beginning before birth and extending to death. At each moment in life, every human being is in a state of personal evolution. Physical changes largely drive the process, as our cognitive abilities advance and decline in response to the brain's growth in childhood and reduced functioning in old age. Psychosocial–spiritual development is also significantly influenced by physical growth, as changing body and brain, together with environment, shape a client's identity and relationships with other people.

Thus, development is the product of the elaborate interplay of biological, psychological, social, and spiritual influences. As children develop physically, gaining greater psychomotor control and increased brain function, they become more sophisticated cognitively—that is, more adept at thinking about and acting upon their environment. These physical and cognitive changes, in turn, allow them to develop psychosocially and spiritually, forming individual identities and relating effectively and appropriately with other people.

BASIC HUMAN NEEDS

Maslow's hierarchy of needs implies that clients are motivated to meet certain needs. When one need is fulfilled, a client seeks to fulfill the next one, and so on. This hierarchy is often depicted as a pyramid. This five stage model can be divided into basic (or deficiency) needs (i.e., physiological, safety, social, and esteem) and growth needs (self-actualization).

1. Deficiency needs—also known as D-Needs

2. Growth needs—also known as "being needs" or B-Needs

Deficiency Needs

- Physiological
- Safety
- Social
- Esteem

Maslow called these needs "deficiency needs" because he felt that these needs arise due to deprivation. The satisfaction of these needs helps to "avoid" unpleasant feelings or consequence.

Growth Needs

- Self-actualization

These needs fall on the highest level of Maslow's pyramid. They come from a place of growth rather than from a place of "lacking."

A client must satisfy lower-level basic needs before moving on to meet higher-level growth needs. After meeting lower levels of needs, a client can reach the highest level of self-actualization, but few people do so.

Every client is capable and has the desire to move up the hierarchy toward a level of self-actualization. Unfortunately, progress is often disrupted by failure to meet lower level needs. Life experiences, including divorce and loss of job, may cause a client to fluctuate between levels of the hierarchy.

Physiological needs: These needs maintain the physical organism. These are biological needs such as food, water, oxygen, and constant body temperature. If a person is deprived of these needs, he or she will die.

Safety needs: There is a need to feel safe from harm, danger, or threat of destruction. Clients need regularity and some predictability.

Social needs: Friendship, intimacy, affection, and love are needed—from one's work group, family, friends, or romantic relationships.

Esteem needs: People need a stable, firmly based level of self-respect and respect from others.

Self-actualization needs: There is a need to be oneself, to act consistently with whom one is. Self-actualization is an ongoing process. It involves developing potential, becoming, and being what one is capable of being. It makes possible true objectivity—dealing with the world as it is, rather than as one needs it to be. You are free to really do what you want to do. There are moments when everything is right (peak experience); a glimmer of what it is like to be complete. One is in a position to find one's true calling (i.e., being an artist, writer, musician). Only 1% of the population consistently operates at this level.

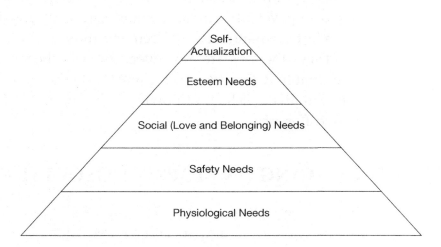

On the examination, Maslow's hierarchy of needs is often not explicitly asked about, but it can be applied when asked about the order of prioritizing problems or issues with a client. A client with an acute medical problem should focus on getting a medical evaluation first; a victim of domestic violence should prioritize medical and safety issues; and a refugee must initially meet basic survival needs (shelter, food, income, clothing, etc.) before working on fulfilling higher level needs.

THE PRINCIPLES OF ATTACHMENT AND BONDING

Attachment theory originated with the seminal work of John Bowlby. Bowlby defined attachment as a lasting psychological connectedness between human beings that can be understood within an *evolutionary* context in which a caregiver provides safety and security for a child. Bowlby suggests that children come into the world biologically preprogrammed to form attachments with others, because this will help them to survive. They initially form only one primary attachment (monotropy) and this attachment figure acts as a secure base for exploring the world. Disrupting this attachment process can have severe consequences because the critical period for developing attachment is within the first 5 years of life.

There is another major theory of attachment that suggests attachment is a set of *learned behaviors*. The basis for the learning of attachments is the provision of food. A child will initially form an attachment to whoever feeds it. This child learns to associate the feeder (usually the mother) with the comfort of being fed and, through the process of classical conditioning, comes to find contact with the mother comforting. The child also finds that certain behaviors (i.e., crying, smiling) bring desirable responses from others and through the process of operant conditioning learns to repeat these behaviors in order to get the things he or she wants.

In both of these theoretical approaches, parents have important impacts on their children's attachment system. Insecure attachment systems have been linked to psychiatric disorders and can result in clients reacting in a hostile and rejecting manner as children or adults.

These theories are, however, criticized because there are cultural influences that may impact on attachment and the ways in which children interact with caregivers. Much of Bowlby and others' work has not fully considered these differences.

THE EFFECT OF AGING ON BIOPSYCHOSOCIAL FUNCTIONING

The process of human aging is complex and individualized, causing biological, psychological, and social changes. Biological aging is characterized by progressive age-changes in metabolism, organ functioning, and so on. It is a natural and irreversible process with biological changes that occur with age in the human body affecting mood, attitude, and social activity.

Social work with older adults is based on comprehensive assessments aimed at gathering information about the quality of their biopsychosocial functioning. Social workers evaluate older adults' capacity to function effectively in their environments and determine what resources are needed to improve interpersonal functioning. The purpose of biopsychosocial assessments is to gather information on functional capacity or everyday competence—the ability of older adults to care for themselves, manage their affairs, and live independent, quality lives in their communities. Assessments may also include diagnostic medical and physical evaluations.

THE IMPACT OF AGING PARENTS ON ADULT CHILDREN

For social workers, there is an increasing need to provide services and supports to adult children as they become caregivers for their parents. In these new roles, adult children may need direct assistance with maintaining adequate nutrition, decent housing, economic stability, and access to appropriate medical care for both their parents and themselves. However, of even greater concern to adult children are a multitude of psychosocial stressors that come with the transitioning of roles and the expectations placed upon them. In these instances, there are often blurred familial roles, boundaries, and expectations.

The responsibility of caring for the aging parent often falls to adult children who are generally accepting of this responsibility. Their reasons for doing so may include fulfilling expectations, religious beliefs, sense of duty, financial rewards, altruism, and/or respect/love.

Adult children may need the assistance of social workers due to feelings of guilt, fatigue, sadness, anxiety, and/or frustration. These feelings are compounded when the assistance of adult children is not appreciated by their aging parents. Often adult children need help getting other family members to share the burden and/or getting their parents' affairs in order.

Seeing parents grow old forces adult children to confront feelings about their own mortality. Feelings can include denial, hostility, resentment, hatred of their parents or themselves, helplessness, fear, anger, and sadness. Clients may have any or all of these emotions at one time and the emotions may vary in range and intensity. In some instances, adult children may feel in a bind and begin to seek reasons for reducing their commitment to their older family members. A social worker can provide help in sorting out these feelings, finding their roots, and reframing them into empowerment, opportunity, and choice.

Clients may want help in areas such as communication (i.e., understanding requests for assistance/resistance of their parents), self-care (i.e., developing coping skills and attending to their own needs), and/or resource identification (i.e., finding services to assist in meeting child/parent needs).

Social workers need to be sensitive to client needs in these situations, since the transforming role of child to adult child of aging parents will most likely leave a client on shaky ground, especially if the role was not expected or anticipated. A social worker may need to act as a consultant, advocate, case manager, catalyst, broker, mediator, facilitator, instructor, mobilizer, and/or clinician in these situations as the family dynamic is complex and the needs are great.

GERONTOLOGY

Aging is scientifically defined as the accumulation of diverse deleterious changes occurring in cells and tissues with advancing age that are responsible for an increased risk of disease and death. Life expectancy is defined as the average total number of years that a human expects to live. The lengthening of life expectancy is mainly due to the elimination of most infectious diseases occurring in youth, better hygiene, and the adoption of antibiotics and vaccines.

The notion that aging requires treatment is based on the false belief that becoming old is undesirable. Aging has at times received a negative connotation and become synonymous with deterioration, approaching pathology, and death. Society should learn to value old age to the same extent as it presently values youth.

There are physical changes that naturally occur. In older adulthood, age-related changes in stamina, strength, or sensory perception may be noticed and will vary based on personal health choices, medical history, and genetics.

Social workers understand that old age is a time of continued growth and that older adults contribute significantly to their families, communities, and society. At the same time, clients face multiple biopsychosocial–spiritual–cultural challenges as they age: changes in health and physical abilities; difficulty in accessing comprehensive, affordable, and high-quality health and behavioral health care; decreased economic security; increased vulnerability to abuse and exploitation; and loss of meaningful social roles and opportunities to remain engaged in society. Social workers are well positioned and trained to support and advocate for older adults and their caregivers.

PERSONALITY THEORIES

Personality theories attempt to explain both personality characteristics and the way these characteristics develop and impact behavior/functioning. Theories that have this aim can be categorized as biological, behavioral, psychodynamic, humanist, or trait focused.

Biological

Biological theories suggest that genetics are responsible for personality. Research on heritability suggests that there is a link between genetics and personality traits.

Behavioral

Behavioral theories suggest that personality is a result of interaction between the individual and the environment. Behavioral theorists study observable and measurable behaviors, rejecting theories that take internal thoughts and feelings into account.

Psychodynamic

Psychodynamic theories emphasize the influence of the unconscious mind and childhood experiences on personality.

Humanist

Humanist theories emphasize the importance of free will and individual experience in the development of personality. Humanist theorists emphasized the concept of self-actualization, which is an innate need for personal growth that motivates behavior.

Trait

Trait theories posit that the personality is made up of a number of broad traits. A trait is basically a relatively stable characteristic that causes an individual to behave in certain ways.

THEORIES OF CONFLICT

Conflict theory, derived from the works of Karl Marx, posits that society is fragmented into groups that compete for social and economic resources. Social order is maintained by consensus among those with the greatest political, economic, and social resources.

According to conflict theory, inequality exists because those in control of a disproportionate share of society's resources actively defend their advantages. The masses are bound by coercion by those in power. This perspective emphasizes social control, not consensus and conformity. Groups and individuals advance their own interests, struggling over control of societal resources.

There is great attention paid to class, race, and gender in this perspective since they relate to the most pertinent and enduring struggles in society.

Conflict theorists challenge the status quo, encourage social change, and believe rich and powerful people force social order on the poor and the weak. Conflict theorists note that unequal groups usually have conflicting values and agendas, causing them to compete against one another. This constant competition between groups forms the basis for the ever-changing nature of society.

FACTORS INFLUENCING SELF-IMAGE (E.G., CULTURE, RACE, RELIGION/SPIRITUALITY, AGE, DISABILITY, TRAUMA)

Self-image is how a client defines himself or herself, which is often tied to physical description (i.e., tall, thin), social roles (i.e., mother, student), personal traits (i.e., worthy, generous), and/or existential beliefs (i.e., one with the world, a spiritual being). It is how a client sees himself or herself.

Self-esteem refers to the extent to which a client accepts or approves of this definition. Self-esteem always involves a degree of evaluation that may produce positive or negative feelings. Thus, self-image and self-esteem are linked throughout the life cycle.

Generally, self-esteem is relatively high in childhood, drops during adolescence, rises gradually throughout adulthood, and then declines sharply in old age.

Childhood: Young children have relatively high self-esteem, which gradually declines over childhood. This high self-image may be because children's self-views are unrealistically positive. As children develop cognitively, they begin to base their self-evaluations on external feedback and social comparisons, and thus form a more balanced and accurate appraisal of their academic competence, social skills, attractiveness, and other personal characteristics.

Adolescence: Self-esteem continues to decline during adolescence, perhaps due to a decrease in body image and other problems associated with puberty, as well as the increasing ability to think abstractly coupled with more academic and social challenges.

Adulthood: Self-esteem increases gradually throughout adulthood, peaking sometime around the late 60s. This increase is tied to assuming positions of power and status that might promote feelings of self-worth. Adulthood also brings an increasing level of maturity and adjustment, as well as emotional stability.

Older Adulthood: Self-esteem declines in old age, beginning to drop around age 70. This decline may be due to loss of employment due to retirement, loss of a spouse or friends, and/or health problems.

Overall, males and females follow essentially the same course during the life cycle. However, there are some interesting gender differences. Although boys and girls report similar levels of self-esteem during childhood, a gender gap emerges by adolescence, with adolescent boys having higher self-esteem than adolescent girls. This gender gap persists throughout adulthood, and then narrows and perhaps even disappears in old age.

Individuals tend to maintain their ordering relative to one another, with those who have relatively high self-esteem at one point in time tending to have relatively high self-esteem years later.

BODY IMAGE AND ITS IMPACT (E.G., IDENTITY, SELF-ESTEEM, RELATIONSHIPS, HABITS)

Body image is the way one perceives and relates to his or her body, and how one thinks he or she is seen.

Body image affects nearly everyone from time to time. Body image is not only influenced by the perceptions of others, but by the media and cultural forces as well. Senses are bombarded by an onslaught of mixed messages about how one "should" look or think about his or her body.

Having a healthy body image is a key to well-being, both mentally and physically. A positive body image means that, most of the time, a client has a realistic perception of, and feels comfortable with, his or her looks.

Factors associated with positive body image:

- Acceptance and appreciation of natural body shape and body differences
- Self-worth not tied to appearance
- Confidence in and comfort with body
- An unreasonable amount of time is not spent worrying about food, weight, or calories
- Judgment of others is not made related to their body weight, shape, and/or eating or exercise habits
- Knowing physical appearance says very little about character and value as a person

Factors of negative body image:

- Distorted perception of shape or body parts, unlike what they really are
- Believing only other people are attractive and that body size or shape is a sign of personal failure
- Feeling body doesn't measure up to family, social, or media ideals
- Ashamed, self-conscious, and anxious about body
- Uncomfortable and awkward in body
- Constant negative thoughts about body and comparisons to others

Some possible effects of a negative body image:

- Emotional distress
- Low self-esteem
- Unhealthy dieting habits
- Anxiety
- Depression
- Eating disorders
- Social withdrawal or isolation

PARENTING SKILLS AND CAPACITIES

Although there are very few actual cause-and-effect links between specific actions of parents and later behavior of children, there are four distinct parenting styles that seem to impact behavior later in life.

Authoritarian Parenting

Children are expected to follow the strict rules established by the parents. Failure to follow such rules usually results in punishment. Authoritarian parents fail to explain the reasoning behind these rules.

Authoritarian parenting styles generally lead to those who are obedient and proficient, but are lower in happiness, social competence, and self-esteem.

Authoritative Parenting

Like authoritarian parents, those with an authoritative parenting style establish rules and guidelines that their children are expected to follow. However, this parenting style is much more democratic. Authoritative parents are responsive to their children and willing to listen to questions. When children fail to meet the expectations, these parents are more nurturing and forgiving rather than punishing.

Authoritative parenting styles generally tend to result in those who are happy, capable, and successful.

Permissive Parenting

Permissive parents have very few demands on their children. These parents rarely discipline their children and are generally nurturing and communicative with their children, often taking on the status of a friend more than that of a parent.

Permissive parenting often results in children who rank low in happiness and self-regulation, experiencing problems with authority and tending fto perform poorly in school.

Uninvolved Parenting

An uninvolved parenting style is characterized by few demands, low responsiveness, and little communication. Although these parents fulfill basic needs, they are generally detached from their children's lives.

Those who have experienced uninvolved parenting styles rank lowest across all life domains. They tend to lack self-control, have low self-esteem, and are less competent than their peers.

Human Behavior in the Social Environment

2

THE FAMILY LIFE CYCLE

The emotional and intellectual stages from childhood to retirement as a member of a family are called the family life cycle. In each stage, clients face challenges in family life that allow the building or gaining of new skills.

Not everyone passes through these stages smoothly. Situations such as severe illness, financial problems, or the death of a loved one can have an effect. If skills are not learned in one stage, they can be learned in later stages.

Stage 1: **Family of origin experiences**
   Main tasks
   - Maintaining relationships with parents, siblings, and peers
   - Completing education
   - Developing the foundations of a family life

Stage 2: **Leaving home**
   Main tasks
   - Differentiating self from family of origin and parents and developing adult-to-adult relationships with parents
   - Developing intimate peer relationships
   - Beginning work, developing work identity, and financial independence

Stage 3: **Premarriage stage**
   Main tasks
   - Selecting partners
   - Developing a relationship
   - Deciding to establish own home with someone

Stage 4: **Childless couple stage**
Main tasks
- Developing a way to live together both practically and emotionally
- Adjusting relationships with families of origin and peers to include partner

Stage 5: **Family with young children**
Main tasks
- Realigning family system to make space for children
- Adopting and developing parenting roles
- Realigning relationships with families of origin to include parenting and grandparenting roles
- Facilitating children to develop peer relationships

Stage 6: **Family with adolescents**
Main tasks
- Adjusting parent–child relationships to allow adolescents more autonomy
- Adjusting family relationships to focus on midlife relationship and career issues
- Taking on responsibility of caring for families of origin

Stage 7: **Launching children**
Main tasks
- Resolving midlife issues
- Negotiating adult-to-adult relationships with children
- Adjusting to living as a couple again
- Adjusting to including in-laws and grandchildren within the family circle
- Dealing with disabilities and death in the family of origin

Stage 8: **Later family life**
Main tasks
- Coping with physiological decline in self and others
- Adjusting to children taking a more central role in family maintenance
- Valuing the wisdom and experience of the elderly
- Dealing with loss of spouse and peers
- Preparing for death, life review, and reminiscence

Mastering the skills and milestones of each stage allows successful movement from one stage of development to the next. If not mastered, clients are more likely to have difficulty with relationships and future transitions. Family life cycle theory suggests that successful transitioning may also help to prevent disease and emotional or stress-related disorders.

The stress of daily living, coping with a chronic medical condition, or other life crises can disrupt the normal life cycle. Ongoing stress or a crisis can delay the transition to the next phase of life.

FAMILY DYNAMICS AND FUNCTIONING AND THE EFFECTS ON INDIVIDUALS, FAMILIES, GROUPS, ORGANIZATIONS, AND COMMUNITIES

Family dynamics are the patterns of relating or interactions between family members. Each family system and its dynamics are unique, although there are some common patterns. All families have some helpful and some unhelpful dynamics.

Even where there is little or no present contact with family, there is almost always an influence on a client by dynamics in previous years. Family dynamics often have a strong influence on the way individuals see themselves, others, and the world, and influence their relationships, their behaviors, and their well-being.

An understanding of the impact of family dynamics on a client's self-perception may help social workers pinpoint and respond to the driving forces behind her or his current needs.

Healthy functioning is characterized by

- Treating each family member as an individual
- Having regular routines and structure
- Being connected to extended family, friends, and the community
- Having realistic expectations
- Spending quality time, which is characterized by fun, relaxed, and conflict-free interactions
- Ensuring that members take care of their own needs and not just the family needs
- Helping one another through example and direct assistance

Family dynamics significantly impact on a client's biological, psychological, and social functioning in both positive and negative ways. Having a close-knit and supportive family provides emotional support, ensures economic well-being, and increases overall health. However, the opposite is also true. When family life is characterized by stress and conflict, well-being can be poor.

Social support is one of the main ways that family positively impacts well-being. Social relationships, such as those found in close families, have been demonstrated to decrease the likelihood of negative outcomes, such as chronic disease, disability, mental illness, and death.

Though good familial relations and social support serve as protective factors and improve overall well-being and health, studies have shown that not all familial relations positively impact these areas. Problematic and nonsupportive familial interactions have a negative impact. For example, growing up in an unsupported, neglectful, or violent home is associated with poor physical health and development.

THEORIES OF COUPLES DEVELOPMENT

Although relationships vary significantly, there are some predictable stages that characterize intimate relationships. Couples interactions follow a developmental model, much like those that explain individual growth throughout the life course.

Stage 1: Romance

The first stage of couples development begins when individuals are introduced and learn that they have common interests and are attracted to one another. Much of this stage consists of conversations and dates to learn more about the other partner. The focus of this stage is attachment. Like early stages of child development, the infancy of couples development is filled with passion, nurturing, and selfless attention to the needs of others. Differences are minimized and partners place few demands on each other. This romantic bond is the foundation that is critical to the health of the relationship in the future.

In this first stage, members engage in *symbiotic or mutualistic relationships*—often putting the needs of others before their own. Individuals who are coupling do not see themselves as unique—much like babies identifying themselves as part of their mothers or caregivers. Differentiation and learning to balance and support the separate needs of others happens in later stages, but is not present initially.

Stage 2: Power Struggle

Soon individuals who are engaged in intimate relationships see that they have differences from their mates. These unique qualities result in unique needs that require an ongoing process of defining oneself and managing conflict which threatens intimacy. As the coupled individuals begin to notice differences and annoyances that were once overlooked, there can be greater separation and loss of romance resulting from self-expression. This stage differs as individuals focus on differences rather than similarities which was the hallmark of the initial romantic stage.

Time away from each other is often needed for the partners and the bliss associated with the initial stage of couples development dissolves. *Differentiation*, or seeing oneself as distinct within a relationship, must be managed so that these new feelings do not result in breakups as the illusion of "being one" fades. Critical effort must be made to balance the desire for self-discovery with the desire for intimacy. To "survive" this stage, individuals must acknowledge differences, learn to share power, forfeit fantasies of complete harmony, and accept partners without the need to change them.

Stage 3: Stability

This stage in couples development is characterized by the redirection of personal attention, time, and activities away from partners and toward one's self. Individuals focus on personal needs in a manner that is respectful of others.

Autonomy and individuality are key. Relationships are seen as more mature as disagreements can occur with both parties "winning." There is acceptance that partners are different from one another and power struggles to minimize these differences are avoided.

Margaret Mahler described *"practicing"* as a subphase of separation-individuation in infant development. Practicing occurs when toddlers begin to explore on their own, but still see themselves as part of their mothers/caregivers. The stability stage of couples development mirrors this subphase as partners learn to live independent lives while still identifying and seeing the value of being part of an intimate relationship.

Another subphase of separation-individuation identified by Mahler, *"rapprochement,"* also relates to the stability stage of couples development. Often, partners who have been successful in achieving a well-defined sense of self in relationships will have crises that will threaten their identities or separateness. They may rely more heavily on companionship and intimacy, seeking more comfort and support from each other. Thus, the stability stage is a time when there is still some back and forth between intimacy and independence with the ultimate goal being intimacy that does not sacrifice separateness.

Stage 4: Commitment

While the commitment stage of couples development is when marriage is ideal, it often occurs earlier in the romance stage, perhaps explaining the high rates of divorce caused by the inability to resolve power struggles. Individuals who have stabilized are able to embrace the reality that both partners are human, resulting in shortcomings in all relationships. Partners acknowledge that they want to be with each other and that the good outweighs the bad. Although much work has been done in building relationships, there is still more needed to effectively function in the next and last stage of couplehood.

Stage 5: Co-Creation

Constancy is the hallmark of this last stage. Just like children who are able to internalize and maintain images of their mothers/caregivers and use them to soothe in stressful moments, couples in this stage are able to do something similar. Each partner is able to value and respect the separateness of the other. The foundation of the relationship is no longer personal need, but the appreciation and love of the other and the support and respect for *mutual growth.*

Often, couples in this stage work on projects together, such as businesses, charities, and/or families. This stage aims to make a contribution beyond the relationship itself. Like Erik Erikson's stage of psychosocial functioning in middle adulthood, which focuses on the crisis of generativity versus stagnation, this stage of couples development aims to create or nurture things that are enduring, often by creating positive change that benefits other people. Success leads to feelings of usefulness and accomplishment.

As with Erikson's and other theories of development, stages are not linear. Lessons learned help couples move forward, but couples can revert back to prior stages, especially those including power struggles.

Homosexual couples also go through these developmental stages, but have unique challenges that impact relationship formation. For example, heterosexual couples have a much wider variety of public role models for their partnerships than their homosexual peers. In addition, there may be heightened concerns by partners about acceptance of their mates or even the very existence of their intimate relationships by their respective families.

THE IMPACT OF PHYSICAL AND MENTAL ILLNESS ON FAMILY DYNAMICS

Physical illness and/or disability places a set of extra demands on the family system. An illness and/or disability can consume a lot of a family's resources of time, energy, and money, so that other individual and family needs may go unmet.

Day-to-day assistance may lead to exhaustion and fatigue, taxing the physical and emotional energy of family members. There can be emotional strain, including worry, guilt, anxiety, anger, and uncertainty about the cause or prognosis of the disability, about the future, about the needs of other family members, and about whether the individual is getting enough assistance.

There can be a financial burden associated with getting health, education, and social services; buying or renting equipment and devices; making accommodations to the home; transportation; and acquiring medications and/or special food. The person or family may be eligible for payment or reimbursement from an insurance company and/or a publicly funded program such as Medicaid or Supplemental Security Income. However, knowing about services and programs and then working to become eligible is another major challenge faced by families.

Working through eligibility issues and coordinating among different providers is a challenge faced by families for which they may want a social worker to assist.

Many communities still lack programs, facilities, and resources that allow for the full inclusion of persons with disabilities. Families often report that one burden comes from dealing with people in the community whose attitudes and behaviors are judgmental, stigmatizing, and rejecting.

There are differential impacts on families. The degree to which a physical illness and/or disability limits activities or functions of daily living or the ages of individuals or parents when an illness/disability emerges are important factors that may impact on adjustment.

The impact of mental illness on family dynamics also can be profound. Mental illness of a family member affects all aspects of family functioning, including physical, financial, and emotional well-being. These impacts often depend upon the relationship of family members to a person with a mental illness. For those closest, there can be considerable time spent addressing some of the practical impacts of mental illness, such as financial problems and disruptions to daily life. This time commitment can result in family members giving up things they care about or missing appointments needed for their own health or well-being.

When mental illness is first diagnosed, family members may deny that there is a continuing illness. If there is a crisis, family members may be upset about what is happening, but the desire to put the incident "behind them" often emerges once the episode is over. Thus, family members may believe that the symptomatic behavior of the mental illness will never return. Some family members often do understand the reality of the illness, whereas others do not. This can cause problems and tension within the family, as well as isolation and loss of meaningful relationships with those who are not supportive of the illness.

Due to the stigma sometimes associated with mental illness, family members may often be reluctant to discuss it with others because they do not know how other people will react. Isolation can also occur because family members may be reluctant to invite anyone to the home for fear of the presence of unpredictable behavior and/or the fear that the activity may be a stressor, triggering behavior related to the illness. This isolation causes families to withdraw from previous relationships to protect both themselves and their loved ones.

Families may have little knowledge about mental illness. They may inappropriately believe that it is a condition that is totally disabling. Without correct information, families may become very pessimistic about the future. They may need assistance from social workers in learning how to manage the illness and to plan for the future.

It is difficult for anyone to deal with strange thinking and bizarre and unpredictable behavior. Family members may be bewildered, frightened, and exhausted. Even when stabilized, those with mental illness may have apathy and lack of motivation that can be frustrating to family members. Family members may become angry and frustrated as they struggle to get back to a routine that previously they took for granted. If the illness is not stable, families go from crisis to crisis, feeling that they have no control over what is happening. Family life can be unsettled and unpredictable. It becomes very difficult, often impossible, to plan for family outings or vacations. The needs of those with mental illness take over the attention of families and siblings can feel that their needs are put off or ignored.

PSYCHOLOGICAL DEFENSE MECHANISMS AND THEIR EFFECTS ON BEHAVIOR AND RELATIONSHIPS

To manage internal conflicts, people use defense mechanisms. **Defense mechanisms** are behaviors that protect people from anxiety. Defense mechanisms are automatic, involuntary, usually unconscious psychological activities to exclude unacceptable thoughts, urges, threats, and impulses from awareness for fear of disapproval, punishment, or other negative outcomes. Defense mechanisms are sometimes confused with coping strategies, which are voluntary.

The following are some defense mechanisms (the list of defense mechanisms is huge, and there is no theoretical consensus on the exact number).

1. **Acting Out**—emotional conflict is dealt with through actions rather than feelings (i.e., instead of talking about feeling neglected, a person will get into trouble to get attention).

2. **Compensation**—enables one to make up for real or fancied deficiencies (i.e., a person who stutters becomes a very expressive writer; a short man assumes a cocky, overbearing manner).

3. **Conversion**—repressed urge is expressed disguised as a disturbance of body function, usually of the sensory, voluntary nervous system (as pain, deafness, blindness, paralysis, convulsions, tics).

4. **Decompensation**—deterioration of existing defenses.

5. **Denial**—primitive defense; inability to acknowledge true significance of thoughts, feelings, wishes, behavior, or external reality factors that are consciously intolerable.

6. **Devaluation**—a defense mechanism frequently used by persons with borderline personality organization in which a person attributes exaggerated negative qualities to self or another. It is the split of primitive idealization.

7. **Dissociation**—a process that enables a person to split mental functions in a manner that allows him or her to express forbidden or unconscious impulses without taking responsibility for the action, either because he or she is unable to remember the disowned behavior, or because it is not experienced as his or her own (i.e., pathologically expressed as fugue states, amnesia, or dissociative neurosis, or normally expressed as daydreaming).

8. **Displacement**—directing an impulse, wish, or feeling toward a person or situation that is not its real object, thus permitting expression in a less threatening situation (i.e., a man angry at his boss kicks his dog).

9. **Idealization**—overestimation of an admired aspect or attribute of another.

10. **Identification**—universal mechanism whereby a person patterns himself or herself after a significant other. Plays a major role in personality development, especially superego development.

11. **Identification With the Aggressor**—mastering anxiety by identifying with a powerful aggressor (such as an abusing parent) to counteract feelings of helplessness and to feel powerful oneself. Usually involves behaving like the aggressor (i.e., abusing others after one has been abused oneself).

12. **Incorporation**—primitive mechanism in which psychic representation of a person is (or parts of a person are) figuratively ingested.

13. **Inhibition**—loss of motivation to engage in (usually pleasurable) activity avoided because it might stir up conflict over forbidden impulses (i.e., writing, learning, or work blocks or social shyness).

14. **Introjection**—loved or hated external objects are symbolically absorbed within self (converse of projection; i.e., in severe depression, unconscious unacceptable hatred is turned toward self).

15. **Intellectualization**—where the person avoids uncomfortable emotions by focusing on facts and logic. Emotional aspects are completely ignored as being irrelevant. Jargon is often used as a device of intellectualization. By using complex terminology, the focus is placed on the words rather than the emotions.

16. **Isolation of Affect**—unacceptable impulse, idea, or act is separated from its original memory source, thereby removing the original emotional charge associated with it.

17. **Projection**—primitive defense; attributing one's disowned attitudes, wishes, feelings, and urges to some external object or person.

18. **Projective Identification**—a form of projection utilized by persons with Borderline Personality Disorder—unconsciously perceiving others' behavior as a reflection of one's own identity.

19. **Rationalization**—third line of defense; not unconscious. Giving believable explanation for irrational behavior; motivated by unacceptable unconscious wishes or by defenses used to cope with such wishes.

20. **Reaction Formation**—person adopts affects, ideas, attitudes, or behaviors that are opposites of those he or she harbors consciously or unconsciously (i.e., excessive moral zeal masking strong, but repressed asocial impulses or being excessively sweet to mask unconscious anger).

21. **Regression**—partial or symbolic return to more infantile patterns of reacting or thinking. Can be in service to ego (i.e., as dependency during illness).

22. **Repression**—key mechanism; expressed clinically by amnesia or symptomatic forgetting serving to banish unacceptable ideas, fantasies, affects, or impulses from consciousness.

23. **Splitting**—defensive mechanism associated with Borderline Personality Disorder in which a person perceives self and others as "all good" or "all bad." Splitting serves to protect the good objects. A person cannot integrate the good and bad in people.

24. **Sublimation**—potentially maladaptive feelings or behaviors are diverted into socially acceptable, adaptive channels (i.e., a person who has angry feelings channels them into athletics).

25. **Substitution**—unattainable or unacceptable goal, emotion, or object is replaced by one more attainable or acceptable.

26. **Symbolization**—a mental representation stands for some other thing, class of things, or attribute. This mechanism underlies dream formation and some other symptoms (such as conversion reactions, obsessions, compulsions) with a link between the latent meaning of the symptom and the symbol; usually unconscious.

27. **Turning Against Self**—defense to deflect hostile aggression or other unacceptable impulses from another to self.

28. **Undoing**—a person uses words or actions to symbolically reverse or negate unacceptable thoughts, feelings, or actions (i.e., a person compulsively washing hands to deal with obsessive thoughts).

ADDICTION THEORIES AND CONCEPTS

There are many risk factors for alcohol and other drug abuse, including, but not limited to:

1. *Family:* Parents, siblings, and/or spouse use substances; family dysfunction (i.e., inconsistent discipline, poor parenting skills, lack of positive family rituals and routine); family trauma (i.e., death, divorce)

2. *Social:* Peers use drugs and alcohol; social or cultural norms condone use of substances; expectations about positive effects of drugs and alcohol; drugs and alcohol are available and accessible

3. *Psychiatric:* Depression, anxiety, low self-esteem, low tolerance for stress; other mental health disorders; feelings of desperation; loss of control over one's life

4. *Behavioral:* Use of other substances; aggressive behavior in childhood; impulsivity and risk-taking; rebelliousness; school-based academic or behavioral problems; poor interpersonal relationships

Different models are believed to explain the causes of substance abuse.

1. *Biopsychosocial model:* There are a wide variety of reasons why people start and continue using substances. This model provides the most comprehensive explanation for the complex nature of substance abuse disorders. It incorporates hereditary predisposition, emotional and psychological problems, social influences, and environmental problems.

2. *Medical model:* Addiction is considered a chronic, progressive, relapsing, and potentially fatal medical disease.

   ■ Genetic causes: Inherited vulnerability to addiction, particularly alcoholism
   ■ Brain reward mechanisms: Substances act on parts of the brain that reinforce continued use by producing pleasurable feelings
   ■ Altered brain chemistry: Habitual use of substances alters brain chemistry and continued use of substances is required to avoid feeling discomfort from a brain imbalance

3. *Self-medication model:* Substances relieve symptoms of a psychiatric disorder and continued use is reinforced by relief of symptoms.

4. *Family and environmental model:* Explanation for substance abuse can be found in family and environmental factors such as behaviors shaped by family and peers, personality factors, physical and sexual abuse, disorganized communities, and school factors.

5. *Social model:* Drug use is learned and reinforced from others who serve as role models. A potential substance abuser shares the same values and activities as those who use substances. There are no controls that prevent use of substances. Social, economic, and political factors, such as racism, poverty, sexism, and so on, contribute to the cause.

Whatever the root causes, a client's substance abuse problem must be addressed before other psychotherapeutic issues. A social worker should also rule out symptoms being related to a substance abuse problem before attributing them to a psychiatric issue.

Substance Use Disorder

Substance Use Disorder in *Diagnostic and Statistical Manual of Mental Disorders* (5th ed.; *DSM-5*) combines the *DSM-IV* categories of Substance Abuse and

Substance Dependence into a single disorder measured on a continuum from mild to severe. Each specific substance (other than caffeine, which cannot be diagnosed as a Substance Use Disorder) is addressed as a separate use disorder (Alcohol Use Disorder, Stimulant Use Disorder, etc.). Mild Substance Use Disorder in *DSM-5* requires two to three symptoms from a list of 11. Drug craving is added to the list, and problems with law enforcement are eliminated because of cultural considerations that make the criteria difficult to apply.

Non-Substance-Related Disorders

Gambling Disorder is the sole condition in a new category on behavioral addictions. Its inclusion here reflects research findings that Gambling Disorder is similar to Substance-Related Disorders in clinical expression, brain origin, comorbidity, physiology, and treatment.

Goals of Treatment

1. Abstinence from substances

2. Maximizing life functioning

3. Preventing or reducing the frequency and severity of relapse

The harm reduction model refers to any program, policy, or intervention that seeks to reduce or minimize the adverse health and social consequences associated with substance use without requiring a client to discontinue use. This definition recognizes that many substance users are unwilling or unable to abstain from use at any given time and that there is a need to provide them with options that minimize the harm that continued drug use causes to themselves, to others, and to the community.

Recovery is an ongoing process, and relapse occurs when attitudes, behaviors, and values revert to what they were during active drug or alcohol use. Relapse most frequently occurs during early stages of recovery, but it can occur at any time. Prevention of relapse is a critical part of treatment.

Stages of Treatment

1. Stabilization: Focus is on establishing abstinence, accepting a substance abuse problem, and committing oneself to making changes

2. Rehabilitation/habilitation: Focus is on remaining substance-free by establishing a stable lifestyle, developing coping and living skills, increasing supports, and grieving loss of substance use

3. Maintenance: Focus is on stabilizing gains made in treatment, relapse prevention, and termination

A social worker should be aware of the signs and symptoms of use, as well as withdrawal. For example, use of cocaine can be associated with dilated pupils, hyperactivity, restlessness, perspiration, anxiety, and impaired judgment.

Delirium tremens (DTs) is a symptom associated with alcohol withdrawal that includes hallucinations, rapid respiration, temperature abnormalities, and body tremors.

Wernicke's encephalopathy and Korsakoff's syndrome are disorders associated with chronic abuse of alcohol. They are caused by a thiamine (vitamin B_1) deficiency resulting from the chronic consumption of alcohol. A person with Korsakoff's syndrome has memory problems. Treatment is administration of thiamine.

Treatment Approaches

1. *Medication-assisted treatment* interventions assist with interfering with the symptoms associated with use. For example, methadone, a synthetic narcotic, can be legally prescribed. A client uses it to detox from opiates or on a daily basis as a substitute for heroin. Antabuse is a medication that produces highly unpleasant side effects (flushing, nausea, vomiting, hypotension, and anxiety) if a client drinks alcohol, it is a form of "aversion therapy." Naltrexone is a drug used to reduce cravings for alcohol; it also blocks the effects of opioids.

2. *Psychosocial or psychological interventions* modify maladaptive feelings, attitudes, and behaviors through individual, group, marital, or family therapy. These therapeutic interventions also examine the roles that are adopted within families in which substance abuse occurs; for example, the "family hero," "scapegoat," "lost child," or "mascot" (a family member who alleviates pain in the family by joking around).

3. *Behavioral therapies* ameliorate or extinguish undesirable behaviors and encourage desired ones through behavior modification.

4. *Self-help groups* (Alcoholics Anonymous, Narcotics Anonymous) provide mutual support and encouragement while becoming abstinent or in remaining abstinent. Twelve-step groups are utilized throughout all phases of treatment. After completing formal treatment, the recovering person can continue attendance indefinitely as a means of maintaining sobriety.

SYSTEMS AND ECOLOGICAL PERSPECTIVES AND THEORIES

A system is a whole comprising component parts that work together. Applied to social work, systems theory views human behavior through larger contexts, such as members of families, communities, and broader society.

Important to this theory is the concept that when one thing changes within a system, the whole system is affected.

Systems tend toward equilibrium and can have closed or open boundaries.

Applications to Social Work

1. Social workers need to understand interactions between the micro, mezzo, and macro levels.

2. Problems at one part of a system may be manifested at another.

3. Ecomaps and genograms can help to understand system dynamics.

4. Understanding "person-in-environment" (PIE) is essential to identifying barriers or opportunities for change.

5. Problems and change are viewed within larger contexts.

Some System Theory Terms

Closed system	Uses up its energy and dies
Differentiation	Becoming specialized in structure and function
Entropy	Closed, disorganized, stagnant; using up available energy
Equifinality	Arriving at the same end from different beginnings
Homeostasis	Steady state
Input	Obtaining resources from the environment that are necessary to attain the goals of the system
Negative entropy	Exchange of energy and resources between systems that promote growth and transformation
Open system	A system with cross-boundary exchange
Output	A product of the system that exports to the environment
Subsystem	A major component of a system made up of two or more interdependent components that interact in order to attain their own purpose(s) and the purpose(s) of the system in which they are embedded
Suprasystem	An entity that is served by a number of component systems organized in interacting relationships
Throughput	Energy that is integrated into the system so it can be used by the system to accomplish its goals

ROLE THEORIES

A role is defined as the collection of expectations that accompany a particular social position. Clients have multiple roles in their lives; in different contexts or with different people, such as being students, friends, employees, spouses, or parents.

Each of these roles carries its own expectations about appropriate behavior, speech, attire, and so on. What might be rewarded in one role would be unacceptable for another (e.g., competitive behavior is rewarded for an athlete but not a preschool teacher). Roles range from specific, in that they only apply to a certain setting, to diffuse, in that they apply across a range of situations. For example, gender roles influence behavior across many different contexts. Role theory examines how these roles influence a wide array of psychological outcomes, including behavior, attitudes, cognitions, and social interaction.

There are some important terms used in role theory.

- *Role ambiguity*: lack of clarity of role
- *Role complementarity*: the role is carried out in an expected way (i.e., parent–child, social worker–client)
- *Role discomplementarity*: the role expectations of others differ from one's own
- *Role reversal*: when two or more individuals switch roles
- *Role conflict*: incompatible or conflicting expectations

When assessing, social workers view problems as differences between clients' behaviors and the expectations of others with regard to roles.

THEORIES OF GROUP DEVELOPMENT AND FUNCTIONING

Humans are small group beings. Group work is a method of social work that helps individuals to enhance their social functioning through purposeful group experiences, as well as to cope more effectively with their personal, group, or community problems. In group work, **individuals help each other** in order to influence and change personal, group, organizational, and community problems.

A social worker focuses on helping each member change his or her environment or behavior through interpersonal experience. Members help each other change or learn social roles in the particular positions held or desired in the social environment.

A therapeutic group provides a unique microcosm in which members, through the process of interacting with each other, gain more knowledge and insight into themselves for the purpose of making changes in their lives.

The goal of the group may be a major or minor change in personality structure or changing a specific emotional or behavioral problem.

A social worker helps members come to agreement regarding the purpose, function, and structure of a group. A group is the major helping agent.

Individual self-actualization occurs through:

- Release of feelings that block social performance
- Support from others (not being alone)
- Orientation to reality and check out own reality with others
- Reappraisal of self

Some types of groups include:

- Groups centered on a shared problem
- Counseling groups
- Activity groups
- Action groups
- Self-help groups
- Natural groups
- Closed versus open groups
- Structured groups
- Crisis groups
- Reference groups (similar values)

Psychodrama is a treatment approach in which roles are enacted in a group context. Members of the group re-create their problems and devote themselves to the role dilemmas of each member.

Despite the differences in goals or purposes, all groups have common characteristics and processes.

The stages of group development are:

1. Preaffiliation—development of trust (known as forming)

2. Power and control—struggles for individual autonomy and group identification (known as storming)

3. Intimacy—utilizing self in service of the group (known as norming)

4. Differentiation—acceptance of each other as distinct individuals (known as performing)

5. Separation/termination—independence (known as adjourning)

Groups help through:

- Instillation of hope
- Universality
- Altruism
- Interpersonal learning
- Self-understanding and insight

Factors affecting group cohesion include:

- Group size
- Homogeneity: similarity of group members
- Participation in goal and norm setting for group
- Interdependence: dependent on one another for achievement of common goals
- Member stability: frequent change in membership results in less cohesiveness

Key Concepts

Groupthink is when a group makes faulty decisions because of group pressures. Groups affected by groupthink ignore alternatives and tend to take irrational actions that dehumanize other groups. A group is especially vulnerable to groupthink when its members are similar in background, when the group is insulated from outside opinions, and when there are no clear rules for decision making.

There are eight causes of groupthink:

1. Illusion of invulnerability—excessive optimism is created that encourages taking extreme risks.

2. Collective rationalization—members discount warnings and do not reconsider their assumptions.

3. Belief in inherent morality—members believe in the rightness of their cause and ignore the ethical or moral consequences of their decisions.

4. Stereotyped views of those "on the out"—negative views of the "enemy" make conflict seem unnecessary.

5. Direct pressure on dissenters—members are under pressure not to express arguments against any of the group's views.

6. Self-censorship—doubts and deviations from the perceived group consensus are not expressed.

7. Illusion of unanimity—the majority view and judgments are assumed to be unanimous.

8. Self-appointed "mindguards"—members protect the group and the leader from information that is problematic or contradictory to the group's cohesiveness, views, and/or decisions.

Group polarization occurs during group decision making when discussion strengthens a dominant point of view and results in a shift to a more extreme position than any of the members would adopt on their own. These more extreme decisions are toward greater risk if individuals' initial tendencies are to be risky and toward greater caution if individuals' initial tendencies are to be cautious.

THEORIES OF SOCIAL CHANGE AND COMMUNITY DEVELOPMENT

There is no one way to define community development. Over the years, community development has been defined as an occupation, a movement, an approach, and a set of values. It has been labeled the responsibility of social workers because it is seen as the most practical framework for creating lasting change for clients.

Community development has been used to the benefit of communities of place, of interest, and of identity. But despite these differences, there are certain principles, characteristics, and values that underpin nearly every definition of community development—neighborhood work aimed at improving the quality of community life through the participation of a broad spectrum of people at the local level.

Community development is a **long-term** commitment. It is not a quick fix to address a community's problems, nor is it a time-limited process. It aims to address imbalances in power and bring about change founded on social justice, equality, and inclusion. Its key purpose is to build communities based on justice, equality, and mutual respect.

Community development is ultimately about getting community members **working together** in collective action to tackle problems that many individuals may be experiencing or to help in achieving a shared dream that many individuals will benefit from.

THE DYNAMICS OF INTERPERSONAL RELATIONSHIPS

Family theory provides a theoretical and therapeutic base for dealing with family-related situations; it is also useful in understanding and managing individual problems by determining the extent to which such problems are related to family issues. A family systems approach argues that in order to understand a family system, a social worker must look at the family as a whole, rather than focusing on its members.

People do not exist in a vacuum. They live, play, go to school, and work with other people. Most anthropologists agree that, next to their peculiar tendency to think and use tools, one of the distinguishing characteristics of human beings is that they are social creatures. The social group that seems to be most universal and pervasive in the way it shapes human behavior is the family. For social workers, the growing awareness of the crucial impact of families on clients has led to the development of family systems theory.

Family systems theory searches for the causes of behavior, not in the individual alone, but in the interactions among the members of a group. The basic rationale is that all parts of the family are interrelated. Further, the family has properties of its own that can be known only by looking at the relationships and interactions among all members.

The family systems approach is based on several basic assumptions:

- Each family is more than a sum of its members.
- Each family is unique, due to the infinite variations in personal characteristics and cultural and ideological styles.
- A healthy family has flexibility, consistent structure, and effective exchange of information.
- The family is an interactional system whose component parts have constantly shifting boundaries and varying degrees of resistance to change.
- Families must fulfill a variety of functions for each member, both collectively and individually, if each member is to grow and develop.
- Families strive for a sense of balance or **homeostasis.**
- Negative feedback loops are those patterns of interaction that maintain stability or constancy while minimizing change. Negative feedback loops help to maintain homeostasis. Positive feedback loops, in contrast, are patterns of interaction that facilitate change or movement toward either growth or dissolution.
- Families are seen as being goal oriented. The concept of **equifinality** refers to the ability of the family system to accomplish the same goals through different routes.
- The concept of hierarchies describes how families organize themselves into various smaller units or **subsystems** that are comprised by the larger family system. When the members or tasks associated with each subsystem become blurred with those of other subsystems, families have been viewed as having difficulties. For example, when a child becomes involved in marital issues, difficulties often emerge that require intervention.
- Boundaries occur at every level of the system and between subsystems. Boundaries influence the movement of people and the flow of information into and out of the system. Some families have

very open boundaries where members and others are allowed to freely come and go without much restriction; in other families, there are tight restrictions on where family members can go and who may be brought into the family system. Boundaries also regulate the flow of information in a family. In more closed families, the rules strictly regulate what information may be discussed and with whom. In contrast, information may flow more freely in families that have more permeable boundaries.

■ The concept of interdependence is critical in the study of family systems. Individual family members and the subsystems comprised by the family system are mutually influenced by and are mutually dependent upon one another. What happens to one family member, or what one family member does, influences other family members.

Genograms are diagrams of family relationships beyond a family tree allowing a social worker and client to visualize hereditary patterns and psychological factors. They include annotations about the medical history and major personality traits of each family member. Genograms help uncover intergenerational patterns of behavior, marriage choices, family alliances and conflicts, the existence of family secrets, and other information that will shed light on a family's present situation.

MODELS OF FAMILY LIFE EDUCATION IN SOCIAL WORK PRACTICE

Family life education aims to strengthen individual and family life through a family perspective. Social workers are well suited to work with a client within the family context, which is essential for such a model.

Much of family life education is delivered through parenting classes, premarriage education, marriage enrichment programs, and/or family financial planning courses. All of these activities focus on improving a client's quality of life individually and, equally as important, within his or her family unit.

Social workers use a strengths perspective, as well as their knowledge of human development, systems and social role theories, and ecological or "PIE" influences, when engaging in family life education.

In order to work effectively with families, social workers must:

1. Understand the development of, as well as the historical, conceptual, and contextual issues influencing, family functioning

2. Have awareness of the impact of diversity in working with families, particularly race, class, culture, ethnicity, gender, sexual preference, aging, and disabilities

3. Understand the impact of a social worker's family of origin, current family structure, and its influence on a social worker's interventions with families

4. Be aware of the needs of families experiencing unique family problems (domestic violence, blended families, trauma and loss, adoptive families, etc.)

When conducting family life education, a social worker must be aware of his or her own cultural values and norms with regard to material covered and not impose these beliefs on others or be judgmental.

STRENGTHS-BASED AND RESILIENCE THEORIES

The strengths perspective is based on the assumption that clients have the capacity to grow, change, and adapt (**humanistic approach**). Clients also have the knowledge that is important in defining and solving their problems (clients or families are experts about their own lives and situations); they are resilient and survive and thrive despite difficulties.

Strength is any ability that helps an individual (or family) to confront and deal with a stressful life situation and to use the challenging situation as a stimulus for growth. Individual strengths include, but are not limited to, cognitive abilities, coping mechanisms, personal attributes, interpersonal skills, or external resources. Families may have other strengths such as kinship bonds, community supports, religious connections, flexible roles, strong ethnic traditions, and so on.

Strengths vary from one situation to another and are contextual. What may be an appropriate strength or coping mechanism in one situation may not be appropriate in another. Ideally, in a given situation, a client selects an appropriate way to cope by drawing from a repertoire of coping mechanisms or strengths. The appropriateness of a particular coping mechanism may vary according to life course stage, developmental tasks, kinds of stressors, situation, and so on. Having a variety of coping mechanisms and resources enables flexibility in the way a client copes with stresses.

The strengths perspective focuses on understanding clients (or families) on the basis of their strengths and resources (internal and external) and mobilizing the resources to improve their situations. There is a systematic assessment of all the strengths and resources available to meet desired goals. Methods to enhance strengths include:

- Collaboration and partnership between a social worker and client
- Creating opportunities for learning or displaying competencies
- Environmental modification—environment is both a resource and a target of intervention

Diversity, Social/Economic Justice, and Oppression

3

FEMINIST THEORY

Feminist theory analyzes the status of women and men in society with the purpose of using that knowledge to better women's lives. Feminist theorists question the differences between women and men, including how race, class, ethnicity, sexuality, nationality, and age intersect with gender. Themes that are studied include discrimination, objectification (especially sexual objectification), oppression, stereotyping, and so on. Feminist theory is used in the fields of social work, sociology, economics, education, and others.

Feminism is a political, cultural, or economic movement aimed at establishing equal rights and legal protection for women.

THE EFFECT OF DISABILITY ON BIOPSYCHOSOCIAL FUNCTIONING THROUGHOUT THE LIFESPAN

With increased age comes increased likelihood of disability as people live longer and do not encounter fatal diseases. Unfortunately, this positive association between age and disability sometimes leads to a negative image of aging. Given that the aging process often results in some type of disability, examinations of differences in aging outcomes have not centered around whether disabilities will occur, but rather when they will happen, how many will occur, and how severe they will be.

Disability occurs when physical or mental health declines associated with aging, illness, or injury restrict ability to perform activities of daily living (ADLs). Mobility impairment is often tied to disability because being able to ambulate and/or use one's upper extremities are critical to engaging in many activities that allow independence.

The most common causes of disability among older adults are chronic diseases, injuries, mental impairment, and/or malnutrition. Major chronic conditions related to disability include cardiovascular diseases, hypertension, stroke, diabetes, cancer, chronic obstructive pulmonary disease, muscular–skeletal conditions including arthritis and osteoporosis, mental health conditions such as dementia and depression, and blindness and visual impairment. Injuries can be due to accidents and/or falls.

There is a relationship between disability and poverty. Poverty can lead to malnutrition, poor or no health services, and/or unsafe living conditions that can result in increased risk for disability. Disability can also result in loss of income and, thus, a greater likelihood of living in poverty.

Interestingly, happiness and well-being tend to be high among older adults overall despite declines in physical and mental health and the onset of disability for some. This discrepancy is due to the fact that not all disability leads to dependence. If the consequences of disability can be reduced or eliminated altogether, its negative effects on quality of life can be minimized.

The environment and improvements in lifestyle are critical. The environment plays an important role in the impact of disability on the lives of older adults, with those remaining outside of institutional settings—such as nursing homes—being more productive and satisfied. In addition, environments based on accessible design promote independent living, which can result in good quality of life for those who are older and/or have disabilities.

Improvements in lifestyle and health behaviors include better nutrition, quitting or reducing smoking, less obesity, and greater physical activity. Benefits from exercise, even when begun later in life, can postpone and/or minimize disability.

THE EFFECT OF CULTURE, RACE, AND ETHNICITY ON BEHAVIORS, ATTITUDES, AND IDENTITY

The United States has a racially and ethnically diverse population. The Census officially recognizes six ethnic and racial categories: White American; American Indian and Alaska Native; Asian; African American; Native Hawaiian and Other Pacific Islander; and people of two or more races. The U.S. Census Bureau also classifies Americans as "Hispanic or Latino" and "Not Hispanic or Latino," which identifies Hispanic and Latino Americans as a racially diverse ethnicity that comprises the largest minority group in the nation.

A social worker must remember that there is tremendous intragroup diversity. In fact, the differences between racial and ethnic groups (intergroup) are often less profound than those found within these groups (intragroup). It is important to view a client as the expert and to not stereotype or make assumptions about values, behaviors, or attitudes based on a client's racial or ethnic group.

The following is an overview of some characteristics recognized as being more prevalent within each of the Census categories/classifications:

White American

- Family: parents with young children; divorce common; personal desires put over family; parents try to be friends with their children; avoid physical punishment
- Communication: language—American Standard English; communication can be long-winded and impersonal
- Spirituality: religion is a private affair, but mainly Protestant and Bible based
- Values: capitalism (i.e., the future is what you make it); poverty is a moral failing and wealth is held in high esteem; physical beauty is valued with white skin, blond hair, and thin body being the ideal; sports are an important part of life (baseball, American football, basketball); democracy and freedom; individual rights

American Indian/Alaska Native

- Family: complex family organizations that include relatives without blood ties; strong kinship bonds (multigenerational, extended families); group valued over individual; husband and wife show a tendency to communicate more with their gender group than with each other; harmony within the group is very important; common sharing of material goods; group decision making
- Communication: indirectness; being still and quiet; comfortable with silence; value listening and nonverbal communication; may avoid making direct eye contact as a show of respect when talking to a higher status person
- Spirituality: fundamental part of life; interconnectedness of all living things; sacredness of all creation; use of traditional and Western healing practices; medicine man, shaman, or spiritual leaders are traditional healers
- Values: holistic; interconnectedness of mind, body, spirit, and heart; time is viewed as a circular flow that is always with us; follow nature's rhythms rather than linear time

Asian

- Family: patriarchal system in which a wife has lower status and is subservient to her father, husband, and oldest son; obligation to parents and respect for elders; hierarchical family structure with strictly prescribed roles and rules of behavior and conduct

- Communication: often indirect in order to avoid direct confrontation and maintain highly valued harmonious relationships; less emotional expressiveness (reserved) and demonstration of affection

- Spirituality: cultures influenced by Confucian and Buddhist philosophies

- Values: shaming and obligation to others are mechanisms for reinforcing cultural norms; adhering to rules of conduct reflects not only on the individual, but also on the family and extended kinship network, including past and future generations; usually seek help from the family or cultural community

Asian clients may respond to psychotropic drugs differently than clients from other ethnic groups. They typically require lower doses of medications and may experience more severe side effects from the same doses given to other clients. It is sometimes recommended to start Asian clients on less than the normally prescribed dosage. They are also sometimes resistant and view treatment of symptoms via homeopathic methods as more acceptable.

African American

- Family: multigenerational family systems; strong kinship bonds, including extended families and relatives without blood ties; informal adoption of children by extended family members; flexible family roles; women are often viewed as being "all sacrificing" and the "strength of the family"

- Communication: animated; individuals try to get their opinions heard; often includes physical touch; direct; show respect at all times; history of racism and sense of powerlessness impacts interactions

- Spirituality: turn to community and/or religious leaders if assistance is needed; church is seen as a central part of community life

- Values: strong kinship bonds; strong work orientation; strong religious orientation; use informal support network—church or community; distrust of government and social services—feel "big brother" doesn't care; don't like to admit they need help—strong sense of pride

Native Hawaiian and Other Pacific Islander

- Family: Western concept of "immediate family" is completely alien to indigenous Hawaiians; family is not restricted to those related by blood; "we are all related"; ties that bind cannot be broken, even by death; cherish their ancestors, with generation upon generation of lineage committed to memory and beautiful chants composed to herald their ancestors' abilities

- Communication: many Native Hawaiian and Pacific Islander subgroups, representing different languages and customs; ability to speak English has a tremendous impact on access to health information, public services; Hawaii is the only state in the United States that has designated a native language, Hawaiian, as one of its two official state languages

- Spirituality: polytheistic, believing in many deities; belief that spirits are found in nonhuman beings and objects such as animals, waves, and the sky

- Values: importance of culture and welfare of all living in a community; focus on ensuring the health of the community as a whole; everyone has a responsibility to use his or her talents to the benefit of the whole; sharing is central

Hispanic/Latino

- Family: extended family system incorporates godparents and informally adopted children; deep sense of commitment and obligation to family; family unity, welfare, and honor are important; emphasis on group rather than individual; male has greater power and authority

- Communication: often speak Spanish (but do not assume that they wish to receive services in native language); display varied emotional expressiveness depending on language being spoken; when speaking Spanish, client may be very expansive/expressive, friendly, playful, but in switching to English, speech may be more businesslike and guarded

- Spirituality: most are Roman Catholic; emphasis on spiritual values; strong church and community orientation/interdependence

- Values: wish to improve their life circumstances; belief in the innate worth of all individuals and that people are born into their lot in life; respect for dignity of self and others; respect for elders; respect for authority; very proud of heritage—never forget where they came from

THE EFFECTS OF DISCRIMINATION AND STEREOTYPES ON BEHAVIORS, ATTITUDES, AND IDENTITY

The negative impacts of discrimination can be seen on both the micro and macro levels. Exposure to discrimination is linked to anxiety and depression as well as other mental health and behavioral problems. In addition, there may be physical effects such as diabetes, obesity, and high blood pressure. These health problems may be caused by not maintaining healthy behaviors (such as physical activity) or engaging in unhealthy ones (such as smoking and alcohol or drug abuse).

On a macro level, discrimination also restricts access to the resources and systems needed for good health, education, employment, social support, and participation in sports, cultural, and civic activities. Discrimination and intolerance can also create a climate of despondence, apprehension, and fear within a community. The social and economic effects of discrimination on one generation may flow on to affect future generations, which can lead to cycles of poverty and disadvantage through those generations.

THE INFLUENCE OF SEXUAL ORIENTATION ON BEHAVIORS, ATTITUDES, AND IDENTITY

Sexuality is a crucial part of who we are. Sexual orientation, sexual behavior, and sexual identity are three parts of sexuality that can help you understand the term better.

Sexual orientation refers to an individual's pattern of physical and emotional arousal toward other persons. People do not choose their sexual orientation—it is simply part of who they are.

Sexual behavior refers to sexual contacts or actions. It is important to realize that people's sexual orientation may not fit perfectly with their sexual behavior (what they do sexually). There are many factors that shape or determine sexual behavior and sexual orientation is only one of those factors. Sexual behavior can be influenced by peer pressure, family expectations, cultural expectations, religious beliefs, and so on.

Sexual identity also may be very different from an individual's sexual orientation. Sexual identity is about the way people present their sexual preferences. People may have private sexual identities which may be different from their public identities. Even private sexual identities can differ from sexual orientation or attractions. Many people who experience same-sex attraction and/or have sexual contact with others of the same sex do not see themselves as homosexual or bisexual.

Sexual orientation often does not fit "neatly" into a label or category. People's attractions can be complicated and often are not clear. Clients may be struggling to determine what feels right for them.

Sexual orientation can be fluid with attractions changing over time. Some people take a while to figure out these attractions. That does not mean people "grow out of" their sexual attractions or that one set of feelings was a stage, it just means people change. *It is important to not use labels and let individuals define their own sexual orientation.*

THE IMPACT OF TRANSGENDER AND TRANSITIONING PROCESS ON BEHAVIORS, ATTITUDES, IDENTITY, AND RELATIONSHIPS

"Transgender" is a term for people whose gender identity, expression, or behavior is different from those typically associated with their assigned sex at birth. "Trans" is sometimes used as shorthand for "transgender."

People might realize they are trans (that their gender identity does not align with their birth sex designation) at any point in their lives. Some people may first experience an internal sense of identity that does not match their external characteristics in early childhood. Others report realizing this in puberty or later. Societal gender norms and expectations may contribute to realization of their true gender identity. These assumptions can also contribute to dysphoria, as people might first attempt to conform to societal expectations by expressing gender identities they do not have. Feelings of distress frequently arise, during which people realize that they cannot meet these gender norms as they do not match their identities.

Transition is a time when individuals begin living as the gender with which they identify rather than the gender they were assigned at birth, which often includes changing one's first name and dressing and grooming differently. Transitioning may or may not also include medical and legal aspects, including taking hormones, having surgery, or changing identity documents (e.g. driver's license, Social Security record) to reflect one's gender identity. Medical and legal steps are costly and, therefore, unaffordable.

Transition, whether social, through hormone therapy, through surgery, or through some combination, often improves feelings of dysphoria, though it may not relieve them completely. The goal of many is for their gender to be perceived correctly by others, which is often referred to as "passing." Typically, people transition to align their physical appearance and characteristics with their gender identities. Many people begin the process after years of dysphoria and distress, and transitioning may help them feel as if they are finally able to be their true selves.

Transitioning can have significant psychological, social, and physical benefits. Anxiety and depression caused by gender dysphoria may diminish as dysphoria improves. Individuals who no longer have to make uncomfortable adjustments—such as hiding unwanted physical characteristics—may not only feel better physically but may have greater confidence and self-esteem.

People's reasons for choosing to transition, and the goals they have regarding transition, are personal and unique. Some individuals may not pursue certain aspects of transition, whether through personal choice, lack of resources, or lack of access. There is no single "right" way to transition. Gender identity does not depend on whether they have had surgery or if they are taking hormones.

Friends and family members who may have little to no understanding of gender transition or of what it means to be trans may ask invasive questions or say things that are invalidating or hurtful, regardless of intention. They may also find people's true genders difficult to accept. "You'll always be ____ to me," a mother might say, without the intention of harm. But this type of remark may be invalidating and cause distress.

Social work services can help individuals who are transgender as they consider and move through the transitioning process. They can also help family members by creating safe spaces where they can ask questions, develop a better understanding of what it means to be transgender, and learn more about what transition entails.

SYSTEMIC (INSTITUTIONALIZED) DISCRIMINATION (E.G., RACISM, SEXISM, AGEISM)

Social workers should not practice, condone, facilitate, or collaborate with any form of discrimination on the basis of race, ethnicity, national origin, color, sex, sexual orientation, gender identity or expression, age, marital status, political belief, religion, immigration status, or mental or physical disability (*NASW Code of Ethics, 2008–4.02 Discrimination*).

Discrimination can occur at the individual or institutional level. Individual discrimination is when an individual is treated differently whereas institutionalized discrimination refers to policies or practices that discriminate against a group of people based on these characteristics (achievement gaps in education, residential segregation, etc.).

THE PRINCIPLES OF CULTURALLY COMPETENT SOCIAL WORK PRACTICE

Cultural competence involves working in conjunction with natural, informal support and helping networks within the minority community (neighborhoods, churches, spiritual leaders, healers, etc.). It extends the concept of self-determination to the community. Only when a community recognizes and owns a problem does it take responsibility for creating solutions that fit the context of the culture.

Social workers should promote conditions that encourage respect for cultural and social diversity and promote policies and practices that demonstrate respect for difference, support the expansion of cultural knowledge and resources, advocate for programs and institutions that demonstrate cultural competence, and promote policies that safeguard the rights of all people.

Social workers should act to prevent and eliminate domination of, exploitation of, and discrimination against any person, group, or class on the basis of race, ethnicity, national origin, color, sex, sexual orientation, gender identity or expression, age, marital status, political belief, religion, immigration status, and mental or physical disability.

Since every client's cultural experiences are different, services must be delivered using a flexible and individualized approach. Social workers should be aware of the standards on cultural competence and social diversity (*NASW Code of Ethics, 2008*).

1. Social workers should understand culture and its function in human behavior and society, recognizing the strengths that exist in all cultures.

2. Social workers should have a knowledge base of their clients' cultures and be able to demonstrate competence in the provision of services that are sensitive to clients' cultures and to differences among people and cultural groups. *When social workers are from different racial or cultural backgrounds than their clients, they must clearly understand how these differences impact the problem-solving process.*

3. Social workers should obtain education about and seek to understand the nature of social diversity and oppression with respect to race, ethnicity, national origin, color, sex, sexual orientation, gender identity or expression, age, marital status, political belief, religion, immigration status, and mental or physical disability.

4. Social workers should also not use derogatory language in their written or verbal communications to or about clients. Social workers should use accurate and respectful language in all communications to and about clients (*NASW Code of Ethics, 2008—1.12 Derogatory Language*).

Social workers should be aware of terminology related to cultural barriers and goals.

Ethnocentrism: an orientation that holds one's own culture, ethnic, or racial group as superior to others

Stratification: structured inequality of entire categories of people who have unequal access to social rewards (e.g., ethnic stratification, social stratification)

Pluralism: a society in which diverse members maintain their own traditions while cooperatively working together and seeing others' traits as valuable (cultural pluralism—respecting and encouraging cultural difference)

Social workers must possess specific knowledge about the cultural groups with whom they work, including diverse historical experiences, adjustment styles, socioeconomic backgrounds, learning styles, cognitive skills, and/or specific cultural customs. This knowledge must include theories and principles concerning human behavior development, psychopathology, therapy, rehabilitation, and community functioning because they relate to cultural group members. Institutions, class, culture, and language barriers that prevent ethnic group members from accessing or using services must be identified and addressed.

Some approaches within organizations to promote cultural competency include recruiting multiethnic staff, including cultural competence requirements in job descriptions and performance/promotion measures, reviewing demographic trends for the geographic area served to determine service needs, creating service delivery systems that are more appropriate to the diversity of the target population, and advocating for clients as major stakeholders in the development of service delivery systems to ensure they are reflective of their cultural heritage.

SEXUAL ORIENTATION CONCEPTS

"Sexual orientation" is a term used to describe patterns of emotional, romantic, and sexual attraction—and a sense of personal and social identity based on those attractions. Sexual orientation exists along a continuum, with exclusive attraction to the opposite sex on one end of the continuum and exclusive attraction to the same sex on the other.

There are a bunch of identities associated with sexual orientation.

- People who are attracted to a different gender (e.g., women who are attracted to men or men who are attracted to women) often call themselves straight or heterosexual.

- People who are attracted to people of the same gender often call themselves gay or homosexual. Gay women may prefer the term "lesbian."

- People who are attracted to both men and women often call themselves bisexual.

- People whose attractions span across many different gender identities (male, female, transgender, genderqueer, intersex, etc.) may call themselves pansexual or queer.

- People who are unsure about their sexual orientation may call themselves questioning or curious.
- People who do not experience sexual attraction often call themselves asexual.

It is also important to note that some people don't think any of these labels describe them accurately. Some people don't like the idea of labels at all. Other people feel comfortable with certain labels and not others.

Social workers must let clients identify and use their own labels to describe their own sexual orientations.

GENDER AND GENDER IDENTITY CONCEPTS

A gender role is a theoretical construct that refers to a set of social and behavioral norms that, within a specific culture, are widely considered to be socially appropriate for individuals of a specific sex. Socially accepted gender roles differ widely between different cultures. Gender role theory asserts that observed gender differences in behavior and personality characteristics are, at least in part, socially constructed, and therefore the product of socialization experiences; this contrasts with other models of gender, which assert that gender differences are "essential" to biological sex. Thus, there is a debate over the environmental or biological causes for the development of gender roles.

Gender role theory posits that boys and girls learn to perform one's biologically assigned gender through particular behaviors and attitudes. Gender role theory emphasizes the environmental causes of gender roles and the impact of socialization, or the process of transferring norms, values, beliefs, and behaviors to group members, in learning how to behave as a male or a female. Social role theory proposes that the social structure is the underlying force in distinguishing genders and that sex-differentiated behavior is driven by the division of labor between two sexes within a society. The division of labor creates gender roles, which, in turn, lead to gendered social behavior.

Gender has several definitions. It usually refers to a set of characteristics that are either seen to distinguish between male and female, one's biological sex, or one's gender identity. Gender identity is the gender(s), or lack thereof, a person self-identifies as; it is not based on biological sex, either real or perceived, nor is it always based on sexual orientation. There are two main genders, masculine (male) and feminine (female), although in some cultures there are more genders. Gender roles refer to the set of attitudes and behaviors socially expected from those with a particular gender identity.

Gender identity usually conforms to anatomic sex in both heterosexual and homosexual individuals. However, individuals who identify as transgender feel themselves to be of a gender different from their biological sex; their gender identity does not match their anatomic or chromosomal sex. **Sexual orientation and gender identity are distinct with those who are transgender exhibiting the same full range of possible sexual orientations and interests of those who are not transgender.**

It is important to let individuals define their own gender identity. For some, gender is not just about being male or female; in fact, identity can change every day or even every few hours. **Gender fluidity**, when gender expression shifts between masculine and feminine, can be displayed in dress, expression, and self-description.

There are lots of misconceptions about gender fluidity. Gender fluidity is also not the equivalent of transgender, in which a person's gender identity is different from the one assigned at birth.

It is the belief that gender exists on a spectrum and is not binary with the ability to change at any time. Some individuals who are gender fluid prefer the pronoun "they."

THE IMPACT OF SOCIAL INSTITUTIONS ON SOCIETY

Many social institutions exist within our society. They have many functions including satisfying individuals' basic needs, defining and promoting dominant social values, defining and promoting individual roles, creating permanent patterns of social behavior, and supporting other social institutions.

The five basic institutions are family, religion, government, education, and economics.

Some of the functions of each of these institutions include the following.

Family

- To control and regulate sexual behavior
- To provide for new members of society (children)
- To provide for the economic and emotional maintenance of individuals
- To provide for primary socialization of children

Religion

- To provide solutions for the unexplained
- To support the normative structure of the society
- To provide a psychological diversion from unwanted life situations
- To sustain the existing class structure
- To promote and prevent social change

Government

- To create norms via laws and enforce them
- To adjudicate conflict via the courts
- To provide for the welfare of members of society
- To protect society from external threats

Education

- To transmit culture
- To prepare for jobs and roles
- To evaluate and select competent individuals
- To transmit functional skills

Economics

- To provide methods for the production and distribution of goods and services
- To enable individuals to acquire goods and services that are produced

THE EFFECT OF POVERTY ON INDIVIDUALS, FAMILIES, GROUPS, ORGANIZATIONS, AND COMMUNITIES

Clients who are poor often do not have resources to meet their basic needs. There are many social problems that contribute to and result from poverty, including, but not limited to, little or no education, poor basic nutrition and hygiene, disability or illness, unemployment, substance abuse, and homelessness.

Family income has selective but, in some instances, quite substantial impacts on child and adolescent well-being. Family income appears to be more strongly related to children's ability and achievement than to their emotional outcomes.

Children who live in extreme poverty or who live below the poverty line for multiple years appear, all other things being equal, to suffer the worst outcomes. The timing of poverty also seems to be important for certain outcomes. Children who experience poverty during their preschool and early school years have lower rates of school completion than children and adolescents who experience poverty only in later years. Although more research is needed, findings to date suggest that interventions during early childhood may be most important in reducing poverty's impact on children.

Social workers must also consider the implications on the biopsychosocial–spiritual–cultural aspects of well-being. Medical care may be neglected in order to meet other needs. Coping skills are needed when there are dramatic changes in income and opportunities to adapt and return to economic stability are critical.

Wealth is often poorly distributed. A small minority has all the money, causing major societal tensions and divisions. There are the "haves" and the "have nots." Communities are often homogeneous—with those comprised of poor people being segregated from those living above the poverty line. Communities comprised of the poor have fewer opportunities and resources to assist their members, leading to a greater likelihood that they will not be able to break out of the cycle that originally resulted in their economic insecurity. Thus, those born into poverty often remain there throughout their life course.

THE IMPACT OF THE ENVIRONMENT (E.G., SOCIAL, PHYSICAL, CULTURAL, POLITICAL, ECONOMIC) ON INDIVIDUALS, FAMILIES, GROUPS, ORGANIZATIONS, AND COMMUNITIES

Social workers must be knowledgeable about human behavior across the life course, the range of social systems in which people live, and the ways social systems promote or deter people in maintaining or achieving health and well-being. Social workers should apply theories and knowledge to understand biological, social, cultural, psychological, and spiritual development.

The ecological perspective is rooted in systems theory, which views coping as a transactional process that reflects the "PIE" relationship. Using this perspective, the focus of intervention is the interface between a client (person, family, group, etc.) and a client's environment. The ecological perspective is also concerned with the issues of power and privilege and how they are withheld from some groups, imposing enormous stress on affected individuals.

Environmental factors can have strong positive or negative impacts on development.

PERSON-IN-ENVIRONMENT (PIE) THEORY

The PIE perspective highlights the importance of understanding individual behavior in light of the environmental contexts in which a client lives and acts. The perspective has historical roots in the social work profession.

The PIE classification system was developed as an alternative to the commonly used disease and moral models (i.e. *DSM*, *International Statistical Classification of Diseases and Related Health Problems* [ICD], civil or penal-codes) to implement social work philosophy and area of expertise. PIE is client-centered, rather than agency-centered.

The PIE classification system is field-tested and examines social role functioning, the environment, mental health, and physical health.

SOCIAL AND ECONOMIC JUSTICE

Social work is a profession aimed at helping people address their problems and match them with the resources they need to lead healthy and productive lives. One of the most important values of the social work profession is social and economic justice. Social justice is the view that everyone deserves equal economic, political, and social rights and opportunities.

Economic justice is a component of social justice. It is a set of moral principles for building economic institutions, the ultimate goal of which is to create an opportunity for each person to create a sufficient material foundation upon which to have a dignified, productive, and creative life.

Social workers promote social justice and social change with and on behalf of clients who are individuals, families, groups, organizations, and/or communities.

Social workers aim to open the doors of access and opportunity for all, particularly those in greatest need.

Social workers also apply social justice principles to structural problems in the social service agencies in which they work. Armed with the long-term goal of empowering clients, they use knowledge of existing legal principles and organizational structure to suggest changes to protect clients, who are often powerless and underserved.

CRIMINAL JUSTICE SYSTEMS

Social work is an essential component of the nation's criminal justice system. For the most part, social work practice as performed in the various criminal (and juvenile) justice systems in the United States is referred to as criminal justice social work, correctional social work, or forensic social work.

Criminal justice social workers serve as frontline staff and administrators in criminal justice settings. There are many thousands of social workers employed in criminal justice settings, serving criminal justice populations, or both.

The criminal justice system encompasses a broad spectrum of public and private agencies, and settings including, but not limited to, state and federal correctional facilities; city and county jails; federal, state, and city parole and probation agencies; federal, state, and local court systems (including drug courts and mental health courts); community-based nonprofit agencies; faith-based agencies; and primary health and behavioral health care providers.

Schools of social work prepare their graduates to address the complex psychosocial needs of individuals in the criminal justice system. Social work is adapting to the evolving changes in the country's philosophy on the best ways to balance the sometimes conflicted dichotomy between the need for public safety and the need to address the biopsychosocial needs of offenders. The ethical challenge to social workers is to weigh the needs of the justice system against those of the offender. The social worker should take on the challenge by participating in legislative action to mold social policy to create a balance between the justice system and the offender. Thus, the social worker can help the justice system provide more effective services to the offender, their families, and their communities as professionals by participating in the process of public policy development.

Two competing, dichotomous schools of thought drive the discussion related to crime prevention. One, the pro-punishment school of thought, postulates that punishment is the means to preventing; whereas the positivist (pro-treatment) philosophy suggests that some instances of criminal behavior are determined by factors, such as mental illness, that offenders find difficult to control. Therefore, treatment becomes a means of preventing future criminal behaviors. Social work has historically been strongly associated with the positivist school of thought of crime prevention. Social work must recognize its professional obligation both to the offender and to the community (from a public safety perspective) and participate in the process of developing crime reduction policies that reflect social work's commitment to both the offender and the community.

THE EFFECTS OF LIFE EVENTS, STRESSORS, AND CRISES ON INDIVIDUALS, FAMILIES, GROUPS, ORGANIZATIONS, AND COMMUNITIES

Crisis is an essential component in the understanding of human growth and development. It has important implications for quality of life and subjective well-being. Crisis situations are viewed as unusual, mostly negative events that tend to disrupt the normal life of a person.

A crisis is an upset to a steady state. When a stressful event becomes a crisis, the individual or family is vulnerable and feels mounting anxiety, tension, and disequilibrium. *A precipitating cause of a crisis does not have to be a major life event.* It may be the "last straw" in a series of events that exceed a client's ability to cope.

An individual or family, at this point, may be emotionally overtaxed, hopeless, and incapable of effective functioning or making good choices and decisions. The person or family is at a "critical turning point" of coping effectively or not effectively.

The way in which life crises are addressed—whether surviving trauma, parental divorce, or a personal loss—has a very significant role to play in determining quality of life. When crises are understood, dealt with, and overcome, clients emerge as healthier and happier.

THE IMPACT OF THE POLITICAL ENVIRONMENT ON POLICY-MAKING

Social work is unique in its dual focus on assisting clients on an individual level while also working to change the policies that adversely impact them. The personal troubles of clients are linked to the public policies which can help to prevent or address them. Social workers are charged with working with and helping individuals and their families directly, but also working within decision-making bodies to promote these policies.

Social workers must be knowledgeable about the political environment if they are to shape public policy based upon the core values of the profession. As there are always competing interest groups who would like to influence policy-makers in their favor, political advocacy is seen as an important and necessary skill.

Advocacy can be defined as attempting to influence public policy through education, lobbying, or political pressure. Social workers are often called upon to educate the general public as well as public policy-makers about the nature of problems, the legislation needed to address problems, and the funding required to provide services or conduct research.

Social workers should engage in social and political action that seeks to ensure that all people have equal access to the resources, employment, services, and opportunities they require to meet their basic human needs and to develop to their full potential. They should be aware of the impact of the political arena on practice and should advocate for changes in policy and legislation to improve social conditions in order to meet basic human needs and promote social justice (*NASW Code of Ethics—6.04 Social and Political Action*).

Assessment (29%)

Biopsychosocial History and Collateral Data

4

THE COMPONENTS OF A BIOPSYCHOSOCIAL ASSESSMENT

The biopsychosocial–spiritual–cultural history is a tool that provides information on the current/presenting issue or issues; a client's past and present physical health, including developmental milestones; a client's emotional functioning; educational or vocational background; cultural issues; spiritual and religious beliefs; environmental issues; and social functioning. Each issue may be reviewed for its relationship and/or impact with the presenting issue.

The *biological section* assesses a client's medical history, developmental history, current medications, substance abuse history, and family history of medical illnesses. Issues related to medical problems should be explored because mental health symptoms can exacerbate them. Referrals should be made to address medical concerns that are not being treated. Clients who are on medications should have care coordinated with the treating provider, and more should be known about the medications because side effects can also mask or exacerbate psychiatric symptoms or illnesses.

The *psychological section* assesses a client's present psychiatric illness or symptoms, history of the current psychiatric illness or symptoms, past or current psychosocial stressors, and mental status. Exploration of how the problem has been treated in the past, past or present psychiatric medications, and the family history of psychiatric and substance-related issues is also included.

The *social section* focuses on client systems and unique client context, and may identify strengths and/or resources available for treatment planning. Included are sexual identity issues or concerns, personal history, family of origin history, support system, abuse history, education, legal history, marital/relationship status and concerns, work history, and risks.

The assessment should also include information about a client's spiritual beliefs, as well as his or her cultural traditions.

THE COMPONENTS AND FUNCTION OF THE MENTAL STATUS EXAMINATION

A mental status examination is a structured way of observing and describing a client's current state of mind under the domains of appearance, attitude, behavior, mood and affect, speech, thought process, thought content, perception, cognition, insight, and judgment. A mental status examination is a necessary part of any client assessment no matter what the presenting problem. It should be documented in the record either in list form or in narrative form. The following client functions should be included:

1. *Appearance*—facial expression, grooming, dress, gait, and so on

2. *Orientation*—awareness of time and place, events, and so on

3. *Speech pattern*—slurred, pressured, slow, flat tone, calm, and so on

4. *Affect/mood*—mood as evidenced in both behavior and client's statements (sad, jittery, manic, placid, etc.)

5. *Impulsive/potential for harm*—impulse control with special attention to potential suicidality and/or harm to others

6. *Judgment/insight*—ability to predict the consequences of her or his behavior, to make "sensible" decisions, to recognize her or his contribution to her or his problem

7. *Thought processes/reality testing*—thinking style and ability to know reality, including the difference between stimuli that are coming from inside herself or himself and those that are coming from outside herself or himself (statements about delusions, hallucinations, and conclusions about whether or not a client is psychotic would appear here)

8. *Intellectual functioning/memory*—level of intelligence and of recent and remote memory functions

A paragraph about mental status in the record might read as follows:

> "Client is a 43-year-old woman who looks older than her stated age. She is well groomed and appropriately dressed for a professional interview. She is well oriented. Her speech is slow as if it is painful to talk. She has had occasional thoughts of 'ending it all,' but has not made any suicidal plans or preparations. She talks about future events with expectation to be alive.

She is aware that she is 'depressed' and recognizes that the source of some of the feeling comes from 'inside moods' although she often refers to the difficulties of her situation. Her thoughts are organized. She is not psychotic."

BIOPSYCHOSOCIAL RESPONSES TO ILLNESS AND DISABILITY

The ways in which clients experience chronic illness or disability are influenced by numerous factors including:

- Personal characteristics (such as gender, race, age, coping style, past experience)
- Social and family supports
- Socioeconomic status
- Culture
- Environment (physical, social, and political)
- Activities (restrictions on those related to daily living, work, school, social)
- Personal goals

The responses to illness or disability are dependent on the interplay between these factors. Limitations faced may not be due to the illness or disability, but instead the environment. In addition, societal attitudes may influence their responses with norms focused more on the limitations than on actual functioning.

Clients also vary in terms of their personal resources such as tolerance of symptoms, functional capabilities, coping strategies, and social supports. Consequently, social workers must assess biopsychosocial responses individually. The health condition or disability is only one factor that determines clients' abilities to function effectively.

BIOPSYCHOSOCIAL FACTORS RELATED TO MENTAL HEALTH

It is not possible to understand mental health and the onset or course of mental disorders without knowing about biological, psychological, and social factors and how they interact across the lifespan.

Biological Factors

There is clear evidence to support the role that genes play as a factor in the development of psychiatric disorders. New information also keeps emerging about how brain structure and functioning relate to the existence of mental disorders. It is thought that brain growth in utero or early life can be affected by exposure to adverse factors, leading to changes in brain structure that increase the risk of development of particular mental disorders.

A social worker must use a systems approach in assessment of client mental health. A change in one aspect of a client's life—such as loss of a job, diagnosis of a physical illness, and so on—can affect his or her mental health. Conversely, mental health problems can have a dramatic impact on earnings, role fulfillment, friendships and social relationships, and even physical health.

Psychological Factors

Personality, relating to others and reacting to the world, includes a wide range of psychological responses to cope with different situations. Psychoanalytic, cognitive, and behavioral theories have all had an influence on how personality is understood, its impact on mental disorders, and how it can be influenced in treatment.

Social Factors

Social factors can influence mental health in dramatic ways and it is necessary to investigate social factors thoroughly to fully understand mental health and disorder. Factors such as socioeconomic situation, age, gender, social networks, level of support, life events, migration, and culture can all play a role in influencing the onset and course of mental illnesses.

THE INDICATORS OF PSYCHOSOCIAL STRESS

Psychosocial stress results when there is a perceived threat (real or imagined). Examples of psychosocial stress include threats to social status, social esteem, respect, and/or acceptance within a group; threats to self-worth; or threats that are perceived as uncontrollable.

Psychosocial stress can be caused by upsetting events, such as natural disasters, sudden health problems or death, and/or breakups or divorce.

Although current upsetting events certainly create stress, events from the past can also still affect clients. Social workers should assess the impacts of events such as childhood abuse, bullying, discrimination, violence, and/or trauma.

Often, psychosocial stress is not caused by single events, but by ongoing problems such as caring for a parent or child with disabilities.

Stress may manifest itself in many different ways, such as high blood pressure, sweating, rapid heart rate, dizziness, and/or feelings of irritability or sadness.

When psychosocial stress triggers a stress response, the body releases a group of stress hormones that lead to a burst of energy, as well as other changes in the body. The changes brought about by stress hormones can be helpful in the short term, but can be damaging in the long run.

It is essential that clients learn to manage psychosocial stress so that the stress response is only triggered when necessary and not for prolonged states of chronic stress.

BASIC MEDICAL TERMINOLOGY

Social workers must recognize the relationship between physical well-being and mental status. Social workers should always rule out medical etiology before making psychiatric diagnoses. A **differential diagnosis** is a systematic diagnostic method used to identify the presence of an entity where multiple alternatives are possible.

Social workers must know the major body systems and medical conditions associated with them that can affect psychological functioning and mood.

1. *Circulatory System*

   The circulatory system is the body's transport system. It is made up of a group of organs that transport blood throughout the body. The heart pumps the blood and the arteries and veins transport it.

2. *Digestive System*

   The digestive system is made up of organs that break down food into protein, vitamins, minerals, carbohydrates, and fats, which the body needs for energy, growth, and repair.

3. *Endocrine System*

   The endocrine system is made up of a group of glands that produce the body's long-distance messengers, or hormones. Hormones are chemicals that control body functions, such as metabolism, growth, and sexual development.

4. *Immune System*

   The immune system is a body's defense system against infections and diseases. Organs, tissues, cells, and cell products work together to respond to dangerous organisms (like viruses or bacteria) and substances that may enter the body from the environment.

5. *Lymphatic System*

   The lymphatic system is also a defense system for the body. It filters out organisms that cause disease, produces white blood cells, and generates disease-fighting antibodies. It also distributes fluids and nutrients in the body and drains excess fluids and protein so that tissues do not swell.

6. *Muscular System*

The muscular system is made up of tissues that work with the skeletal system to control movement of the body. Some muscles—like those in arms and legs—are voluntary, meaning that an individual decides when to move them. Other muscles, like the ones in the stomach, heart, intestines, and other organs, are involuntary. This means that they are controlled automatically by the nervous system and hormones—one often does not realize they are at work.

7. *Nervous System*

The nervous system is made up of the brain, the spinal cord, and nerves. One of the most important systems in the body, the nervous system is the body's control system. It sends, receives, and processes nerve impulses throughout the body. These nerve impulses tell muscles and organs what to do and how to respond to the environment.

8. *Reproductive System*

The reproductive system allows humans to produce children. Sperm from the male fertilizes the female's egg, or ovum, in the fallopian tube. The fertilized egg travels from the fallopian tube to the uterus, where the fetus develops over a period of 9 months.

9. *Respiratory System*

The respiratory system brings air into the body and removes carbon dioxide. It includes the nose, trachea, and lungs.

10. *Skeletal System*

The skeletal system is made up of bones, ligaments, and tendons. It shapes the body and protects organs. The skeletal system works with the muscular system to help the body move.

11. *Urinary System*

The urinary system eliminates waste from the body in the form of urine. The kidneys remove waste from the blood. The waste combines with water to form urine.

THE INDICATORS OF MENTAL AND EMOTIONAL ILLNESS THROUGHOUT THE LIFESPAN

Although the *Diagnostic and Statistical Manual of Mental Disorders* (*DSM*) provides a framework and criteria for applying uniform labels to psychiatric dysfunction, the process of social work assessment and diagnosis is much broader.

Diagnosis refers to the process of identifying problems, with their underlying causes and practical solutions.

A diagnosis is generally obtained after a social worker utilizes information gained through the assessment. Diagnosing includes drawing inferences and reaching conclusions based on the data available. A social worker should not diagnose if adequate information or data is not available.

A social worker must consider biological, psychological, and social factors when identifying the root causes of client problems.

Diagnostic information should always be shared with clients and used to facilitate the establishment of intervention plans.

Assessment and diagnosis must be a continual part of the problem-solving process.

The assessment process must focus on client strengths and resources for addressing problems.

There are some terms and concepts that a social worker should be familiar with when making assessments and/or diagnosing.

1. *Comorbid*: existing with or at the same time; for instance, having two different illnesses at the same time

2. *Contraindicated*: not recommended or safe to use (a medication or treatment that is contraindicated would not be prescribed because it could have serious consequences)

3. *Delusion*: false, fixed belief despite evidence to the contrary (believing something that is not true)

4. *Disorientation*: confusion with regard to person, time, or place

5. *Dissociation*: disturbance or change in the usually integrative functions of memory, identity, perception, or consciousness (often seen in clients with a history of trauma)

6. *Endogenous depression*: depression caused by a biochemical imbalance rather than a psychosocial stressor or external factors

7. *Exogenous depression*: depression caused by external events or psychosocial stressors

8. *Folie à deux*: shared delusion

9. *Hallucinations*: hearing, seeing, smelling, or feeling something that is not real (auditory most common)

10. *Hypomanic*: elevated, expansive, or irritable mood that is less severe than full-blown manic symptoms (not severe enough to interfere with functioning and not accompanied by psychotic symptoms)

11. *Postmorbid*: subsequent to the onset of an illness

12. *Premorbid*: prior to the onset of an illness

13. *Psychotic*: experiencing delusions or hallucinations

THE TYPES OF INFORMATION AVAILABLE FROM OTHER SOURCES (E.G., AGENCY, EMPLOYMENT, MEDICAL, PSYCHOLOGICAL, LEGAL, OR SCHOOL RECORDS)

Assessment is ongoing within the problem-solving process. In order to ensure that all relevant information is considered, social workers often rely on information available from clients' existing records in addition to the data that they collect directly.

In order to access this information, it is critical that social workers are aware of laws governing the release of such information and get the informed consent of clients prior to requesting these documents. The consent process must make clients aware of the reasons for such requests and the benefits and risks of social workers obtaining this information.

When information is obtained, it becomes part of the client record. Though protected by the Health Insurance Portability and Accountability Act (HIPAA), these client records can be subject to subpoenas and/or court orders. Thus, inclusion of this information in their records can have some additional risks associated with the legal duty to release them if court-ordered to do so.

Despite this risk, using existing employment, medical, psychological, psychiatric, and educational records can be very helpful when completing a biopsychosocial–spiritual–cultural history.

Employment records may help social workers construct clients' work histories and obtain data about income earned from their jobs. These records may be essential if clients need assistance with applying for Unemployment Insurance or other public benefits (Temporary Assistance for Needy Families [TANF], Supplemental Nutrition Assistance Program [SNAP], and so on).

Medical records are essential to ensure that client problems are not a result of health issues and to better understand the impact of past or current medical problems on client functioning.

Psychological records can be helpful as they can contain the results of any psychological testing that has been completed and whether any mental health diagnoses have been assigned. Whether or not a client has been prescribed psychotropic medications and/or received any subsequent treatment for behavioral health concerns would also be contained in psychiatric records.

When working with children, educational records are often consulted to determine performance in school and whether any problems experienced at home or elsewhere are being manifested in this setting as well. When working with adults, educational records can provide clues as to the age at which problems or difficulties began. Historical educational records are often used to diagnose adults with intellectual or developmental disabilities if they were not appropriately identified while in school.

Components of a Sexual History

Some clients may not be comfortable talking about their sexual history, sex partners, or sexual practices. It is critical that social workers try to put clients at ease and let them know that taking a sexual history may be an important part of the assessment process. A history is usually obtained through a face-to-face interview, but can also be gotten from a pencil-and-paper document.

Questions included in a sexual history may vary depending upon client issues. However, they usually involve collecting information about partners (number, gender, risk factors, length of relationships), practices (risk behaviors, oral/vaginal/anal intercourse, satisfaction with practices, desire/arousal/orgasm), protection from and past history of sexually transmitted diseases (STDs; condom use), and prevention of pregnancy (if desired)/reproductive history.

If clients are experiencing dissatisfaction or dysfunction, social workers will need to understand the reasons for dissatisfaction and/or dysfunction. Medical explanations must be ruled out before psychological factors are considered as causes. A systems perspective should be used to understand issues in this area. For example, a medical/biological condition that decreases satisfaction or causes dysfunction may heavily impact on psychological and social functioning. In addition, a psychological or social issue can lead to a lack of desire, inability to become aroused, or failure to attain orgasm.

Alcohol and/or drug use should also be considered related to concerns about desire, arousal, or orgasm because they can cause decreased interest or abilities in these areas.

Components of a Family History

Understanding a client's family history is an important part of the assessment process. A client is part of a larger family system. Thus, gaining a better understanding of the experiences of other family members may prove useful in understanding influences imposed on a client throughout his or her life course.

One tool used by social workers to depict a client as part of a larger family system is a **genogram**. A genogram is a graphic representation of a family tree that displays the interaction of generations within a family. It goes beyond a traditional family tree by allowing the user to analyze family, emotional, and social relationships within a group. It is used to identify repetitive patterns of behavior and to recognize hereditary tendencies. A social worker can also ask about these relationships, behaviors, and tendencies without using a genogram.

There are no set questions that must be included in a family history; often, they relate to the problem or issue experienced by a client at the time. However, they may include identifying family members':

- Ethnic backgrounds (including immigration) and traditions
- Biological ties (adoption, blended family structures, foster children)
- Occupations and educational levels
- Unusual life events or achievements
- Psychological and social histories, as well as current well-being
- Past and present substance use behaviors
- Relationships with other family members
- Roles within the immediate and larger family unit
- Losses such as those from death, divorce, or physical separation
- Current and past significant problems, including those due to medical, financial, and other issues
- Values related to economic status, educational attainment, and employment
- Coping skills or defense mechanisms

Finding out which adults and/or children get the most attention or recognition and which get the least may also provide insight.

Assessment Methods and Techniques

5

THE FACTORS AND PROCESSES USED IN PROBLEM FORMULATION

In both micro and macro practice, social workers must work with clients to identify the problem(s) to be addressed. Problem identification concerns determining the problem targeted for intervention. Although this seems straightforward, it is often difficult to isolate the issue that, when addressed, will result in a change in the symptomology of a client and/or client system.

Part of problem identification is determining the issue in exact definable terms, when it occurs, and its magnitude. When doing macro practice, a social worker may often need to get consensus from the group regarding whether there is agreement as to the nature of the problem and its occurrence and magnitude.

It is often useful in problem identification to determine that which is not the problem. Such a technique will ensure that these elements are not grouped in with those that are targeted and will assist in narrowing down the focus.

The problem should always be considered within the person-in-environment perspective and using a strengths-based approach. It should not blame a client and/or client system for its existence.

METHODS OF INVOLVING CLIENTS/CLIENT SYSTEMS IN PROBLEM IDENTIFICATION (E.G., GATHERING COLLATERAL INFORMATION)

Social workers focus on assisting clients to identify problems and areas of strength, as well as increasing problem-solving strategies.

It is essential that, throughout the problem-solving process, social workers view clients as experts in their lives.

Clients should be asked about what they would like to see changed in their lives and clients' definitions of problems should be accepted.

Clients should be asked about what will be different in their lives when their problems are solved. Social workers should listen carefully for, and work hard to respect, the directions in which clients want to go with their lives (their goals) and the words they use to express these directions.

Clients should be asked about the paths that they would like to take to make desired changes. Clients' perceptions should be respected and clients' inner resources (strengths) should be maximized as part of treatment.

Use of Collateral Sources

Social workers often use collateral sources—family, friends, other agencies, physicians, and so on—as informants when collecting information to effectively treat clients. These sources can provide vital information because other professionals or agencies may have treated clients in the past. Family members and friends may also provide important information about the length or severity of issues or problems.

Collateral information is often used when the credibility and validity of information obtained from a client or others is questionable. For example, child custody cases are inherently characterized by biased data within an adversarial process. Thus, it is often necessary to evaluate the integrity of information gathered through use of collateral information.

However, social workers should always assess the credibility of collateral informants, because data from more neutral parties has higher integrity. In addition, informants who have greater access to key information may produce more valid data.

When an account by a collateral informant agrees with information gathered from a client, it enhances the trustworthiness of the data collected.

Using multiple information sources (or triangulation) is an excellent method for social workers to have accurate accounts upon which to make assessments or base interventions.

It is essential that a social worker get a client's informed consent prior to reaching out to collateral sources. However, they can be a valuable source of data to supplement that obtained directly from a client, as well as provide contextual or background information that a client may not know.

TECHNIQUES AND INSTRUMENTS USED TO ASSESS CLIENTS/ CLIENT SYSTEMS

There are many psychological tests in existence for assessment and diagnostic purposes. The following are a few of the most well known.

Beck Depression Inventory

The Beck Depression Inventory (BDI) is a 21-item test, presented in multiple-choice formats, that assesses the presence and degree of depression in adolescents and adults.

The Minnesota Multiphasic Personality Inventory

The Minnesota Multiphasic Personality Inventory (MMPI) is an objective verbal inventory designed as a personality test for the assessment of psychopathology consisting of 550 statements, 16 of which are repeated.

Myers–Briggs Type Indicator

The Myers–Briggs Type Indicator (MBTI) is a forced-choice, self-report inventory that attempts to classify individuals along four theoretically independent dimensions. The first dimension is a general attitude toward the world, either extraverted (E) or introverted (I). The second dimension, perception, is divided between sensation (S) and intuition (N). The third dimension is that of processing. Once information is received, it is processed in either a thinking (T) or feeling (F) style. The final dimension is judging (J) versus perceiving (P).

Rorschach Inkblot Test

Client responses to inkblots are used to assess perceptual reactions and other psychological functioning. It is one of the most widely used projective tests.

Stanford–Binet Intelligence Scale

The Stanford–Binet Intelligence Scale is designed for the testing of cognitive abilities. It provides verbal, performance, and full scale scores for children and adults.

Thematic Apperception Test

The Thematic Apperception Test (TAT) is another widely used projective test. It consists of a series of pictures of ambiguous scenes. Clients are asked to make up stories or fantasies concerning what is happening, has happened, and is going to happen in the scenes, along with a description of their thoughts and feelings. The TAT provides information on a client's perceptions and imagination for use in the understanding of a client's current needs, motives, emotions, and conflicts, both conscious and unconscious. Its use in clinical assessment is generally part of a larger battery of tests and interview data.

Wechsler Intelligence Scale

The Wechsler Intelligence Scale (WISC) is designed as a measure of a child's intellectual and cognitive ability. It has four index scales and a full scale score.

METHODS TO INCORPORATE THE RESULTS OF PSYCHOLOGICAL AND EDUCATIONAL TESTS INTO ASSESSMENT

Social workers use both tests and assessments to help formulate diagnoses and to guide treatment for their clients.

Psychological tests are instruments used to measure an assortment of mental abilities and characteristics, such as personality, achievement, intelligence, and neurological functioning. They often take the form of questionnaires. They may be written, verbal, or pictorial tests (like the famous Rorschach test that uses inkblot images). The tests may also be referred to as scales, surveys, screens, checklists, assessments, measures, inventories, and so on.

Educational tests measure cognitive (thinking) abilities and academic achievement. These measurements provide a profile of strengths and weaknesses that accurately identify areas for academic remediation and insight into the best learning strategies. They provide details into the learning process that will provide clients, family members, and school staff the best learning strategies. Educational assessments provide the necessary documentation for the legal purposes of establishing the presence of disabilities, but they do not guarantee that their findings will be accepted by schools and/or accommodations provided. Reaching decisions to have educational testing is often arrived at after a period of struggle, distress, and different efforts at improving the educational process with limited success.

Social work assessment is a more comprehensive process that may utilize the results from educational and psychological tests, but can also involve interviewing a client and/or family, reviewing a client's history, checking existing records, and consulting with previous or concurrent providers.

Some common tests are:

- *Achievement/Aptitude tests*: typically used in education, measure how much clients know (have *achieved*) in a certain subject or subjects, or have ability (*aptitude*) to learn
- *Intelligence tests*: measure intelligence (IQ)

- *Job/Occupational tests*: match interests with careers
- *Personality tests*: measure basic personality traits/characteristics
- *Neuropsychological tests*: assess and measure cognitive functioning (e.g., how a particular problem with the brain affects recall, concentration, etc.)
- *Specialized clinical tests*: investigates areas of clinical interest, such as anxiety, depression, Posttraumatic Stress Disorder (PTSD), and so on.

COMMUNICATION THEORIES AND STYLES

Communication theory involves the ways in which information is transmitted; the effects of information on human systems; how people receive information from their own feelings, thoughts, memories, physical sensations, and environments; how they evaluate this information; and how they subsequently act in response to the information.

Effective communication skills are one of the most crucial components of a social worker's job. Every day, social workers must communicate with clients to gain information, convey critical information, and make important decisions. Without effective communication skills, a social worker may not be able to obtain or convey that information, thereby causing detrimental effects on clients.

One cannot not communicate. Even when one is silent one is communicating, and another person is reacting to the silence. **Silence** is very effective when faced with a client who is experiencing a high degree of emotion, because the silence indicates acceptance of these feelings. On the other hand, silence on the part of a client can indicate a reluctance to discuss a subject. A social worker should probe further with a client who is silent for an unusually long period of time. If persons do not communicate clearly, mutual understanding, acceptance, or rejection of the communication will not occur, and relationship problems can arise.

Some communication styles can serve to inhibit effective communication with clients.

1. Using "shoulds" and "oughts" may be perceived as moralizing or sermonizing by a client and elicit feelings of resentment, guilt, or obligation. In reaction to feeling judged, a client may oppose a social worker's pressure to change.

2. Offering advice or solutions prematurely, before thorough exploration of the problem, may cause resistance because a client is not ready to solve the problem.

3. Using logical arguments, lecturing, or arguing to convince a client to take another viewpoint may result in a power struggle with a client. A better way of helping a client is to assist him or her in exploring options in order to make an informed decision.

4. Judging, criticizing, and blaming are detrimental to a client, as well as to the therapeutic relationship. A client could respond by becoming defensive or, worse yet, internalizing the negative reflections about himself or herself.

5. Talking to a client in professional jargon and defining a client in terms of his or her diagnosis may result in a client viewing himself or herself in the same way (as "sick").

6. Providing reassurance prematurely or without a genuine basis is often for a social worker's benefit rather than a client's. It is a social worker's responsibility to explore and acknowledge a client's feelings, no matter how painful they are. A client may also feel that a social worker does not understand his or her situation.

7. Ill-timed or frequent interruptions disrupt the interview process and can annoy clients. Interruptions should be purposive, well-timed, and done in such a way that they do not disrupt the flow of communication.

8. It is counterproductive to permit excessive social interactions rather than therapeutic interactions. In order for a client to benefit from the helping relationship, he or she has to self-disclose about problematic issues.

9. Social workers must provide structure and direction to the therapeutic process on a moment-to-moment basis in order to maximize the helping process. Passive or inactive social workers may miss fruitful moments that could be used for client benefit. Clients may lose confidence in social workers who are not actively involved in the helping process.

The following are some communication concepts that are critical to social work practice.

Acceptance

An acknowledgment of "what is." Acceptance does not pass judgment on a circumstance and allows clients to let go of frustration and disappointment, stress and anxiety, regret and false hopes. Acceptance is the practice of recognizing the limits of one's control. Acceptance is not giving up or excusing other people's behavior and allowing it to continue. Acceptance is not about giving in to circumstances that are unhealthy or uncomfortable. The main thing that gets in the way of acceptance is wanting to be in control.

Cognitive dissonance

Arises when a person has to choose between two contradictory attitudes and beliefs. The most dissonance arises when two options are equally attractive. Three ways to reduce dissonance are to (a) reduce the importance of conflicting beliefs, (b) acquire new beliefs that change the balance, or (c) remove the conflicting attitude or behavior. This theory is relevant when making decisions or solving problems.

Context
The circumstances surrounding human exchanges of information.

Double bind
Offering two contradictory messages and prohibiting the recipient from noticing the contradiction.

Echolalia
Repeating noises and phrases. It is associated with Catatonia, Autism Spectrum Disorder, Schizophrenia, and other disorders.

Information
Anything people perceive from their environments or from within themselves. People act in response to information.

Information processing
Responses to information that are mediated through one's perception and evaluation of knowledge received.

Information processing block
Failure to perceive and evaluate potentially useful new information.

Metacommunication
The context within which to interpret the content of the message (i.e., nonverbal communication, body language, vocalizations).

Nonverbal communications
Facial expression, body language, and posture can be potent forms of communication.

In communication, there are two types of content, manifest and latent. Manifest content is the concrete words or terms contained in a communication, whereas latent content is that which is not visible, the underlying meaning of words or terms.

Relying just on the manifest content to understand client experiences or problems may result in not really understanding their meaning to individuals.

There are social work techniques such as clarifying, paraphrasing, confronting, and interpreting that can assist social workers in developing a better understanding of the meaning of clients' communication.

In addition, therapeutic techniques, such as psychoanalysis, focus on the hidden meaning of fantasies or dreams.

THE CONCEPT OF CONGRUENCE IN COMMUNICATION

Communication can be verbal and nonverbal, so an assessment of clients' communication skills must involve both. Role playing is a good way to assess and enhance clients' communication skills. It also allows a social worker to see if there is congruence between nonverbal and verbal communication.

Congruence is the matching of awareness and experience with communication. It is essential that a client is able to express himself or herself and that this communication is reflective of his or her feelings. *Congruence is essential for the vitality of a relationship and to facilitate true helping as part of the problem-solving process.*

RISK ASSESSMENT METHODS

Social workers are often called upon to assess risks of clients to themselves and others. Such assessments are not easy, because there are no indicators that definitively predict whether a client will act on his or her feelings or desires to hurt himself or herself. A social worker must review all assessment data in order to determine the appropriate level of care and a treatment plan. Such an assessment must include examining risk and protective factors, as well as the presence of behavioral warning signs. Such an assessment may include examining:

- Frequency, intensity, and duration of suicidal or violent thoughts
- Access to or availability of method(s)
- Ability or inability to control suicidal/violent thoughts
- Ability not to act on thoughts
- Factors making a client feel better or worse
- Consequences of actions
- Deterrents to acting on thoughts
- Whether client has been using drugs or alcohol to cope
- Measures a client requires to maintain safety

In situations where a client is seen to be a danger to self or others, a social worker may limit a client's right to self-determination and seek involuntary treatment such as commitment to an inpatient setting. If a client is deemed to be a danger to an identifiable third party, a social worker should consider this as a "duty to warn" situation (under the Tarasoff decision), as well as the party in danger.

METHODS TO ASSESS THE CLIENT'S/CLIENT SYSTEM'S STRENGTHS, RESOURCES, AND CHALLENGES (E.G., INDIVIDUAL, FAMILY, GROUP, ORGANIZATION, COMMUNITY)

Clients typically seek social work services for help with problems or difficulties. As a result, the assessment generally focuses on the problems. This focus can lead to an overemphasis on client pathology and dysfunction without the same attention to client strengths, capabilities, and achievements. Information on both strengths and challenges are needed to get a full understanding of the client situation.

Social workers must be sensitive to client strengths and skillful in using them to achieve service goals. Social workers who do not attend to client strengths will not be able to determine clients' potential for growth and the steps needed to get there. Often clients are experiencing self-doubt or poor self-esteem. To assist with helping clients view themselves more positively, social workers must be able to emphasize their strengths.

Strengths which may be overlooked include clients:

- Facing problems by seeking help—rather than denying them;
- Taking risks by sharing problems with social workers;
- Persevering under difficult situations;
- Being resourceful;
- Meeting family and financial obligations;
- Seeking to understand the actions of others;
- Functioning in stressful situations; and/or
- Considering alternative courses of action.

Methods to identify more about client strengths, resources, and challenges can be obtained by:

- Seeking exceptions—determining when the problem does not exist or occur (locations, times, contexts);
- Scaling the problem—identifying the severity of the problem on a scale from 1 to 10 according to the client;
- Scaling motivation—estimating the degree to which client feels hopeful about resolution; and/or
- Miracle question—having the client determine what would be different if problem did not exist.

When conducting community assessments, it is essential for social workers to identify strengths and challenges. Strengths are positive features of the community that can be leveraged to develop solutions to problems. Strengths can include organizations, people, partnerships, facilities, funding, policies, regulations, and culture.

A social worker should consider the current assets that are already in existence to promote the quality of life of community members. For example, organizations that provide after-school programs that help youth graduate on time would be included in a community assessment focused on keeping kids in school. In some instances, a social worker may want to look at experiences of other communities with similar demographics that have successfully addressed similar problems. Examining the presence and utilization of strengths in these communities can assist a social worker in determining if similar assets can be found in its target community.

A social worker must also develop an informed understanding of the gaps or needs that exist within a community. These needs serve as challenges that can affect a large or small number of community members. If community needs affect a large number of community members, there may be more support for addressing them. Collaboration and community building are essential in addressing community challenges.

There are a number of methods for data collection related to community strengths and challenges including interviews, observation, and surveys. Ensuring that the data collection procedures are robust is essential in conducting a complete and accurate community assessment.

THE INDICATORS OF MOTIVATION, RESISTANCE, AND READINESS TO CHANGE

Social workers should not assume that clients are ready or have the skills needed to make changes in their lives. Clients may be oppositional, reactionary, noncompliant, and/or unmotivated. These attitudes or behaviors are often referred to as resistance.

There are indicators that a social worker should use as evidence that a client may be resistant or not ready/able to fully participate in services. These indicators include:

- Limiting the amount of information communicated to a social worker
- Silence/minimal talking during sessions
- Engaging in small talk with a social worker about irrelevant topics
- Engaging in intellectual talk by using technical terms/abstract concepts or asking questions of a social worker that are not related to client issues or problems
- Being preoccupied with past events, instead of current issues
- Discounting, censoring, or editing thoughts when asked about them by a social worker
- False promising
- Flattering a social worker in an attempt to "soften" him or her so client will not be pushed to act
- Not keeping appointments
- Payment delays or refusals

It is essential to determine the extent to which this resistance or these inabilities are caused by a client, a social worker, and/or the conditions present.

A client may be resistant due to feelings of guilt or shame and may not be ready to recognize or address the feelings and behaviors being brought up by a social worker. Clients may be frightened of change and may be getting some benefit from the problems that they are experiencing.

Social workers may experience a lack of readiness, as they have not developed sufficient rapport with clients. There also may not be clear expectations by clients of their role versus those of social workers. Social workers need to use interventions that are appropriate for clients.

Sometimes, a lack of readiness or ability is a result of external factors such as changes in clients' living situations, physical health problems, lack of social support, and/or financial problems.

Whatever the causes, a social worker must address these barriers as clients will not make changes until they are ready and able.

METHODS TO ASSESS MOTIVATION, RESISTANCE, AND READINESS TO CHANGE

Motivation and resistance exist along a continuum of readiness. When assessing motivation and resistance of a client, it is important to determine what stage of change a client is in. This will provide a social worker with appropriate clinical strategies to use to address these issues. If social workers push clients at a faster pace than they are ready to take, the therapeutic alliance may break down.

A lack of motivation and resistance are often found in *precontemplation* and *contemplation* before making the decision to change. There can also be motivational challenges during preparation, action, and maintenance, but they are more easily addressed. When resistance occurs in these latter stages of change, a social worker should reassess the problem and appropriateness of the intervention to ensure that there have not been new developments in a client's life that need to be considered. They may be distracting a client from making progress or serving as barriers to making real change.

In precontemplation, a client is unaware, unable, and/or unwilling to change. In this stage, there is the greatest resistance and lack of motivation. It can be characterized by arguing, interrupting, denial, ignoring the problem, and/or avoiding talking or thinking about it. A client may not even show up for appointments and does not agree that change is needed.

A social worker can best deal with lack of motivation and resistance in this stage by establishing a rapport, acknowledging resistance or ambivalence, keeping conversation informal, trying to engage a client, and recognizing a client's thoughts, feelings, fears, and concerns.

In contemplation, a client is ambivalent or uncertain regarding behavior change; thus, his or her behaviors are unpredictable. In this stage, a client may be willing to look at the pros and cons of behavior change, but is not committed to working toward it.

A social worker can best deal with lack of motivation and resistance in this stage by emphasizing a client's free choice and responsibility, as well as discussing the pros and cons of changing. It is also useful to discuss how change will assist a client in achieving his or her goals in life. Fear can be reduced by producing examples of change and clarifying what change is and is not.

METHODS TO ASSESS THE CLIENT'S/CLIENT SYSTEM'S COMMUNICATION SKILLS

Social workers must involve clients in every aspect of treatment. In order to do so, social workers must assess clients' communication skills and determine effective methods to gather needed information, as well as to ensure that clients understand data that is presented to them. Thus, the expressive and receptive communication of clients must be considered.

As many clients may have experienced trauma, it is essential that social workers understand how such experiences may impact on clients' communication styles and patterns. Much of communication is also cultural and should be viewed within the context of clients' backgrounds and experiences.

Silence is a form of communication and should be considered by a social worker when used by a client.

Social workers should understand how to communicate with clients who are upset and angry, as well as how some wording choices and tones can be upsetting to clients based on their ethnic backgrounds and/or past experiences, such as victimization.

METHODS TO ASSESS THE CLIENT'S/CLIENT SYSTEM'S COPING ABILITIES

Social workers can learn a lot about clients' difficulties by determining how clients have attempted to cope with their problems in the past. The coping abilities that clients employ give valuable clues about their levels of stress and functioning. Investigation may indicate that clients have few coping abilities, but rely on rigid patterns that are unhelpful or cause further problems. Some clients follow avoidance pattern by immersing themselves in work, withdrawing, or using drugs or alcohol. Others attempt to cope by being aggressive or acting out. Lastly, others become dependent and rely on family members or friends to manage difficulties for them.

Exploring how clients have attempted to cope with problems may reveal that they have struggled with the same or similar problems in the past. As they are no longer able to manage, it is important to find out what has changed ("why now?"). In order to assess coping skills, social workers might want to ask about the extent to which clients:

- Turn to work or other substitute activities to take their minds off things
- Get upset and let their emotions out
- Get advice from others about what to do
- Concentrate on doing something about their problems
- Put their trust in high beings
- Laugh about their situations
- Discuss their feelings with others
- Use alcohol or drugs to make themselves feel better
- Pretend that their problems do not exist
- Seek out others who have similar experiences

THE INDICATORS OF CLIENT'S/CLIENT SYSTEM'S STRENGTHS AND CHALLENGES

Strength is the capacity to cope with difficulties, to maintain functioning under stress, to return to equilibrium in the face of significant trauma, to use external challenges to promote growth, and to be resilient by using social supports.

There is not a single approach to the assessment of strengths. However, social workers can view all of these areas as strengths or protective factors that can assist clients when they experience challenges. These characteristics can also be abilities that need to be bolstered as a focus of treatment.

1. *Cognitive and appraisal skills*

- Intellectual/cognitive ability
- Creativity and curiosity
- Initiative, perseverance, and patience
- Common sense
- Ability to anticipate problems
- Realistic appraisal of demands and capacities
- Ability to use feedback

2. *Defenses and coping mechanisms*

- Ability to regulate impulses and affect
- Self-soothing
- Flexible; can handle stressors

3. *Temperamental and dispositional factors*

- Belief in trustworthiness of others
- Belief in justice
- Self-esteem and self-worth

- Sense of mastery, confidence, and optimism
- Ability to tolerate ambiguity and uncertainty
- Ability to make sense of negative events
- Sense of humor
- Lack of hostility, anger, and anxiety
- Optimistic and open
- Ability to grieve
- Lack of helplessness
- Responsibility for decisions
- Sense of direction, mission, and purpose

4. *Interpersonal skills and supports*

- Ability to develop/maintain good relationships
- Ability to confide in others
- Problem-solving skills
- Capacity for empathy
- Presence of an intimate relationship
- Sense of security

5. *Other factors*

- Supportive social institutions, such as church
- Good physical health
- Adequate income
- Supportive family and friends

Methods to Assess Ego Strengths

Ego strength is the ability of the ego to effectively deal with the demands of the id, the superego, and reality. It is a basis for resilience and helps maintain emotional stability by coping with internal and external stress.

Traits usually considered to be indicators of positive ego strength include tolerance of pain associated with loss, disappointment, shame, or guilt; forgiveness of others, with feelings of compassion rather than anger; persistence and perseverance in the pursuit of goals; and/or openness, flexibility, and creativity in learning to adapt. Those with positive ego strength are less likely to have psychiatric crises.

Other indicators of positive ego strength include clients:

- Acknowledging their feelings—including grief, insecurity, loneliness, and anxiety
- Not getting overwhelmed by their moods
- Pushing forward after loss and not being paralyzed by self-pity or resentment

- Using painful events to strengthen themselves
- Knowing that painful feelings will eventually fade
- Empathizing with others without trying to reduce or eliminate their pain
- Being self-disciplined and fighting addictive urges
- Taking responsibility for actions
- Holding themselves accountable
- Not blaming others
- Accepting themselves with their limitations
- Setting firm limits even if it means disappointing others or risking rejection
- Avoiding people who drain them physically and/or emotionally

METHODS USED TO ASSESS TRAUMA

Trauma is the response that a client has to an extremely negative event. Although trauma is a normal reaction to a horrible event, the effects can be so severe that they interfere with a client's ability to live life. Thus, a social worker is needed to treat the stress and dysfunction caused by the traumatic event and to restore a client to his or her previous emotional state.

Emotional reactions are the common effects of trauma. Impacts of trauma on clients' self-image include, but are not limited to:

- Anxiety
- Denial
- Agitation
- Irritability or rage
- Flashbacks or intrusive memories
- Feeling disconnected from the world
- Unrest in certain situations
- Being "shut down"
- Being very passive
- Feeling depressed
- Guilt/shame/self-blame
- Unusual fears
- Impatience
- Having a hard time concentrating
- Wanting to hurt oneself
- Being unable to trust anyone
- Feeling unlikable
- Feeling unsafe

Trauma often manifests physically, including both physiological and behavioral symptoms. Behavioral manifestations of trauma include, but are not limited to:

- Insomnia or fatigue
- Using harmful substances
- Keeping to oneself
- Overworking
- Lethargy
- Eating problems
- Drug or alcohol use
- Needing to do certain things over and over
- Always having to have things a certain way
- Doing strange or risky things

Clients may have anxiety or panic attacks and be unable to cope in certain circumstances. Social workers must often work with clients to address the underlying emotional impacts of the trauma in order for clients to make behavioral changes.

Clients who experience trauma often believe that they cannot trust, the world is not safe, and they are powerless to change their circumstances. Beliefs about themselves, others, and the world diminish their sense of competency. Thus, clients view themselves as powerless or "damaged" and have trouble feeling hopeful.

Clients who have experienced trauma may display intense emotions toward others, such as friends or family members. Clients can also emotionally retreat from these individuals, choosing to isolate themselves. Thus, trauma can be difficult for those who are close to clients as well.

PLACEMENT OPTIONS BASED ON ASSESSED LEVEL OF CARE

Social workers must assess the client's needed level of care, with the belief that there should be a continuum of intensity depending upon the level of crisis. Clients should enter treatment at a level appropriate to their needs and then step up to more intense treatment or down to less intense treatment as needed. An effective continuum of care features successful transfer of a client between levels of care.

Levels of care for behavioral health services, for example, vary from early intervention services/outpatient services to intensive outpatient/partial hospitalization to residential/inpatient services.

Early intervention or outpatient services are appropriate unless a client is experiencing crisis or at risk for residential/inpatient services, which may then warrant a step up to intensive outpatient or partial hospitalization. The goal is to serve clients in the least restrictive environment, while ensuring health and safety.

THE EFFECTS OF ADDICTION AND SUBSTANCE ABUSE ON INDIVIDUALS, FAMILIES, GROUPS, ORGANIZATIONS, AND COMMUNITIES

There are biopsychosocial–spiritual–cultural impacts of substance abuse or dependence on clients themselves. Clients who use drugs experience a wide array of physical effects other than those expected. The excitement or high that results from the use of cocaine is followed by a "crash": a period of anxiety, fatigue, depression, and an acute desire for more cocaine to alleviate these continued feelings. Marijuana and alcohol interfere with motor control and are factors in many automobile accidents. Users of hallucinogenic drugs may experience flashbacks, which are unwanted recurrences of the drug's effects weeks or months after use. Sudden abstinence from certain drugs results in withdrawal symptoms. For example, heroin withdrawal can cause vomiting, muscle cramps, convulsions, and delirium. With the continued use of substances that are physically addictive, tolerance develops; that is, constantly increasing amounts of the drug are needed to duplicate the initial effect.

Substance abuse or dependence also impacts mental health because it causes irrational behavior, violence, and lapses in memory. Chronic use of some substances can cause long-lasting changes in the brain, which may lead to paranoia, depression, aggression, and hallucinations.

In addition, because the purity and dosage of illegal drugs are uncontrolled, drug overdose is a constant risk. Many drug users also engage in criminal activity, such as burglary and prostitution, to raise money to buy drugs.

Substance use can disrupt family life and destroy relationships. A client's preoccupation with the substance, plus its impacts on mood and performance, can lead to relationship/marital problems. A client may spend more time on getting and using substances than attending to his or her relationships with others. Drug use can also create destructive patterns of codependency. Codependency occurs when a partner/spouse or members of the family, out of love or fear of consequences, inadvertently enables a client to continue using substances by covering up, supplying money, or denying there is a problem.

In addition, substance abuse or dependence can result in accidental injury, disability, legal involvement, and/or loss of income or employment, which negatively impacts on those who are friends or family members of a client. Neglect of friends and family, as well as anger that can lead to verbal assaults or physical violence, are also seen as a result of substance abuse or dependence.

Clients who are using or dependent on substances may also tend to neglect "old" relationships and find those who also engage in similar behaviors.

THE INDICATORS OF ADDICTION AND SUBSTANCE ABUSE

Some people are able to engage in behaviors or use substances without abusing them and/or becoming addicted.

There are signs when clients are addicted to behaviors and/or substances are being abused. These include, but are not limited to, indications that the behavior or substance use is:

- Causing problems at work, home, school, and in relationships
- Resulting in neglected responsibilities at school, work, or home (i.e., flunking classes, skipping work, neglecting children)
- Dangerous (i.e., driving while on drugs, using dirty needles, having unprotected sex, binging/purging despite medical conditions)
- Causing financial and/or legal trouble (i.e., arrests, stealing to support shopping, gambling, or drug habit)
- Causing problems in relationships, such as fights with partner or family members or loss of old friends
- Creating tolerance (more of the behavior or substance is needed to produce the same impact)
- Out of control or causing a feeling of being powerless
- Life-consuming, resulting in abandoned activities that used to be enjoyed
- Resulting in psychological issues such as mood swings, attitude changes, depression, and/or paranoia

Signs of Drug Use

- Marijuana: glassy, red eyes; loud talking, inappropriate laughter followed by sleepiness; loss of interest, motivation; weight gain or loss
- Cocaine: dilated pupils; hyperactivity; euphoria; irritability; anxiety; excessive talking followed by depression or excessive sleeping at odd

times; may go long periods of time without eating or sleeping; weight loss; dry mouth and nose

- Heroin: contracted pupils; no response of pupils to light; needle marks; sleeping at unusual times; sweating; vomiting; coughing, sniffling; twitching; loss of appetite

CO-OCCURRING DISORDERS AND CONDITIONS

Co-occurring disorders and conditions are present when there are two or more disorders occurring at the same time. For example, clients may have one or more disorders relating to the use of alcohol and/or other drugs, as well as one or more mental disorders. In order for a disorder or condition to be co-occurring, it must be independent and not symptomatology resulting from the other disorder(s)/condition(s).

Co-occurring disorders used to be called dual diagnoses or dual disorders. Just as the field of treatment for substance use and mental disorders has evolved to become more precise, so too has the terminology used to describe clients with both substance use and mental disorders. Many clients with severe mental illness are further impaired by Substance Use Disorders. However, co-occurring can also be used to describe clients with other conditions, such as those with physical and/or intellectual disabilities.

Though co-occurring, disorders and conditions may not be equivalent in severity, chronicity, and/or degree of impairment in functioning. For example, disorders or conditions may each be severe or mild, or one may be more severe than the other. The severity of both disorders or conditions may also change over time.

Compared with clients who have a single disorder or condition, clients with co-occurring disorders or conditions often require longer treatment, have more crises, and progress more gradually in treatment. Integrated treatment or treatment that considers the presence of all the disorders or conditions at the same time is associated with lower costs and better outcomes.

THE DIAGNOSTIC AND STATISTICAL MANUAL OF THE AMERICAN PSYCIATRIC ASSOCIATION

The *Diagnostic and Statistical Manual of Mental Disorders* (5th ed.; *DSM®-5*) was published in 2013 and is the current diagnostic framework used by social workers. It has many revisions in content and format from the *DSM-IV-TR*, which was used previously.

The *DSM-5* deleted a separate section for "Disorders Usually First Diagnosed in Infancy, Childhood, or Adolescence" and now lists them in other chapters.

The *DSM-5* replaces the Not Otherwise Specified (NOS) categories with two options: Other Specified Disorder and Unspecified Disorder. The first allows a social worker to specify the reason that the criteria for a specific disorder is not met, whereas the second allows a social worker the option to forgo specification.

The *DSM-5* has discarded the multiaxial system of diagnosis (formerly Axis I, Axis II, and Axis III) and combines the first three axes outlined in past editions of the *DSM* into one axis with all mental and other medical diagnoses.

It has replaced Axis IV with significant psychosocial and contextual features and dropped Axis V (Global Assessment of Functioning, known as GAF).

The *World Health Organization Disability Assessment Schedule 2.0 (WHODAS 2.0)* is added to Section III, Emerging Measures and Models, under Assessment Measures.

The following are some categories of disorders included in the *DSM-5.*

1. *Neurodevelopmental Disorders*

2. *Schizophrenia Spectrum and Other Psychotic Disorders*

3. *Bipolar and Related Disorders*

4. *Depressive Disorders*

5. *Anxiety Disorders*

6. *Obsessive-Compulsive and Related Disorders*

7. *Trauma- and Stressor-Related Disorders*

8. *Dissociative Disorders*

9. *Somatic Symptom and Related Disorders*

10. *Feeding and Eating Disorders*

11. *Elimination Disorders*

12. *Sleep–Wake Disorders*

13. *Sexual Dysfunctions*

14. *Gender Dysphoria*
    Now its own category

15. *Disruptive, Impulse-Control, and Conduct Disorders*

16. *Substance-Related and Addictive Disorders*

17. *Neurocognitive Disorders*

18. *Personality Disorders*

19. *Paraphilic Disorders*

20. *Other Mental Disorders*

21. *Medication-Induced Movement Disorders and Other Adverse Effects of Medication*

22. *Other Conditions That May Be a Focus of Clinical Attention*

THE INDICATORS OF BEHAVIORAL DYSFUNCTION

"Normal" and "abnormal" depend on the person, place, and situation, and are largely shaped by social standards. Definitions of "normal" change with societal standards and norms. Normality is often viewed as good, whereas abnormality is seen as bad. When people do not conform to what is perceived as "normal," they are often given a number of negative labels, including unusual, sick, or disabled. These labels can lead to that individual being marginalized, or stigmatized.

The most comprehensive attempt to distinguish normality from abnormality is the *DSM*. The *DSM* shows how normality has changed throughout history and how it often involves value judgments. The *DSM* explicitly distinguishes mental disorders and nondisordered conditions.

THE INDICATORS OF SOMATIZATION

Somatization is the unconscious process by which psychological distress is expressed as physical symptoms. Somatic symptoms often occur as reactions to stressful situations and are not considered abnormal if they occur sporadically. However, some clients experience continuing somatic symptoms and even seek medical care for them.

Persistent somatization is associated with considerable distress and disability. Somatization may lead to overutilization of medical care, including unnecessary medical tests, and even increased hospitalization rates.

Not all somatizing clients are motivated by an unconscious wish to adopt the sick role, as is observed in clients with Factitious Disorder. Clients may vary in their degree of conviction that their symptoms are caused by a physical illness or disease. Clients may also present in multiple ways, including having multiple unexplained somatic symptoms, exhibiting predominantly illness worry or hypochondriacal beliefs, and/or displaying somatization as a manifestation of a variety of mental disorders.

THE INDICATORS OF FEIGNING ILLNESS

Malingering is not considered a mental illness. In the *DSM-5*, malingering receives a V code as one of the other conditions that may be a focus of clinical attention. The *DSM-5* defines malingering as intentionally falsely or grossly exaggerating physical or psychological problems. Motivation for malingering is usually external, such as avoiding work/military, obtaining reward (financial resources, medications, etc.), avoiding legal action, and so on. On the other hand, malingering also may be an adaptive response such as an inmate with mental illness trying to obtain relatively sparse and difficult-to-obtain mental health resources in prison.

Malingering varies in intensity, from all symptoms being falsified to some symptoms being falsified or symptoms being exaggerated. Malingering is not easy to diagnose because of the difficulty in gathering external evidence.

Prolonged direct observation can reveal evidence of malingering because it is difficult for a client who is malingering to maintain consistency with the false or exaggerated claims for extended periods. Malingering can be detected by discrepancies between the claimed distress and the objective findings or lack of cooperation during evaluation and in complying with prescribed treatment. Clues may be reports of rare or improbable symptoms. Rare symptoms—by definition—occur very infrequently, and clients almost never report improbable symptoms. In addition, social workers should watch closely for internal or external inconsistent presentation of symptoms. Often diagnosis comes as a result of the use of collateral data beyond the social work interview.

Malingering is different from Factitious Disorder (in which the motive is the desire to occupy a sick role, rather than some form of material gain) and Somatic Symptom and Related Disorders (in which symptoms are not produced willfully).

Three categories of malingering are:

- Pure malingering (feigning a nonexistent disorder)
- Partial malingering (consciously exaggerating real symptoms)
- False imputation (ascribing real symptoms to a cause a client knows is unrelated to the symptoms)

COMMON PSYCHOTROPIC AND NON-PSYCHOTROPIC PRESCRIPTIONS AND OVER-THE-COUNTER MEDICATIONS AND THEIR SIDE EFFECTS

Psychotropic medications affect brain chemicals associated with mood and behavior. Psychotropic drugs are prescribed to treat a variety of mental health problems and typically work by changing the amounts of important chemicals in the brain called neurotransmitters. Psychotropic drugs are usually prescribed by psychiatrists, though other physicians and professionals may be allowed to prescribe them in certain jurisdictions. Psychotropic drugs may be needed to treat disorders such as Schizophrenia or Bipolar Disorder, but are often combined with other supports, such as that from family and friends, therapy, lifestyle changes, and other treatment protocols, to ensure healthy everyday living.

Antipsychotics

Used for the treatment of Schizophrenia and mania

Typical

Haldol (haloperidol)

Haldol Decanoate (long-acting injectable)

Loxitane (loxapine)

Mellaril (thioridazine)

Moban (molindone)

Navane (thiothixene)

Prolixin (fluphenazine)

Serentil (mesoridazine)

Stelazine (trifluoperazine)

Thorazine (chlorpromazine)

Trilafon (perphenazine)

Atypical

Abilify (aripiprazole)

Clozaril (clozapine)

Geodon (ziprasidone)

Risperdal (risperidone)

Seroquel (quetiapine)

Zyprexa (olanzapine)

With Clozaril, there is an increased risk of agranulocytosis that requires blood monitoring.

Some antipsychotics are available in injectable forms; these are useful for clients who are noncompliant with oral medications.

Tardive dyskinesia (abnormal, involuntary movements of the tongue, lips, jaw, and face, as well as twitching and snakelike movement of the extremities and occasionally the trunk) may result from taking high doses of antipsychotic medications over a long period of time. Symptoms may persist indefinitely after discontinuation of these medications. Thus, antipsychotic use should be closely monitored and prescribed at low doses if possible.

Antimanic Agents (Mood Stabilizers)

Used for the treatment of Bipolar Disorder

Depakene (valproic acid, divalproex sodium), Depakote sprinkles

Lamictal (lamotrigine)

Lithium (lithium carbonate), Eskalith, Lithobid

Tegretol (carbamazepine), Carbotrol

Topamax (topiramate)

There is a small difference between toxic and therapeutic levels (narrow therapeutic index) that necessitates periodic checks of blood levels of lithium. Also, there is a need for periodic checks of thyroid and kidney functions, because lithium can affect the functioning of these organs.

Antidepressants

Used for the treatment of Depressive Disorders

Selective Serotonin Reuptake Inhibitors

Celexa (citalopram)

Lexapro (escitalopram)

Luvox (fluvoxamine)

Paxil (paroxetine)

Prozac (fluoxetine)

Zoloft (sertraline)

Tricyclics

Anafranil (clomipramine)

Asendin (amoxapine)

Elavil (amitriptyline)

Norpramin (desipramine)

Pamelor (nortriptyline)

Sinequan (doxepin)

Surmontil (trimipramine)

Tofranil (imipramine)

Vivactil (protriptyline)

Monoamine Oxidase Inhibitors (MAOIs)

Nardil (phenelzine)

Parnate (tranylcypromine)

There are dietary restrictions of foods that contain high levels of tyramine (generally food that has been aged). Foods to avoid may include beer, ale, wine (particularly Chianti), cheese (except cottage and cream cheese), smoked or pickled fish (herring), beef or chicken liver, summer (dry) sausage, fava or broad bean pods (Italian green beans), and yeast vitamin supplements (brewer's yeast).

Others

Desyrel (trazodone)

Effexor (venlafaxine)

Remeron (mirtazapine)

Serzone (nefazodone)

Wellbutrin (bupropion)

Antianxiety Drugs

Used for the treatment of Anxiety Disorders

Benzodiazepines are a class of drugs primarily used for treating anxiety, but they also are effective in treating several other conditions.

Ativan (lorazepam)

Buspar (buspirone)

Klonopin (clonazepam)

Valium (diazepam)

Xanax (alprazolam)

There is a high abuse potential of these drugs and they can be dangerous when combined with alcohol or illicit substances. It is critical to look for signs of impaired motor or other functioning.

Stimulants

Used for the treatment of Attention-Deficit/Hyperactivity Disorder

Adderall (amphetamine, mixed salts)

Concerta (methylphenidate, long acting)

Dexedrine (dextroamphetamine)

Dexedrine Spansules (dextroamphetamine, long acting)

Metadate (methylphenidate, long acting)

Ritalin (methylphenidate)

Common Prescription Medications

The vast majority of Americans take at least one prescription medication, with more than half of Americans taking two or more. The most commonly prescribed include the following medications:

Advair Diskus is a prescription used to treat asthma and chronic obstructive pulmonary disease (COPD).

Crestor is a lipid-lowering agent taken orally.

Cymbalta is a selective serotonin and norepinephrine reuptake inhibitor (SSNRI) for oral administration.

Diovan is used to treat heart disease or heart failure.

Hydrocodone/acetaminophen is the most popular painkiller used to treat moderate to severe pain. Hydrocodone, a narcotic analgesic, relieves pain through the central nervous system, and it also is used to stop or prevent coughing. This drug can become habit-forming when used over an extended period of time.

Levothyroxine sodium is used to treat hypothyroidism, a condition where the thyroid gland does not produce enough of the thyroid hormone. This drug also is used to treat thyroid cancer and to help shrink an enlarged thyroid gland.

Lantus is a sterile solution of insulin glargine for use as a subcutaneous injection for diabetes.

Lisinopril (which used to be sold under the brand names Zestril and Prinivil) is a high blood pressure medication. Its main function is to block chemicals in the body that trigger the tightening of blood vessels. Lisinopril also is used to help treat heart failure.

Lyrica is used to control seizures, as well as treat nerve pain and fibromyalgia.

Metoprolol, the generic version of Lopressor, is used to treat high blood pressure and also helps reduce the risk of repeated heart attacks. Metoprolol also treats heart failure and heart pain or angina.

Nexium is used to treat symptoms of gastroesophageal reflux disease (GERD) and other conditions involving excessive stomach acid.

Simvastatin (generic form of Zocor) is prescribed to treat high cholesterol and is typically recommended in conjunction with diet changes. This drug is believed to have a variety of benefits including helping to prevent heart attacks and strokes.

Synthroid is a prescription, man-made thyroid hormone that is used to treat hypothyroidism.

Ventolin solution is used in inhalers for asthma.

Vyvanse is used to treat hyperactivity and impulse control disorders.

Concepts of Abuse and Neglect

6

INDICATORS AND DYNAMICS OF ABUSE AND NEGLECT THROUGHOUT THE LIFESPAN

There are various forms of abuse and neglect: **physical abuse** (infliction of physical injury); **sexual abuse** (inappropriate exposure or sexual contact, activity, or behavior without consent); **psychological abuse** (emotional/verbal/mental injury); and **neglect** (failing to meet physical, emotional, or other needs).

Different forms of abuse occur separately, but are often seen in combinations. Psychological abuse almost always accompanies other forms of abuse.

Indicators and Dynamics of Sexual Abuse

Physical or anatomical signs/injuries associated with the genital and rectal areas are signs of physical or sexual abuse. Behavioral signs include any extreme changes in behavior, including regression, fears and anxieties, withdrawal, sleep disturbances, and/or recurrent nightmares. If the victim is a child, he or she may also show an unusual interest in sexual matters or know sexual information inappropriate for his or her age group. Sexual promiscuity, sexual victimization, and prostitution can also be signs.

Some factors influencing the effect of sexual abuse include:

- Age of the victim (at time of abuse and time of assessment)
- Extent and duration of sexual abuse
- Relationship of offender to victim
- Reaction of others to the abuse
- Other life experiences

Immediately after disclosing the abuse, an individual is at risk for:

■ Disbelief by others (especially if victim is a child or perpetrator is a spouse/partner of an adult)

■ Being rejected by others

■ Being blamed for the abuse and the consequences of disclosing the sexual abuse

For a child, one of the most significant factors contributing to adjustment after sexual abuse is the level of parental support.

Some of the effects of sexual abuse can be:

■ Aversive feelings about sex; overvaluing sex; sexual identity problems; and/or hypersexual behaviors

■ Feelings of shame and guilt or feeling responsible for the abuse, which are reflected in self-destructive behaviors (such as substance abuse, self-mutilation, suicidal ideation and gestures, and acts that aim to provoke punishment)

■ Lack of trust, unwillingness to invest in others; involvement in exploitive relationships; angry and acting-out behaviors

■ Perceived vulnerability and victimization; phobias; sleep and eating problems

Indicators and Dynamics of Psychological Abuse and Neglect

Psychological abuse/neglect is sustained, repetitive, and inappropriate behavior aimed at threatening, isolating, discrediting, belittling, teasing, humiliating, bullying, confusing, and/or ignoring. Psychological abuse/neglect can be seen in constant criticism, belittling, teasing, ignoring or withholding of praise or affection, and placing excessive or unreasonable demands, including expectations above what is appropriate.

It can impact intelligence, memory, recognition, perception, attention, imagination, and moral development. Individuals who have been psychologically abused are likely to be fearful, withdrawn, and/or resentful, distressed, and despairing. They are likely to feel unloved, worthless, and unwanted, or only valued in meeting another's needs.

Those who are victims of psychological abuse and neglect often:

■ Avoid eye contact and experience deep loneliness, anxiety, and/or despair

■ Have a flat and superficial way of relating, with little empathy toward others

■ Have a lowered capacity to engage appropriately with others

- Engage in bullying, disruptive, or aggressive behaviors toward others
- Engage in self-harming and/or self-destructive behaviors (i.e., cutting, physical aggression, reckless behavior showing a disregard for self and safety, drug taking)

Indicators and Dynamics of Physical Abuse and Neglect

Physical abuse is defined as nonaccidental trauma or physical injury caused by punching, beating, kicking, biting, or burning. It is the most visible form of abuse because there are usually physical signs.

With a child, physical abuse can result from inappropriate or excessive physical discipline.

Indicators of physical abuse include:

- Unexplained bruises or welts on the face, lips, mouth, torso, back, buttocks, or thighs, sometimes reflecting the shape of the article used to inflict them (electric cord, belt buckle, etc.)
- Unexplained burns from a cigar or cigarette, especially on soles, palms, back, or buttocks—sometimes patterned like an electric burner, iron, or similar
- Unexplained fractures to the skull, nose, or facial structure
- Unexplained lacerations or abrasions to the mouth, lips, gums, eyes, and/or external genitalia

Behavioral indicators include being wary of individuals (parent or caretaker if a child is being abused) and behavioral extremes (aggressiveness or withdrawal), as well as fear related to reporting injury.

THE EFFECTS OF PHYSICAL, SEXUAL, AND PSYCHOLOGICAL ABUSE ON INDIVIDUALS, FAMILIES, GROUPS, ORGANIZATIONS, AND COMMUNITIES

Abuse and neglect have both immediate and long-term consequences. The impacts are often influenced by various factors including the extent and type of abuse or neglect, whether it was continual or infrequent, the age at which it occurred, the relationship to the perpetrator (if abuse), and how the abuse or neglect was discovered and addressed upon disclosure. Client personality traits, inner strength, and support systems also influence the effects.

For many, the impacts of abuse and neglect will not be immediately evident. Physical injuries, if there are any, are usually temporary. The more damaging and lasting impacts are those that result from impaired language, cognitive, and physical development due to the abuse and neglect.

Children who have been abused and neglected are at risk of academic problems and school failure due to difficulty following rules, being respectful, staying in their seats and keeping on-task, temper tantrums, and/or difficult peer relationships.

In addition, social and emotional problems, poor relationships, substance use and dependency, risky or violent behaviors, and delinquency are manifestations of abuse and neglect. The psychological consequences of abuse and neglect include isolation, fear, inability to trust, low self-esteem, anxiety, depression, and hopelessness. These difficulties can lead to relationship problems and the possibility of antisocial behavioral traits.

It is important to note that not all those who have been abused and neglected will experience physical, behavioral, and/or psychological problems—though they are more likely. Thus, a lack of these problems should not be used as evidence that abuse or neglect did not occur.

THE INDICATORS, DYNAMICS, AND IMPACT OF EXPLOITATION ACROSS THE LIFESPAN (E.G., FINANCIAL, IMMIGRATION STATUS, SEXUAL TRAFFICKING)

Exploitation is treating someone badly in order to benefit from his or her resources or work. It is when someone uses a situation to gain unfair advantage for himself or herself. Exploitation is more common when there is a power differential between parties due to social status, abilities, income, education, job position, and so on.

Social workers have ethical mandates not to exploit clients, supervisees, students, and others who they come in contact with in their work.

They also may be asked to assess exploitation of clients by others and intervene when needed. For example, a form of maltreatment sometimes seen with older adults is financial/material exploitation or unauthorized use of an older person's resources. Individuals may befriend an older person to gain his or her trust so that the older adult's money or items of value can be inappropriately used for the individual's wants or needs and not the care of the older adult.

On a macro level, it is also important to see the relationship between discrimination and exploitation of individuals. When individuals are not provided the same access to social rewards, they are inherently exploited. Most social problems are aggravated by the status of particular groups in the society, including that:

- There is a greater prevalence of poverty among people of color and female household heads.
- Poverty decreases the opportunities for employment, education, goods, and so on.

- Poverty creates greater stresses that lead to physical and mental illnesses, family breakdown, inability to work, and other problems.
- Discrimination creates deficits in social power.

THE CHARACTERISTICS OF PERPETRATORS OF ABUSE, NEGLECT, AND EXPLOITATION

Many individuals with these characteristics do not commit acts of abuse. However, some factors are more likely to be present in those who commit abusive acts. Thus, having one of these risk factors does not mean that an individual will become an abuser, but an abuser is likely to have one or more of these risk factors.

A past history of violent behavior is the best predictor of future violence. Each prior act of violence increases the chance of future episodes of violence. In addition, those who suffered some form of abuse as children are more likely to be perpetrators of abuse as adults.

Risk factors include:

1. History of owning weapons and using them against others

2. Criminal history, repetitive antisocial behavior

3. Drug and alcohol use (substance use is associated with the most violent crimes)

4. Psychiatric disorder with coexisting substance abuse

5. Certain psychiatric symptoms such as psychosis, intense suspiciousness, anger, and/or unhappiness

6. Personality Disorders (Borderline and Antisocial Personality Disorders)

7. History of impulsivity; low frustration tolerance; recklessness; inability to tolerate criticism; entitlement

8. Angry affect without empathy for others—high anger scores associated with increased chance of violence

9. Environmental stressors: lower socioeconomic status or poverty, job termination

A social worker should take all reports of abuse and all threats for harm seriously.

A social worker can distinguish between static and dynamic risk factors.

Static risk factors: factors that cannot be changed by interventions such as past history of violent behavior or demographic information.

Dynamic risk factors: factors that can be changed by interventions such as change in living situation, treatment of psychiatric symptoms, abstaining from drug and alcohol use, access to weapons, and so on. Each client presents with a unique set of risk factors that require an individualized plan.

Some of the risk factors include the following:

- *Stressors*: history of abuse; isolated with lack of social supports; low sense of self-competence and self-esteem; financial problems
- *Poor skills*: rigid, authoritarian; low intelligence quotient (IQ); poor self-control; poor communication, problem-solving, and interpersonal skills
- *Family issues*: marital discord, imbalanced relationship with marital partner (dominant or noninvolved); domestic violence; substance abuse

The victim is often blamed for the abuse by the perpetrator.

Interventions to reduce dynamic risk factors include:

- Pharmacological interventions
- Substance use treatment
- Psychosocial interventions
- Removal of weapons
- Increased level of supervision

Interventions With Clients/ Client Systems (26%)

Indicators and Effects of Crisis and Change

7

THE IMPACT OF OUT-OF-HOME PLACEMENT (E.G., HOSPITALIZATION, FOSTER CARE, RESIDENTIAL CARE, CRIMINAL JUSTICE SYSTEM) ON CLIENTS/CLIENT SYSTEMS

The use of out-of-home placement is generally viewed as an intervention that only occurs when there is a health or safety risk in the home. This risk can be due to the individual who is being removed (caused by a medical or behavioral health issue of the individual being removed) or his or her family members (caused by child abuse or neglect, medical or behavioral health issues of a family member, etc.). Often, out-of-home placement occurs after in-home interventions have been tried and failed.

Individuals who are placed outside of their homes often experience significant life problems. Determining whether these issues are directly caused by the removal is difficult as these individuals are likely to be at-risk for such problems prior to the placements.

For example, children who are removed from their homes due to abuse and/or neglect typically are higher users of mental health or other social services than before they were placed away from their parents. These children often report a high level of stress, which may manifest in substance abuse, chronic aggressive or destructive behavior, suicidal ideation or acting out, and/or patterns of runaway behavior. Academic problems are also common among these children.

For all those leaving their homes, regardless of age, there is a disruption of emotional bonds with other family members, which is often accompanied by rage, grief, sadness, and/or despair.

THE IMPACT OF STRESS, TRAUMA, AND VIOLENCE

Emotional and psychological trauma is the result of extraordinarily stressful events that destroy a sense of security, making a client feel helpless and vulnerable in a dangerous world.

Traumatic experiences often involve a threat to life or safety, but **any situation that leaves a client feeling overwhelmed and alone can be traumatic, even if it does not involve physical harm**. It is not the objective facts that determine whether an event is traumatic, but a subjective emotional experience of the event.

An event will most likely lead to emotional or psychological trauma if:

- It happened unexpectedly
- There was not preparation for it
- There is a feeling of having been powerless to prevent it
- It happens repeatedly
- Someone was intentionally cruel
- It happened in childhood

Emotional and psychological trauma can be caused by one-time events or ongoing, relentless stress.

Not all potentially traumatic events lead to lasting emotional and psychological damage. Some clients rebound quickly from even the most tragic and shocking experiences. Others are devastated by experiences that, on the surface, appear to be less upsetting.

A number of risk factors make clients susceptible to emotional and psychological trauma. Clients are more likely to be traumatized by a stressful experience if they are already under a heavy stress load or have recently suffered a series of losses.

Clients are also more likely to be traumatized by a new situation if they have been traumatized before—especially if the earlier trauma occurred in childhood. Experiencing trauma in childhood can have a severe and long-lasting effect. Children who have been traumatized see the world as a frightening and dangerous place. When childhood trauma is not resolved, this fundamental sense of fear and helplessness carries over into adulthood, setting the stage for further trauma.

THEORIES OF TRAUMA-INFORMED CARE

Trauma-informed care organizations, programs, and services are based on an understanding of the vulnerabilities or triggers of trauma survivors that traditional service delivery approaches may exacerbate, so that these services and programs can be more supportive and avoid re-traumatization.

Trauma-informed care also can be viewed as an overarching philosophy and approach based on the understanding that many clients have suffered traumatic experiences and providers must be responsible for being sensitive to this issue, regardless of whether clients are being treated specifically for the trauma. Therefore, social workers should initially approach all of their clients as if they have a trauma history, regardless of the services for which the clients are being seen.

It is important for social workers to understand trauma and how it affects people regardless of their diagnoses or identified needs. Thus, in everyday practice, social workers need to recognize how the organizations, programs, and environments in which they practice could potentially act as trauma triggers for their clients and should make every effort to minimize these triggers.

An important component of trauma-informed care is recognizing trauma's centrality to clients and how this plays into their perception of physical and emotional safety, relationships, and behaviors. When trauma goes unrecognized, it can be difficult to understand clients' behaviors or attitudes, and social workers may be tempted to assign unfounded pathologies to clients. Clients even may end up being barred from services as a result of what appears to be bizarre behavior or unfounded beliefs. Often, however, clients' otherwise challenging behavior is provoked by a legitimate trigger that easily could have been avoided.

CRISIS INTERVENTION THEORIES

A "crisis" is an acute disruption of psychological homeostasis in which a client's usual coping mechanisms fail and there is evidence of distress and functional impairment. While there are many theories used to explain and address crises, there are seven critical stages through which clients typically pass on the road to crisis stabilization, resolution, and mastery. These stages are essential, sequential, and sometimes overlapping in the process of crisis intervention:

1. *Plan and conduct a thorough biopsychosocial–spiritual–cultural and lethality/imminent danger assessment*

   A social worker must conduct a biopsychosocial–spiritual–cultural assessment covering a client's environmental supports and stressors, medical needs and medications, current use of drugs and alcohol, and internal and external coping methods and resources. Assessing lethality is first and foremost.

2. *Make psychological contact and rapidly establish the collaborative relationship*

   In a crisis, a social worker must do this quickly, generally as part of assessment.

3. *Identify the major problems, including crisis precipitants*

   A social worker should determine from a client why things have "come to a head." There is usually a "last straw," but a social worker should also find out what other problems a client is concerned about.

It can also be useful to prioritize the problems in terms of which problems a client wants to work on first.

4. *Encourage an exploration of feelings and emotions*

A social worker should validate a client's feelings and emotions and let him or her vent about the crisis. The use of active listening skills, paraphrasing, and probing questions is essential. A social worker should also challenge maladaptive beliefs.

5. *Generate and explore alternatives and new coping strategies*

A social worker and a client must come up with a plan for what will help improve the current situation. Brainstorming possibilities and finding out what has been helpful in the past are critical.

6. *Restore functioning through implementation of an action plan*

This stage represents a shift from a crisis to a resolution. A client and a worker will begin to take the steps negotiated in the previous stage. This is also where a client will begin to make meaning of the crisis event.

7. *Plan follow-up*

Follow-up can take many forms as it can involve phone or in-person visits at specific intervals. A postcrisis evaluation may look at a client's current functioning and assess a client's progress.

THE INDICATORS OF TRAUMATIC STRESS AND VIOLENCE

Stress is a typical response to feeling overwhelmed or threatened. Fight, flight, and freeze are survival responses to protect individuals from danger. Individuals react and respond to stress in different ways. There are many disadvantages to a stressful lifestyle that creates constant feelings of being overwhelmed, as well as physiological stimulation. Interventions aimed at social and lifestyle changes can usually restore physiological and psychological balance in order to address stress.

This is not the case when traumatization occurs. Traumatization is when a client experiences neurological distress that does not go away or when he or she is not able to return to a state of equilibrium. Traumatization can lead to mental, social, emotional, and physical disability. Like stress, trauma is also experienced differently by different individuals.

There are many indicators of traumatic stress and violence, including:

1. Addictive behaviors related to drugs, alcohol, sex, shopping, and gambling

2. An inability to tolerate conflicts with others or intense feelings

3. A belief of being bad, worthless, without value or importance

4. Dichotomous "all or nothing" thinking

5. Chronic and repeated suicidal thoughts/feelings

6. Poor attachment

7. Dissociation

8. Eating disorders—anorexia, bulimia, and obesity

9. Self-blame

10. Intense anxiety and repeated panic attacks

11. Depression

12. Self-harm, self-mutilation, self-injury, or self-destruction

13. Unexplained, but intense, fears of people, places, or things

When trauma or violence occurs during childhood, children may have problems regulating their behaviors and emotions. They may be clingy and fearful of new situations, easily frightened, difficult to console, aggressive, impulsive, sleepless, delayed in developmental milestones, and/or regressing in functioning and behavior.

In order to practice competently in this area, social workers must

1. Realize the widespread impact of trauma and understand potential paths for recovery

2. Recognize the signs and symptoms of trauma in clients, families, staff, and other systems

3. Respond by fully integrating knowledge about trauma into social work policies, procedures, and practices

4. Seek to actively resist retraumatization

THE IMPACT OF OUT-OF-HOME DISPLACEMENT (E.G., NATURAL DISASTER, HOMELESSNESS, IMMIGRATION) ON CLIENTS/ CLIENT SYSTEMS

The homes in which clients live are part of their self-definition. They are decorated to reflect likes or dislikes, telling others about their occupants and accommodating interests such as gardening, cooking, and others. Homes are seen as extensions of their residents and distinguish people from each other.

Behavior is also cued by the physical environment. Homes remind inhabitants of experiences which took place in the past, as well as what to do in the future. Homes are familiar and are often viewed as safe havens where clients can behave without being judged.

Thus, involuntary displacement outside the home due to hospitalization, incarceration, needed safety, or long-term care needs can be traumatic for many reasons. First, such movement may be associated with losses such as those due to health issues, financial concerns, or safety problems. These losses alone can cause depression, anxiety, confusion, and/or other emotional reactions, which are compounded from having to move from the communities or homes in which clients live.

In out-of-home placements, clients may have changes in roles, causing them to develop poor self-image. For example, the roles of neighbor, community leader, gardener, and so on, which provided fulfillment and recognition, may be lost and no longer possible. Since there is status attached to these roles, their loss can negatively affect self-image.

There also may be a loss of possessions associated with displacement. Precious items that represent a lifetime of memories may have been destroyed, such as by a natural disaster, or sold/given away as there may be no room to keep them in the new settings—especially if they are shared with others.

There also may be a cost associated with involuntary displacement. For example, long-term care can drain client assets and make clients feel guilty about spending money on themselves or fearful about running out of funds for sustained care and housing.

Out-of-home displacement also often accompanies loss of relationships. Relatives and friends who interfaced with clients in their homes may find it inconvenient or impossible to see them in the new settings. Sometimes the lack of private space in which to visit puts up barriers. Visitors may also be intimidated by the sights and sounds of hospitals, jails, or nursing homes.

Clients frequently do not have the same freedom or control that they had when they were at home. In congregate settings, meals, activities, room cleaning, and bathing may be overseen and scheduled for the sake of organization and efficiency, and there are usually numerous rules, policies, and procedures to follow with less individual autonomy and choice.

THE INDICATORS AND RISK FACTORS OF THE CLIENT'S/CLIENT SYSTEM'S DANGER TO SELF AND OTHERS

There are risk factors that must be considered in any assessment, because they are linked to a risk of suicide or violence.

Danger to Self: Suicide

Risk Factors

- History of previous suicide attempt (best predictor of future attempt; medical seriousness of attempt is also significant)

- Lives alone; lack of social supports
- Presence of psychiatric disorder—depression (feeling hopeless), Anxiety Disorder, Personality Disorder (*A client is also at greater risk after being discharged from the hospital or after being started on antidepressants as he or she may now have the energy to implement a suicide plan.*)
- Substance abuse
- Family history of suicide
- Exposure to suicidal behavior of others through media or peers
- Losses—relationship, job, financial, social
- Presence of firearm or easy access to other lethal methods

Some Protective Factors

- Effective and appropriate clinical care for mental, physical, and Substance Use Disorders
- Easy access to a variety of clinical interventions and support (i.e., medical and mental health care)
- Restricted access to highly lethal methods
- Family and community support
- Learned coping and stress reduction skills
- Cultural and religious beliefs that discourage suicide and support self-preservation

Some Behavioral Warning Signs

- Change in eating and sleeping habits
- Drug and alcohol use
- Unusual neglect of personal appearance
- Marked personality change
- Loss of interest in pleasurable activities
- Not tolerating praise or rewards
- Giving away belongings
- Isolation from others
- Taking care of legal and other issues
- Dramatic increase in mood (might indicate a client has made a decision to end his or her life)
- Verbalizes threats to commit suicide or feelings of despair and hopelessness
    - "I'm going to kill myself."
    - "I wish I were dead."

- "My family would be better off without me."
- "The only way out for me is to die."
- "It's just too much for me to put up with."
- "Nobody needs me anymore."

Danger to Others: Violence

Risk Factors

- Youth who become violent before age 13 generally commit more crimes, and more serious crimes, for a longer time; these youth exhibit a pattern of escalating violence throughout childhood, sometimes continuing into adulthood.
- Most highly aggressive children or children with behavioral disorders do not become serious violent offenders.
- Serious violence is associated with drugs, guns, and other risky behaviors.
- Involvement with delinquent peers and gang membership are two of the most powerful predictors of violence.

Some Protective Factors

- Effective programs combine components that address both individual risks and environmental conditions; building individual skills and competencies; changes in peer groups
- Interventions that target change in social context appear to be more effective, on average, than those that attempt to change individual attitudes, skills, and risk behaviors
- Effective and appropriate clinical care for mental, physical, and substance abuse disorders
- Easy access to a variety of clinical interventions and support (i.e., medical and mental health care)
- Restricted access to highly lethal methods
- Family and community support
- Learned coping and stress reduction skills

Some Behavioral Warning Signs

- Drug and alcohol use
- Marked personality changes
- Angry outbursts
- Preoccupation with killing, war, violence, weapons, and so on

- Isolation from others
- Obtaining guns or other lethal methods

METHODS AND APPROACHES TO TRAUMA-INFORMED CARE

A good trauma-informed approach is multidimensional. Several elements that indicate a good, trauma-informed program are:

Environment of Care

- Soothing colors for decor and paint
- Overall quiet; soft music
- Neutral or pleasant aroma
- Individual chairs with discrete seating areas
- Individual bathroom options

Staff Appearance

- Attire connotes professionalism; easy to identify staff members
- Clothing not sexually provocative

Staff Behavior

- Clearly demonstrate proper manners and respect
- Make every effort to minimize delays
- Speak in clear, nonthreatening tones
- Make eye contact
- Smile and demonstrate a generally pleasant demeanor
- Open physical stance, nodding
- Open to change/not rigid

Organizational Understanding

- Trauma policy/philosophy in place
- Commitment to trauma-informed care articulated
- All staff/clients/family members taught about trauma and its impact
- Universal trauma screenings for all clients
- Trauma status continually assessed
- Clear organization plan for dealing with behavioral crises
- Discrete areas for calming or crisis management identified
- Feedback valued and concerted outreach efforts made

Treatment Considerations

- Treatment goals reflect consumer preferences
- Treatment integrated across disciplines
- Offering choice of treatment provider when possible
- Everyday language used
- All statements of abuse acknowledged and addressed
- Sensitivity to seating configuration and proximity of seating options
- Co-occurring treatment needs assessed and incorporated into service provided
- Culture of origin respected and incorporated into service planning
- Recognize the importance of physical boundaries and aware that touch—sometimes even a handshake—could trigger trauma
- Avoid jokes and stories which can serve as triggers

THE IMPACT OF CAREGIVING ON FAMILIES

Although caregiving is at the heart of family functioning, the dynamics of families can be greatly altered when family members experience physical illness or disability. For example, when a primary family caregiver becomes ill or disabled, family roles must shift to redistribute the tasks he or she is unable to perform. This redistribution includes both instrumental and emotional tasks, as the family may face a loss of both financial and emotional support that was provided by the primary family caregiver.

When a child is ill or disabled, parents can be overwhelmed by the added responsibilities to typical childrearing. In addition, healthy siblings may also feel the strain and may feel that they should not "burden" parents any further, so they ignore their own emotional and/or physical needs.

The stage when physical illness or disability occurs within the life course can also have differential impacts. For example, parents of children born ill or disabled may be more accepting of the situation than those who are faced with the illness or disability of children that occurs later. At any time, it is a major challenge for a family to tend to its members' individual developmental needs and meet the caregiving demands of a serious illness or disability. Some families may be paralyzed at the time of the illness or onset of the disability. Crisis intervention may be needed to stabilize the situation and develop coping skills.

Addressing the grief or loss that can accompany chronic illness or disability may also be needed. In addition, families may seek help from social workers to identify critical resources because they are not able to meet family members' needs and/or their own without them. Lastly, illness and disability can be isolating for an individual, as well as his or her family.

THE DYNAMICS AND EFFECTS OF LOSS, SEPARATION, AND GRIEF

Elisabeth Kübler-Ross outlined what has been the traditional five stages of grief. She originally developed this model based on her observations of people suffering from terminal illness. She later expanded her theory to apply to any form of personal loss, such as the death of a loved one, the loss of a job or income, major rejection, the end of a relationship or divorce, drug addiction, incarceration, the onset of a disease or chronic illness, and/or an infertility diagnosis, as well as many tragedies and disasters (and even minor losses).

Denial and isolation: Shock is replaced with the feeling of "this can't be happening to me."

Anger: The emotional confusion that results from this loss may lead to anger and finding someone or something to blame—"why me?"

Bargaining: The next stage may result in trying to negotiate with one's self (or a higher power) to attempt to change what has occurred.

Depression: A period of sadness and loneliness will then occur, in which a person reflects on his or her grief and loss.

Acceptance: After time feeling depressed about the loss, a person will eventually be at peace with what happened.

Hope is not a separate stage, but is possible at any stage.

Intervention Processes and Techniques

8

THE PRINCIPLES AND TECHNIQUES OF INTERVIEWING (E.G., SUPPORTING, CLARIFYING, FOCUSING, CONFRONTING, VALIDATING, FEEDBACK, REFLECTING LANGUAGE DIFFERENCES, USE OF INTERPRETERS, REDIRECTING)

In social work, an interview is always purposeful and involves verbal and nonverbal communication between a social worker and client, during which ideas, attitudes, and feelings are exchanged. The actions of a social worker aim to gather important information and keep a client focused on the achievement of the goal.

A social work interview is designed to serve the interest of a client; therefore, the actions of a social worker during the interview must be planned and focused. Questions in a social work interview should be tailored to the specifics of a client, not generic, "one size fits all" inquiries. The focus is on the uniqueness of a client and his or her unique situation.

The purpose of the social work interview can be informational, diagnostic, or therapeutic. The same interview may serve more than one purpose.

Communication during a social work interview is interactive and interrelational. A social worker's questions will result in specific responses by a client that, in turn, lead to other inquiries. The message is formulated by a client, encoded, transmitted, received, processed, and decoded. The importance of words and messages may be implicit (implied) or explicit (evident). *A social worker should listen, being nonjudgmental, throughout a social work interview.*

There are a number of techniques that a social worker may use during an interview to assist clients.

- *Universalization*—the generalization or normalization of behavior
- *Clarification*—reformulate problem in a client's words to make sure that the social worker is on the same wavelength
- *Confrontation*—calling attention to something
- *Interpretation*—pulling together patterns of behavior to get a new understanding
- *Reframing and relabeling*—stating problem in a different way so a client can see possible solutions

Social workers must be proficient in the languages spoken by clients or use qualified interpreters. *It is not appropriate to use family members to interpret or provide services in which social workers are not linguistically competent as valuable information may be missed during social work interviews.* When working with interpreters, social workers should face clients and speak directly to them—not the interpreters. Social workers also should have ask for the opinions of the interpreters or have conversations with them as their focus must clients.

METHODS TO INVOLVE CLIENTS/CLIENT SYSTEMS IN INTERVENTION PLANNING

The participation of clients in the process of identifying what is important to them now and in the future, and acting upon these priorities, is paramount. Clients' participation in the process will reduce resistance, increase motivation to change, and ensure sustainability of progress made.

In order to involve clients, social workers must continually listen to, learn about, and facilitate opportunities with clients who they are serving. Client involvement should not just occur during intervention planning, but instead during the entire problem-solving process.

In *engagement,* a social worker should be actively involved with a client in determining why treatment was sought; what has precipitated the desire to change now; the parameters of the helping relationship, including defining the roles of a social worker and client; and the expectations for treatment (what will occur and when it will happen). Client involvement is essential in determining what is important to a client now and in the future.

In *assessment,* a client is the source of providing essential information upon which to define the problem and solutions, as well as identifying collateral contacts from which gaps in data can be collected.

In *planning,* a client and social worker must develop a common understanding of a client's preferred lifestyle. Goals are developed from this common understanding in order to provide a direction to help a client move toward this lifestyle. Specific action plans are developed and agreed upon in order to specify who will do what, what and how resources will be needed and used, and timelines for implementation and review.

In *intervention*, a client must be actively involved in mobilizing his or her support network to realize continued progress and sustainable change. A client must bring to the attention of a social worker issues that arise which may threaten goal attainment. Progress, based upon client reports, must be tracked and plans/timelines adjusted accordingly.

In *evaluation*, subjective reports of a client, in conjunction with objective indicators of progress, should be used to determine when goals or objectives have been met and whether new goals or objectives should be set. Client self-monitoring is a good way to involve a client so he or she can see and track progress himself or herself.

In *termination*, a client should reflect on what has been achieved and anticipate what supports are in place if problems arise again. Although this is the last step in the problem-solving process, it still requires active involvement by both a social worker and client.

CULTURAL CONSIDERATIONS IN THE CREATION OF AN INTERVENTION PLAN

It is essential that a social worker address cultural considerations into treatment or intervention planning. These considerations should include the identification of cross-cultural barriers, which may hinder a client's engagement and/or progress in treatment.

Social workers also have an ethical mandate to take information learned when working with individual clients and adapt agency resources to meet others who may also have similar cultural considerations and/or language assistance needs.

A social worker should understand and validate each client's cultural norms, beliefs, and values. Areas in treatment or intervention planning that can be greatly influenced by cultural factors include identification of client strengths and problems, goals and objectives, and modalities of treatment.

For example, a client's culture can provide him or her with strengths that can be brought to the intervention process. These strengths can include, but are not limited to:

- Supportive family and community relations
- Community and cultural events and activities
- Faith and spiritual or religious beliefs
- Multilingual capabilities
- Healing practices and beliefs

- Participation in rituals (religious, cultural, familial, spiritual, community)
- Dreams and aspirations

A culturally informed intervention plan must be based on a therapeutic relationship in which a client feels safe to explore his or her problems within his or her cultural context.

Intervention will be most effective when it is consistent with a consumer's culture. A social worker should consider the following given their cultural appropriateness:

- Individual versus group treatment
- Alternative treatment approaches (yoga, aromatherapy, music, writing)
- Medication (western, traditional, and/or alternative)
- Family involvement
- Location/duration of intervention

The *DSM-5* incorporates a greater cultural sensitivity throughout the manual rather than a simple list of culture-bound syndromes.

Different cultures and communities exhibit or explain symptoms in various ways. Because of this, it is important for social workers to be aware of relevant contextual information stemming from clients' cultures, races, ethnicities, religious affiliations, and/or geographical origins so social workers can more accurately diagnose client problems, as well as more effectively treat them.

In the *DSM-5*, specific diagnostic criteria were changed to better apply across diverse cultures. *The Cultural Formulation Interview Guide* is included to help social workers assess cultural factors influencing clients' perspectives of their symptoms and treatment options. It includes questions about clients' backgrounds in terms of their culture, race, ethnicity, religion, or geographical origin. The Interview provides an opportunity for clients to define their distress in their own words and then relate this distress to how others, who may not share their culture, see their problems.

THE CRITERIA USED IN THE SELECTION OF INTERVENTION/ TREATMENT MODALITIES (E.G., CLIENT/CLIENT SYSTEM ABILITIES, CULTURE, LIFE STAGE)

A social worker develops an intervention plan by consulting the relevant practice research and then flexibly implementing an approach to fit a client's needs and circumstances. The intervention plan is driven by the data collected as part of assessment. Assessment is informed by current human behavior and development research that provides key information about how clients behave and research about risk and resilience factors that affect human functioning. These theories inform social workers about what skills, techniques, and strategies must be used by social workers, clients, and others for the purpose of improving well-being. These techniques and strategies are outlined in an intervention plan.

An intervention plan should be reviewed during the intervention, at termination, and, if possible, following the termination of services to make adjustments, ensure progress, and determine the sustainability of change after treatment.

THE COMPONENTS OF INTERVENTION, TREATMENT, AND SERVICE PLANS

The goals of intervention and means used to achieve these goals are incorporated in a contractual agreement between a client and a social worker. The contract (also called an intervention or service plan) may be informal or written. The contract specifies problem(s) to be worked on; the goals to reduce the problem(s); client and social worker roles in the process; the interventions or techniques to be employed; the means of monitoring progress; stipulations for renegotiating the contract; and the time, place, fee, and frequency of meetings.

PSYCHOTHERAPIES

Psychotherapy aims to treat clients with mental disorders or problems by helping them understand their illness or situation. Social workers use verbal techniques to teach clients strategies to deal with stress, unhealthy thoughts, and dysfunctional behaviors. Psychotherapy helps clients manage their symptoms better and function optimally in everyday life.

Sometimes, psychotherapy alone may be the best treatment for a client, depending on the illness and its severity. Other times, psychotherapy is combined with the use of medication or a psychopharmacological approach.

There are many kinds of psychotherapy, so social workers must determine which is best to meet a client's need. A social worker should not use a "one size fits all approach" or a particular type of psychotherapy because it is more familiar or convenient. Some psychotherapies have been scientifically tested more than others for particular disorders.

For example, cognitive behavioral therapy (CBT), a blend of cognitive and behavioral therapy, is used for depression, anxiety, and other disorders. Dialectical behavior therapy (DBT), a form of CBT developed by Marsha Linehan, was developed to treat people with suicidal thoughts and actions. It is now also used to treat people with Borderline Personality Disorder. A social worker assures a client that his or her feelings are valid and vunderstandable, but coaches him or her to understand that they are unhealthy or disruptive and a balance must be achieved. A client understands that it is his or her personal responsibility to change the situation.

Some psychotherapies are effective with children and adolescents and can also be used with families.

THE IMPACT OF IMMIGRATION, REFUGEE, OR UNDOCUMENTED STATUS ON SERVICE DELIVERY

Social workers may have a general concept of immigration requirements, but this area of law is both complex and volatile. Laws and policies affecting the status of immigrants have evolved over time in response to various social, political, and economic pressures. Most recently, immigration policy has had an exclusionary focus that has turned toward conflating criminality and undocumented immigration status. Although immigration laws are within the exclusive purview of the federal government, some states have attempted to address concerns by passing their own measures. This situation creates legal questions and ethical dilemmas for social workers who are employed in programs or areas serving immigrants.

Professional social work standards support immigration and refugee policies that uphold and support equity and human rights, while protecting national security. The social work profession recognizes the challenge of competing claims; however, immigration policies must promote social justice and avoid racism and discrimination or profiling on the basis of race, religion, country of origin, gender, or other grounds. The impact of refugee and immigration policies on families and children have to be closely monitored. Policies that encourage family reunification and ensure that children do not grow up unduly disadvantaged by the immigration status of their parents must be enacted and upheld.

Given the great diversity and myriad needs of the growing immigrant population, it is essential that social workers understand the legal and political, as well as psychological and social, issues surrounding immigration. Undocumented immigrants represent a large and vulnerable population in the United States. When conducting individual practice with undocumented immigrants, social workers must be aware of the laws that impact service provision and the unique psychosocial stressors that are experienced by this population.

Numerous immigrant households are comprised of mixed-status families in which family members hold different legal statuses. Each status carries different benefit entitlements, services, and legal rights.

DISCHARGE, AFTERCARE, AND FOLLOW-UP PLANNING

Discharge may occur for a variety of reasons; for example, a client may have met his or her goals or no longer needs the services; decides not to continue to receive them from a particular social worker or in general; and/or requires a different level of care. In addition, when a social worker leaves an agency, a client may continue to receive the same service from this agency, but from another worker. Although this is not a "discharge" from services, there is careful planning and standards that need to be followed to ensure continuity of care and prevent gaps in service.

The 2008 *NASW Code of Ethics* provides some guidance with regard to discharge or terminations, as well as aftercare and follow-up services.

Social workers should terminate services to clients and professional relationships with them when such services and relationships are no longer required or no longer serve client needs or interests (*NASW Code of Ethics, 2008—1.16 Termination of Services*).

Social workers should take reasonable steps to avoid abandoning clients who are still in need of services. Social workers should withdraw services precipitously only under unusual circumstances, giving careful consideration to all factors in the situation and taking care to minimize possible adverse effects. Social workers should assist in making appropriate arrangements for continuation of services when necessary (*NASW Code of Ethics, 2008—1.16 Termination of Services*).

Social workers in fee-for-service settings may terminate services to clients who are not paying an overdue balance if the financial contractual arrangements have been made clear to a client, if a client does not pose an imminent danger to self or others, and if the clinical and other consequences of the current nonpayment have been addressed and discussed with a client (*NASW Code of Ethics, 2008—1.16 Termination of Services*).

Social workers should not terminate services to pursue a social, financial, or sexual relationship with a client (*NASW Code of Ethics, 2008—1.16 Termination of Services*).

Social workers who anticipate the termination or interruption of services to clients should notify clients promptly and seek the transfer, referral, or continuation of services in relation to client needs and preferences (*NASW Code of Ethics, 2008—1.16 Termination of Services*).

Social workers who are leaving an employment setting should inform clients of appropriate options for the continuation of services and of the benefits and risks of the options (*NASW Code of Ethics, 2008—1.16 Termination of Services*).

It is unethical to continue to treat clients when services are no longer needed or in their best interests.

Another standard that is relevant to termination of services (*NASW Code of Ethics, 2008—1.15 Interruption of Services*) mandates that social workers should make reasonable efforts to ensure continuity of services in the event that services are interrupted by factors such as unavailability, relocation, illness, disability, or death.

Social workers must involve clients and their families (when appropriate) in making their own decisions about follow-up services or aftercare. Involvement must include, at a minimum, discussion of client and family preferences (when appropriate).

Social workers are often responsible for coordination of clients' follow-up services, when needed.

A return of clients to services quickly may suggest either that they did not receive needed follow-up services or that these services were inadequate. Termination may have occurred prematurely.

Clients who are at high risk for developing problems after services have ended should receive regular assessments after discharge to determine whether services are needed or discharge plans are being implemented as planned.

THE PHASES OF INTERVENTION AND TREATMENT

Social work aims to assist with making change on the micro, mezzo, or macro levels to enhance well-being. Despite the level of intervention, the steps that a social worker takes are similar.

Step 1	Engagement with client, group, or community
Step 2	Assessment of strengths and needs to be used in the intervention process
Step 3	Planning or design of intervention to address problem
Step 4	Intervention aimed at making change
Step 5	Evaluation of efforts
Step 6	Termination and anticipation of future needs

Usually change does not occur easily and there are stages of change that occur. Understanding these stages can help achieve goals.

Precontemplation	Denial, ignorance of the problem
Contemplation	Ambivalence, conflicted emotion
Preparation	Experimenting with small changes, collecting information about change
Action	Taking direct action toward achieving a goal
Maintenance	Maintaining a new behavior, avoiding temptation
Relapse	Feelings of frustration and failure

In order for real change to occur, all intervention steps must occur and change must be understood in these sequential stages.

THE PRINCIPLES AND TECHNIQUES FOR BUILDING AND MAINTAINING A HELPING RELATIONSHIP

Helping is based on acceptance of a client's situation and the ability of him or her to make changes only if desired. In a helping relationship, a social worker is trying to constructively assist a client—that is, to have an impact on or to influence his or her thinking and acting. The influence is further presumed to be in the direction of increasing the autonomy, understanding, effectiveness, and skill of a client.

Helping is distinguished from the more common concepts of advice giving, reprimanding, or punishing. These often involve threats and seldom result in more than outward conformity or superficial change. They generally do not increase strength or willingness and ability to carry responsibility.

The core of the helping process is the relationship between a social worker and a client.

The relationship between a social worker and a client is expressed through interaction. This interaction is commonly thought of in terms of verbal communication, which is natural, because the greater part of treatment consists of talking. However, nonverbal behavior is also very important. Body posture, gestures, facial expressions, eye movements, and other reactions often express feelings and attitudes more clearly than do spoken words. It is often for these reasons that a social worker must be aware of his or her own feelings, attitudes, and responses, as well as those of a client if he or she is to understand what is taking place and be of assistance.

A social worker cannot be useful in helping others unless he or she understands and is willing to accept the difficulties that all human beings encounter in trying to meet their needs. A social worker must know that the potential for all the weaknesses and strengths known to humanity exists at some level in every person. Social workers must also understand that human beings become more capable of dealing with their problems as they feel more adequate. Social workers recognize positive, as well as negative, aspects of a client, which will influence efforts to change and successful achievement of goals.

The interaction between a social worker and a client that takes place about a problem involves and is affected by the relationship between the two persons. Human beings act in terms of their feelings, attitudes, and understandings; hence, these must be taken into account and explored if the helping process is to result in change. Both a social worker and a client have objectives; a social worker's perceived objective is to be of assistance. Clarification and definition of these objectives often become important parts of the helping process. Both a social worker and a client have a degree of power (i.e., ability to influence the situation and the results).

Process of Engagement in Social Work Practice

The beginning of the problem-solving process includes activities of a social worker and a client to be helped that are directed at (a) becoming engaged with each other (engagement), (b) assessing a client's situation in order to select appropriate goals and the means of attaining them (assessment), and (c) planning how to employ these means (planning). During engagement, the limits to confidentiality must be explicitly stated at the beginning of this stage. Social workers must also explain their roles and how they can assist clients in addressing their problems.

It is important to consider how a client feels about coming for help and to deal with any negative feelings a client may feel (particularly if a client is involuntarily seeking help). A social worker must be open to discussing these feelings openly, because very little in a client can be changed until negative feelings are addressed. If a social worker is empathic with a client, it may be possible to find a common ground between what a client wishes and what a social worker can legitimately do.

A social worker and a client establish a therapeutic alliance in which a client views himself or herself as an ally of a social worker. A working alliance or a willingness by a client to work with a social worker should be established. A working alliance is sometimes referred to as a treatment alliance.

A social worker should express hopefulness that change can occur.

Resistance may occur during this stage. If clients are resistant to engage, social workers should clarify the process or specify what will happen and discuss this ambivalence.

THE CLIENT'S/CLIENT SYSTEM'S ROLE IN THE PROBLEM-SOLVING PROCESS

Clients often tend to think of themselves and their problems as unique. A client may think his or her difficulties are so different from those of others that no one else could ever understand them. He or she may even enjoy this feeling of uniqueness. It may be a defense against the discomfort of exploring his or her fears of being like others. At this point, a client may not be ready to look at the problem. It is hard to admit difficulties, even to oneself.

There may also be concerns as to whether social workers can really be trusted. Some people, because of unfortunate experiences in their childhoods, grow up with distrust of others. Furthermore, people are generally afraid of what others will think of them.

A client may only be looking for sympathy, support, and/or empathy, rather than searching for a new way to solve his or her difficulties. A client may not see that change must occur. When a social worker points out some of the ways in which a client is contributing to his or her own problems, he or she stops listening. Solving the problem often requires a client to uncover some aspects of himself or herself that he or she has avoided thinking about in the past and wants to avoid thinking about in the future.

A client may have struggled very hard to make himself or herself an independent person. The thought of depending on or receiving help from another individual seems to violate something. A client must constantly defend against a sense of weakness and may have difficulty listening to and using the assistance of another person.

There are also many clients who have strong needs to lean on others. Some spend much of their lives looking for others on whom they can be dependent. In the helping situation, they may constantly and inappropriately seek to repeat this pattern.

PROBLEM-SOLVING MODELS AND APPROACHES (E.G., BRIEF, SOLUTION-FOCUSED METHODS OR TECHNIQUES)

The problem-solving approach is based on the belief that an inability to cope with a problem is due to some lack of motivation, capacity, or opportunity to solve problems in an appropriate way. Clients' problem-solving capacities or resources are maladaptive or impaired.

The goal of the problem-solving process is to enhance client mental, emotional, and action capacities for coping with problems and/or making accessible the opportunities and resources necessary to generate solutions to problems.

A social worker engages in the problem-solving process via the following steps:

1. Engaging
2. Assessing (includes a focus on client strengths and not just weaknesses)
3. Planning
4. Intervening
5. Evaluating
6. Terminating

Short-Term Interventions

The growing need for time-limited treatment, fueled by the widening influence of managed care in the behavioral health field, has produced a renewed focus on short-term therapy. Short-term interventions vary greatly in their duration.

Research has suggested that a social worker's and client's views on the time of treatment are more important than the duration of treatment itself. Sometimes these approaches are used because of organizational or financial constraints. In other instances, clients are choosing them over open-ended approaches. Although some have been wary of the effectiveness of these techniques to instill long-lasting change, they are being used more broadly than ever before. Some short-term interventions include a crisis intervention model and a cognitive behavioral model.

Although psychoanalysis is often thought of as long term, this was not the case with Freud's early work, and psychoanalysis did not start out this way. A number of short-term psychodynamic approaches focus on the belief that childhood experiences are the root of adult dysfunction.

METHODS TO ENGAGE AND MOTIVATE CLIENTS/CLIENT SYSTEMS

A motivational approach aims to help clients realize what needs to change and to get them to talk about their daily lives, as well as their satisfaction with current situations. Social workers want to create doubt that everything is "OK" and help clients recognize consequences of current behaviors or conditions that contribute to dissatisfaction.

It is much easier if clients believe goals can be achieved and life can be different. Sometimes clients are incapacitated by conditions that need to be addressed first (i.e., depression). Social workers can help clients think of a time when things were better or create a picture of what their lives could look like with fewer stresses.

The role of a social worker is to create an atmosphere that is conducive to change and to increase a client's intrinsic motivation, so that change arises from within rather than being imposed from without.

Motivation is a state of readiness or eagerness to change, which may fluctuate from one time or situation to another.

Some additional techniques include:

- Clearly identifying the problem or risk area
- Explaining why change is important
- Advocating for specific change
- Identifying barriers and working to remove them
- Finding the best course of action
- Setting goals
- Taking steps toward change
- Preventing relapse

Empathy is a factor that increases motivation, lowers resistance, and fosters greater long-term behavioral change.

METHODS TO ENGAGE AND WORK WITH INVOLUNTARY CLIENTS/CLIENT SYSTEMS

Social workers often find themselves providing services to those who did not choose to receive them, but instead have to do so as mandated by law, including families in the child protection system, people in the criminal justice system, and so on. Working with involuntary clients can be challenging because they may want to have no contact or may only participate because they feel that they have no other choice.

Often these situations require social workers to receive peer support or supervision to process struggles encountered, as well as reassert their professionalism, because clients may try to test and exhibit anger at social workers, who represent the mandates placed upon them.

Some methods that can be helpful in working with involuntary clients include:

- Acknowledging clients' circumstances and understanding how they came about given clients' histories
- Listening to clients' experiences in order to try to understand how they feel about intervention
- Engaging in clear communication because involuntary clients struggle to understand what is happening to them
- Making clear what the purpose of the intervention is, what clients have control over and what they do not, what is going to happen next, and what the likely consequences will be if they do not participate
- Assisting at an appropriate pace as progress may be slow
- Building trust, even on the smallest scale, by consistently being honest and up-front about the situation and why a social worker is involved
- Giving clients practical assistance when needed to help them fight for their rights
- Paying attention to what is positive in clients' behavior and celebrating achievements
- Showing empathy and viewing clients as more than the problems that brought them into services

METHODS TO OBTAIN AND PROVIDE FEEDBACK

Social workers interface with professionals and others in order to achieve the best possible outcomes for clients. Feedback is essential in order to learn what works and what can be done better.

There is no single method for social workers to seek feedback. Many factors may impact on how such feedback is solicited and incorporated into practice. However, there are some important principles that social workers should adhere to when obtaining or providing feedback.

1. Feedback may be either verbal or nonverbal, so social workers must make efforts to see what clients are trying to convey verbally

or via their behavior and nonverbal cues in order to see whether interventions should be altered.

2. When social workers involve consultants or others in the feedback process related to client care, clients should provide consent.

3. Social workers should ask for feedback in difficult circumstances— not just when circumstances appear neutral or positive. It can be tempting only to ask for feedback from people who will say something positive. Sometimes the best learning can be from those who will be critical. Talking through difficult feedback in supervision is important.

4. Feedback is especially critical at key decision points (such as when transferring or closing cases).

5. It is important to guard against influencing people to respond in a particular way; this influence may be unintentional, because a social worker may have more influence or power than the individual from whom feedback is sought.

6. Confidentiality should be respected if the informant wants it.

7. Always be clear about why feedback is needed and what will be done with the information.

8. Documentation of feedback is essential.

9. Be aware that the feedback may be very different depending upon when it is solicited. It is critical to realize how recent events may have influenced information received. Getting feedback repeatedly at several different times may be needed to see if responses differ.

10. A social worker must make sure that the communication method is appropriate. For a younger person, texting, email, or an online questionnaire may work, whereas a face-to-face conversation may be needed for others. The language should be jargon free and issues such as language, culture, and disability may affect the ways in which people both understand and react to requests for feedback. A social worker may want to use close-ended questions and/or open ones to capture needed data.

THE PRINCIPLES OF ACTIVE LISTENING AND OBSERVATION

Active listening skills are an essential part of building relationships and trust. The active part in the listening process can be achieved by showing interest in clients' words. Once clients notice that social workers are understanding what is said and really taking an interest, communication will be more open.

Active listening establishes trust and respect, so clients will feel comfortable confiding in social workers. Thus, it helps build a therapeutic alliance.

Active listening can also include speaking by using mirroring techniques to paraphrase and reflect back to clients what they have just said. For example, a client may say, "I hate my job and my boss yells at me all the time." An active listening response might involve saying something such as, "So you feel like your boss doesn't appreciate you or treat you with respect." Responses need to be tailored to what clients are saying to demonstrate listening and engagement in what is being said.

Although most information that a social worker uses during assessment comes from the social work interview, direct observation of interactions between family members and the client's nonverbal behavior can produce a lot of information about emotional states and interaction patterns.

Social workers also may use observation as part of macro-level intervention in order to assess the extent of a problem/issue, driving and restraining forces for change, key policy influencers, and community members who can work as part of a task group for reform.

When functioning as an observer, a social worker can take many roles, including *complete participant* (living the experience as a participant), *participant as observer* (interacting with those who are participating), *observer as participant* (limited relationship with others participating—primarily observer), or *complete observer* (removed from activity—observer only). Observation is also a method used in scientific inquiry to collect data.

VERBAL AND NONVERBAL COMMUNICATION TECHNIQUES

In order to facilitate change through the problem-solving process, a social worker must use various verbal and nonverbal communication techniques to assist clients to understand their behavior and feelings. In addition, to ensure clients are honest and forthcoming during this process, social workers must build trusting relationships with clients. These relationships develop through effective verbal and nonverbal communication. Social workers must be adept at using both forms of communication successfully, as well as understanding them, because verbal and nonverbal cues will be used by clients throughout the problem-solving process. Insight into their meaning will produce a higher degree of sensitivity to clients' experiences and a deeper understanding of their problems.

There are many verbal and nonverbal communication methods, including:

- **Active listening**, in which social workers are sitting up straight and leaning toward clients in a relaxed and open manner. Attentive listening can involve commenting on clients' statements, asking open-ended questions, and making statements that show listening is occurring.

- **Silence** by social workers, which can show acceptance of clients' feelings and promotes introspection or time to think about what has been learned (*very effective when used with a client who is displaying a high degree of emotion*).

- **Questioning** using open- and closed-ended formats to get relevant information in a nonjudgmental manner.

- **Reflecting** or **validating** to show empathetic understanding of clients' problems. These techniques can also assist clients in understanding negative thought patterns.

- **Paraphrasing** and **clarifying** by social workers to rephrase what clients are saying in order to join together information. Clarification uses questioning, paraphrasing, and restating to ensure full understanding of clients' ideas and thoughts.

- **Reframing** by social workers shows clients that there are different perspectives and ideas that can help to change negative thinking patterns and promote change.

- Exhibiting desirable **facial expressions**, which include direct eye contact if culturally appropriate, warmth and concern reflected, and varied facial expressions.

- Using desirable **postures or gestures**, which include appropriate arm movements and attentive gestures.

There are many methods that social workers use to facilitate communication with clients. Central to the formation of a therapeutic alliance is displaying empathy. Empathy is distinguished from sympathy as the latter denotes pity or feeling bad for a client, whereas the former means that a social worker understands the ideas expressed, as well as the feelings of a client. To be empathetic, a social worker must accurately perceive a client's situation, perspective, and feelings, as well as communicate this understanding in a helpful (therapeutic) way.

A social worker should also display *genuineness* in order to build trust. Genuineness is needed in order to establish a therapeutic relationship. It involves listening to and communicating with clients without distorting their messages, as well as being clear and concrete in communications.

Another method is the use of *positive regard*, which is the ability to view a client as being worthy of caring about and as someone who has strengths and achievement potential. It is built on respect and is usually communicated nonverbally.

Communication is also facilitated by *listening*, *attending*, *suspending value judgments*, and *helping* clients develop their own resources. A social worker should always use culturally appropriate communication.

It is also essential to clearly establish *boundaries* with clients to facilitate a safe environment for change.

LIMIT SETTING TECHNIQUES

Clients of all ages are frequently desperate for an environment with consistent boundaries. For this reason, it is helpful if social workers can learn limit-setting skills. Limit setting is facilitative as clients do not feel safe or accepted in a completely permissive environment.

In addition, although compassion is important for a social worker, it is important to maintain a client–social worker relationship. Understanding boundaries and being able to maintain those boundaries with clients are essential.

THE TECHNIQUE OF ROLE PLAY

Role playing is a teaching strategy that offers several advantages. Role playing in social work practice may be seen between supervisor and supervisee or social worker and client.

In all instances, role playing usually raises interest in a topic as clients are not passive recipients in the learning process. In addition, role playing teaches empathy and understanding of different perspectives as clients take on the role of another, learning and acting as that individual would in the specified setting. In role playing, participation helps embed concepts. Role playing gives clarity to information that may be abstract or difficult to understand.

The use of role playing emphasizes personal concerns, problems, behavior, and active participation. It improves interpersonal and communication skills, and enhances communication.

Role playing activities can be divided into four stages.

1. Preparation and explanation of the activity

2. Preparation of the activity

3. Role playing

4. Discussion or debriefing after the role play activity

ROLE MODELING TECHNIQUES

Role modeling emphasizes the importance of learning from observing and imitating and has been used successfully in helping clients acquire new skills, including those associated with assertiveness.

Role modeling works well when it is combined with role play and reinforcement to produce lasting change.

There are different types of modeling, including live modeling, symbolic modeling, participant modeling, or covert modeling.

Live modeling refers to watching a real person perform the desired behavior.

Symbolic modeling includes filmed or videotaped models demonstrating the desired behavior. Self-modeling is another form of symbolic modeling in which clients are videotaped performing the target behavior.

In *participant modeling*, an individual models anxiety-evoking behaviors for a client and then prompts the client to engage in the behavior.

In *covert modeling*, clients are asked to use their imagination, visualizing a particular behavior as another describes the imaginary situation in detail.

Models in any of these forms may be presented as either a coping or a mastery model. The coping model is shown as initially fearful or incompetent, and then is shown as gradually becoming comfortable and competent performing the feared behavior. The mastery model shows no fear and is competent from the beginning of the demonstration.

METHODS TO OBTAIN SENSITIVE INFORMATION (E.G., SUBSTANCE ABUSE, SEXUAL ABUSE)

Clients are often reluctant to reveal sensitive information about themselves and others in their families. However, this information may be vital to understanding client problems and designing interventions that will be effective. While there is no set road map of how to elicit this information, there are some techniques that may assist.

- A social worker should start off with some open-ended and nonthreatening questions to gather needed background and get a client used to talking about his or her situation before having to disclose more sensitive material. This initial questioning will also give a client time to "test the waters" with a social worker and gauge his or her reaction as more sensitive information is provided. Trust is often needed in a therapeutic relationship before a client can be completely honest about his or her situation.

- A social worker should be aware of verbal and nonverbal clues when speaking with a client. A client may avoid eye contact, fail to completely answer a question, look down when speaking, or laugh nervously when feeling anxious about a topic. A social worker may want to repeat a question or probe further into this area to see if there is something undisclosed which is causing this behavior.

- A client who is engaged in couples, family, or group treatment may worry about the confidentiality of revealing sensitive information, as well as the reactions of others to such disclosure. In these instances, a social worker may want to explore with a client whether individual treatment in lieu of or in conjunction with couples, family, or group treatment may be appropriate.

- A social worker may want to review with a client the professional mandate for confidentiality and what information will be stored in a client file.

- A client may be reluctant to reveal sensitive information if he or she thinks there could be negative repercussions as a result of the information being disclosed to others verbally or lack of security related to the file.

- A client is much more likely to disclose sensitive information if a social worker reacts to such disclosures with acceptance and a neutral stance, being neither judgmental nor confrontational and not interrupting when information is being gathered.

TECHNIQUES FOR HARM REDUCTION FOR SELF AND OTHERS

A harm reduction approach refers to any program, policy, or intervention that seeks to reduce or minimize the adverse health and social consequences associated with an illness, condition, and/or behavior, such as substance use, without requiring a client to practice abstinence, discontinue use, or completely extinguish the behavior. This definition recognizes that many clients are not unwilling or unable to abstain from behaviors or use at any given time and that there is a need to provide them with options that minimize the harm caused by their condition to themselves, to others, and to the community.

Harm reduction complements prevention approaches because it is based on the acceptance that, despite best efforts, clients will engage in behaviors such as substance use, and are unable or unwilling to stop using substances at any given time.

In addition, clients who use substances may prefer to use informal and nonclinical methods to reduce their consumption or reduce the risks associated with use. Harm reduction is practical, feasible, effective, safe, and cost-effective. Most harm reduction approaches are inexpensive, easy to implement, and have a high impact on individual and community health.

Harm reduction acknowledges the significance of ANY positive change that clients make in their lives; these interventions are designed to "meet clients where they are" currently.

Harm reduction recognizes that intervention can be seen as a continuum with the more feasible options at one end and less feasible, but desirable, ones at the other end. Though desirable, abstinence can be considered difficult to achieve. Thus, social workers should partner with clients to identify actions that can be taken to minimize impacts of their illnesses, conditions, and/or behaviors.

METHODS TO TEACH COPING AND OTHER SELF-CARE SKILLS TO CLIENTS/CLIENT SYSTEMS

Social workers assist clients in realizing how their lives can improve and/or how they can learn from mistakes that they have made. The techniques that social workers employ are a form of informal or didactic teaching.

For example, social workers may help clients see:

- How their histories have shaped them
- Needs associated with medical and/or behavioral health conditions
- Developmental issues related to various phases across the lifespan
- The workings of systems in which they operate
- Ways of coping in various situations

A social worker must use the problem-solving process to teach clients skills needed to make changes in their lives.

In addition, social workers may collaborate with or inform clients of colleagues who may also assist with more formal teaching, such as learning to read, obtaining a driver's license, and so on.

CLIENT/CLIENT SYSTEM SELF-MONITORING TECHNIQUES

Clients are encouraged to pay attention to any subtle shift in feelings. Clients frequently keep thought or emotion logs that include three components: (a) disturbing emotional states, (b) the exact behaviors engaged in at the time of the emotional states, and (c) thoughts that occurred when the emotions emerged. In cognitive behavioral therapy, homework is often done between sessions to record these encounters. This homework involves client self-monitoring, which is central to this approach.

METHODS TO DEVELOP, REVIEW, AND IMPLEMENT CRISIS PLANS

A crisis is defined as an acute *disruption of psychological homeostasis (steady state) in which usual coping mechanisms fail* and there exists evidence of distress and functional impairment. The subjective reaction to a stressful life is a compromised stability and ability to cope or function.

Given such a definition, it is imperative that social workers have a framework or blueprint to guide them in responding. When confronted by clients in crisis, social workers need to address their distress, impairment, and instability by operating in a logical and orderly process. Social workers can easily exacerbate crises with well-intentioned, but haphazard responding. Comprehensive plans allow for responses that are active and directive, but do not take problem ownership away from clients. Finally, plans should meet clients where they are at, assessing their levels of risk, mobilizing client resources, and moving strategically to stabilize the crisis and improve functioning.

The development, review, and implementation of crises plans require actions aimed at crisis stabilization, resolution, and mastery. Social workers should:

1. Plan and conduct a thorough biopsychosocial and lethality/imminent danger assessment;

2. Make psychological contact and rapidly establish the collaborative relationship;

3. Identify the major problems, including crisis precipitants;

4. Encourage an exploration of feelings and emotions;

5. Generate and explore alternatives and new coping strategies;

6. Restore functioning through implementation of an action plan; and

7. Plan follow-up and "booster" sessions.

METHODS OF CONFLICT RESOLUTION

Management of conflict entails four steps:

1. The recognition of an existing or potential conflict

2. An assessment of the conflict situation

3. The selection of an appropriate strategy

4. Intervention

When previous attempts to resolve a conflict have only escalated the conflict, a useful technique is to structure the interactions between the parties. Structuring techniques include:

1. Decreasing the amount of contact between the parties in the early stages of conflict resolution

2. Decreasing the amount of time between problem-solving sessions

3. Decreasing the formality of problem-solving sessions

4. Limiting the scope of the issues that can be discussed

5. Using a third-party mediator

CRISIS INTERVENTION AND TREATMENT APPROACHES

A state of crisis is time limited. Brief intervention during a crisis usually provides maximum therapeutic effect. Crisis intervention is a process of actively influencing the psychosocial functioning of clients during a period of disequilibrium or crisis. *A crisis does not need to be precipitated by a major life event.* The goals are to alleviate stress and mobilize coping skills, psychological capabilities, and social resources.

The goals of crisis intervention are to (a) relieve the impact of stress with emotional and social resources, (b) return a client to a previous level of functioning (regain equilibrium), (c) help strengthen coping mechanisms during the crisis period, and (d) develop adaptive coping strategies.

Crisis intervention focuses on the here and now, is time limited (most crises last from 4 to 6 weeks), is directive, and requires high levels of activity and involvement from a social worker. A social worker sets specific goals and tasks in order to increase a client's sense of mastery and control.

ANGER MANAGEMENT TECHNIQUES

Although everyone gets angry, clients may come to social workers because they are not able to control their anger, causing problems. Anger can also increase risk for developing physical health problems, such as heart disease, stress-related illnesses, insomnia, digestive issues, and/or headaches.

Social workers can assist clients to develop action or treatment plans to change these behaviors. Techniques for assisting clients can include one or more of the following:

Relaxation Exercises

- Deep breathing
- Meditation or repeating calming words/phrases
- Guided imagery
- Yoga
- Stretching or physical exercise

Assisting clients to practice these techniques regularly will result in using them automatically in tense situations.

Cognitive Techniques

- Replacing destructive thoughts, such as "This is the end of the world" with healthy ones like "This is frustrating, but it will pass"

- Focusing on goals as a way of finding solutions to problems
- Using logic to get a more balanced perspective
- Not using an "all or nothing" approach
- Putting situations into perspective

Communication Skills

- Slowing down speech to avoid saying something not meant or that one will regret
- Listening to what others are saying
- Thinking about what to say before speaking
- Avoiding defensiveness
- Using humor to lighten the situation

Environmental Change

- Walking away or leaving situation
- Avoiding people or situations in the future that evoke anger
- Not starting conversations or entering situations that may cause anger when tired or rushed

STRESS MANAGEMENT TECHNIQUES

Stress is a psychological and/or physical reaction to life events, with most people experiencing it regularly in their own lives. When a life event is seen as a threat, it signals the release of hormones aimed at generating a response. This process has been labeled the "fight-or-flight" response.

Once the threat is gone, clients should return to typical relaxed states, but this may not happen if other threats are presented immediately thereafter. Thus, stress management is important because it provides tools to deal with threats and minimize the impacts of psychological and/or physical reactions.

The first step in stress management is for clients to monitor their stress levels and identify their stress triggers. These can be major life events, but also those associated with day-to-day life, such as job pressures, relationship problems, or financial difficulties. Positive life events, such as getting a job promotion, getting married, or having children, also can be stressful.

The second step in stress management is to assist clients in identifying what aspects of a situation they can control. Clients can make these changes, as well as benefit from stress-reduction techniques, such as deep breathing, exercise, massage, tai chi, or yoga, to manage those aspects of a situation that cannot be altered. Maintaining a healthy lifestyle is essential to helping manage stress.

Stress will always be a part of life, but assisting clients to manage it can increase their ability to cope with challenges and enhance their psychological and/or physical well-being.

COGNITIVE AND BEHAVIORAL INTERVENTIONS

Cognitive behavioral therapy (CBT) is a hands-on, practical approach to problem solving. Its goal is to change patterns of thinking or behavior that are responsible for clients' difficulties, and so change the way they feel. CBT works by changing clients' attitudes and their behavior by focusing on the thoughts, images, beliefs, and attitudes that are held (cognitive processes) and how this relates to behavior, as a way of dealing with emotional problems.

CBT can be thought of as a combination of psychotherapy and behavioral therapy. Psychotherapy emphasizes the importance of the personal meaning placed on things and how thinking patterns begin in childhood. Behavioral therapy pays close attention to the relationship between problems, behaviors, and thoughts.

This approach is active, collaborative, structured, time limited, goal oriented, and problem focused. This approach lends itself to the requirements posed by managed care companies, including brief treatment, well-delineated techniques, goal and problem oriented, and empirically supported evidence of its effectiveness.

Steps in Cognitive Restructuring

Assist clients in:

1. Accepting that their self-statements, assumptions, and beliefs determine or govern their emotional reaction to life's events

2. Identifying dysfunctional beliefs and patterns of thoughts that underlie their problems

3. Identifying situations that evoke dysfunctional cognitions

4. Substituting functional self-statements in place of self-defeating thoughts

5. Rewarding themselves for successful coping efforts

Foundational to this treatment is client self-monitoring. Clients are encouraged to pay attention to any subtle shift in feelings. Clients frequently keep thought or emotion logs that include three components: (a) disturbing emotional states, (b) the exact behaviors engaged in at the time of the emotional states, and (c) thoughts that occurred when the emotions emerged. Homework is often done between sessions to record these encounters.

STRENGTHS-BASED AND EMPOWERMENT STRATEGIES AND INTERVENTIONS

The primary mission of the social work profession is to enhance human well-being and help meet the basic human needs of all people, with particular attention to the needs and empowerment of people who are vulnerable, oppressed, and living in poverty (*NASW Code of Ethics, 2008—Preamble*).

Empowerment aims to ensure a sense of control over well-being and that change is possible. A social worker can help to empower individuals, groups, communities, and institutions.

On an individual level, social workers can engage in a process with a client aimed at strengthening his or her self-worth by making a change in life that is based on his or her desires (self-determination).

To facilitate empowerment, a social worker should:

- Establish a relationship aimed at meeting a client's needs and wishes such as access to social services and benefits or to other sources of information
- Educate a client to improve his or her skills, thereby increasing the ability for self-help
- Help a client to secure resources, such as those from other organizations or agencies, as well as natural support networks, to meet needs
- Unite a client with others who are experiencing the same issues when needed to enable social and political action

Social workers should also use an empowerment process with groups, communities, and institutions so they may gain or regain the capacity to meet human needs, enhance overall well-being and potential, and provide individuals control over their lives to the extent possible.

A social worker needs many skills that focus on the activation of resources, the creation of alliances, and the expansion of opportunities in order to facilitate empowerment.

CLIENT/CLIENT SYSTEM CONTRACTING AND GOAL-SETTING TECHNIQUES

A social worker and client work together to develop a contract (intervention or service plan), including an agreement on its implementation or the activities used to help a client attain his or her goals. Modification of the contract may be required as new information about a client's situation emerges and/ or as the situation changes.

When clients seek to attain their goals, changes may need to be made to themselves, groups, families, and/or systems in the larger environment. This choice of targets is an even more complex issue than it first appears because the process of changing one system may bring about changes in others.

Change Strategies

- *Modify systems:* The decision to help a client on a one-to-one basis or in the context of a larger system must take into consideration a client's preferences and previous experiences, as well as the degree to which a client's problem is a response to forces within the larger system and whether change can be readily attained by a change in the larger system.
- *Modify individual thoughts:* A social worker may teach how to problem solve, alter his or her self-concepts by modifying self-defeating statements, and/or make interpretations to increase a client's understanding about the relationship between events in his or her life.
- *Modify individual actions:* A social worker may use behavior modification techniques such as reinforcement, punishment, modeling, role playing, and/or task assignments. *Modeling and role modeling are very effective methods for teaching. They should be used whenever possible.*
- Thoughts can be modified by *feedback from others* and behaviors can be modified through the *actions of others* in a system (by altering reinforcements).
- A social worker can also *advocate* for a client and seek to secure a change in a system on his or her behalf.
- A social worker can be a *mediator* by helping a client and another individual or system to negotiate with each other so that each may attain their respective goals.

PARTIALIZING TECHNIQUES

During the problem-solving process, a social worker may need to assist a client to break down problems or goals into less overwhelming and more manageable components. This is known as partialization and aims to break complex issues into simpler ones.

Partialization is useful because it may assist a social worker and a client to identify the goals that are easier to achieve first, enabling a client to see results more quickly and gain some success in making harder changes. Partialization can also help individuals to order the problems or goals that need more immediate help from those that can be addressed later. A social worker can use Maslow's hierarchy of needs as one tool to assist in making decisions about more pressing needs. In addition, a client should be asked to prioritize his or her concerns or goals.

ASSERTIVENESS TRAINING

Assertiveness training is when procedures are used to teach clients how to express their positive and negative feelings and to stand up for their rights in ways that will not alienate others.

Assertiveness training typically begins with clients thinking about areas in their life in which they have difficulty asserting themselves. The next stage usually involves role plays designed to help clients practice clearer and more direct forms of communicating with others. Feedback is provided to improve responses, and the role play is repeated. Clients are asked to practice assertive techniques in everyday life.

Assertiveness training promotes the use of "I" statements as a way to help clients express their feelings. "I" statements tell others how their actions may cause clients to be upset, but are in contrast with "you" statements, which are often seen as blaming or aggressive.

Learning specific techniques and perspectives, such as self-observation skills, awareness of personal preferences, and assuming personal responsibility, are important components of the assertiveness training process.

TASK-CENTERED APPROACHES

A task-centered approach aims to quickly engage clients in the problem-solving process and to maximize their responsibility for treatment outcomes. In this modality, the duration of treatment is usually limited due to setting constraints, limitations imposed by third-party payers, or other reasons. Thus, at the outset, the expectation is that interventions from learning theory and behavior modification will be used to promote completion of a well-defined task to produce measurable outcomes. The focus is on the "here and now." This type of practice is often preferred by clients, as they are able to see more immediate results.

The problem is partialized into clearly delineated tasks to be addressed consecutively (assessment leads to goals, which lead to tasks). A client must be able to identify a precise psychosocial problem and a solution confined to a specific change in behavior or a change of circumstances. A client must also be willing to work on the problem. It is essential that a social worker and client establish a strong working relationship quickly. A social worker's therapeutic style must be highly active, empathic, and sometimes directive in this approach.

Assessment focuses on helping a client identify the primary problem and explore the circumstances surrounding the problem. Specific tasks are expected to evolve from this process. Consideration is given to how a client would ideally like to see the problem resolved. Termination, in this modality, begins almost immediately upon the onset of treatment.

PSYCHOEDUCATION METHODS (E.G., ACKNOWLEDGING, SUPPORTING, NORMALIZING)

One of the ways that social workers provide information to clients is through psychoeducation. This model allows a social worker to provide clients with information necessary to make informed decisions that will allow them to reach their respective goals. In addition to focusing on clients' education, it also provides support and coping skills development.

Psychoeducation is delivered in many service settings and with many types of client populations. It is provided to those who are experiencing some sort of issue or problem with the rationale that, with a clear understanding of the problem, as well as self-knowledge of strengths, community resources, and coping skills, clients are better equipped to deal with problems and to contribute to their emotional well-being.

The core psychoeducational principle is that education has a role in emotional and behavioral change. With an improved understanding of the causes and effects of problems, psychoeducation broadens clients' perception and interpretation of them, positively influencing clients' emotions and behavior. In other words, clients feel less helpless about the situation and more in control of themselves.

GROUP WORK TECHNIQUES AND APPROACHES (E.G., DEVELOPING AND MANAGING GROUP PROCESSES AND COHESION)

Group work is a method of working with two or more people for personal growth, the enhancement of social functioning, and/or for the achievement of socially desirable goals.

Social workers use their knowledge of group organization and functioning to affect the performance and adjustment of individuals. Individuals remain the focus of concern and the group is the vehicle of growth and change. *When individual problems arise, they should be directed to the group for possible solutions as the group is the agent of change. Social workers must remind group members that confidentiality cannot be guaranteed—though seeing an agreement among group members concerning preserving the confidentiality of information shared should be an initial goal of any group process.*

Contraindications for group: *client* who is *in crisis; suicidal;* compulsively needy for attention; actively psychotic; and/or paranoid

There are different kinds of groups. For example:

Open Versus Closed

Open groups are those in which new members can join at any time. Closed groups are those in which all members begin the group at the same time.

Short-Term Versus Long-Term

Some groups have a very short duration, whereas others meet for a longer duration.

A social worker takes on different roles throughout the group process, which has a beginning, middle, and end.

Beginning

A social worker identifies the purpose of the group and his or her role. This stage is characterized as a time to convene, to organize, and to set a plan. Members are likely to remain distant or removed until they have had time to develop relationships.

Middle

Almost all of the group's work will occur during this stage. Relationships are strengthened as a group so that the tasks can be worked on. Group leaders are usually less involved.

End

The group reviews its accomplishments. Feelings associated with the termination of the group are addressed.

FAMILY THERAPY MODELS, INTERVENTIONS, AND APPROACHES

Working with families has always been central to social work practice. Family interventions require treating not just an individual but all those within a family unit, with the focus of assessment and intervention directed at the interaction of family members.

In order to work effectively with families, social workers must:

1. Understand the development of, as well as the historical, conceptual, and contextual issues influencing, family functioning

2. Have awareness of the impact of diversity in working with families, particularly race, class, culture, ethnicity, gender, sexual preference, aging, and disabilities

3. Understand the impact of a social worker's family of origin, current family structure, and its influence on a social worker's interventions with families

4. Be aware of the needs of families experiencing unique family problems (domestic violence, blended families, trauma and loss, adoptive families, etc.)

Social workers use a variety of techniques to work with families. Family therapy treats the family as a unified whole—a system of interacting parts in which change in any part affects the functioning of the overall system. The family is the unit of attention for diagnosis and treatment. Social roles and interpersonal interaction are the focus of treatment. Real behaviors and communication that affect current life situations are addressed. The goal is to interrupt the circular pattern of pathological communication and behaviors and replace it with a new pattern that will sustain itself without the dysfunctional aspects of the original pattern.

Key clinical issues include:

- Establishing a contract with the family
- Examining alliances within the family
- Identifying where power resides
- Determining the relationship of each family member to the problem
- Seeing how the family relates to the outside world
- Assessing influence of family history on current family interactions
- Ascertaining communication patterns
- Identifying family rules that regulate patterns of interaction
- Determining meaning of presenting symptom in maintaining family homeostasis
- Examining flexibility of structure and accessibility of alternative action patterns
- Finding out about sources of external stress and support

The following are some types of family therapy.

Strategic Family Therapy

In strategic family therapy, a social worker initiates what happens during therapy, designs a specific approach for each person's presenting problem, and takes responsibility for directly influencing people.

It has roots in structural family therapy and is built on communication theory.

It is active, brief, directive, and task-centered. Strategic family therapy is more interested in creating change in behavior than change in understanding.

Strategic family therapy is based on the assumption that families are flexible enough to modify solutions that do not work and adjust or develop. There is the assumption that all problems have multiple origins; a presenting problem is viewed as a symptom of and a response to current dysfunction in family interactions.

Therapy focuses on problem resolution by altering the feedback cycle or loop that maintains the symptomatic behavior. The social worker's task is to formulate the problem in solvable, behavioral terms and to design an intervention plan to change the dysfunctional family pattern.

Concepts/Techniques

- Pretend technique—encourage family members to "pretend" and encourage voluntary control of behavior
- First-order changes—superficial behavioral changes within a system that do not change the structure of the system
- Second-order changes—changes to the systematic interaction pattern so the system is reorganized and functions more effectively
- Family homeostasis—families tend to preserve familiar organization and communication patterns; resistant to change
- Relabeling—changing the label attached to a person or problem from negative to positive so the situation can be perceived differently; it is hoped that new responses will evolve
- Paradoxical directive or instruction—prescribe the symptomatic behavior so a client realizes he or she can control it; uses the strength of the resistance to change in order to move a client toward goals

Structural Family Therapy

This approach stresses the importance of family organization for the functioning of the group and the well-being of its members. A social worker "joins" (engages) the family in an effort to restructure it. Family structure is defined as the invisible set of functional demands organizing interaction among family members. Boundaries and rules determining who does what, where, and when are crucial in three ways.

1. Interpersonal boundaries define individual family members and promote their differentiation and autonomous, yet interdependent, functioning. Dysfunctional families tend to be characterized by either a pattern of rigid enmeshment or disengagement.

2. Boundaries with the outside world define the family unit, but boundaries must be permeable enough to maintain a well-functioning open system, allowing contact and reciprocal exchanges with the social world.

3. Hierarchical organization in families of all cultures is maintained by generational boundaries, the rules differentiating parent and child roles, rights, and obligations.

Restructuring is based on observing and manipulating interactions within therapy sessions, often by enactments of situations as a way to understand and diagnose the structure and provide an opportunity for restructuring.

Bowenian Family Therapy

Unlike other models of family therapy, the goal of this approach is not symptom reduction. Rather, a Bowenian-trained social worker is interested in improving the intergenerational transmission process. Thus, the focus within this approach is consistent whether a social worker is working with an individual, a couple, or the entire family. It is assumed that improvement in overall functioning will ultimately reduce a family member's symptomatology. Eight major theoretical constructs are essential to understanding Bowen's approach. These concepts are differentiation, emotional system, multigenerational transmission, emotional triangle, nuclear family, family projection process, sibling position, and societal regression. These constructs are interconnected.

Differentiation is the core concept of this approach. The more differentiated, the more a client can be an individual while in emotional contact with the family. This allows a client to think through a situation without being drawn to act by either internal or external emotional pressures.

Emotional fusion is the counterpart of differentiation and refers to the tendency for family members to share an emotional response. This is the result of poor interpersonal boundaries between family members. In a fused family, there is little room for emotional autonomy. If a member makes a move toward autonomy, it is experienced as abandonment by other members of the family.

Multigenerational transmission stresses the connection of current generations to past generations as a natural process. Multigenerational transmission gives the present a context in history. This context can focus a social worker on the differentiation in the system and on the transmission process.

An **emotional triangle** is the network of relationships among three people. Bowen's theory states that a relationship can remain stable until anxiety is introduced. However, when anxiety is introduced into the dyad, a third party is recruited into a triangle to reduce the overall anxiety. It is almost impossible for two people to interact without triangulation.

The **nuclear family** is the most basic unit in society and there is a concern over the degree to which emotional fusion can occur in a family system. Clients forming relationships outside of the nuclear family tend to pick mates with the same level of differentiation.

Family projection process describes the primary way parents transmit their emotional problems to children. The projection process can impair child functioning and increase vulnerability to clinical symptoms.

Sibling position is a factor in determining personality. Where a client is in birth order has an influence on how he or she relates to parents and siblings. Birth order determines the triangles that clients grow up in.

Societal regression, in contrast to progression, is manifested by problems such as the depletion of natural resources. Bowen's theory can be used to explain societal anxieties and social problems, because Bowen viewed society as a family—an emotional system complete with its own multi-generational transmission, chronic anxiety, emotional triangles, cutoffs, projection processes, and fusion/differentiation struggles.

PERMANENCY PLANNING

Permanency planning is an approach to child welfare that is based on the belief that children need permanence to thrive. Child protection services should focus on getting children into, and maintaining, permanent homes. Permanency planning received a lot of attention in the 1970s. Legislation in the United States, such as the Adoption Assistance and Child Welfare Act of 1980, promotes permanency planning and creates mandates related to child placements.

In permanency planning, the first goal is to get children back into their original homes. This can be achieved with a thorough investigation into child protection situations to determine if homes are safe and, if needed, exploring ideas for making them safer or more enriching for children.

Supports can include getting caregivers services for meeting needs or providing education, if needed, to ensure adequate and quality care. If children cannot return to their original homes, steps need to be made so that they can get into permanent living situations as quickly as possible with adults with whom they have continuous and reciprocal relationships, including those made available through adoption.

MINDFULNESS AND COMPLEMENTARY THERAPEUTIC APPROACHES

Social workers continue to provide the bulk of mental health services in the United States. A significant number of persons seek services expecting providers to be aware and knowledgeable about alternatives and complements to Western medical approaches for symptom relief and healing when their medical or behavioral health is disrupted and/or compromised. An ever increasing number of people are seeking complementary and alternative medicine (CAM) or integrated health care (IHC) to address health/behavioral health issues. Not only are clients receptive to the use of complementary approaches, they often request diverse approaches that go beyond medications and psychotherapy to address their overall concerns. Thus, social workers must have knowledge mindfulness and complementary therapeutic approaches.

Interventions and remedies that some cultures and populations consider conventional others view as alternative, and what some clients assess as successful outcomes, some professionals may not concur.

Mindfulness is the practice of paying close attention to what is being experienced in the present, both inside the body and mind and in the external world. It is a conscious effort to be with whatever is going on right now, without judging or criticizing what we find. In each moment, mindfulness invites being awake, aware, and accepting of ourselves.

The practice of mindfulness is integral to efforts to reduce stress and to increase capacity to cope. Mindfulness can stand alone as a treatment tool or may be incorporated with other treatment modalities. Most settings where social workers practice would be conducive to mindfulness practice.

Social workers and other health/behavioral health providers are increasingly including the practice of mindfulness as a useful tool, not only in building a self-care routine, but also in addressing the needs of their clients.

The multitude of complementary approaches to maintaining health are vast and it is unrealistic for social workers to be informed and knowledgeable about all of them, but it is expected that social workers will be aware of the predominant practices and methods being used among the populations they are serving. Just as important, social workers need to be instilled with a respect for clients' authority in determining the best method to treat their problems when there are no indications of harm to self and/or others. Knowing how to integrate empirically tested and validated medical interventions, along with indigenous approaches preserved for generations, is essential to ensuring culturally competent, holistic treatment.

THE COMPONENTS OF CASE MANAGEMENT

Case management has been defined in many ways. However, all models are based on the belief that clients often need assistance in accessing services in today's complex systems, as well as the need to monitor duplication and gaps in treatment and care.

Although there may be many federal, state, and local programs available, there are often serious service gaps. A client might have a specific need met in one program and many related needs ignored because of the lack of coordination. Systems are highly complex, fragmented, duplicative, and uncoordinated.

Social workers provide case management services to different client populations in both nonprofit and for-profit settings.

The primary goal of social work case management is to optimize client functioning and well-being by providing and coordinating high-quality services, in the most effective and efficient manner possible, to individuals with multiple complex needs (*NASW Standards for Social Work Case Management*, 2013).

Five case management activities are (a) assessment, (b) planning, (c) linking, (d) monitoring, and (e) advocacy.

TECHNIQUES USED FOR FOLLOW-UP

The standard of practice is that social workers must involve clients and their families (when appropriate) in making their own decisions about follow-up services or aftercare. Involvement must include, at a minimum, discussion of client and family preferences (when appropriate).

Follow-up meetings are often important to ensure change maintenance. Many clients continue to progress after termination and follow-up meetings provide opportunities to acknowledge these gains and encourage continuation of such efforts.

Follow-up meetings also provide valuable interactions which can mitigate any unanticipated difficulties. Follow-up meetings provide clients with reassurance that they are not alone as they implement what they have learned. They allow for longitudinal evaluation of practice effectiveness.

It is important that social workers explain to clients that follow-up meetings may be important in the problem-solving process. Social workers must not be intrusive or send messages that clients cannot function on their own. Clients who have difficulty terminating may use follow-up meetings as ways to prolong social worker–client relationships beyond what is needed.

Social workers must set clear boundaries and treat follow-up meetings with professionalism—having clearly stated goals for these sessions.

Clients who tell social workers during follow-up about new problems that have arisen should be seen for assessment. Social workers who have already assisted clients resolve issues are often the first ones to which clients disclose new problems which have emerged.

THE ELEMENTS OF A CASE PRESENTATION

When a social worker communicates with others in order to ensure comprehensive and complete care for clients, he or she completes a case presentation. Case presentations are also used in professional development and learning to provide input into options for treatment and to ensure services are being delivered effectively and efficiently.

There is no universal format for a case presentation in social work practice. However, there are some standard elements, including:

- Identifying data (demographics, cultural considerations)
- History of the presenting problem (family history)
- Significant medical/psychiatric history (diagnoses)
- Significant personal and/or social history (legal issues, academic/ work problems, crisis/safety concerns)
- Presenting problem (assessment, mental status, diagnosis)
- Impressions and summary (interview findings)
- Recommendations (treatment plan/intervention strategies, goals, theoretical models used)

Content areas can be added or eliminated based on the reasons for the case presentation and input sought. Information for a case presentation is usually information that a social worker has obtained directly from a client during an interview and/or observation, as well as that collected from collateral contacts, other professionals, and/or case records.

METHODS OF SERVICE DELIVERY

The context of social work practice clearly has a profound influence on the quality and standards of professional activities and the ability of social workers to practice ethically and effectively. Social work takes place in a wide variety of settings, including, but not limited to, private practices, public sector organizations (government), schools, hospitals, correctional facilities, and private nonprofit agencies.

To meet the needs of clients, social workers must have work environments that support ethical practice and are committed to standards and good quality services. A positive working environment is created where the values and principles of social workers are reinforced in agency policies and procedures.

To achieve this aim, employers must understand social work practice and provide supervision, workload management, and continuing professional development consistent with best practices.

Policies setting out standards of ethical practice should be written and clear. Social workers should never be required to do anything that would put at risk their ability to uphold ethical standards, including those in the areas of confidentiality, informed consent, and safety/risk management.

The public, including clients, should be regularly informed of agency policies and procedures and provided with information about how to raise concerns or make complaints about them.

Policies that do not tolerate dangerous, discriminatory, and/or exploitative behavior must be in place so that social workers and their clients are safe from harm.

The adoption and implementation of policies and procedures on workload and caseload management contribute greatly to the provision of quality services to clients. In addition, policies and procedures for confidential treatment and storage of records should be established.

Continuing professional development and further training enable social workers to strengthen and develop their skills. Orientation and other relevant training provided to social workers upon hire and when assuming other jobs within the setting are essential.

Good quality, regular social work supervision by professionals who have the necessary experience and qualifications in social work practice is a critical tool to ensure service quality.

Rates of pay for social workers need to be comparable with similar professionals, and the skill and qualifications of social workers must be recognized, while ensuring services are affordable to clients.

CONCEPTS OF SOCIAL POLICY DEVELOPMENT AND ANALYSIS

Policy analysis is a systematic approach to solving problems through policies.

It involves identifying the problem, developing alternatives, assessing the impacts of the alternatives (such as conducting a cost/benefit analysis), selecting the desired option, designing and implementing the policy, and evaluating the outcomes.

Critical to social policy analysis is the identification of alternative policy options and the evaluation of these alternatives. Analyses include developing an understanding of who "wins" and who "loses." Some of the values upon which alternatives are weighed include equity, efficiency, and liberty.

The policy analysis field has become more diversified; thus, it is highly influenced by theories from other fields. Often there are many stakeholders involved, such as federal, state, and local government agencies, stakeholders, community leaders, and clients, all of which will bring in their own set of values. Thus, the chosen approach will be influenced by who participates.

THEORIES AND METHODS OF ADVOCACY FOR POLICIES, SERVICES, AND RESOURCES TO MEET CLIENTS'/CLIENT SYSTEMS' NEEDS

Advocacy is one of a social worker's most important tasks. Social workers may advocate when working with an individual client to ensure that his or her needs are met. However, social workers have an ethical mandate to make systematic changes to address the problems experienced by groups of individuals who are vulnerable and/or who are unable to speak for themselves.

A social worker may engage in advocacy by convincing others of the legitimate needs and rights of members of society. Such work can occur on the local, county, state, or national levels. Some social workers are even involved in international human rights and advocacy for those in need in other countries.

Fundamental to social work is advocating to change the factors that create and contribute to problems.

Sometimes advocacy can be achieved by working through the problem-solving process as it relates to a problem, including acknowledging the problem, analyzing and defining the problem, generating possible solutions, evaluating each option, implementing the option of choice, and evaluating the outcomes.

In other instances, social workers may engage in obtaining legislative support or using the media to draw attention to a concern.

In all instances, social workers should be working with clients to have their voices heard and should not be speaking for them. *Often social workers need to help clients to advocate with third-party payers to have their needs met when resources are not adequate.* Social workers must inform clients of appeal processes when services are denied and support them as they advocate to meet their needs. When clients feel that they have not been treated fairly, social workers should empower them by providing education about appeal processes and other methods to change policies, fix services, and/or increase services to meet their needs.

The goal of social work advocacy is to assist clients to strengthen their own skills in this area. Social workers may assist by locating sources of power that can be shared with clients to make changes.

COMMUNITY ORGANIZING AND SOCIAL PLANNING METHODS

Community organizing is focused on harnessing the collective power of communities to tackle issues of shared concern. It challenges government, corporations, and other power-holding institutions in an effort to tip the power balance more in favor of communities.

It is essential for social workers to understand sources of power in order to access them for the betterment of the community. Organizing members to focus these sources of power on the problem(s) and mobilizing resources to assist is critical.

- **Coercive:** power from control of punishment
- **Reward:** power from control of rewards
- **Expert:** power from superior ability or knowledge
- **Referent:** power from having charisma or identification with others who have power
- **Legitimate:** power from having legitimate authority
- **Informational:** power from having information

Community organization enhances participatory skills of local citizens by working with and not for them, thus developing leadership with particular emphasis on the ability to conceptualize and act on problems. It strengthens communities so they can better deal with future problems; community members can develop the capacity to resolve problems.

Social planning is defined as the process by which a group or community decides its goals and strategies relating to societal issues. It is not an activity limited to government, but includes activities of the private sector, social movements, professions, and other organizations focused specifically on social objectives.

Models of social planning in social work practice include those that are based on community participation. Rather than planning "for" communities, social workers as planners engage "with" community members. Social planning does not merely examine sociological problems that exist, but also includes the physical and economic factors that relate to societal issues.

All issues confronting those who are served by social workers are really human or social issues. Social workers can help facilitate the process of planning through all stages: organizing community members; data gathering related to the issue—including identifying economic, political, and social causes; problem identification; weighing of alternatives; policy/program implementation; and evaluation of effectiveness.

TECHNIQUES FOR MOBILIZING COMMUNITY PARTICIPATION

Community participation is critical in social work practice. Community participation informs others about needed changes that must occur. Policies, programs, and services that were effective or appropriate previously may have become ineffective or inappropriate.

Community participation also creates relationships and partnerships among diverse groups who can then work together, but may not usually do so.

Community participation puts decision-making power partly or wholly with the community, ensuring that individuals will remain interested and involved over time.

When engaging in community-based decision making, individuals will typically go through various stages.

Orientation stage—Community members meet for the first time and start to get to know each other.

Conflict stage—Disputes, little fights, and arguments may occur. These conflicts are eventually worked out.

Emergence stage—Community members begin to see and agree on a course of action.

Reinforcement stage—Community members finally make a decision and justify why it was correct.

Community members are far more likely to buy into policy that has been created with their participation. Their support over time will lead to permanent change.

Community participation energizes communities to continue to change in positive directions. Once involved in a successful change effort, community members see what they can accomplish collectively and take on new challenges.

Lastly, community members must inform policy-makers and planners of the real needs of the community, so that the most important problems and issues can be addressed. They must also provide information about what has been tried before and worked or not worked.

METHODS TO DEVELOP AND EVALUATE MEASURABLE OBJECTIVES FOR CLIENT/CLIENT SYSTEM INTERVENTION, TREATMENT, AND/OR SERVICE PLANS

When social workers are creating intervention or service plans, it is essential that goals are written in observable and measurable terms. In order to achieve this aim, the following should be included in each goal contained in the intervention or service plan.

■ *Criteria:* What behavior must be exhibited, how often, over what period of time, and under what conditions to demonstrate achievement of the goal?

■ *Method for evaluation:* How will progress be measured?

■ *Schedule for evaluation:* When, how often, and on what dates or intervals of time will progress be measured?

There may also be benchmarks or the intermediate knowledge, skills, and/or behaviors that must be learned/achieved in order for a client to reach his or her ultimate goal.

Objectives break down the goals into discrete components or subparts, which are steps toward the final desired outcome.

TECHNIQUES USED TO EVALUATE A CLIENT'S/CLIENT SYSTEM'S PROGRESS

Evaluating progress is a critical part of the problem-solving process. Examining with a client what has occurred and what still needs to occur involves him or her in treatment decisions.

Evaluation methods can be simple or complex. They can rely on quantitative information that shows data on reductions in target behaviors, health care improvements, or psychiatric symptom increases, and/or qualitative information in which a client and/or social worker subjectively report on progress made in various areas.

When evaluating progress, a social worker and client should gather all needed information and identify factors that helped or hindered progress. Goals outlined in the contract/service plan should be modified, if needed, based upon the outcome of the evaluation.

Social workers should assist clients to understand the progress they have made so they can clearly understand and celebrate their accomplishments, as well as identify areas that need attention. This process should ensure that clients understand why progress has happened, as well as include a dialogue about any changes that need to occur in the problem-solving process to facilitate continued growth.

PRIMARY, SECONDARY, AND TERTIARY PREVENTION STRATEGIES

There are three major types of prevention strategies—primary, secondary, and tertiary. Optimally, all three types are needed to create comprehensive strategies of prevention and protection.

Primary Prevention

The goal is to protect people from developing a disease, experiencing an injury, or engaging in a behavior in the first place.

Examples:
- Immunizations against disease
- Education promoting the use of automobile passenger restraints and bicycle helmets
- Screenings for the general public to identify risk factors for illness
- Controlling hazards in the workplace and home
- Regular exercise and good nutrition
- Counseling about the dangers of tobacco and other drugs

Since successful primary prevention helps avoid the disease, injury, or behavior and its associated suffering, cost, and burden, it is typically considered the most cost-effective.

Secondary Prevention

Secondary prevention occurs after a disease, injury, or illness has occurred. It aims to slow the progression or limit the long-term impacts. It is often implemented when asymptomatic, but risk factors are present. Secondary prevention also may focus on preventing reinjury.

Examples:
- Telling those with heart conditions to take daily, low-dose aspirin
- Screenings for those with risk factors for illness
- Modifying work assignments for injured workers

Tertiary Prevention

Tertiary prevention focuses on managing complicated, long-term diseases, injuries, or illnesses. The goal is to prevent further deterioration and maximize quality of life because disease is now established and primary prevention activities have been unsuccessful. However, early detection through secondary prevention may have minimized the impact of the disease.

Examples:
- Pain management groups
- Rehabilitation programs
- Support groups

METHODS TO CREATE, IMPLEMENT, AND EVALUATE POLICIES AND PROCEDURES THAT MINIMIZE RISK FOR INDIVIDUALS, FAMILIES, GROUPS, ORGANIZATIONS, AND COMMUNITIES

Social workers should create, implement, and evaluate policies that minimize risk for clients, workers, and practice settings. One critical feature of implementing a comprehensive risk management strategy is conducting a comprehensive ethics audit. An ethics audit entails examining risks through the following steps:

1. Appointing a committee or task force of concerned and informed staff and colleagues

2. Gathering information from agency documents, interviews with staff and clients, accreditation reports, and other sources to assess risks associated with client rights; confidentiality and privacy; informed consent; service delivery; boundary issues; conflicts of interest; documentation; client records; supervision; staff development and training; consultation; client referral; fraud; termination of services; professional impairment; misconduct, or incompetence; and so on

3. Reviewing all collected information

4. Determining whether there is no risk, minimal risk, moderate risk, or high risk in each area

5. Preparing action plans to address each risk, paying particular attention to policies that need to be created to prevent risk in the future and steps needed to mitigate existing risk

6. Monitoring policy implementation and progress made toward reducing existing risk, as well as ensuring that procedures adhere to social work's core ethical principles

Risk management is an ongoing process and must consist of preventive strategies as well as corrective actions that result from audits done routinely or in response to particular concerns or complaints.

THE IMPACT OF DOMESTIC, INTIMATE PARTNER, AND OTHER VIOLENCE ON THE HELPING RELATIONSHIP

A type of trauma is that resulting from intimate partner abuse (heterosexual, gay, lesbian, dating, married, cohabiting). The common thread in all abusive relationships is the abuser's need for power and control over his or her partner. Domestic violence occurs across all racial, cultural, and socioeconomic groups and can involve physical, sexual, psychological/emotional, and economic/financial abuse.

Signs of abuse are varied.

- Suspicious injury (not consistent with history of injury, unusual locations, various stages of healing, bites, repeated minor injuries, delay in seeking treatment, old scars, or new injuries from weapons)
- Somatic complaints without a specific diagnosis (such as chronic pain—head, abdomen, pelvis, back, or neck)
- Behavioral presentation (crying, minimizing, no emotional expression, anxious or angry, defensive, fearful eye contact)
- Controlling/coercive behavior of partner (partner hovers, overly concerned, won't leave client unattended, client defers to partner, fear of speaking in front of partner or disagreeing with him or her)

Cycle of Violence

Phase I: Tension building

Phase II: Battering incident—shortest period of the cycle, lasts a brief time

Phase III: "Loving–contrition" (absence of tension or "honeymoon" phase)—batterer offers profuse apologies; assures attacks will never happen again and declares love and caring

Batterers often learn abusive behavior from their families of origin, peers, and media, as well as from personal experience of being abused as children. Batterers view their victims as "possessions" and treat them like objects. Victims are dehumanized to justify the battering. Batterers are very self-centered and feel entitled to have their needs (physical, emotional, sexual) met "no matter what." Batterers have control over their impulses and give themselves permission to be abusive.

Some of the reasons that clients stay in abusive relationships are:

- Hope that the abuser will change. If the batterer is in a treatment program, the client hopes the behavior will change; leaving represents a loss of the committed relationship
- Isolation and lack of support systems
- Fears that no one will believe the seriousness of abuse experienced
- Abuser puts up barricades so client won't leave the relationship (escalates threats of violence, threatens to kill, withholds support, threatens to seek custody of children, threatens suicide, etc.)
- Dangers of leaving may pose a greater danger than remaining with the batterer
- Client may not have the economic resources to survive on his or her own

Leaving is a process. Over time, the client comes to the conclusion that the abuser will not change; each time the client tries to leave, he or she gathers more information that is helpful.

Social exchange theory is based on the idea of totaling potential benefits and losses to determine behavior. People make decisions about relationships based on the amount of rewards they receive from them. A client remains in an abusive relationship because the high cost of leaving lowers the attractiveness (outweighs the benefits) of the best alternative. A client will leave when the best alternative promises a better life (rewards outweigh the costs).

Guidelines for Interventions

- **According to most literature on domestic violence, traditional marital/couples therapy is not appropriate in addressing abuse in the family. It puts victims in greater danger of further abuse.**
- Medical needs and safety are priorities. Note: Consider domestic violence in the context of Maslow's hierarchy of needs.
- In working with a victim of abuse, trust is a major issue in establishing a therapeutic alliance.

THE INDICATORS OF CLIENT/CLIENT SYSTEM READINESS FOR TERMINATION

Readiness for termination may be marked when meetings between a social worker and client seem uneventful and the tone becomes one closer to cordiality rather than challenge, as well as when no new ground has been discovered for several sessions in a row.

In termination, a social worker and client (a) evaluate the degree to which a client's goals have been attained, (b) acknowledge and address issues related to the ending of the relationship, and (c) plan for subsequent steps a client may take relevant to the problem that do not involve a social worker (such as seeking out new services, if necessary).

The process of evaluation helps a client determine if his or her goals have been met and if the helping relationship was beneficial. As a result of the evaluation process, a social worker can become a more effective practitioner and provide better services. There must always be a method to evaluate the effectiveness of the services received. Evaluation measures, when compared with those taken at baseline, assist in determining the extent of progress and a client's readiness for termination.

A social worker helps a client cope with the feelings associated with termination. This process may help a client cope with future terminations.

By identifying the changes accomplished and planning how a client is going to cope with challenges in the future, a social worker helps a client maintain these changes.

METHODS, TECHNIQUES, AND INSTRUMENTS USED TO EVALUATE SOCIAL WORK PRACTICE

Social workers have an ethical mandate to ensure that they are providing the most efficient and effective services possible. They also must do no harm and ensure that the intervention provided enhances the well-being of clients.

These goals require the evaluation of practice. Routine practice evaluation by social workers can enhance treatment outcomes and agency decision making, planning, and accountability.

There are two main types of evaluations—formative and summative. Formative evaluations examine the process of delivering services, whereas summative evaluations examine the outcomes.

Formative evaluations are ongoing processes that allow for feedback to be implemented during service delivery. These types of evaluations allow social workers to make changes as needed to help achieve program goals. Needs assessments can be viewed as one type of formative evaluation.

Summative evaluations occur at the end of services and provide an overall description of their effectiveness. Summative evaluation examines outcomes to determine whether objectives were met. Summative evaluations enable decisions to be made regarding future service directions that cannot be made during implementation. Impact evaluations and cost-benefit analyses are types of summative evaluations.

There are ethical standards that must be followed when evaluating practice (*NASW Code of Ethics, 2008—5.02 Evaluation and Research*). Some of these guidelines include:

1. Obtaining voluntary and written informed consent from clients, when appropriate, without any implied or actual deprivation or penalty for refusal to participate; without undue inducement to participate; and with due regard for participants' well-being, privacy, and dignity

2. Informing clients of their right to withdraw from evaluation and research at any time without penalty

3. Ensuring clients in evaluations have access to appropriate supportive services

4. Avoiding conflicts of interest and dual relationships with those being evaluated

EVIDENCE-BASED PRACTICE

Evidence-based social work practice combines research knowledge, professional/clinical expertise, social work values, and client preferences/circumstances. It is a dynamic and fluid process whereby social workers seek, interpret, use, and evaluate the best available information in an effort to make the best practice decisions.

The promotion of evidence-based research within social work is widespread. Evidence-based research gathers evidence that may be informative for clinical practice or clinical decision making. It also involves the process of gathering and synthesizing scientific evidence from various sources and translating it to be applied to practice.

The use of evidence-based practice places the well-being of clients at the forefront, desiring to discover and use the best practices available. The use of evidence-based practice requires social workers to only use services and techniques that were found effective by rigorous, scientific, empirical studies—that is, outcome research.

Social workers must be willing and able to locate and use evidence-based interventions. In areas in which evidence-based interventions are not available, social workers must still use research to guide practice. Applying knowledge gleaned from research findings will assist social workers in providing services informed by scientific investigation and lead to new interventions that can be evaluated as evidence-based practices.

Decisions are based on the use of many sources, ranging from systematic reviews and meta-analyses to less rigorous research designs.

Social workers often use "evidence-based practice" to refer to programs that have a proven track record. However, it takes a long time for a program or intervention to be "evidence-based." Thus, most interventions in social work need more empirically supported research in order to accurately apply the term. "Evidence-informed practice" may be more appropriate.

Some questions guide the selection of intervention modalities:

- How will the recommended modality assist with the achievement of the treatment goal and will it help get the outcomes desired?
- How does the recommended treatment modality promote client strengths, capabilities, and interests?
- What are the risks and benefits associated with the recommended modality?
- Is there research or evidence to support the use of this modality for this target problem?
- Is this modality appropriate and tested on those with the same or similar cultural background as the client?

- What training and experience does a social worker have with the recommended modality?
- Is the recommended modality evidence-based or consistent with available research? If not, why?
- Was the recommended modality discussed with and selected by a client?
- Will the use of the recommended modality be assessed periodically? When? How?
- Is the recommended treatment modality covered by insurance? What is the cost? How does it compare to the use of other options?

Use of Collaborative Relationships

9

THE BASIC TERMINOLOGY OF PROFESSIONS OTHER THAN SOCIAL WORK (E.G., LEGAL, EDUCATIONAL)

Social workers should maintain access to professional case consultation. Often, this consultation may be from qualified professionals in other disciplines. Each discipline has its own set of assumptions, values, and priorities; in order to ensure that the assessment of a client's problems considers all possible root causes (including medical) and all needs of a client are met, the social worker should consult with experts in other fields, as well as refer a client to them when needed.

Social workers often work together with others from various professions. This is known as an interdisciplinary approach. Some interdisciplinary teams interface daily, whereas others may only meet periodically.

Sometimes social workers form interdisciplinary relationships that do not constitute team practice, but are nevertheless necessary for effective service. These relationships may be with legal or educational professionals. To practice effectively, social workers must be prepared to work with professionals from all other disciplines that may be needed by a client.

In turn, social work knowledge is influenced by, and in turn influences, other disciplines, including family studies, medicine, psychiatry, sociology, education, and psychology.

THE EFFECT OF THE CLIENT'S DEVELOPMENTAL LEVEL ON THE SOCIAL WORKER–CLIENT RELATIONSHIP

Social workers must be sensitive to the developmental levels of clients. Development levels refer to the functional abilities at which clients find themselves at given moments. The problem-solving process must take these developmental levels into account. Social workers should not rely on chronological age as clients may be functioning at very different developmental levels. Social workers must use engagement and intervention strategies which are appropriate given clients' developmental functioning. Assessments should include determining the psychosocial levels of clients. Clients' development may be delayed or advanced across all domains or inconsistent with some areas more behind than others. Understanding causes for discrepancies between chronological and developmental age also may be important for insight into clients' problems.

METHODS TO CLARIFY THE ROLES AND RESPONSIBILITIES OF THE SOCIAL WORKER AND CLIENT/CLIENT SYSTEM IN THE INTERVENTION PROCESS

A social worker can be supportive in these roles, but is not supposed to be the client's support system. Instead, a social worker should assist the client to mobilize or build his or her own natural supports. People generally like to give advice. It gives them the feeling of being competent and important. Hence, social workers may easily fall into this inappropriate role without taking into account the abilities, the fears, and the interests of clients and/or their circumstances.

Social workers should also not be insensitive to clients' resistance. When a client does not claim any difficulties, is unable or refuses to talk, explains that it is someone else's fault, and/or denies what has happened, a social worker may try to argue or in other ways exert pressure. This response tends to increase a client's resistance. This approach does nothing for a client.

A social worker may also confuse the situation and hinder clarification of the problem. In an effort to establish a relationship, a social worker may overpraise or fail to confront a client. A client must look at his or her own role in the situation and recognize his or her own limitations.

CONSULTATION APPROACHES (E.G., REFERRALS TO SPECIALISTS)

Social workers are often called upon to seek consultation for a problem related to a client, service, organization, and/or policy. Consultation is the utilization of an "expert" in a specific area to assist with developing a solution to the issue. Consultation is usually time limited and the advice of the consultant can be used by a social worker in the problem-solving process. Although a consultant does not have any formal authority over a social worker, he or she has informal authority as an "expert."

However, a social worker is not required to follow the recommendations of a consultant.

Four things are critical in consultation:

1. Defining the purpose of the consultation

2. Specifying the consultant's role

3. Clarifying the nature of the problem

4. Outlining the consultation process

Social workers should seek the advice and counsel of colleagues whenever such consultation is in the best interests of clients, but should only do so from colleagues who have demonstrated knowledge, expertise, and competence related to the subject of the consultation (*NASW Code of Ethics, 2008—2.05 Consultation*).

When seeking consultation, social workers need to get the permission of clients if any identifying or specific information will be shared. In addition, social workers should only disclose information that is absolutely necessary when interacting with consultants.

Social workers may also provide consultation. They should have the appropriate knowledge and skill to do so and should follow all ethical standards, including avoiding conflicts of interest and maintaining boundaries (*NASW Code of Ethics, 2008—3.01 Supervision and Consultation*).

METHODS OF NETWORKING

The importance of networking has been stressed heavily in business, but it has received far less attention in social work practice. This void is interesting, because it is critical to the effective delivery of services. Networking involves building relationships with other professionals who share areas of interest. It is about creating a community around common interests and building alliances. It is also about creating opportunities to work with others toward the achievement of mutual goals.

Although networking in business is a way to attract patrons/customers or to get jobs, it has a broader, and more altruistic, focus in social work.

For example, learning about others who do similar or complementary work can result in a sharing of resources and expertise, which could be beneficial to clients by keeping the cost of services contained and/or increasing the skills of practitioners. Learning about the skills of others and establishing professional relationships through networking can also provide resources for clients who may need referrals to other professionals.

Networking helps improve social skills and the ability to relate to others in a variety of settings. It puts social workers "out there" so that others can be aware of the important work that they do. Educating others about social problems is an important part of making systematic changes. Lastly, networking can identify individuals who would be good candidates for jobs. Recruiting qualified individuals into the agencies where social workers are employed results in clients receiving quality care.

THE PROCESS OF INTERDISCIPLINARY AND INTRADISCIPLINARY TEAM COLLABORATION

Social workers often work together with others from various professions. This is known as an interdisciplinary approach. Some interdisciplinary teams interface daily, whereas others may only meet periodically. Sometimes social workers form interdisciplinary relationships that do not constitute team practice but are nevertheless necessary for effective service. These relationships may be with legal or educational professionals. To practice effectively, social workers must be prepared to work with professionals from all other disciplines that may be needed by a client. In turn, social work knowledge is influenced by, and in turn influences, other disciplines, including family studies, medicine, psychiatry, sociology, education, and psychology.

Interdisciplinary teams are often seen as advantageous to clients because they do not have the burden of navigating multiple service systems and communicating to multiple professionals involved in their care. Interdisciplinary teams can also be cost-effective and can increase positive outcomes.

An interdisciplinary approach may also have benefits for social workers as they:

1. Provide peer support, especially when working with stressful problems associated with involuntary service delivery, violence, suicide, and so on

2. Allow for work to be assigned across multiple professionals

3. Fulfill professional goals by ensuring all aspects of a client's biopsychosocial–spiritual–cultural care are delivered

4. Create cross-fertilization of skills between professionals

5. Facilitate decision making related to all aspects of client care, which can lead to increased job satisfaction

6. Streamline work practices through sharing of information

Interdisciplinary collaboration is a rewarding, yet challenging, social work activity. Collaboration, a learned skill that can be improved through practice, is a vehicle for improving services for all clients. It means working with others for the betterment of a client. Collaborative teams are more likely to develop important new and innovative approaches to dealing with problems.

Collaboration goes beyond people sitting around a table. It includes pre-meeting work (i.e., making telephone calls), how members typically conduct themselves (i.e., being friendly), and how meetings proceed (i.e., choosing to ignore minor irritations in order to get on with the agenda).

Social workers must understand their own styles and focus on their own behavior as part of a group, rather than on how other members should change.

Collaboration involves strong interpersonal communication and group process skills, as well as being able to understand the perspectives of others. It can be discrete (distinct or separate; limited to single occurrence or action) or continuous (ongoing or repetitive).

The following list provides some guidelines that can be helpful when social workers participate in such collaboration.

1. Social workers should clearly articulate their roles on interdisciplinary teams.

2. Social workers should understand the roles of professionals from other disciplines on these teams.

3. Social workers should seek and establish common ground with these professionals, including commonalities in professional goals.

4. Social workers should acknowledge the differences within the field and across other disciplines.

5. Social workers should address conflict within teams so that it does not interfere with the collaborative process and the teams' outcomes.

6. Social workers should establish and maintain collegial relationships.

There are also ethical guidelines that must be followed when social workers are part of interdisciplinary collaboration (*NASW Code of Ethics, 2008—2.03 Interdisciplinary Collaboration*).

1. Social workers who are members of an interdisciplinary team should participate in and contribute to decisions that affect the well-being of clients by drawing on the perspectives, values, and experiences of the social work profession. Professional and ethical obligations of the interdisciplinary team as a whole and of its individual members should be clearly established.

2. Social workers for whom a team decision raises ethical concerns should attempt to resolve the disagreement through appropriate channels. If the disagreement cannot be resolved, social workers should pursue other avenues to address their concerns consistent with client well-being.

Intradisciplinary teams are composed exclusively of social workers who may have different levels of training and skill within the profession. Intradisciplinary teams are often referred to as unidisciplinary. Unfortunately, the terms "intradisciplinary," "multidisciplinary," and "interdisciplinary" are often used interchangeably, causing confusion. Intradisciplinary teams in social work practice can be useful in professional development, mentorship, and the provision of supervision. However, working on a team with others in the profession has advantages and disadvantages. Members share the same professional orientation and values, which can facilitate consensus and cohesion within the group, but the ability to generate alternative solutions to problems when viewing problems from multiple professional perspectives can be reduced.

METHODS TO ASSESS THE AVAILABILITY OF COMMUNITY RESOURCES

Social workers must respect the rights to self-determination of clients. In order for clients to make informed decisions, it is critical that they understand the range of services available and be informed about any opportunities they have to obtain services from other service providers. Clients should also understand their right to be referred to other professionals for assistance, as well as their right to refuse services and possible consequences of such refusals.

Throughout the problem-solving process, social workers should be assisting clients to access available resources, as well as create new ones if they do not exist or are not appropriate. In order for clients to choose between alternative resources, social workers must review the advantages and disadvantages of using each.

There are important steps, as well as ethical concerns, that must be taken when referring clients for services.

Step 1: Clarifying the Need or Purpose for the Referral
Social workers should refer clients to other professionals when the other professionals' specialized knowledge or expertise is needed to serve clients fully or when social workers believe that they are not being effective or making reasonable progress with clients and additional service is required (*NASW Code of Ethics, 2008—2.06 Referral for Services*).

Step 2: Researching Resources

When making a referral, it is critical that a social worker refers to a competent provider, someone with expertise in the problem that a client is experiencing. When researching resources, a client's right to self-determination should be paramount. In addition, if a client is already receiving services from an agency, it may be advisable to see if there are available services provided by this agency in order to avoid additional coordination and fragmentation for a client.

Step 3: Discussing and Selecting Options

Social workers are prohibited from giving or receiving payment for a referral when no professional service is provided by the referring social worker (*NASW Code of Ethics, 2008—2.06 Referral for Services*).

Step 4: Planning for Initial Contact

Social workers may want to work with a client to prepare for the initial meeting. Preparation may include helping a client to understand what to expect or reviewing needs and progress made so that it can be discussed with the new provider.

Step 5: Initial Contact

Social workers who refer clients to other professionals should take appropriate steps to facilitate an orderly transfer of responsibility. Social workers who refer clients to other professionals should disclose, with clients' consent, all pertinent information to the new service providers (*NASW Code of Ethics, 2008—2.06 Referral for Services*).

Step 6: Follow-Up to See If Need Was Met

Social workers should always follow up to ensure that there was not a break in service and that the new provider is meeting a client's needs.

METHODS TO ESTABLISH SERVICE NETWORKS OR COMMUNITY RESOURCES

The need for services to not be duplicative and complement one another is central to meeting client needs. Social workers are often called upon to assist with developing or navigating service networks, as well as creating community resources where they are lacking. Integrating services takes sustained effort and hard work. Though the concept of service integration may seem simple, it is not and usually takes several administrative and operational strategies. Strong leadership and sound management are critical.

In order to effectively meet client needs, organizations are increasingly recognizing collaborations, networks, alliances, and/or partnerships. There are two distinct network forms—mandated network arrangements and self-organizing networks.

Within each of these forms, there may be a lead organization or a model in which all organizations share decision-making power. The former is often associated with a centralized structure, whereas the latter is more indicative of a decentralized one. Networks can also have strong and weak arrangements in which the parameters of integration may or may not be highly regulated.

The willingness and ability of social service organizations to form networks often depends on organizational size, resource dependency, and collaborative experience.

THE EFFECTS OF POLICIES, PROCEDURES, REGULATIONS, AND LEGISLATION ON SOCIAL WORK PRACTICE AND SERVICE DELIVERY

Social workers should be fully informed of existing laws, policies, practices, and procedures that impact or govern service delivery.

Social workers are also expected to keep up-to-date with new public laws and policies.

Many laws affect social work practice. Although social workers may not be responsible for implementing these pieces of legislation, they provide protections or programs that are critical to those served.

Some relevant federal legislation is listed in chronological order in the following list.

1. *Title VI of the Civil Rights Act of 1964* states that no person shall "on the grounds of race, color, or national origin, be excluded from participation in, denied the benefits of, or be subjected to discrimination under any program or activity receiving federal financial assistance." It desegregated all schools and public buildings and required all agencies that receive federal funds to terminate discriminatory hiring practices. Social workers are charged with challenging discriminatory practices and upholding the belief of equal rights for all.

2. The *Older Americans Act (OAA) of 1965* offers services to older Americans. It established the Administration on Aging, which empowers the federal government to distribute funds to the states for supportive services for individuals over the age of 60. The Administration achieves its aim by awarding grants to states, which pass them along to local Area Agencies on Aging (AAA). Some programs target vulnerable older adults who need help staying in their homes. Other programs provide access services, in-home services, community services, caregiver services, and opportunities for volunteer work.

3. The *Child Abuse Prevention and Treatment Act of 1974* is key legislation for addressing child abuse and neglect. It has been amended several times and provides federal funding to states in support of prevention, assessment, investigation, prosecution, and treatment activities; it also provides grants to public agencies and nonprofit organizations for demonstration programs and projects.

4. The *Family Educational Rights and Privacy Act (FERPA) of 1974* protects the privacy of educational records. The law applies to all schools that receive funds under an applicable program of the United States Department of Education. FERPA gives parents certain rights with respect to their children's education records. These rights transfer to the student when he or she reaches the age of 18 or attends a school beyond the high school level. Prior to 18, parents have the right to inspect and review a student's education records maintained by the school. Schools are not required to provide copies of records unless, for reasons such as great distance, it is impossible for parents to review the records. Schools may charge a fee for copies. Parents also have the right to request that a school correct records that they believe to be inaccurate or misleading. If the school decides not to amend the record, the parent or eligible student then has the right to a formal hearing. After the hearing, if the school still decides not to amend the record, the parent has the right to place a statement with the record setting forth his or her view about the contested information. Generally, schools must have written permission from the parent in order to release any information from a student's education record, though there are some exceptions related to the student's care.

5. The *Education for All Handicapped Children Act of 1975* (which is now known as the *Individuals with Disabilities Education Act* [IDEA]) guarantees a free, appropriate public education to all children with disabilities between the ages of 3 and 21. Children receiving such services should be provided with Individual Educational Programs (IEPs) which are outlined in plans that are revised annually. A team composed of a social worker, teacher, administrator, and other relevant school personnel typically create the IEP. The parents, and often the child, also participate. The IEP includes goals, means of attaining goals, and ways of evaluating goal attainment. A child who has an IEP must also be educated in the "least restrictive environment." Thus, the child should either spend part or all of his or her time in a regular classroom or in an environment that is as close to this as possible while still leading to the attainment of the educational goals. Services that are needed, such as speech therapy and others related to educational goals, are provided at no extra cost to the family.

6. The *Indian Child Welfare Act of 1978* gives American Indian/Native American/Indigenous nations or organizations jurisdiction over child welfare cases that involve an American Indian/Native American/Indigenous child in order to protect the integrity of American Indian/Native American/Indigenous families. The law specifies a hierarchical procedure for placement of an American Indian/Native American/Indigenous child: (a) verify the ethnic and tribal identity of the child; (b) allow tribal jurisdiction over case; (c) if tribe rejects jurisdiction, placement with family member; or (d) if that is impossible, placement with family of the same tribe. The last resort is placing the child in a home with a family that is not American Indian/Native American/Indigenous.

7. The *Adoption Assistance and Child Welfare Act of 1980* focuses on family preservation efforts to help keep families together and children out of foster care or other out-of-home placements. This law also focuses on family reunification or adoption if a child is removed from a home. The act requires courts to review child welfare cases more regularly and mandates that states make "reasonable efforts" to keep families together via prevention and family reunification services. States are also required to develop reunification and preventive programs for foster care and assure that children in nonpermanent settings are seen at least every 6 months. An adoption subsidy reimbursed by the federal government is also provided through this law for children with complex needs or disabilities.

8. The *Americans with Disabilities Act (ADA) of 1990* is civil-rights legislation that prohibits discrimination on the basis of disability. It has been amended and affords similar protections as the Civil Rights Act of 1964 for discrimination based on race, religion, sex, national origin, and other characteristics. Unlike the Civil Rights Act of 1964, the ADA also requires covered employers to provide reasonable accommodations to employees with disabilities and imposes accessibility requirements on public accommodations. ADA disabilities include both mental and physical conditions. A condition does not need to be severe or permanent to be a disability.

9. The *Patient Self-Determination Act (PSDA) of 1991* introduced a new set of federal requirements intended to implement advance directive policies at all health care facilities that receive federal funding through Medicaid and Medicare programs. The Act specified that these facilities must inform clients of their rights to make decisions concerning their own health care, ask and document whether a client has an advance directive, and provide education for staff and the community.

Advance directives are a legal way of indicating that a person has given the legal rights to a designated person to make decisions on his or her behalf about continuation of support measures should the individual be incapable physically or mentally of making wants known.

The purpose of advance directives is to respond to judicial decisions that have been made indicating that if a person has not told someone of his or her wishes, in case of severe physical injury, the decision to remove a person from life supports or to place the person on life supports cannot be made. Therefore, it has become increasingly imperative that people indicate their wishes and identify individuals that they designate to make these decisions if needed.

Advance directives have been paired with living wills to give people control over what happens to them in a severe illness or injury. A living will allows individuals to retain some control over what happens at the end of their lives, even if the individuals are then no longer competent to make personal choices for terminal care, by specifying their wishes while they are still healthy and at a time when there is no doubt of their mental competence.

10. The *Family and Medical Leave Act (FMLA) of 1993* requires covered employers to provide up to 12 weeks of unpaid, job-protected leave to "eligible" employees for certain family and medical reasons with continuation of group health insurance coverage under the same terms and conditions as if the employee had not taken leave.

11. The *Multiethnic Placement Act (MEPA) of 1994* and its subsequent amendments prohibit agencies from refusing or delaying foster or adoptive placements because of a child's or foster/adoptive parent's race, color, or national origin, and prohibits agencies from considering race, color, or national origin as a basis for denying approval as a foster and/or adoptive parent. It also requires agencies to diligently recruit a diverse base of foster and adoptive parents to better reflect the racial and ethnic makeup of children in out-of-home care.

12. The *Violence Against Women Act (VAWA) of 1994* has improved the criminal justice response to violence against women by strengthening federal penalties for repeat sex offenders and creating a federal "rape shield law," which is intended to prevent offenders from using victims' past sexual conduct against them during a rape trial; keeping victims safe by requiring that a victim's protection order will be recognized and enforced in all state, tribal, and territorial jurisdictions; increasing rates of prosecution, conviction, and sentencing of offenders by helping communities develop dedicated law enforcement and prosecution units and domestic violence dockets; training law enforcement officers, prosecutors, victim advocates, and judges; and ensuring access to the services needed by victims to achieve safety and rebuild their lives.

This law, reauthorized in 2013, now includes a landmark addition that empowers Native American tribal authorities to prosecute non-Native Americans for abuses committed on tribal lands. In addition, it includes additional protections for those who are gay, lesbian, bisexual, or transgender.

13. The *Personal Responsibility and Work Opportunity Reconciliation Act (PRWORA) of 1996* was considered to be a fundamental shift in both the method and goal of federal cash assistance to the poor. It added a workforce development component to welfare legislation, encouraging employment among the poor. PRWORA instituted Temporary Assistance for Needy Families (TANF), which became effective July 1, 1997. TANF replaced the Aid to Families With Dependent Children (AFDC) program, which had been in effect since 1935, and also supplanted the Job Opportunities and Basic Skills (JOBS) Training Program of 1988. It also imposed a lifetime 5-year limit on the receipt of benefits.

14. The *Health Insurance Portability and Accountability Act (HIPAA) of 1996* provides individuals with access to their medical records and more control over how their personal health information is used and disclosed. It represents a uniform, federal floor of privacy protections for individuals across the country. State laws providing additional protections are not affected by HIPAA, which took effect on April 14, 2003.

15. The *Patient Protection and Affordable Care Act (ACA) of 2010* expands access to insurance, increases protections, emphasizes prevention and wellness, improves quality and system performance, expands the health workforce, and curbs rising health care costs. Key provisions of the ACA that intend to address rising health costs include providing more oversight of health insurance premiums and practices; emphasizing prevention, primary care, and effective treatments; reducing health care fraud and abuse; reducing uncompensated care to prevent a shift onto insurance premium costs; fostering comparison shopping in insurance exchanges to increase competition and price transparency; implementing Medicare payment reforms; and testing new delivery and payment system models in Medicaid and Medicare.

16. The *Workforce Innovation and Opportunity Act (WIOA) of 2014* reauthorizes the Workforce Investment Act (WIA) of 1998 with several key changes in areas such as the structure of Workforce Development Boards; One-Stop Operations; Job-Driven Training for Adults and Dislocated Workers; and Integrated Performance and Youth Services.

THE RELATIONSHIP BETWEEN FORMAL AND INFORMAL POWER STRUCTURES IN THE DECISION-MAKING PROCESS

Formal power is received in accordance with position in an organization and the authority associated with that position. Conversely, informal power stems from the relationships built and respect earned from coworkers.

Formal Power

Organizations typically have organizational charts that list the relationship and ranks of positions. The charts detail the lines of authority and responsibilities and outline the formal power structures of the organizations. Formal power may refer to position in the organizational hierarchy, corporate structure, or even job function. A chief executive officer, for example, has decision-making power in many areas. Even in small agencies without official organizational charts, employees can easily recognize formal power because of job roles, titles, and functions.

Informal Power

The most powerful person in an organizational unit is not necessarily a supervisor. Instead, persons with the most influence, who can lead others to achieve goals or accomplish tasks, may have the greatest influence. Informal power refers to the ability to lead, direct, or achieve without official authority. It is derived from relationships that are built. Employees with informal power may be the most experienced or knowledgeable or the most respected because of personality traits.

All forms of power within an organization are beneficial when used appropriately. Formal power is necessary to achieve goals. Informal power can be equally useful. Workers may be more apt to accept criticism or take direction when they receive guidance from a colleague that is respected and trusted. It is often easier to get employee "buy-in" when suggestions come from those with informal power.

Documentation

10

THE PRINCIPLES OF CASE RECORDING, DOCUMENTATION, AND MANAGEMENT OF PRACTICE RECORDS

The proper documentation of client services is paramount to competent practice. Without proper case recording or record-keeping, the quality of service may be compromised, the continuity of service may be disrupted, there may be misinterpretation that can cause harm, client confidentiality may be breached, and a client's confidence in the integrity of a social worker may be impacted.

In addition to client harm, a social worker, as well as his or her agency, if applicable, may be at risk of liability due to malpractice, negligence, and/or breach of confidentiality.

Some important "rules" about case recording include that it is:

- A clear, accurate, and unbiased representation of the facts
- A written record of all decisions
- Free of value judgments and subjective comments
- Timely

It should also include only information that is directly relevant to the delivery of services.

The release and storage of case recordings is also critical. Social workers must make sure that records are not released without proper client consent and records are properly stored during and following the termination of services. Records should be maintained for the number of years required by state statutes and regulations and relevant contracts.

THE ELEMENTS OF CLIENT/CLIENT SYSTEM REPORTS

There is no one way to organize information or client files. Some client information and files are obtained and stored in paper format. However, increasingly client records are kept electronically with software to assist professionals in organizing and accessing data.

Whether paper or electronic, client files are usually stored with the following in separate sections or folders:

1. Demographic information and intake materials

2. Assessments, quarterly reviews, and reassessments

3. Service plan(s) with goals

4. Discharge plan

5. Releases of information and referrals

6. Correspondence

Social workers should keep psychotherapy notes in a secure location outside of client files to provide added confidentiality protection.

Often agency policies or requirements imposed by funders dictate the organizational structure for client files. However, regardless of the schema, it is essential that files are secure, up-to-date, and complete, with a format that makes locating information easy and evident.

Social workers are expected to communicate effectively, including in the preparation of written reports for external organizations. Poorly written reports or the inclusion of irrelevant or inappropriate information can have an adverse impact on a client. In the preparation of reports, including those for the courts, social workers are expected to communicate accurately and professionally. Reports generated by social workers must be taken seriously and will not be treated legitimately if there are spelling or grammatical mistakes, or the content is not based on critical thought and analysis.

Social workers also must develop reports as requested or needed, adhering to the standards of confidentiality, as failure to provide professional observations may hinder opportunities for clients. Often, social workers are reluctant to generate reports even when requested by clients and legally allowed to do so.

Critical to developing reports is the knowledge that they must be understandable and useful to recipients with a wide range of educational backgrounds and literacy levels. In addition, social workers must have a keen awareness of the purposes of reports, who they are being written for, and how they should be presented differently depending on the purposes and the audience.

Social workers should avoid irrelevant and inappropriate information, meaningless phrases or slang words, and illogical conclusions in the preparation and writing of reports. Social workers should plan what should and should not be included in the final documents prior to starting to develop them. It is also helpful to prepare drafts for later editing. Having others review draft reports can help catch errors and ensure the clarity of all material.

Social workers' competence and the value of social work services are often judged by the quality of written reports. Thus, it is essential that thought and care be taken in their preparation, and that they adhere to best practices and standards.

Administrative reports, such as annual reports from public and private social service organizations, are critical to the fulfillment of the social work mission. They provide accountability to the public about the number of people served, the services delivered, and how funds were allocated. They also may be used by social workers to document unmet needs which should be addressed.

Social workers may be required to prepare grant reports, evaluations, program proposals, and accreditation reports. While each of these documents serves a different purpose, they all require social workers to use their written communication skills and critical thinking/analysis to help clients directly or indirectly.

For example, a program proposal sets forth a plan of activities needed to begin or modify services in order to (better) meet clients' needs. It includes recommendations to organize or arrange a program in an effective and efficient manner. It describes and recommends procedures and ways to organize services for maximum client benefit. To ensure that it is implemented as intended, it must be clear, accurate, and well-written.

THE PRINCIPLES AND PROCESSES FOR DEVELOPING FORMAL DOCUMENTS (E.G., PROPOSALS, LETTERS, BROCHURES, PAMPHLETS, REPORTS, EVALUATIONS)

Social workers are expected to communicate effectively and be able to prepare formal documents. Being able to provide quality services is not the only important aspect of social work; all work is undermined by poor recording or documentation.

A good document begins with careful planning—jotting down the report's purpose and some notes about key content to be contained. Many times, drafts need to be made to ensure that the formal document meets its purpose and is written clearly, without punctuation and other mistakes. Editing is usually required before finalizing for dissemination.

Typing reports is always preferred for a more professional appearance and to avoid "illegible" handwriting.

From court reports, to grant proposals, to public relations pamphlets, social workers are expected to communicate accurately with others. Poor English skills can affect the quality of reports. Social workers need to be able to write reports that can be taken "seriously" by others.

Quality of content is just as critical as spelling and punctuation. Time must be allotted to be able to do critical analyses which many formal reports require. It is easy to describe something, but much harder to indicate its significance. Repeating facts may not provide needed professional opinions and observations.

Formal documents will only count if they get to the right people. Social workers must be aware of the purpose of documents to be prepared and to whom they are being written, and then write accordingly. Social workers should avoid irrelevant, inappropriate information; meaningless phrases; and illogical conclusions.

Social workers should expect that their documents may be scrutinized. Thus, they should write just enough to make their points, but not "overdocument" with irrelevant details. Social workers should be specific and avoid characterizations such as "poor outcome," "good result," "moderate compliance," "drunk," "aggressive," and "combative." They should also avoid acronyms and abbreviations and use precise description and specific language (not "it seems," "I suppose," "it appears," "I believe," "I feel," and so on).

Social workers must prepare documents in a timely fashion and consider ethical issues that can be related to their preparation and distribution. Documents should not contain bias wording. Social workers should not alter documents after they are written unless it is appropriate to do so. Social workers must know when communication is "privileged" and should not share information with those without a need to know.

THE PRINCIPLES AND FEATURES OF OBJECTIVE AND SUBJECTIVE DATA

A social worker uses both objective and subjective data throughout the problem-solving process. For example, in assessment, a social worker must understand the "facts" related to a client's situation (objective data), but also how those "facts" are perceived by the client through descriptions of his or her feelings, experiences, and perceptions (subjective data). It is not the objective facts that determine whether an event is traumatic, but a subjective emotional experience of the event. Thus, having a client describe the meaning of an event to him or her is critically important.

Treatment plans are often developed and progress is often assessed based upon objective and subjective data gathered by a social worker. For example, in health care, a **SOAP format** is often used.

S (Subjective): The subjective component is a client's report of how he or she has been doing since the last visit and/or what brought a client into treatment.

O (Objective): In health care, the objective component includes vital signs (temperature, blood pressure, pulse, and respiration), documentation of any physical examinations, and results of laboratory tests. In other settings, this section may include other objective indicators of problems such as disorientation, failing school, legal issues, and so forth.

A (Assessment): A social worker pulls together the objective and subjective findings and consolidates them into a short assessment.

P (Plan): The plan includes what will be done as a consequence of the assessment.

Lastly, in evaluation, subjective reports of a client, in conjunction with objective indicators of progress, should be used to determine when goals or objectives have been met and whether new goals or objectives should be set. Client self-monitoring (subjective data) is a good way to involve a client so he or she can see and track progress himself or herself.

Unit IV

Professional Relationships, Values, and Ethics (20%)

Unit IV

Professional Relationships, Value
and Ethics (20%)

Professional Values and Ethical Issues

LEGAL AND/OR ETHICAL ISSUES RELATED TO THE PRACTICE OF SOCIAL WORK, INCLUDING RESPONSIBILITY TO CLIENTS/CLIENT SYSTEMS, COLLEAGUES, THE PROFESSION, AND SOCIETY

Social workers frequently encounter ethical and legal issues. In most instances, ethical and legal standards complement each other. However, in some circumstances, ethical and legal standards conflict. The ethical standards for social workers are outlined in the *NASW Code of Ethics* (2008). With regard to legal mandates, social workers must be aware of five distinct sets of requirements: constitutional law, statutory law, regulatory law, court-made/common law, and executive orders.

Ethical and legal issues encountered by social workers fall into four distinct categories:

1. Actions that are compatible with both legal and ethical standards in social work (legal and ethical)

2. Actions that are neither legal nor ethical in social work according to prevailing standards (not legal and not ethical)

3. Actions that are legal, but not ethical according to prevailing standards (legal, but not ethical)

4. Actions that are ethical, but not legal according to standards and laws (ethical, but not legal)

When there are conflicts between ethical and legal standards, a social worker should identify the mandates that conflict. A social worker should also identify the individuals, groups, and organizations that are likely to be affected by the outcome of the conflict. All possible courses of action and the benefits and risks of each alternative should be considered, including the reasons supporting and in opposition to each possibility. Resolution of conflicts should not be done in a vacuum and a social worker should consult with colleagues and appropriate experts. All steps in the decision-making process should be documented. Once a decision is made, the results should be monitored and evaluated.

PROFESSIONAL VALUES AND PRINCIPLES (E.G., COMPETENCE, SOCIAL JUSTICE, INTEGRITY, AND DIGNITY AND WORTH OF THE PERSON)

The mission of the social work profession is rooted in a set of core values. These core values are the foundation of social work practice:

- Service
- Social justice
- Dignity and worth of the person
- Importance of human relationships
- Integrity
- Competence

Professional ethics are based on these basic values and guide social workers' conduct. These standards are relevant to all social workers, regardless of their professional functions, the settings in which they work, or the populations they serve.

Professional ethics are "rules" based on the core values of the profession that should be adhered to by social workers. They are statements to the general public about what they can expect from a social worker. These standards tell new social workers what is essential for practice based on the profession's core values. Social workers are judged with regard to competency based on these standards.

Professional standards are also helpful in guiding social workers when they are unsure about a course of action or conflicts arise.

The social work profession is based on the belief that every person has dignity and worth. It is essential that social workers respect this value and treat everyone in a caring and respectful fashion. Social workers should also be mindful of individual differences, as well as cultural and ethnic diversity.

Social workers should promote clients' right to self-determination and act as a resource to assist clients to address their own needs. Social workers have a dual responsibility to clients and to the broader society and must resolve any conflicts, in a socially responsible and ethical manner, that arise due to this dual mandate.

THE INFLUENCE OF THE SOCIAL WORKER'S OWN VALUES AND BELIEFS ON THE SOCIAL WORKER–CLIENT/CLIENT SYSTEM RELATIONSHIP

Social workers must recognize values that may inhibit the therapeutic relationship.

1. **Universalism—There is one acceptable norm or standard for everyone** versus there are other valid standards that have been developed by people that they have determined to be most useful to them.

2. **Dichotomous "either-or" thinking; differences are inferior, wrong, bad** versus differences are just different and coexist.

3. **Heightened ability/value on separating, categorizing, numbering, "left-brain"** versus "right-brain" or "whole picture." Mental activity is highly valued to the exclusion of physical and spiritual experiences. Persons are studied in isolation, not as part of a group or interrelated with their environment.

4. **High value on control, constraint, restraint** versus value on flexibility, emotion/feelings, expressiveness, spirituality. What cannot be controlled and definitively defined is deemed nonexistent, unimportant, unscientific, or deviant/inferior. Reality is defined with the assumption of objectivity; subjective reality is viewed as invalid because it cannot be consistently replicated by many people.

5. **Measure of self comes from outside, and is only in contrast to others** versus value comes from within—you are worthwhile because you were born, and you strive to live a life that is in harmony with others and the environment. Worth is measured by accumulation of wealth or status (outside measures)—therefore, one can only feel good if one is better than someone else, or accumulates more than someone else, or has a higher status.

6. **Power is defined as "power over" others, mastery over environment** versus "power through" or in harmony with others; by sharing power, power can be expanded, and each becomes more powerful.

THE DYNAMICS OF DIVERSITY IN THE SOCIAL WORKER–CLIENT/ CLIENT SYSTEM RELATIONSHIP

A social worker's self-awareness about his or her own attitudes, values, and beliefs about cultural differences and a willingness to acknowledge cultural differences are critical factors in working with diverse populations. A social worker is responsible for bringing up and addressing issues of cultural difference with a client and is also ethically responsible for being culturally competent by obtaining the appropriate knowledge, skills, and experience. Social workers should:

1. Move from being culturally unaware to being aware of their own heritage and the heritage of others

2. Value and celebrate differences of others rather than maintaining an ethnocentric stance

3. Have an awareness of personal values and biases and how they may influence relationships with clients

4. Demonstrate comfort with racial and cultural differences between themselves and clients

5. Have an awareness of personal and professional limitations

6. Acknowledge their own racial attitudes, beliefs, and feelings

TECHNIQUES TO IDENTIFY AND RESOLVE ETHICAL DILEMMAS

An ethical dilemma is a predicament when a social worker must decide between two viable solutions that seem to have similar ethical value. Sometimes two viable ethical solutions can conflict with each other. Social workers should be aware of any conflicts between personal and professional values and deal with them responsibly.

In instances where social workers' ethical obligations conflict with agency policies or relevant laws or regulations, they should make a responsible effort to resolve the conflict in a manner that is consistent with ethical values, principles, and standards.

In order to resolve this conflict, ethical problem solving is needed.

Essential Steps in Ethical Problem Solving

1. Identify ethical standards, as defined by the professional code of ethics, that are being compromised (always go to the *NASW Code of Ethics* first—do not rely on supervisor or coworkers)

2. Determine whether there is an ethical issue or dilemma

3. Weigh ethical issues in light of key social work values and principles as defined by the *NASW Code of Ethics*

4. Suggest modifications in light of the prioritized ethical values and principles that are central to the dilemma

5. Implement modifications in light of prioritized ethical values and principles

6. Monitor for new ethical issues or dilemmas

CLIENT/CLIENT SYSTEM COMPETENCE AND SELF-DETERMINATION (E.G., FINANCIAL DECISIONS, TREATMENT DECISIONS, EMANCIPATION, AGE OF CONSENT, PERMANENCY PLANNING)

Self-determination, the concept that clients are qualified to make their own decisions about their lives, is a central concept in the social work profession. It is described in the *NASW Code of Ethics* as one of a social worker's primary ethical responsibilities. Using a strengths-based perspective, all clients are assumed to be competent to make their own decisions, including those about financial matters and treatment options.

When working with clients, there may be, at times, some concerns about their cognitive or functional abilities to perform life tasks. For example, clients who are not able to complete activities of daily living independently may need services to assist them in these areas. The need to rely on others to assist may limit clients' independence. An assessment which can assist social workers in determining assistance needed in functional life domains is the *World Health Organization Disability Assessment Schedule 2.0 (WHODAS 2.0)* which was added to the *Diagnostic and Statistical Manual of Mental Disorders* (5th ed.; *DSM-5*) in "Section III, Emerging Measures and Models," under Assessment Measures.

When limitations are not physical, but involve mental processes, there may be some unease about clients' abilities to provide consent related to financial, medical, and/or legal treatment. All those over the age of majority (adults) are presumed to be competent to provide consent unless legal proceedings have found otherwise. When clients lack the capacity to provide consent, social workers should protect clients' interests by seeking permission from an appropriate third party and informing clients in a manner consistent with the clients' level of understanding. In such instances, social workers should seek to ensure that the third party acts in a manner consistent with clients' wishes and interests. Social workers should take reasonable steps to enhance such clients' ability to give informed consent (*NASW Code of Ethics, 2008—1.03 Informed Consent*).

Emancipation and Age of Consent

Treating minors requires social workers to be well versed in state and federal laws related to consent and confidentiality. The age at which minors can obtain services without parental/guardian permission varies by state and the type of service being delivered. Minors also do not have the same legal rights to confidentiality in some instances because parents/guardians may have access to minors' records.

Even when parental/guardian consent is needed for treatment, social workers should provide explanations to minors of all elements required in a consent procedure, using language that can easily be understood. Social workers should also seek the minor's assent or willingness to participate.

During the problem-solving process, social workers treating minors must make clear to them all the limits to their self-determination imposed by legal, financial, and other constraints.

Within our society, minors do not have the same rights as adults. Emancipation is a legal process that ends the rights and responsibilities of parents or guardians over minor children. However, there can be either a partial or complete emancipation. Emancipation involves decision-making authority. Upon achieving emancipation, the minor assumes the rights, privileges, and duties of adulthood before actually reaching the "age of majority" (adulthood). An emancipated minor can enter into a contract, sue others, make health care decisions, and so on. However, the emancipated minor still has to follow other laws and still cannot get a driver's license or drink alcohol prior to the legal age to do so.

All states have laws dealing with the emancipation of minors; that is, laws that specify when and under what conditions children can become independent of their parents or guardians for important legal purposes. Approximately half of the states regulate emancipation by statutes specifically designed for that purpose. These statutes set forth the conditions required or the procedures for seeking emancipation. Statutes vary considerably from state to state, but most states allow for the possibility of court-reviewed emancipation. The age at which minors can apply for or petition for emancipation varies between states.

Under normal circumstances, a minor is presumed to become emancipated from his or her parents upon reaching the age of majority. In most states, the age of majority is 18.

TECHNIQUES FOR PROTECTING AND ENHANCING CLIENT/ CLIENT SYSTEM SELF-DETERMINATION

Social workers respect and promote the right of clients to self-determination and assist clients in their efforts to identify and clarify their goals. Social workers may limit clients' right to self-determination when, in social workers' professional judgment, clients' actions or potential actions pose serious, foreseeable, and imminent risk to themselves or others (*NASW Code of Ethics, 2008–1.02 Self-Determination*).

THE CLIENT'S/CLIENT SYSTEM'S RIGHT TO REFUSE SERVICES (E.G., MEDICATION, MEDICAL TREATMENT, COUNSELING, PLACEMENT, ETC.)

Social workers should provide services to clients only in the context of a professional relationship based, when appropriate, on valid informed consent. Social workers should use clear and understandable language to inform clients of the purpose of the services, risks related to the services, limits to services because of the requirements of a third-party payer, relevant costs, reasonable alternatives, clients' right to refuse or withdraw consent, and the time frame covered by the consent. Social workers should provide clients with an opportunity to ask questions (*NASW Code of Ethics, 2008–1.03 Informed Consent*).

In instances when clients are receiving services involuntarily, social workers should provide information about the nature and extent of services and about the extent of clients' right to refuse service (*NASW Code of Ethics, 2008–1.03 Informed Consent*).

THE DYNAMICS OF POWER AND TRANSPARENCY IN THE SOCIAL WORKER–CLIENT/CLIENT SYSTEM RELATIONSHIP

Social workers have power and privileges associated with their roles, titles, and education. Being conscious of these privileges is critical because there is a responsibility to challenge hierarchical assumptions and power dynamics inherent in social worker–client relationships. Social workers should use egalitarian and collaborative approaches that give clients choices, decision-making power, and opportunities for honest feedback.

If social workers are transparent and honest about their positions of privilege, they help to undercut the power differentials. Transparency about the process and intent of social work interventions is essential. Role expectations should be discussed and power differences should be acknowledged.

Transparency and power are linked. If clients are not informed about what is going to occur in each stage of the problem-solving process and do not understand the theoretical models which help explain their situations, they cannot be full participants in the change process. Thus, transparency or the provision of all available information is the underpinning of the therapeutic relationship. If social workers deliberately withhold observations or knowledge from clients, they are reinforcing the power differential which inherently exists and disempowering clients. This is not helpful to clients or in accordance with the values of social work practice.

PROFESSIONAL BOUNDARIES IN THE SOCIAL WORKER–CLIENT/ CLIENT SYSTEM RELATIONSHIP (E.G., POWER DIFFERENCES, CONFLICTS OF INTEREST, ETC.)

Many standards speak to the professional boundaries that social workers should maintain with clients. These include those related to sexual relationships, physical contact, and sexual harassment.

The standards that govern social work practice address the use of physical contact with clients. Setting clear, appropriate, and sensitive boundaries that govern physical contact are essential for professional practice (*NASW Code of Ethics, 2008–1.10 Physical Contact*). Social workers should not engage in physical contact with clients when there is a possibility of psychological harm to a client as a result of the contact (such as cradling or caressing clients).

Physical contact or other activities of a sexual nature with clients are clearly not allowed by social workers.

Social workers should under no circumstances engage in sexual activities or sexual contact with current clients, whether such contact is consensual or forced (*NASW Code of Ethics, 2008–1.09 Sexual Relationships*).

Social workers should not engage in sexual activities or sexual contact with clients' relatives or other individuals with whom clients maintain a close personal relationship when there is a risk of exploitation or potential harm to a client. Sexual activity or sexual contact with clients' relatives or other individuals with whom clients maintain a personal relationship has the potential to be harmful to a client and may make it difficult for a social worker and client to maintain appropriate professional boundaries. Social workers—not their clients, their clients' relatives, or other individuals with whom a client maintains a personal relationship—assume the full burden for setting clear, appropriate, and culturally sensitive boundaries (*NASW Code of Ethics, 2008–1.09 Sexual Relationships*).

Social workers should not engage in sexual activities or sexual contact with former clients because of the potential for harm to a client. If social workers engage in conduct contrary to this prohibition or claim that an exception to this prohibition is warranted because of extraordinary circumstances, it is social workers—not their clients—who assume the full burden of demonstrating that the former client has not been exploited, coerced, or manipulated, intentionally or unintentionally (*NASW Code of Ethics, 2008–1.09 Sexual Relationships*).

Social workers should not provide clinical services to individuals with whom they have had a prior sexual relationship. Providing clinical services to a former sexual partner has the potential to be harmful to the individual and is likely to make it difficult for a social worker and individual to maintain appropriate professional boundaries (*NASW Code of Ethics, 2008–1.09 Sexual Relationships*).

In addition, social workers should not sexually harass clients, including sexual advances, sexual solicitation, requests for sexual favors, and other verbal or physical conduct of a sexual nature (*NASW Code of Ethics, 2008–1.11 Sexual Harassment*).

ETHICAL ISSUES RELATED TO DUAL RELATIONSHIPS

Social workers must ensure that they do not engage in dual or multiple relationships that may impact on the treatment of clients. The standards related to this area provide guidelines that can assist social workers if such relationships emerge (*NASW Code of Ethics, 2008—1.06 Conflicts of Interest*).

Social workers should be alert to and avoid conflicts of interest that interfere with the exercise of professional discretion and impartial judgment. Social workers should inform clients when a real or potential conflict of interest arises and take reasonable steps to resolve the issue in a manner that makes clients' interests primary and protects clients' interests to the greatest extent possible. In some cases, protecting clients' interests may require termination of the professional relationship with proper referral of clients (*NASW Code of Ethics, 2008—1.06 Conflicts of Interest*).

Social workers should not take unfair advantage of any professional relationship or exploit others to further their personal, religious, political, or business interests (*NASW Code of Ethics, 2008—1.06 Conflicts of Interest*).

Social workers should not engage in dual or multiple relationships with clients or former clients in which there is a risk of exploitation or potential harm to a client. In instances when dual or multiple relationships are unavoidable, social workers should take steps to protect clients and are responsible for setting clear, appropriate, and culturally sensitive boundaries. Dual or multiple relationships occur when social workers relate to clients in more than one relationship, whether professional, social, or business. Dual or multiple relationships can occur simultaneously or consecutively (*NASW Code of Ethics, 2008—1.06 Conflicts of Interest*).

When social workers provide services to two or more people who have a relationship with each other (e.g., couples, family members), social workers should clarify with all parties which individuals will be considered clients and the nature of social workers' professional obligations to the various individuals who are receiving services. Social workers who anticipate a conflict of interest among the individuals receiving services or who anticipate having to perform in potentially conflicting roles (e.g., when a social worker is asked to testify in a child custody dispute or divorce proceedings involving clients) should clarify their role with the parties involved and take appropriate action to minimize any conflict of interest (*NASW Code of Ethics, 2008—1.06 Conflicts of Interest*).

In addition, social workers engaged in evaluation or research should be alert to and avoid conflicts of interest and dual relationships with participants, should inform participants when a real or potential conflict of interest arises, and should take steps to resolve the issue in a manner that makes participants' interests primary (*NASW Code of Ethics, 2008—5.02 Evaluation and Research*).

LEGAL AND/OR ETHICAL ISSUES REGARDING MANDATORY REPORTING (E.G., ABUSE, THREAT OF HARM, IMPAIRED PROFESSIONALS, ETC.)

Social workers are required to disclose confidential information, sometimes against a client's wishes, to comply with mandatory reporting laws. Laws not only require social workers to report suspected cases of abuse and neglect, but there can be varying levels of civil and criminal liability for failing to do so.

This mandate causes ethical issues for social workers who have a commitment to their clients' interests as well as a responsibility to the larger society.

The majority of all reports of abuse and/or neglect came from professionals including medical personnel, law enforcement agents, educators, lawyers, and social workers.

Social workers who have direct knowledge of a social work colleague's impairment that is due to personal problems, psychosocial distress, substance abuse, or mental health difficulties and that interferes with practice effectiveness should consult with that colleague when feasible and assist the colleague in taking remedial action. Social workers who believe that a social work colleague's impairment interferes with practice effectiveness and that the colleague has not taken adequate steps to address the impairment should take action through appropriate channels established by employers, agencies, NASW, licensing and regulatory bodies, and other professional organizations (*NASW Code of Ethics, 2008–2.09 Impairment of Colleagues*).

LEGAL AND/OR ETHICAL ISSUES REGARDING DOCUMENTATION

In addition to maintaining confidentiality of client records, there are many other obligations related to documentation that social workers must consider in order to follow legal and/or ethical standards.

It is important to document the purpose, goals, plans, services, interventions, and referrals offered and provided to clients. Assessments, evaluations, recommendations, and circumstances of termination should also be documented in the case record. Consultations with supervisors and other professionals and rationale for case-related decisions should be documented as well.

Case records should include informed consent and release of information documents. All information relevant to client contact should be stated in clear, accurate terms. False, inaccurate, or misleading information in a client record is unethical and may be potentially harmful to clients and pose a liability risk to social workers. It is unethical to alter case notes after the fact. If necessary, social workers should add new notes with current dates indicating that, in review, past entries were found to be inaccurately documented and correction of those inaccuracies should be clearly stated.

In an effort to ensure continuity of service, it is imperative that client contact be documented in a timely, thorough, and accurate manner. Timely documentation is required for optimal service continuity when clients are transferred from one staff member to another in an agency or when clients are referred out of the agency to collaborating agencies. In addition, accurate and timely records are required by insurers, funding agencies, and so on. Lastly, documentation of significant aspects of client contact is also critical to protecting social workers in the event of lawsuits or ethics' complaints.

Client contact documentation should include social history, assessment, treatment plans, intervention strategies, dates and times of contacts, methods of evaluation of progress, reasons for termination, documentation of informed consent and release of information signatures, contacts with all third parties, consultation with collaborating professionals, explanation of social worker's reasoning regarding decisions, recommendations, interventions, and referrals and documentation of any critical incidents. Documentation should be completed as soon as possible after contact so as to ensure accuracy and to maintain up-to-date information in the record in the event of an emergency or the social workers' absence or incapacitation that would require another professional to intervene.

Social workers should only include relevant information that is directly related to client issues for the purpose of service provided. Case records should not include subjective or speculative observation, or any extraneous and irrelevant information.

Social workers must be familiar with legal and ethical protections available for clients—including keeping psychotherapy notes in locations which are secure, but separate from clients' files to provide additional confidentiality protections.

LEGAL AND/OR ETHICAL ISSUES REGARDING TERMINATION

Social workers should terminate services to clients and professional relationships with them when such services and relationships are no longer required or no longer serve client needs or interests (*NASW Code of Ethics, 2008–1.16 Termination of Services*).

Social workers should take reasonable steps to avoid abandoning clients who are still in need of services. Social workers should withdraw services precipitously only under unusual circumstances, giving careful consideration to all factors in the situation and taking care to minimize possible adverse effects. Social workers should assist in making appropriate arrangements for continuation of services when necessary (*NASW Code of Ethics, 2008–1.16 Termination of Services*).

Social workers in fee-for-service settings may terminate services to clients who are not paying an overdue balance if the financial contractual arrangements have been made clear to a client, if a client does not pose an imminent danger to self or others, and if the clinical and other consequences of the current nonpayment have been addressed and discussed with a client (*NASW Code of Ethics, 2008–1.16 Termination of Services*).

Social workers should not terminate services to pursue a social, financial, or sexual relationship with a client (*NASW Code of Ethics, 2008–1.16 Termination of Services*).

Social workers who anticipate the termination or interruption of services to clients should notify clients promptly and seek the transfer, referral, or continuation of services in relation to client needs and preferences (*NASW Code of Ethics, 2008–1.16 Termination of Services*).

Social workers who are leaving an employment setting should inform clients of appropriate options for the continuation of services and of the benefits and risks of the options (*NASW Code of Ethics, 2008–1.16 Termination of Services*).

It is unethical to continue to treat clients when services are no longer needed or in their best interests.

Another standard also relevant to termination of services mandates that social workers should make reasonable efforts to ensure continuity of services in the event that services are interrupted by factors such as unavailability, relocation, illness, disability, or death (*NASW Code of Ethics, 2008–1.15 Interruption of Services*).

LEGAL AND/OR ETHICAL ISSUES RELATED TO DEATH AND DYING

There are many legal and/or ethical issues related to death and dying. Some legal issues involved with dying include, but are not limited to, clients' right to have informed consent to receive or refuse treatment, advance directives, and establishing living wills. Treating professionals, by law, must give clients the opportunity for informed consent. It involves explaining the options for treatment, the possible benefits as well as risks for each treatment, and any recommendations, with rationales, for one treatment over another. Furthermore, clients must know that they have the right to choose whatever treatment they want or to choose to refuse treatment. Particularly when discussing chronic or terminal illness, conditions over which there is little control over the ultimate outcome of care provided, having clients feel as much control over their treatment options as possible is of great importance.

Clients can give written directions, called advance directives, about the type of care they do and do not want to receive when dying. Advance directives are legal written agreements that will be honored in the future when people can no longer communicate their wishes. For example, advance directives can prohibit resuscitation (the act of trying to revive a person whose heart has stopped) or tube feeding, if clients wish. Advance directives may be in the form of living wills, which express clients' preferences for medical care; a durable power of attorney, in which clients designate other people to make health care decisions; or both.

Clients whose death may occur soon should also have Physician Orders for Life-Sustaining Treatment (POLST) documents. These documents are written doctors' orders that reflect preferences for medical care (particularly whether to receive care or not). The documents are kept in clients' medical records and in the home and are used to direct emergency medical personnel in following the clients' preferences. For example, these documents may contain the doctors' orders as to whether people should receive cardiopulmonary resuscitation (CPR), transportation to hospitals, or aggressive treatments (such as blood transfusions or chemotherapy) to relieve symptoms even if death is inevitable.

Although very few people actually take any steps toward causing their own death, many clients who are dying at least consider suicide. Discussing suicide may help sort out the issues and often correct certain problems that prompted consideration of suicide. Pain medicine can be prescribed if clients are uncomfortable and spiritual guidance can help clients find meaning in the remainder of their lives. Making decisions to forgo life-sustaining treatment, forgo food and fluids when near death, or take many drugs or large doses of drugs to relieve symptoms is not considered suicide. Several states have passed laws which allow those who are terminally ill to receive lethal combinations of drugs to take when they decide to die.

RESEARCH ETHICS (E.G., INSTITUTIONAL REVIEW BOARDS, USE OF HUMAN SUBJECTS, INFORMED CONSENT)

Social workers have an ethical mandate to monitor and evaluate policies, the implementation of programs, and practice interventions. They also must promote and facilitate evaluation and research to contribute to the development of knowledge. In addition to doing research themselves, social workers must keep current with emerging knowledge relevant to social work and fully use evaluation and research evidence in their professional practice.

When doing research and evaluation, social workers must consider possible consequences and should follow guidelines developed for the protection of evaluation and research participants. Social workers must protect participants from unwarranted physical or mental distress, harm, danger, or deprivation (*NASW Code of Ethics, 2008—5.02 Evaluation and Research*). Appropriate institutional review boards should be consulted.

For example, social workers engaged in evaluation or research should obtain voluntary and written informed consent from participants, when appropriate, without any implied or actual deprivation or penalty for refusal to participate or without undue inducement to participate. Informed consent should include information about the nature, extent, and duration of the participation requested and disclosure of the risks and benefits of participation in the research (*NASW Code of Ethics, 2008—5.02 Evaluation and Research*). When evaluation or research participants are incapable of giving informed consent, social workers should provide an appropriate explanation to the participants, obtain the participants' assent to the extent they are able, and obtain written consent from an appropriate proxy (*NASW Code of Ethics, 2008—5.02 Evaluation and Research*).

Social workers should never design or conduct evaluation or research that does not use consent procedures, such as certain forms of naturalistic observation and archival research, unless rigorous and responsible review of the research has found it to be justified because of its prospective scientific, educational, or applied value and unless equally effective alternative procedures that do not involve waiver of consent are not feasible (*NASW Code of Ethics, 2008—5.02 Evaluation and Research*).

Social workers should inform participants of their right to withdraw from evaluation and research at any time without penalty (*NASW Code of Ethics, 2008—5.02 Evaluation and Research*).

Social workers should take appropriate steps to ensure that participants in evaluation and research have access to appropriate supportive services (*NASW Code of Ethics, 2008—5.02 Evaluation and Research*).

Social workers engaged in evaluation or research should ensure the anonymity or confidentiality of participants and of the data obtained from them. Social workers should inform participants of any limits of confidentiality, the measures that will be taken to ensure confidentiality, and when any records containing research data will be destroyed (*NASW Code of Ethics, 2008—5.02 Evaluation and Research*).

Social workers engaged in evaluation or research should be alert to and avoid conflicts of interest and dual relationships with participants, should inform participants when a real or potential conflict of interest arises, and should take steps to resolve the issue in a manner that makes participants' interests primary (*NASW Code of Ethics, 2008—5.02 Evaluation and Research*).

ETHICAL ISSUES IN SUPERVISION AND MANAGEMENT

Social workers must follow all ethical standards when providing and receiving supervision, as well as engaging in management tasks. These include, but are not limited to, those regarding commitment to clients, self-determination, informed consent, competence, cultural competence and social diversity, conflicts of interest, privacy and confidentiality, access to records, sexual relationships, physical contact, sexual harassment, derogatory language, payments, clients who lack decision-making capacity, and interruption or termination of services.

Social workers who provide supervision should have the necessary knowledge and skill to supervise or consult appropriately, and they should do so only within their areas of competence. They should also evaluate supervisees' performance in a manner that is fair and respectful (*NASW Code of Ethics, 2008–3.01 Supervision and Consultation*). Social workers who are in managerial roles should take reasonable steps to ensure that adequate agency resources are available to provide appropriate staff supervision (*NASW Code of Ethics, 2008–3.07 Administration*).

Social workers who provide supervision are responsible for setting clear, appropriate, and culturally sensitive boundaries. They should not engage in any dual or multiple relationships with supervisees when there is a risk of exploitation of or potential harm to the supervisee (*NASW Code of Ethics, 2008–3.01 Supervision and Consultation*).

Social workers in managerial roles should advocate within and outside their agencies for adequate resources to meet clients' needs and ensure resource allocation procedures are open, fair, and nondiscriminatory. Social work managers should ensure that working environments are consistent with the *NASW Code of Ethics* and eliminate conditions which are not (*NASW Code of Ethics, 2008–3.07 Administration*).

Sometimes in practice, ethical issues can arise related to the payment of services. These standards indicate what rules social workers should follow in these situations.

When setting fees, social workers should ensure that the fees are fair, reasonable, and commensurate with the services performed. Consideration should be given to clients' ability to pay (*NASW Code of Ethics, 2008–1.13 Payment for Services*).

Social workers should avoid accepting goods or services from clients as payment for professional services. Bartering arrangements, particularly involving services, create the potential for conflicts of interest, exploitation, and inappropriate boundaries in social workers' relationships with clients. Social workers should explore and may participate in bartering only in very limited circumstances when it can be demonstrated that such arrangements are an accepted practice among professionals in the local community, considered to be essential for the provision of services, negotiated without coercion, and entered into at a client's initiative and with a client's informed consent. Social workers who accept goods or services from clients as payment for professional services assume the full burden of demonstrating that this arrangement will not be detrimental to a client or the professional relationship (*NASW Code of Ethics, 2008–1.13 Payment for Services*).

Social workers should not solicit a private fee or other remuneration for providing services to clients who are entitled to such available services through social workers' employers or agencies (*NASW Code of Ethics, 2008–1.13 Payment for Services*).

Social workers should obtain information on procedures for using insurance coverage when a client wants to use an employee benefit package for behavioral health services.

METHODS TO CREATE, IMPLEMENT, AND EVALUATE POLICIES AND PROCEDURES FOR SOCIAL WORKER SAFETY

Social workers provide services in increasingly complex, dynamic social environments with many client populations. The number and variety of people to whom social workers provide services and the variety of settings in which these services are provided contribute to an increasingly unpredictable, and often unsafe, environment for social work practice. Social workers have been the targets of verbal and physical assaults in agencies, as well as during field visits with clients. Tragically, some social workers have also been permanently injured or have lost their lives.

Most clients and families that social workers serve do not present threats or pose danger. In cases where threats are present, most employers address these issues appropriately. There are, however, social work settings where social workers face increased risks of violence.

Social workers have the right to work in safe environments and to advocate for safe working conditions. Social workers who report concerns regarding their personal safety, or who request assistance in assuring their safety, should not fear retaliation, blame, or questioning of their competency from their supervisors or colleagues. Social workers should routinely practice universal safety precautions in their work. Violence occurs in every economic, social, gender, and racial group. To avoid stereotyping particular groups of people and to promote safety, social workers should practice safety assessment and risk reduction with all clients and in all settings. A thorough understanding of the risk factors associated with elevated risk for violence can inform safety assessments. Social workers should also be aware of the potential that their personal information on the Internet, particularly social networking sites, can be accessed by anyone. Universal safety precautions also include the establishment of safety plans as a matter of routine planning. The adoption of universal safety precautions should not preclude agencies from establishing particular safeguards when social workers are asked to perform dangerous tasks. In those situations, agencies should establish specific policies to reduce the risk of harm.

Confidentiality

12

THE PRINCIPLES AND PROCESSES OF OBTAINING INFORMED CONSENT

In instances when clients are not literate or have difficulty understanding the primary language used in the practice setting, social workers should take steps to ensure clients' comprehension. This may include providing clients with a detailed verbal explanation or arranging for a qualified interpreter or translator whenever possible (*NASW Code of Ethics, 2008–1.03 Informed Consent*).

In instances when clients lack the capacity to provide informed consent, social workers should protect clients' interests by seeking permission from an appropriate third party, informing clients consistent with clients' level of understanding. In such instances, social workers should seek to ensure that the third party acts in a manner consistent with the clients' wishes and interests. Social workers should take reasonable steps to enhance such clients' ability to give informed consent (*NASW Code of Ethics, 2008–1.03 Informed Consent*).

Social workers who provide services via electronic media (such as computer, telephone, radio, and television) should inform recipients of the limitations and risks associated with such services (*NASW Code of Ethics, 2008–1.03 Informed Consent*).

Social workers should obtain clients' informed consent before audiotaping or videotaping clients or permitting observation of services to clients by a third party (*NASW Code of Ethics, 2008–1.03 Informed Consent*).

When social workers act on behalf of clients who lack the capacity to make informed decisions, social workers should take reasonable steps to safeguard the interests and rights of those clients (*NASW Code of Ethics, 2008–1.14 Clients Who Lack Decision-Making Capacity*).

In order to obtain informed consent, social workers must use clear and understandable language related to service purpose, risks, limits due to third-party payers, time frame, and right of refusal or withdrawal. If the client lacks capacity or is a minor, informed **consent** must be obtained by a responsible third party and **assent** must be obtained from the client.

THE USE OF CLIENT/CLIENT SYSTEM RECORDS

Social workers should provide clients with reasonable access to their records. Social workers who are concerned that clients' access to their records could cause serious misunderstanding or harm to a client should provide assistance in interpreting the records and consultation with a client regarding the records. **Social workers should limit clients' access to their records, or portions of their records, only in exceptional circumstances when there is compelling evidence that such access would cause serious harm to a client.** Both clients' requests and the rationale for withholding some or all of the record should be documented in clients' files (*NASW Code of Ethics, 2008–1.08 Access to Records*).

When providing clients with access to their records, social workers should take steps to protect the confidentiality of other individuals identified or discussed in such records.

The *NASW Code of Ethics* **states that a social worker should only solicit information essential for providing services (minimum necessary to achieve purpose).**

LEGAL AND/OR ETHICAL ISSUES REGARDING CONFIDENTIALITY, INCLUDING ELECTRONIC INFORMATION SECURITY

Social workers should respect clients' right to privacy. Social workers should not solicit private information from clients unless it is essential to providing services or conducting social work evaluation or research. Once private information is shared, standards of confidentiality apply (*NASW Code of Ethics, 2008–1.07 Privacy and Confidentiality*).

Social workers may disclose confidential information when appropriate with valid consent from a client or a person legally authorized to consent on behalf of a client (*NASW Code of Ethics, 2008–1.07 Privacy and Confidentiality*).

Social workers should protect the confidentiality of all information obtained in the course of professional service, except for compelling professional reasons. The general expectation that social workers will keep information confidential does not apply when disclosure is necessary to prevent serious, foreseeable, and imminent harm to a client or other identifiable person. In all instances, social workers should disclose the least amount of confidential information necessary to achieve the desired purpose; only information that is directly relevant to the purpose for which the disclosure is made should be revealed (*NASW Code of Ethics, 2008–1.07 Privacy and Confidentiality*).

Social workers should inform clients, to the extent possible, about the disclosure of confidential information and the potential consequences, when feasible, before the disclosure is made. This applies whether social workers disclose confidential information on the basis of a legal requirement or client consent (*NASW Code of Ethics, 2008–1.07 Privacy and Confidentiality*).

Social workers should discuss with clients and other interested parties the nature of confidentiality and limitations of clients' right to confidentiality. Social workers should review circumstances with clients where confidential information may be requested and where disclosure of confidential information may be legally required. This discussion should occur as soon as possible in a social worker–client relationship and as needed throughout the course of the relationship (*NASW Code of Ethics, 2008–1.07 Privacy and Confidentiality*).

When social workers provide counseling services to families, couples, or groups, social workers should seek agreement among the parties involved concerning each individual's right to confidentiality and obligation to preserve the confidentiality of information shared by others. Social workers should inform participants in family, couples, or group counseling that social workers cannot guarantee that all participants will honor such agreements (*NASW Code of Ethics, 2008–1.07 Privacy and Confidentiality*).

Social workers should inform clients involved in family, couples, marital, or group counseling of a social worker's, employer's, and agency's policy concerning a social worker's disclosure of confidential information among the parties involved in the counseling (*NASW Code of Ethics, 2008–1.07 Privacy and Confidentiality*).

Social workers should not disclose confidential information to third-party payers unless clients have authorized such disclosure (*NASW Code of Ethics, 2008–1.07 Privacy and Confidentiality*).

Social workers should not discuss confidential information in any setting unless privacy can be ensured. Social workers should not discuss confidential information in public or semipublic areas such as hallways, waiting rooms, elevators, and restaurants (*NASW Code of Ethics, 2008–1.07 Privacy and Confidentiality*).

Social workers should protect the confidentiality of clients during legal proceedings to the extent permitted by law. When a court of law or other legally authorized body orders social workers to disclose confidential or privileged information without a client's consent and such disclosure could cause harm to a client, social workers should request that the court withdraw the order or limit the order as narrowly as possible or maintain the records under seal, unavailable for public inspection (*NASW Code of Ethics, 2008–1.07 Privacy and Confidentiality*).

A subpoena and court order are not the same. When receiving a subpoena, a social worker should respond and claim privilege, but not turn over records unless the court issues a subsequent order to do so. As stated, when a social worker gets a court order, he or she should try to limit its scope and/or ask that the records be sealed.

Social workers should protect the confidentiality of clients when responding to requests from members of the media (*NASW Code of Ethics, 2008–1.07 Privacy and Confidentiality*).

Social workers should protect the confidentiality of clients' written and electronic records and other sensitive information. Social workers should take reasonable steps to ensure that clients' records are stored in a secure location and that clients' records are not available to others who are not authorized to have access (*NASW Code of Ethics, 2008–1.07 Privacy and Confidentiality*).

Social workers should take precautions to ensure and maintain the confidentiality of information transmitted to other parties through the use of computers, electronic mail, facsimile machines, telephones and telephone answering machines, and other electronic or computer technology. Disclosure of identifying information should be avoided whenever possible (*NASW Code of Ethics, 2008–1.07 Privacy and Confidentiality*).

Social workers should transfer or dispose of clients' records in a manner that protects clients' confidentiality and is consistent with state statutes governing records and social work licensure (*NASW Code of Ethics, 2008–1.07 Privacy and Confidentiality*).

Social workers should take reasonable precautions to protect client confidentiality in the event of a social worker's termination of practice, incapacitation, or death (*NASW Code of Ethics, 2008–1.07 Privacy and Confidentiality*).

Social workers should not disclose identifying information when discussing clients for teaching or training purposes unless a client has consented to disclosure of confidential information (*NASW Code of Ethics, 2008–1.07 Privacy and Confidentiality*).

Social workers should not disclose identifying information when discussing clients with consultants unless a client has consented to disclosure of confidential information or there is a compelling need for such disclosure (*NASW Code of Ethics, 2008–1.07 Privacy and Confidentiality*).

Social workers should protect the confidentiality of deceased clients consistent with the preceding standards (*NASW Code of Ethics, 2008–1.07 Privacy and Confidentiality*).

If a client sues a social worker, a social worker has the right to defend himself/herself and may need to release client information as part of this defense. A social worker should limit this disclosure only to information required for defense.

Confidentiality of minor records can be challenging, especially if a parent wants access to them and/or consents to their release. Social workers must be knowledgeable about ethical standards and laws that relate to the protection and release of minor records. Parents may have access to these records depending upon the age of the minor and the type of treatment or setting. Social workers treating minors with parents who may have joint or limited custody must also be aware of the rights of all parties to access and/or consent to their release.

Professional Development and Use of Self

13

THE COMPONENTS OF THE SOCIAL WORKER–CLIENT/CLIENT SYSTEM RELATIONSHIP

A social worker–client relationship is an emotional or connecting bond. The relationship is the communication bridge whereby messages pass over the bridge with greater or lesser difficulty, depending on the nature of the emotional connection or alliance.

A positive relationship is an important tool of helping. Social workers must create a warm, accepting, trustworthy, and dependable relationship with clients.

In working with a client, a social worker must convey a sense of respect for a client's individuality, as well as his or her right and capacity for self-determination and for being fully involved in the helping process from beginning to end.

The most consistent factor associated with beneficial outcomes of a helping relationship is a positive relationship between a social worker and a client, but other factors, such as a social worker's competence and the motivation and involvement of a client, are also influential.

THE SOCIAL WORKER'S ROLE IN THE PROBLEM-SOLVING PROCESS

Social worker roles in the problem-solving process include consultant, advocate, case manager, catalyst, broker, mediator, facilitator, instructor, mobilizer, resource allocator, and so on.

Key social work practice roles include:

Advocate

In the advocate role, social workers champion the rights of others with the goal of empowering the client system being served. Social workers speak on behalf of clients when others will not listen or when clients are unable to do so. Social workers have a particular responsibility to advocate on behalf of those disempowered by society.

Broker

In the role of broker, social workers are responsible for identifying, locating, and linking client systems to needed resources in a timely fashion. Once client needs are assessed and potential services identified, the broker assists in choosing the most appropriate service option and assists in negotiating the terms of service delivery. Social workers are concerned with the quality, quantity, and accessibility of services.

Change Agent

A change agent participates as part of a group or organization seeking to improve or restructure some aspect of service provision. A change agent, working with others, uses the problem-solving model to identify the problem, solicit input, and plan for change. A change agent acts in a coordinated manner to achieve planned change at multiple levels that helps to shift the focus of institutional resources to meet identified goals.

Counselor

The role of the counselor focuses on improving social functioning. Social workers help client systems articulate their needs, clarify their problems, explore resolution strategies, and apply intervention strategies to develop and expand the capacities of client systems to deal with problems more effectively. A key function of this role is to empower clients by affirming their personal strengths and their capacities to deal with problems more effectively.

Mediator

When dispute resolution is needed in order to accomplish goals, social workers will carry out the role of mediator. Social workers intervene in disputes between parties to help them find compromises, reconcile differences, and reach mutually satisfying agreements. The mediator takes a neutral stance among the involved parties.

The primary role of social workers is to act as a resource—assuming various roles depending upon the nature of client problems.

THE CONCEPT OF ACCEPTANCE AND EMPATHY IN THE SOCIAL WORKER–CLIENT/CLIENT SYSTEM RELATIONSHIP

Empathic understanding involves being nonjudgmental, accepting, and genuine.

Empathic Communication

- Establishes rapport with clients—empathic communication is one means of bridging the gap between a social worker and client
- Starts where a client is and stays attuned to a client throughout the encounter (being perceptive to changes in frame of mind)
- Increases the level at which clients explore themselves and their problems
- Responds to a client's nonverbal messages (a social worker can observe body language and make explicit a client's feelings)
- Decreases defensiveness and engages a client in processing and testing new information
- Defuses anger that represents obstacles to progress

Empathic responding encourages more rational discussion and sets the stage for problem solving. For those clients who have learned to cope with feelings of helplessness and frustration by becoming angry and/or violent, an empathic response may be the first step in engaging in helping relationships.

THE IMPACT OF TRANSFERENCE AND COUNTERTRANSFERENCE IN THE SOCIAL WORKER–CLIENT/CLIENT SYSTEM RELATIONSHIP

Transference refers to redirection of a client's feelings for a significant person to a social worker. Transference was first described by Sigmund Freud, who acknowledged its importance for a better understanding of a client's feelings.

Transference is often manifested as an erotic attraction toward a social worker, but can be seen in many other forms such as rage, hatred, mistrust, parentification, extreme dependence, or even placing a social worker in an esteemed status.

When Freud initially encountered transference in his therapy with clients, he felt it was an obstacle to treatment success. But what he learned was that the analysis of the transference was actually the work that needed to be done. The focus in psychoanalysis is, in large part, a social worker and a client recognizing the transference relationship and exploring the relationship's meaning.

Since the transference between a client and a social worker happens on an unconscious level, a social worker doing psychoanalysis uses transference to reveal unresolved conflicts a client has with childhood figures.

Countertransference is defined as redirection of a social worker's feelings toward a client, or more generally as a social worker's emotional entanglement with a client. A social worker's recognition of his or her own countertransference is nearly as critical as understanding a client's transference. Not only does this help a social worker regulate his or her emotions in the therapeutic relationship, but it also gives a social worker valuable insight into what a client is attempting to elicit in him or her.

For example, a social worker who is sexually attracted to a client must understand this as countertransference, and look at how a client may be eliciting this reaction. Once it has been identified, a social worker can ask a client what his or her feelings are toward a social worker, and/or explore how they relate to unconscious motivations, desires, or fears.

SOCIAL WORKER SELF-CARE PRINCIPLES AND TECHNIQUES

Self-care is essential for social workers so that they can practice effectively and honor their professional and personal commitments. Self-care refers to activities and practices that are done on a regular basis to reduce stress and maintain and enhance short- and longer-term health and well-being.

Practicing self-care helps social workers:

- **Identify and manage the general challenges** that hard-working professionals face such as the potential for stress and burnout or interpersonal difficulties

- **Become aware of personal vulnerabilities** such as the potential for retraumatization (if trauma history exists), vicarious or secondary traumatization (if working with individuals who report their own traumatic experiences), and compassion fatigue (which can be developed from a combination of burnout and vicarious traumatization)

- **Achieve balance in life** by maintaining and enhancing the attention paid to different domains of life in a way that meets personal needs

Self-care is not simply about limiting or addressing professional stressors. It is also about **enhancing overall well-being**. There are common aims to almost all self-care efforts including:

- Taking care of physical and psychological health
- Managing and reducing stress
- Honoring emotional and spiritual needs
- Fostering and sustaining relationships
- Achieving an equilibrium between meeting personal needs and school/work demands

BURNOUT, SECONDARY TRAUMA, AND COMPASSION FATIGUE

Burnout, secondary trauma, and compassion fatigue have been used interchangeably to express adverse impacts that result from constantly working with those who are experiencing problems or trauma or are in crisis.

Burnout is a state of physical, emotional, psychological, and/or spiritual exhaustion. It can be manifested by cynicism or a lack of satisfaction in working with clients to resolve their problems. Burnout is characterized by emotional fatigue and feeling inadequate due to not being able to change clients' life circumstances. Many factors can contribute to burnout, including client, organizational, and/or contextual variables.

Secondary trauma relates to the behaviors and emotions that result from knowledge about traumatizing events experienced by clients and the stress resulting from helping or wanting to help them. Secondary trauma results from engaging in empathic relationships with clients who have had traumatic experiences and witnessing the effects of those experiences. The symptoms of secondary trauma mirror those experienced by the primary victim of trauma, including, but not limited to, insomnia, chronic irritability or angry outbursts, fatigue, difficulty concentrating, and/or avoidance.

Compassion fatigue is best defined as a syndrome consisting of a combination of the symptoms of secondary trauma and burnout. It usually represents the overall experience of emotional and physical fatigue that social workers can experience due to the prevalent use of empathy when treating clients who are distraught and experiencing emotional pain. Social workers also encounter bureaucratic hurdles that exacerbate agency stress and upset the balance between practice and administrative demands. Much like burnout, compassion fatigue tends to occur cumulatively over time, whereas secondary trauma may have a more immediate onset. Social workers may develop empathy or compassion fatigue as they repeatedly see little or no improvement in client situations. Social workers who treat victims of trauma can find that secondary trauma may contribute to overall compassion fatigue. However, social workers who do not treat those who have experienced trauma may experience compassion fatigue without experiencing secondary trauma.

In order to manage the effects of burnout and secondary trauma, and in an attempt to prevent compassion fatigue, social workers must engage in *self-care* activities which should include, but not be limited to, receiving support from mentors or peers, obtaining therapy, engaging in relaxation and personal endeavors that are nonprofessional activities, and balancing work demands with one's personal life.

THE COMPONENTS OF A SAFE AND POSITIVE WORK ENVIRONMENT

To practice effectively and ethically, social workers need a working environment that upholds ethical practice and is committed to standards and good quality services. A positive working environment is created where the values and principles of employers and social workers are consistent with each other and mutually reinforcing. There is substantial evidence that the most effective social work services are provided in situations where employers understand social work practice, respect their employees, and are committed to implementing professional values.

A framework for supporting good practice needs to take account of ethical principles and ensure effective induction, supervision, workload management, and continuing professional development.

The following are some elements which enable social workers to practice ethically:

- Written policies setting out standards of ethical practice provide clarity and protection for clients, social workers, and agencies. Social workers should never be required to do anything that would put at risk their ability to uphold such ethical standards, including policies on confidentiality, equal opportunities and risk management.

- Quality social work services draw on research and practice evidence. Policies should be informed by research and practice evidence.

- The public, including clients, should be regularly informed about these standards, policies, and procedures and provided with information about how to raise concerns or make complaints about standards of practice.

- People employed as social workers must be suitable to enter the workforce, hold appropriate recognized qualifications that entitles them to practice as social workers, provide references (including evidence that they are not a risk to clients), and demonstrate that they understand their roles and responsibilities, including their ethical duties.

- Dangerous, discriminatory, or exploitative behavior and practice must be dealt with promptly through the implementation of policies and procedures. Such policies should provide measures to prevent and minimize violence, making it clear to staff, social workers, and clients that violence, threats, or abusive behavior is not acceptable.

■ Social workers have a right for their health and occupational safety to be protected. Social workers frequently experience trauma or violence in their work and they are vulnerable to work-related stress and burnout due to the nature of their work.

■ The adoption and implementation of policies on workload management make a major contribution to the provision of quality services to clients. Workload practices must consider the basic tenets of social work intervention, including the centrality of human relationships, the need to manage risk and complexity, and the duty to highlight unmet need.

■ The physical working environment has an important part to play in the support of effective and ethical practice including, for example, the physical arrangements and procedures required for confidential interviewing and storage of confidential records.

■ Continuing professional development and further training enable social workers to strengthen and develop their skills and knowledge and ensure that agencies adapt to the changing needs of clients and changing organizational realities. Orientation and induction training provided to new employees and those changing jobs are essential, including the management of risk, making complex professional judgments, and the fulfillment of statutory obligations such as the protection of minors and vulnerable adults.

■ Good quality, regular social work supervision by people who have the necessary experience and qualifications in social work practice is an essential tool to ensure accountable and ethical practice. Research has confirmed that supervision is an important vehicle for supporting the management function in promoting creative and reflective practice, supporting staff resilience and well-being and continuous professional development.

■ Systematic reviews of services and practice, led by social workers who have experience of the field, should be held regularly. These activities identify needed support, training, and action when poor or unethical practice is identified.

■ Career development opportunities for social workers wishing to develop advanced practice skills need to be available. These not only meet the individual needs of social workers, but can also constitute an effective tool for retaining valuable practice knowledge and experience and for preventing high staff turnover and difficulties in recruitment that are typical challenges constantly being faced by social work services.

■ Rates of pay or fees for social work practice need to be comparable with similar professionals and recognize the skill and qualifications of social workers.

PROFESSIONAL OBJECTIVITY IN THE SOCIAL WORKER–CLIENT/ CLIENT SYSTEM RELATIONSHIP

Social worker communication should not be burdened with emotional investment; instead, social workers should be interested, genuinely concerned, and encouraging, while neither condemning nor praising.

The relationship between a social worker and a client must be productive, and must have certain characteristics. There must be mutual acceptance and trust. A client must feel he or she is understood and valued as a person, though his or her performance may be unsatisfactory. If a client feels judged, he or she will not speak freely, and his or her response will be to find ways to defend himself or herself and his or her acts.

A social worker accepts and understands a client's problems, recognizes the demands and the requirements of the situation, and assists a client to examine alternatives and potential consequences. A social worker does not tell a client what he or she should do. Only a client can and will decide, because he or she acts upon his or her feelings, insights, and/or understanding of himself or herself and the problem.

SELF-DISCLOSURE PRINCIPLES AND APPLICATIONS

The decision about whether to disclose personal information by a social worker often arises in practice because the social worker–client relationship involves the discussion of intimate topics. Some self-disclosure by a social worker may be harmless and even therapeutically useful as it can help clients connect during engagement and/or realize that they are not the only ones who have experienced similar problems.

However, some self-disclosure is exploitative, self-serving, and harmful to clients. Many boundary violations begin as a result of social workers discussing personal information with clients. Though not intended to be the start of friendships or more intimate relationships, self-disclosure by social workers, perhaps well meaning, can blur the boundaries between professional and personal relationships.

Sometimes social workers disclose personal information because they have experienced trauma or other problems which have not been adequately addressed and they are looking to connect with others in order to cope with their own challenges. Social workers may also self-disclose about problems because they think that clients can help them in some way, such as giving them legal advice if the clients are lawyers.

Sometimes clients learn personal information about social workers unexpectedly. For example, a social worker may run into a client at his or her children's activities. These events cannot be anticipated and provide personal information to a client about a social worker that he or she would prefer not to have been revealed.

Most therapeutic situations require no self-disclosure by a social worker. In fact, a client having information about a social worker's family, personal interests, and/or relationship status can be an indication of a potential boundary violation.

Prior to disclosing any information about themselves, social workers should engage in consultation or supervision about why such disclosure is being considered and why it is professionally justified in this instance. Only when it will clearly assist clients and there are no other methods for achieving the same outcome should it be contemplated. Better understanding by social workers about their own desire to self-disclose is necessary in order to prevent boundary crossings which are harmful to clients.

THE INFLUENCE OF THE SOCIAL WORKER'S OWN VALUES AND BELIEFS ON INTERDISCIPLINARY COLLABORATION

Social workers are increasingly recognized as beneficial members of interdisciplinary teams in addressing the complex needs of clients. A social worker may be on the team because he or she is a direct service provider (counselor, case manager), an administrator, and/or a consultant.

Interdisciplinary teams can compromise those from many professions including law, psychology, and education. When working collaboratively, social workers can work "hand-in-hand" or "side-by-side" with others. In the former, social workers and others work together on most issues, whereas in the latter, each discipline works separately to accomplish what needs to be done.

Often when working with others, there can be potential conflicts in both personal and professional values of the team members. In order to mitigate these conflicts, it is important to:

- Outline the parameters that will govern the functioning of the collaborative team, including frequency of contact, other forms of communication, delineation of responsibilities, and leadership positions
- Understand and define the roles of those who are collaborating
- Understand and articulate the professional values of each member
- Agree upon methods of decision making
- Determine means for resolving disagreements

The importance of role boundaries, role maintenance, and role clarity are essential in collaborative relationships. These issues should be openly discussed among team members, and obstacles to effective team functioning should be identified and addressed.

In all instances, it is the responsibility of a social worker to understand and reflect upon his or her own values, ensure that they do not interfere with the collaborative process, and that they are always aligned with ensuring outcomes in the best interest of a client. Areas of sensitivity that require self-reflection include beliefs about differing status among team members, unequal benefits for participation, different levels of personal and time commitments, insecurity about the value of the team approach, and/or lack of administrative support.

GOVERNANCE STRUCTURES

Governance concerns those structures, functions, processes, and customs that exist within an organization to ensure it operates in a way that achieves its objectives, and does so in an effective and transparent manner. It is a framework of accountability to clients, stakeholders, and the wider community, within which organizations make decisions and control their functions and resources to achieve their objectives.

Good governance adds value by improving the performance of an organization through more efficient management, more strategic and equitable resource allocation and service provision, and other improvements that lend themselves to improved outcomes and impacts.

Social workers should advocate within and outside their agencies for adequate resources to meet clients' needs and for resource allocation procedures that are open and fair (*NASW Code of Ethics, 2008—3.07 Administration*). When not all clients' needs can be met, an allocation procedure should be developed that is nondiscriminatory, appropriate, and consistent. Social workers should take reasonable steps to ensure that adequate agency or organizational resources are available to provide appropriate staff supervision and that the working environment for which they are responsible is consistent with and encourages compliance with the *NASW Code of Ethics (2008)*.

ACCREDITATION AND/OR LICENSING REQUIREMENTS

Administrative reviews, such as annual reviews from public and private social service organizations, are critical to the fulfillment of the social work mission. They provide accountability to the public about the number of people served, the services delivered, and how funds were allocated. They also may be used by social workers to document unmet needs that should be addressed.

Social workers may be required to engage in grant monitoring, evaluations, program inspections, and accreditation reviews. While each of these reviews serves a different purpose, they all require social workers to use critical thinking/analysis to help clients directly or indirectly.

TIME MANAGEMENT APPROACHES

Time management is planning and consciously controlling the amount of time spent on specific activities, especially to increase effectiveness, efficiency, or productivity. Though time management initially focused on business or work activities, it is now increasingly used to control personal activities as well.

Most time management approaches focus on creating conducive or effective environments, modifying behaviors, setting priorities, and/or reducing time spent on nonpriorities.

The approaches to time management have evolved. Initially, approaches consisted of checklists and notes to recognize the demands on time. These then evolved into calendars and appointment books that focused on looking ahead to anticipate future events. The third approach, often used today, examines efficiency with the focus on prioritizing, planning, controlling, and taking steps toward a goal.

The last approach requires the categorization of daily activities by importance and urgency. Those activities that are urgent and important can be stressful and require immediate action; those who deal with these exclusively will think they are just "putting out fires." Activities that are not urgent or important require little or no attention, and time spent on these activities will result in feelings of disengagement. Activities that are urgent but not important often take up a lot of attention but tend to yield little difference or progress. The last grouping—those things that are important but not urgent—are likely to be put aside yet are critical to personal fulfillment. Time management should include minimizing time spent on activities that are not important and ensuring those that are not urgent but are important, such as building relationships, recreation and leisure, and so on, are also prioritized.

MODELS OF SUPERVISION AND CONSULTATION (E.G., INDIVIDUAL, PEER, GROUP)

There are many and varied supervision models, each with its own benefits and limitations. In order for supervision to be effective, it is necessary to take into account both the needs of social workers and the requirements and constraints of organizations when considering the model to be utilized.

Individual supervision has traditionally been the cornerstone of professional skill development. Supervision can be provided in groups, peer-led or facilitated by professional leaders. Group and peer supervision, as well as intensive case consultation on a case-by-case basis, are useful and less costly additions to individual supervision, but they may be inadequate as substitutes for one-on-one support.

Individual

Benefits

- Full attention on the skill development, strengths, challenges, and professional enhancement of the individual supervisee
- More time and potentially safer environment in which to explore supervisee's interpersonal dynamics with clients and the impact of the work (e.g., countertransference issues, secondary trauma, compassion fatigue, burnout)
- Less exposure to poor practices of peers which could be inappropriately modeled or interfere with supervision process

Challenges

- Potential for supervisee to feel intimidated by the supervisor, with no one else present to observe, or break up the intensity of the one-to-one focus
- Costly and time consuming
- No input from others outside the dyad
- No opportunity for supervisee to compare self with others, or gain support from peers

Peer Group

Benefits

- Each group member can offer and receive wisdom, experience, and ideas (i.e., enjoy both "teacher" and "student" roles)
- Shared influence and responsibility regarding how the group is run
- Avoids chance of getting stuck with an unwanted supervisor
- Opportunities for personal growth via group dynamics
- Participants as equals encourages lateral help and peer support

Challenges

- Potential for unconscious designation of more experienced/skilled members as "de facto" supervisors
- Success is dependent upon how group members exercise their responsibilities

- Mutual trust, openness, and respect are essential
- Usually requires that groups remain closed, at least for a period of time
- Competition, defensiveness, and criticism between peers can occur
- Clinical case discussion frequency, depth, and intensity is limited by the time available and the number of members participating in the group

Facilitated Group

Benefits

- Learning occurs from others' practice examples and ways of working
- Self-confirmation occurs through giving feedback
- Opportunities for role play and other action techniques are present
- Less expensive and time consuming than individual supervision
- Opportunities for personal growth via group dynamics

Challenges

- Supervisor must be skilled in working systemically with groups and must be able to facilitate while also supervising (dual tasks)
- Supervisor's anxiety about his or her own competence may pose a barrier, as there is greater exposure of the supervisor's abilities and experience
- Less time for each supervisee, as the group must balance the needs of each member
- Group needs to have a high level of trust in order for supervisees to feel safe

THE SUPERVISEE'S ROLE IN SUPERVISION (E.G., IDENTIFYING LEARNING NEEDS, SELF-ASSESSMENT, PRIORITIZING, ETC.)

The short-term objectives of supervision are to increase a social worker's capacity to work more effectively, to provide a work context conducive to productivity, and to help a social worker take satisfaction in his or her work. The ultimate objective is to assure the delivery of the most effective and efficient client services.

Social workers who are administrators should take reasonable steps to ensure that adequate agency or organizational resources are available to provide appropriate staff supervision.

Competence is essential for ethical social work practice and social workers must be competent in the services that they are providing (*NASW Code of Ethics, 2008–1.04 Competence*). In order to be competent, they must keep abreast of new developments in the field and obtain supervision.

Social workers should provide services and represent themselves as competent only within the boundaries of their education, training, license, certification, consultation received, supervised experience, or other relevant professional experience (*NASW Code of Ethics, 2008–1.04 Competence*).

Social workers should provide services in substantive areas or use intervention techniques or approaches that are new to them only after engaging in appropriate study, training, consultation, and supervision from people who are competent in those interventions or techniques (*NASW Code of Ethics, 2008–1.04 Competence*).

When generally recognized standards do not exist with respect to an emerging area of practice, social workers should exercise careful judgment and take responsible steps (including appropriate education, research, training, consultation, and supervision) to ensure the competence of their work and to protect clients from harm (*NASW Code of Ethics, 2008–1.04 Competence*).

If a supervisor needs to talk with a social worker about a problem situation, he or she should meet privately with the social worker to discuss the matter.

THE IMPACT OF TRANSFERENCE AND COUNTERTRANSFERENCE WITHIN SUPERVISORY RELATIONSHIPS

Transference and countertransference within supervisory relationships can be a parallel process of what is occurring between a social worker and a client. The transference occurs when a social worker recreates, within a supervisory relationship, a presenting problem and emotions occurring in a therapeutic relationship. Countertransference occurs when a supervisor responds to a social worker in the same manner that a social worker responds to a client. Thus, a supervisory interaction replays, or is parallel with, a social worker–client interaction. In essence, the processes at work in the relationship between a social worker and a client are reflected in the relationship between a social worker and his or her supervisor.

Parallel process is an unconscious identification with a client and can be used as an important part of the supervisory process. Examining it will assist a social worker and his or her supervisor in identifying issues that exist in a therapeutic relationship and allow for techniques to resolve these issues to be identified and discussed.

PROFESSIONAL DEVELOPMENT ACTIVITIES TO IMPROVE PRACTICE AND MAINTAIN CURRENT PROFESSIONAL KNOWLEDGE (E.G., IN-SERVICE TRAINING, LICENSING REQUIREMENTS, REVIEWS OF LITERATURE, WORKSHOPS)

Professions enjoy a high social status, regard, and esteem conferred upon them by society. This high esteem arises primarily from the higher social function of their work, which is regarded as vital to society as a whole and, thus, special and valuable in nature. All professions involve technical, specialized, and highly skilled work, often referred to as "professional expertise." Training for this work involves obtaining degrees and professional qualifications (i.e., licensure) without which entry to the profession is barred. Training also requires regular updating of skills through continuing education.

Professional development refers to skills and knowledge attained for effective service delivery and career advancement. Professional development encompasses all types of learning opportunities, ranging from formal coursework and conferences to informal learning opportunities situated in practice. There are a variety of approaches to professional development, including consultation, coaching, communities of practice, mentoring, reflective supervision, and technical assistance.

Social workers often go through various stages of professional development, including:

1. Orientation and job induction

2. Autonomous worker

3. Member of a service team (independence to interdependence)

4. Development of specialization

5. Preparation to be mentor or supervisor

Practice Test

170-Question Practice Test

This practice test contains 170 questions, but remember that your score on the actual examination will be based on 150 questions because 20 items are being piloted. As you won't know which items will be scored and determine whether or not you pass, you will need to complete all 170 questions. Thus, this test has 170 questions so that you can gauge the length of time that it takes you to complete an equivalent number of questions. The questions in each domain or area are in random order on this practice test, as they are on the actual examination, and there is a similar distribution of questions from each section as will appear on your actual examination.

Human Development, Diversity,
and Behavior in the Environment

43 Questions

Assessment

49 Questions

Interventions With Clients/Client Systems

44 Questions

Professional Relationships, Values, and Ethics

34 Questions

The best way to use this practice test is as a mock examination, which means:

a. Take it AFTER you have completed your studying—do not memorize answers to these questions.

b. Do not apply the answers to these questions to the actual examination or you may miss subtle differences in each question that can distinguish the correct from the incorrect answer.

c. Take it in its entirety during a 4-hour block of time to show yourself that you can finish in the allotted time period for the examination.

d. Do not look up the answers until you are completely finished with the entire practice test, and do not worry if you get incorrect answers. Remember, this examination is not one in which you can expect to get all of the answers correct. **The number of questions that you will need to answer correctly generally varies from 93 to 106 correct of the 150 scored items**.

1. Social workers should refer clients to other professionals in all of the following instances EXCEPT when:

   A. Professionals' specialized knowledge or expertise is needed to meet the clients' needs.
   B. Social workers believe they are not being effective in addressing clients' concerns.
   C. Professionals believe that other modalities of treatment may be more effective to resolve clients' issues.
   D. Social workers are not making reasonable progress in addressing clients' problems.

2. A social worker is working with a second grade child who is having trouble staying in her seat in the classroom. The social worker, in conjunction with the teacher, indicates that the immediate objective is that the child "will remain seated after being reminded to do so by the teacher while in the classroom." The social worker's supervisor, after reviewing the objective, would judge it to be:

   A. Adequate as it addresses the target problem
   B. Inadequate as it puts too much responsibility on the teacher
   C. Adequate since the teacher was involved in the process
   D. Inadequate as it lacks some elements of a measurable objective

3. A social worker may limit a client's self-determination when the client's actions:

   A. Pose a serious and imminent risk to self or others according to the social worker's judgment
   B. Cause significant family dysfunction which threatens to impact on the psychological well-being of its members
   C. Result in legal action such as arrests, fines, and/or civil penalties
   D. Violate agency procedures and policies as established by the chief executive officer

4. During assessment, partialization can be used by a social worker to assist a client with all of the following EXCEPT:

   A. Recognizing the next action to take when intervening in a situation
   B. Helping to clarify the specific cause(s) of a problem
   C. Identifying issues that need immediate attention
   D. Distinguishing areas that require further inquiry

5. According to Erikson, which of the following is seen as the last stage in psychosocial development?

   A. Ego integrity versus despair
   B. Trust versus mistrust
   C. Intimacy versus isolation
   D. Autonomy versus shame and doubt

6. Psychological abuse is MOST often detected by:

   A. Confessions of perpetrators
   B. Information supplied by collateral contacts
   C. Behavioral characteristics of victims
   D. Bruises or marks left by comorbid physical mistreatment

7. A client shows a social worker a list of reasons why she should and should not leave her abusive husband. She says that she is preparing the list to see if the benefits are greater than the risks. The client is basing her decision on which of the following theories?

   A. Systems
   B. Functionalist
   C. Harm reduction
   D. Social exchange

8. Which of the following is TRUE about human trafficking?

   A. Human trafficking involves sexual exploitation.
   B. Victims of human trafficking are poor females.
   C. Human trafficking occurs in all countries except the United States.
   D. Human trafficking is not the same as human smuggling.

9. Role complementarity occurs when:

   A. An individual takes on a new role that is appreciated by another
   B. Two individuals act in an expected manner
   C. There is confusion in the role definition of an individual
   D. An individual successfully exits an existing role

10. A social worker needs to contact a client who has not shown up for services in many weeks. He calls the number provided, only to get a household answering machine. The social worker leaves a simple message including his name, his agency name, and his contact information. The social worker's actions were:

    A. Unethical because members of the household are now aware of the client's affiliation with the agency
    B. Ethical since the client provided the phone number upon intake
    C. Ethical as no details about the nature of the call were included in the message
    D. Unethical because the reason for the call should have been fully disclosed

11. Which is NOT a primary purpose of social work licensure?

    A. Create parity with other helping professions to ensure that social workers receive comparable compensation
    B. Identify standards for the safe professional practice of social work

C. Ensure social workers have the knowledge and skills to practice competently

D. Provide an avenue for investigating complaints and taking action to ensure continued safe and professional practice

12. Which of the following is NOT typically part of the sensorimotor stage of cognitive development?

    A. Actions are imitative in nature.

    B. Intentional actions begin to emerge.

    C. Difference between past, present, and future is learned.

    D. Primitive ability to manipulate objects is seen.

13. What is the MOST significant difference between a formative and summative evaluation?

    A. A summative evaluation is more scientifically rigorous than a formative evaluation.

    B. A formative evaluation examines processes while a summative evaluation is focused on outcomes.

    C. A summative evaluation examines processes while a formative evaluation is focused on outcomes.

    D. A formative evaluation is more scientifically rigorous than a summative evaluation.

14. When a social worker receives a subpoena, he or she must:

    A. Send the client his or her records so the client can respond to the subpoena

    B. Claim privilege and not release any information until court-ordered to do so

    C. Send the records immediately to the court in order to avoid being sanctioned

    D. Submit a written summary of services rendered to the court in lieu of sending the records

15. A client tells a social worker that he feels "alone" and does not think that anyone else is having the same problems that he is experiencing. In order to assist the client, it is BEST that the social worker:

    A. Ask the client to explain further what he means by feeling "alone"

    B. Determine whether the client is at risk for suicide and in need of hospitalization

    C. Refer the client to counseling for depression

    D. State that many people have encountered similar difficulties and that the social worker is there to help

16. A client who is going through a bitter divorce tells a social worker that she "does not know how this will ever turn out well." The social

worker, who is divorced, remembers when she also felt that way. To appropriately assist the client, the social worker should:

A. Discuss with the client how she envisions the client's life after the divorce without disclosing her own past

B. Speak candidly to the client about her own marital struggles so the client does not feel alone

C. Tell the client that she also felt that way when she was getting divorced in an effort to normalize the client's emotions

D. Make a referral to another social worker in the agency because the client's experiences are eliciting an emotional reaction in the social worker

17. Which of the following is NOT true about early childhood development?

A. Receptive communication skills usually develop at an earlier age than expressive language.

B. Play is important to cognitive, social, and physical development.

C. Behavioral outbursts can be signs of psychological disturbance.

D. Personality or temperament results from both biological and environmental factors.

18. Which of the following is TRUE about Do Not Resuscitate (DNR) orders?

A. They provide legal permission for euthanasia.

B. They must be done in conjunction with a durable power of attorney.

C. They do not allow any medications to be given.

D. They permit clients to refuse mechanical ventilation or artificial hydration.

19. An elderly client is being discharged from the hospital. She has memory loss and trouble performing activities of daily living, and therefore needs significant support. She would like to return home. In this situation, what should the social worker do FIRST?

A. Identify natural and other community supports that can assist her at home

B. Help to develop a long-term plan to meet her increasing care needs

C. Evaluate why she is failing to recognize the need for out-of-home care

D. Recommend that she visit an assisted living program to see if she might like it

20. A social worker receives a lot of background and collateral data on a client's presenting problem. However, in the assessment interview, the social worker asks the client extensively about the current situation. This questioning is MOST likely being done to:

A. Learn about the client's perception of the problem and impetus for seeking help

B. Determine if the client is aware of all the information that is contained in the records received

C. See if the client feels comfortable enough with the social worker to reveal all relevant information

D. Gather information that is missing from the files in order to generate a complete record of the situation

21. A teenager begins high school and is having behavioral problems in school. He has trouble following directions and keeping up with the academic demands placed upon him. A referral is made to a school social worker to assist. When identifying the problem, it is BEST for the social worker to:

A. Compare it with symptoms of disorders with childhood onset

B. Complete a drug and alcohol evaluation because the boy is at an age when substance use commonly begins

C. Determine whether the boy's behavior is a result of an undiagnosed learning disability

D. View the boy's behavior within an ecological framework—being caused by the "degree of fit" between the boy and his environment

22. Which of the following accurately defines "people first language"?

A. Ensuring that all public documents are appropriately translated into the first languages of citizens

B. Using proper names when speaking to others as a way of personalizing communication

C. Naming the person before a diagnosis, disability, or condition so as not to define him or her by this trait

D. Referring to the verbal and nonverbal communication of American Indians/Native Americans/Indigenous nations

23. A social worker is required by the court to provide summaries detailing compliance with mandated services. In order to appropriately release this information, the social worker should:

A. Show the client the summaries prior to sending them to the court

B. Get the client to provide written consent prior to sending

C. Submit the summaries directly to the court without showing them to the client because the court should decide if they are to be shared

D. Ask the court if this requirement can be waived in order to protect the client's confidentiality

24. Which of the following is NOT true about family functioning?

A. Families struggle against homeostasis in order to be healthy.

B. Each family is unique, with variations in communication styles, cultural practices, and values.

C. Families must fulfill a variety of functions in order for their members to grow and develop.

D. Families can accomplish the same goals through different paths, which is known as equifinality.

25. Negative entropy within a system is BEST described as:

    A. A steady state in which balance is achieved
    B. An exchange of energy and resources that promotes growth and transformation
    C. A closed system that is using up its energy and deteriorating
    D. A product of a system that can subsequently be used as an input

26. Which of the following in NOT an indicator that a client may be resistant or not ready to participate in services?

    A. False promising
    B. Discussing current, as opposed to past, problems
    C. Engaging in casual conversation
    D. Not keeping appointments for or showing up late to services

27. A school social worker has been informed that a student has been involved in an accident which has caused permanent physical disability. In order to BEST meet this student's needs, the social worker should be sure to assess the:

    A. Impacts on the student's psychological and/or social functioning
    B. Special physical accommodations required in school to facilitate maximum independence
    C. Need for physical therapy, given that the accident occurred early in the life course
    D. Mobility of both the arms and legs, given that physical limitations exist

28. Which of the following is TRUE about stereotypes?

    A. Negative stereotypes are harmful when perpetuated, but good stereotypes should be used to highlight strengths about groups of people.
    B. Stereotypes preserve social hierarchies and the interests of dominant groups.
    C. Stereotypes are based on data or factual information.
    D. Stereotypes do not change with the shifting interests and concerns of society.

29. A school social worker learns that a 10-year-old student has just been placed in foster care because physical abuse by her parents has been substantiated. The social worker has had many referrals for this student in recent weeks concerning incidents of bullying other children. This student's behavior is MOST likely a result of:

    A. Displacement
    B. Reaction formation
    C. Projection
    D. Incorporation

30. A social worker and her supervisor are meeting when a teenager comes into the office and wants "to talk." The teenager reports that she is "being tortured" at home and is the victim of emotional and physical abuse. The supervisor tells the social worker that this child made similar allegations several years ago and they were not substantiated by the child protection agency. The supervisor tells the social worker to "monitor" the situation and keep the supervisor informed if any subsequent allegations are made by the teenager. The social worker should:

   A. Follow the supervisor's direction and meet with the teenager regularly to see if subsequent allegations are made
   B. Report the allegations to the child protection agency immediately, informing both the teenager and the supervisor of the need to do so
   C. Anonymously report the allegations to the child protection agency after hours so that they are aware of the teenager's continued concerns
   D. Speak to the parents to try to determine why these allegations keep being made by the teenager

31. Which perspective of bonding is based on the belief that humans come into the world preprogrammed to form attachments because they help them survive by providing security and safety?

   A. Systems
   B. Learned behavioral
   C. Evolutionary
   D. Cognitive dissonance

32. Needle exchange programs for intravenous drug users are based on which of the following models of treatment?

   A. Harm reduction
   B. Social exchange
   C. Operant conditioning
   D. Aversion therapy

33. A social worker has been asked by the court to supply a family history and overview of current functional relationships in a client's life. In preparation of this document, the social worker will likely rely on which document contained in the client's file?

   A. Histogram
   B. Flowchart
   C. Venn diagram
   D. Genogram

34. A social worker sees in a client file that he is taking hydrocodone. The client is MOST likely taking this prescription for which of the following medical issues?

    A. Diabetes
    B. Physical injury
    C. High blood pressure
    D. Tardive dyskinesia

35. Pansexuality is defined as:

    A. Being attracted to members of the opposite gender, but only engaging in sexual activity with those of the same gender
    B. Being attracted to only members of the same gender throughout the life course
    C. Being attracted to others regardless of gender
    D. Choosing not to engage in sexual activity with either gender, regardless of attraction

36. What is the MOST common form of child maltreatment?

    A. Physical abuse
    B. Sexual abuse
    C. Neglect
    D. Psychological abuse

37. A social worker in a private adoption agency has been informed by her supervisor that a client is far behind in paying overdue balances and must be terminated. The client has received many reminders about these balances and was informed of the payment policies and consequences for nonpayment upon the onset of treatment. In order to appropriately deal with the situation, the social worker should:

    A. Continue to provide services with the understanding that the client will owe the agency the money and pay it after the adoption occurs
    B. Terminate the client unless the overdue balances are paid according to the policy
    C. Help the client identify loan programs and other methods for paying the outstanding amount
    D. Determine if the client can provide services in lieu of payment

38. A social worker receives a written letter from a client. Although the client does not state that she is depressed, the social worker is concerned that the "tone" of the letter and the underlying meaning of some of the content are consistent with feeling hopeless. The social worker is focusing on the:

    A. Latent content
    B. Asynchronous communication
    C. Manifest content
    D. Double bind messages

39. Which of the following is TRUE about child sexual abuse?

    A. It is a problem that is limited to certain cultural or socioeconomic groups.

    B. Victims are likely to have physical injuries of the genitals.

    C. Most child molestation is done by unknown perpetrators.

    D. Most children who are sexually victimized do not perpetrate against others.

40. When a social worker delivers services to a client from a different cultural background, what is MOST important to the delivery of effective services?

    A. The social worker has spoken to others from the client's cultural group in order to understand its customs.

    B. The social worker recognizes that strengths exist in all cultures.

    C. The social worker has educated himself or herself on the nature of social diversity and oppression.

    D. The social worker acknowledges how cultural differences between the client and herself or himself may impact on the problem-solving process.

41. A client who has been receiving case management services from a social worker stops coming to the agency abruptly. Several weeks later, the client comes to see the social worker and asks for a copy of her record. Although the social worker does not think that there is anything in the record that would be harmful to the client, he is concerned about the client's abrupt termination. The social worker should:

    A. Tell the client that the record will be provided once appropriate termination has occurred

    B. Refuse to provide a copy of the record to the client directly, but agree that it will be sent to a new service provider once selected

    C. Inform the client that the record is confidential and cannot be provided because it is needed for administrative purposes

    D. Provide a copy of the record to the client after including a summary of the recent interaction for its request

42. A foundation that funds an Alzheimer's support program is doing an audit to ensure that funds were spent appropriately. They ask to review client files as part of their evaluation. The social worker can allow such reviews to occur:

    A. Without client consent because the foundation funding is needed for services to continue

    B. Only after client consent has been obtained

C. Without client consent if clients are informed about the reviews after they occur

D. With written consent from the agency director

43. A social worker meets with a family whose 21-year-old daughter with significant developmental disabilities is leaving her educational entitlement and has been found unemployable at this time due to medical concerns. She has never had a job and financial assistance is needed to pay for her living expenses. She has no income or assets. Her parents are working and receive no public benefits. The daughter will MOST likely be eligible for which of the following?

A. Unemployment insurance
B. Workers' compensation
C. Social Security Disability
D. Supplemental Security Income

44. A social worker does not agree with a supervisor's directive. The social worker should:

A. Obtain feedback from colleagues to see if the social worker's assessment is valid
B. Speak to the supervisor about the concerns
C. Meet with the agency director to make him or her aware of the disagreement
D. Respect the supervisor's position and comply with the directive

45. Transference can BEST be defined as the:

A. Inability of a social worker to engage in appropriate boundaries with a client
B. Inability of a client to engage in appropriate boundaries with a social worker
C. Redirection of a client's feelings toward a social worker
D. Redirection of a social worker's feelings toward a client

46. Which of the following is NOT an advantage of working in an intradisciplinary group?

A. Mentorship opportunities
B. Groupthink
C. Peer consultation
D. Greater cohesion and consensus

47. Which of the following is NOT true related to culture?

A. It is critical not to overgeneralize cultural information or perpetuate stereotypical beliefs.
B. Most individuals are exposed to multiple cultures that impact on their identity formation.

    C. Culture is both learned and transmitted across generations.
    D. Culture is static, staying constant over time.

48. An agency social worker is asked by a supervisee if he knows any candidates for a job opening in the supervisee's program. The social worker's sister has recently graduated and is looking for employment. She is an outstanding student and a hard worker. The social worker should:

    A. Recommend her as he knows that she will be an outstanding employee
    B. Not recommend her, but tell his sister to send in her résumé to the supervisee
    C. Not recommend her and help the supervisee identify other sources for qualified candidates
    D. Tell the supervisee that he cannot recommend his sister as it would be a conflict, but will ask her for the names of friends who would be good candidates

49. Upon entering school for the first time, a boy has ongoing incidents of urinating in his pants. After having him examined by a doctor who states that there are no medical problems, a social worker should NEXT:

    A. Discuss options for addressing the behavior
    B. Engage in a discussion with the boy about his emotions related to starting school
    C. Explore the reasons for the behavior
    D. Suggest a behavioral program aimed at rewarding continence

50. When a client is receiving services involuntarily, a social worker must provide all of the following as part of the informed consent procedure EXCEPT:

    A. A copy of the court order
    B. The consequences for refusing service provision
    C. The frequency and duration of service delivery
    D. A description of the types of services to be provided

51. A client in her mid-20s tells a social worker that she feels like a failure. She does not have a boyfriend, has been unable to find a full-time job after graduating from college, and is living at home. During the assessment process, the social worker praises the client for facing her problems and asks her about her accomplishments and positive skills, rather than her deficits. The social worker's actions are rooted in a(n):

    A. Functionalist approach
    B. Ecological perspective
    C. Resiliency model of treatment
    D. Strengths-based approach

52. Which of the following is NOT an advantage of using an existing scale or instrument in the evaluation of social work practice?

    A. They have undergone reliability and validity testing.
    B. There are usually time and cost savings because they have already been developed.
    C. They are readily available for use.
    D. They have often been tested on a unique cultural group.

53. The service needs of a client should be primarily based on all of the following EXCEPT:

    A. Client's desires and motivations
    B. Results of the assessment process
    C. Prioritization of the client's basic and safety needs
    D. All services are available at the social worker's agency

54. A client is telling a social worker about her childhood. When asked about her relationship with her siblings, the client does not say anything for a long period of time. In this situation, the social worker should:

    A. Remain silent to allow the client time to reflect on the question
    B. Ask a question on another topic because it is obvious that the client does not want to discuss her sibling relationships
    C. Probe the client about the reason for the silence
    D. State that many children have problems with their siblings and urge the client to express any issues that existed

55. Which of the following is TRUE about the interplay of biological, psychological, social, and spiritual functioning of clients throughout their life course?

    A. Changes in physical abilities will likely impact on psychological, social, and spiritual functioning that will need to be addressed in order to assist clients effectively.
    B. Changes in physical functioning must be addressed before other life domains in order to ensure maximum independence.
    C. Spiritual functioning is constant and not influenced by biological, psychological, or social changes throughout the life course.
    D. There is a strong relationship between these areas of functioning during childhood and early adulthood, but the strength of these relationships gradually decreases thereafter.

56. A young man comes to see a social worker because he feels "lost" and would like the social worker to help with his problems. In order to best assist the client, the social worker should:

    A. Ask the client what he would like to see changed in his life
    B. Give the client some suggestions for addressing his problems

C. Refer the client for an evaluation for depression

D. Praise the client for coming to seek help

57. Which of the following is NOT true about age of majority?

   A. It is the age at which a client is recognized by law to be capable of managing his or her own affairs.

   B. It dictates when a client is legally responsible for his or her own actions.

   C. It is the same for every activity in every state.

   D. It usually indicates when parental legal responsibilities end.

58. What type of power is obtained by associating with others who have power?

   A. Coercive

   B. Legitimate

   C. Reward

   D. Referent

59. Which of the following is the MOST current *Diagnostic and Statistical Manual of Mental Disorders* used by social workers?

   A. *DSM-IV-TR*

   B. *DSM-IV*

   C. *DSM-6*

   D. *DSM-5*

60. A social worker is collecting information on dynamic risk factors when completing an assessment on a perpetrator of abuse. Which of the following characteristics will NOT be asked about in the interview?

   A. Current substance use

   B. Past history of violent behavior

   C. Access to weapons

   D. Living situation

61. The Personal Responsibility and Work Opportunity Reconciliation Act (PRWORA) created the Temporary Assistance for Needy Families (TANF) program. Which of the following was NOT one of the restructured elements of this program?

   A. A lifetime limit on the number of years that benefits could be paid out of federal funds was imposed.

   B. Strict work requirements to qualify for federal aid were mandated.

   C. States could set their own benefit levels.

   D. A block grant to the states, which removed much of the federal regulatory authority over the design of the program, replaced a matching grant.

62. When helping a supervisee to use empathic communication when interacting with clients, a social worker is MOST effective by:

    A. Engaging in role playing with the supervisee to provide feedback on verbal and nonverbal communication skills used
    B. Explaining to the supervisee why clients need social work services
    C. Helping the supervisee understand how service delivery is perceived from clients' perspectives
    D. Suggesting the supervisee keep a journal to record feelings that interfere with therapeutic alliances when working with clients

63. When a social worker is referred a client who is a different race or ethnicity from his or her own, the social worker should:

    A. Ask the client if he or she is comfortable working with the social worker given these differences
    B. Seek supervision and consultation to learn more about the client's race or ethnicity
    C. Acknowledge and recognize how the racial or ethnic differences between the social worker and client may impact on stages in the problem-solving process
    D. Refer the client to a social work colleague who shares the client's race or ethnicity

64. A client is having trouble at her job as her boss is asking her to do tasks that she does not feel qualified to do. The client has been afraid to say anything to her boss as she is worried about being fired. The BEST way for a social worker to help this client is to:

    A. Assist her with conducting a job search to locate other employment that is better suited to her qualifications
    B. Help her identify resources to enhance her skills in areas in which she does not feel qualified
    C. Explore with her why she feels inadequate to perform the requested tasks
    D. Engage in role playing with her to enhance her assertiveness skills

65. Which of the following communication styles is characterized by using criticism, blaming others, and having a low tolerance for frustration?

    A. Assertive
    B. Aggressive
    C. Passive
    D. Passive-aggressive

66. A client is reporting feeling very tired and having trouble getting out of bed. He has recently experienced a lot of stress at work. In order to best serve the client, a social worker should FIRST:

    A. Refer the client to a health care professional to rule out any medical causes for the lethargy

    B. Determine if the source of the stress could be coming from other changes in the client's life

    C. Begin teaching him techniques to deal with stress

    D. Explore with the client what issues at work may be causing the stress

67. Which of the following is the BEST definition of environmental justice?

    A. Environmental justice is the duty of those who are members of societal groups with greater access to economic rewards to ensure that the environments of those who do not share this privileged status are clean, free of crime, safe, and rich in natural resources.

    B. Environmental justice is the fair treatment and meaningful involvement of all people, regardless of race, color, national origin, or income, with respect to the development, implementation, and enforcement of environmental laws, regulations, and policies.

    C. Environmental justice is the responsibility to ensure that the remediation of toxins and other harmful chemical agents that have contaminated natural resources occurs, and that policies are put in place to prevent such violations from occurring again.

    D. Environmental justice is the recognition that the surroundings of individuals and their families are essential to their well-being and must be free from physical impediments that limit access for all.

68. Those who are gender nonconforming are:

    A. Likely to be attracted to or engaged in relationships with those of the same sex

    B. Confused about their sexual orientation

    C. Seen dressing in clothing or wearing items that are usually worn by those of the opposite gender

    D. Prone to be subject to discrimination and bias due to societal views about gender roles

69. A client comes to a social worker with concerns about food and housing insecurity, her inability to pursue her passion for writing, her relationship with her boyfriend, and her self-esteem. The social worker should FIRST assist the client with:

    A. Relationship issues that are affecting her day-to-day life

    B. Pursuing her passion for writing

    C. Concerns related to hunger and homelessness

    D. Problems concerning self-image and self-esteem

70. A social worker provides home-based services and is having trouble with a family in the program that needs immediate attention. The social worker is far away from the agency offices and needs to discuss the situation with the supervisor immediately. The supervisor suggests meeting at a local restaurant. The social worker should:

    A. Agree because the situation warrants immediate attention
    B. Agree because the location was suggested by the supervisor
    C. Disagree because it is a boundary crossing to go to a restaurant with the supervisor
    D. Disagree and suggest another location that is not as public

71. A social worker has decided to use a behavioral approach to identify sources of psychosocial stress for a client. During assessment, the social worker's questions will focus on identifying the:

    A. Defense mechanisms in place that will impede change
    B. Age at which stress first occurred
    C. Psychological reasons for the stress
    D. Identification of antecedents that precede indicators

72. In order for social workers to assist with addressing the power imbalance and systemic racism that are at the roots of economic and social injustice, they must do all of the following EXCEPT:

    A. Use "color-blind" ideology when providing services
    B. Understand how social programs maintain poverty and institutional structures that limit access to wealth
    C. Recognize that racism is the glue that holds classism/poverty together and is maintained through structures and systems of racial inequity
    D. Acknowledge that racism has a negative impact on all races

73. An emancipated minor can do all of the following EXCEPT:

    A. Make health care decisions without parental permission
    B. Obtain a driver's license at a younger age than typically required
    C. Enter into legally binding contracts such as real estate purchases or apartment rentals
    D. Take legal action against others, such as suing them

74. A community has a number of problems, including rampant drug addiction, high crime rates, and poor school achievement. In order to assist, a social worker should FIRST:

    A. Gain support for change by using the media to call attention to the existing problems
    B. Determine how the magnitude of these problems compares to those experienced by other similar and neighboring communities

    C. Speak with community residents to assist them to prioritize their concerns

    D. Assess what has been done before to attempt to address the identified problems and concerns

75. A client reports stopping the use of cannabis 2 days ago, after heavy and prolonged use over several years. This client is MOST likely to experience:

    A. Both physical and psychological withdrawal symptoms
    B. Physical withdrawal symptoms only
    C. Psychological withdrawal symptoms only
    D. No physical or psychological withdrawal symptoms

76. A client who always said that she loves her job now reports that she is quitting because she "can't stand it anymore." A social worker replies with, "This is surprising because you have always said that you were happy there." The statement by the social worker is a(n):

    A. Reflection
    B. Validation
    C. Interpretation
    D. Confrontation

77. A client gets into a fight with his wife and buys her flowers and a ring several days later. These gifts are an example of:

    A. Symbolization
    B. Undoing
    C. Reaction formation
    D. Projective identification

78. A social worker uses a puppet when playing with a 6-month-old infant. The social worker quickly hides the puppet behind her back. The infant begins to cry. This behavior is MOST likely a result of the child not yet developing which of the following?

    A. Coping skills
    B. Object permanence
    C. Conscious thought
    D. Fine motor skills

79. Which of the following actions is MOST critical when using an empowerment approach with a client?

    A. Helping a client learn skills that can be used to solve future problems
    B. Listening to a client who is expressing a high degree of emotion
    C. Referring a client to a needed resource or service
    D. Providing direction when a client is struggling with alternatives

80. After completion of an assessment, a client is placed in an intensive outpatient program, as opposed to an inpatient program, for his Substance Use Disorder. This decision is MOST likely based on:

    A. Utilization rates
    B. A level of care determination
    C. Service availability
    D. Client recommendations

81. Which of the following statements is NOT accurate about mental status examinations?

    A. Mental status examinations describe the psychological functioning of clients at specific points in time.
    B. Mental status examinations are important components of all assessment processes with clients.
    C. Mental status examinations are objective without subjective judgments about the developmental levels of clients.
    D. Mental status examinations are important in determining clients' functional capacity and whether follow-up is needed.

82. A teenage client states that she is having trouble "getting along" at home. She is always fighting with her parents, despite doing well in school and having a group of good friends. She ends by saying, "I am not sure how much more I can stand." In order to BEST address the situation, the social worker should:

    A. Suggest that the client enter individual therapy to discuss how to better cope with her stressful home life
    B. Explain to the client that a lot of teenagers have the same feelings and that her situation is not atypical
    C. Make a referral for a mental health screening to rule out dangerousness to self or others
    D. Arrange for her and her parents to be seen together to discuss the issues

83. A client is very distressed by how often she worries about her children throughout the day. A social worker tells her to keep track of the frequency that these thoughts occur. The social worker is most likely using this technique because:

    A. It is less costly than other methods to track behavior frequency.
    B. It will help her better understand the problem, including its magnitude and scope.
    C. It can be done easily, making it more likely that the frequency will be accurate.
    D. It will help reduce exaggeration as the client will know how often the thoughts occur.

84. A client whose husband has recently passed away reports feeling lonely and isolated. She tells a social worker that she does not know what to do with herself as all of her friends are married and socialize as couples. The social worker should suggest:

    A. Learning a new hobby or taking up an old one to keep busy
    B. Speaking to her friends about feeling uncomfortable
    C. Group therapy with others who have experienced similar losses
    D. Individual therapy to deal with the loss of her husband

85. All of the following are appropriate social work roles during the development of an Individualized Education Plan (IEP) EXCEPT:

    A. Completing a family history during the assessment phase
    B. Testing the child to determine developmental lags or delays
    C. Observing a child's ability to participate in class and get along with other students
    D. Ensuring participation by and explaining the IEP process to the family

86. In the *DSM-5*, the multiaxial system used in previous versions of the manual has:

    A. Been eliminated
    B. Been revised to include more specificity on each axis
    C. Been expanded to include more axes
    D. Remained unchanged

87. Which of the following is TRUE of collectivist cultures?

    A. They value individual self-determination and rights.
    B. Traits that are helpful to working in groups are rewarded.
    C. Competition among members is encouraged.
    D. They are consistent with the principles of capitalism.

88. A social worker is provided with flowcharts to assist with determining why the agency is not meeting its performance targets. The social worker is MOST likely being asked to assess organizational:

    A. Processes
    B. Structures
    C. Outcomes
    D. Inputs

89. Which of the following is NOT true related to social worker self-disclosure to a client?

    A. Self-disclosure can be an indicator of blurred boundaries between a social worker and a client.
    B. Even when handled judiciously and skillfully, self-disclosure cannot enhance the therapeutic alliance.

C. There are no clear guidelines about when self-disclosure by a social worker is acceptable, making the issue complex.

D. Most situations can be handled appropriately with little or no self-disclosure by a social worker.

90. A client reports that she has been diagnosed with fibromyalgia. Which of the following systems within the body are MOST affected by this medical condition?

    A. Muscular/skeletal
    B. Circulatory
    C. Reproductive
    D. Immune

91. An 8-year-old child who was physically abused several years ago before being removed from his home is in need of services to address anger issues. Based on the cognitive development of the child, the BEST modality to meet the child's needs is:

    A. Play therapy
    B. Insight-oriented psychotherapy
    C. Cognitive behavioral
    D. Existential

92. A client reports that he is having problems with neurological functioning and is being seen by his physician for additional testing. Which of the following is NOT a physical neurological symptom?

    A. Confusion or delirium
    B. Pain or weakness
    C. Involuntary movements
    D. Visual or auditory changes

93. Which of the following is TRUE about disorders related to addiction in the *DSM-5*?

    A. Legal involvement is eliminated in the *DSM-5* as a criterion of Substance Use Disorder.
    B. Caffeine Use Disorder is new in the *DSM-5*.
    C. The *DSM-5* does not include behavioral addictions.
    D. The *DSM-5* contains two Substance Use Disorders, Substance Abuse and Substance Dependence, which are distinguished by the severity of the symptoms.

94. Which of the following is NOT a physical sign of abuse or neglect?

    A. Avoiding eye contact or interaction
    B. Feeling lonely or disconnected
    C. Aggression toward others
    D. Self-destruction, such as cutting

95. A social worker who is leaving employment to work at another agency must do which of the following related to termination with clients?

   A. Inform clients of appropriate options for the continuation of services
   B. Encourage clients to receive services from the social worker's new employer in the future
   C. Ask his or her supervisor about what would be appropriate
   D. End relationships with clients as quickly as possible so that they can move on and form new alliances

96. A social worker using a strengths approach during assessment would:

   A. Suggest coping strategies that can assist in enhancing resiliency
   B. Collect information from all collateral contacts
   C. Ask the client to identify areas of concern
   D. Ensure that the client has signed all confidentiality forms

97. Which of the following is a core value of social work as cited in the preamble of the professional code of ethics?

   A. Reverence
   B. Integrity
   C. Loyalty
   D. Obedience

98. An 11-year-old student is performing well below her academic potential as she lacks confidence in her abilities and is fearful to take on assigned tasks. She is MOST likely experiencing a crisis in which of the following stages of psychosocial development?

   A. Autonomy versus shame and doubt
   B. Initiative versus guilt
   C. Generativity versus stagnation
   D. Industry versus inferiority

99. When a client develops a strong sense of his or her cultural, racial, and ethnic identity, and is comfortable socializing with those with diverse identities, a client is in which stage of his or her development?

   A. Pre-encounter
   B. Internalization and commitment
   C. Immersion–emersion
   D. Encounter

100. A client firmly believes something despite evidence to the contrary. This is known as a:

   A. Defense mechanism
   B. Disoriented thought

    C. Hallucination

    D. Delusion

101. The PRIMARY purpose of supervision in social work practice to:

    A. Make certain that clients' concerns are addressed when raised

    B. Ensure that clients are getting the most efficient and effective services possible

    C. Help social workers learn about agency and funding requirements

    D. Serve as a support for social workers when they face compassion fatigue

102. A social worker who believes that a colleague's impairment interferes with practice effectiveness, and that this colleague has not taken adequate steps to address this impairment, should take action through appropriate channels. This includes all of the following EXCEPT:

    A. Reporting the impairment to the employing agency and helping the colleague to access employee assistance programs

    B. Informing licensing and regulatory bodies

    C. Accessing impairment programs through professional organizations

    D. Determining the reasons for the impairment and providing supportive services as needed

103. All of the following are not true about consultation in social work practice EXCEPT:

    A. A consultant has formal authority in an agency setting.

    B. A consultant's recommendations must be followed by an agency.

    C. Consultation is aimed at solving a problem identified by the agency.

    D. Consultation is ongoing within an agency to address continual concerns.

104. A client who acts in a manner opposite of his or her unconscious beliefs is MOST likely using which of the following defense mechanisms?

    A. Substitution

    B. Splitting

    C. Reaction formation

    D. Undoing

105. Delirium tremens are associated with withdrawal from:

    A. Cocaine

    B. Alcohol

    C. Barbiturates

    D. Marijuana

106. A social worker employed in a child care agency sees that a mother is very distressed by her toddler's separation anxiety. In order to BEST assist, the social worker should:

    A. Determine whether there are other issues in the mother's life that are causing her to react in this manner

    B. Design a behavioral intervention for the child to reduce the symptoms of separation anxiety

    C. Assess the reactions of other family members to the child's behavior

    D. Teach the mother coping strategies aimed at reducing her distress

107. In the first step of the problem-solving process, all of the following occurs EXCEPT:

    A. Finding out why the client is seeking services

    B. Completing a biopsychosocial–spiritual–cultural assessment

    C. Explaining the limits of confidentiality

    D. Clarifying the role of the social worker

108. During a group session, a client states that he "is tired of being here" and does not know if he wants to continue. In this situation, it is BEST for the social worker to:

    A. Ask the client to speak to the social worker after the group session to discuss his concerns further

    B. Tell the client that these feelings often occur at some point during the course of group participation

    C. Encourage the client to discuss his feelings further with the other members of the group

    D. Assess whether the group is meeting his and other group members' needs

109. A social worker who is employed in an after-school program documents in a client's file that he is having problems concentrating when completing his homework as a result of issues at home with his same-gender parents. The social worker's supervisor would consider this entry to be:

    A. Justification for a referral to a family counseling agency

    B. Critical in understanding how to support the child within the program

    C. Inappropriate because it contains information not relevant for service provision

    D. Incomplete as it did not describe the nature of the problems experienced in the home

110. A social worker learns that a family served by his agency is having problems. They are arguing a lot and have strained interactions.

In the last year, the husband, who has had a long-standing problem with alcohol addiction, has been sober and actively engaged in treatment. He is working after being unemployed for an extended period. This family is most likely experiencing problems due to a change in:

A. Homeostasis
B. Entropy
C. Complementarity
D. Negative feedback loops

111. Which of the following questions is NOT typically asked when taking a spiritual history?

A. "Do you attend religious services on a regular basis?"
B. "How has your spiritual life been a factor in the concerns that you are raising now?"
C. "How did your spirituality inform your life choices throughout your life?"
D. "Have there been any changes in your spirituality recently?"

112. When a social worker restates a client's ideas or thoughts in order to get a fuller understanding, the social worker is using which technique?

A. Generalization
B. Interpretation
C. Paraphrasing
D. Clarification

113. When assessing the functioning of a community, which of the following is MOST important?

A. Recognizing the assets that exist and can be leveraged
B. Isolating problems that have to be addressed in the future
C. Determining outside resources that can help in any change effort
D. Identifying strategies that have been successful and unsuccessful in solving problems in the past

114. A social worker discovers that a client has been absent from services because she is having trouble getting transportation to the agency. The social worker learns that other clients also may be having this problem. In order to address this concern, the social worker should FIRST:

A. Conduct a needs assessment to determine the magnitude of the problem
B. Speak to the agency director about purchasing a van to fill the transportation gap
C. Get permission from the client to advocate with a supervisor on her behalf
D. Meet with local officials to see if public transportation options are available

115. When using a qualified interpreter to provide services to a client who speaks a different language, a social worker should do all of the following EXCEPT:

    A. Stand near the interpreter and face the client so the client can clearly see the social worker and interpreter without having to move his or her head
    B. Avoid using slang expressions or abbreviated terms that can be difficult to translate
    C. Ask the interpreter for his or her comments to ensure that information is gathered from collateral contacts
    D. Speak clearly with typical tone and volume so that the conversation does not appear strained or unnatural

116. A social worker feels overwhelmed by the amount of paperwork that he needs to complete. He is tired, stressed, and overwhelmed by day-to-day tasks. The social worker is MOST likely experiencing:

    A. Burnout
    B. Secondary trauma
    C. Compassion fatigue
    D. Psychological neurosis

117. A client reports that her husband has just been diagnosed with Alzheimer's disease and she will be the primary caregiver for him. What will be MOST helpful for the social worker to do in assisting the client?

    A. Identify others who are caregivers so the client can learn from their experiences
    B. Educate the client about the medical etiology of the disease
    C. Help the client to identify other family members who can assist her
    D. Listen to the client's feelings about her husband's behavioral and personality changes

118. A client tells a social worker that she is attracted to him and would like to terminate services to "see if it would go anywhere." The social worker should:

    A. Terminate services, but not pursue a relationship with the client since it appears that the therapeutic alliance has broken down
    B. Continue to serve the client, but explore whether termination may be needed in the future if the personal relationship develops further
    C. Terminate services after another provider has been identified and explore the personal relationship at that time
    D. Continue to serve the client while reconfirming professional boundaries that prohibit such a personal relationship from occurring

119. A client reports that her boyfriend brutally beat her a year ago but is very remorseful and there have been no signs of violence since that time.

He has been attentive to her needs and promised that "nothing like that will ever happen again." In this situation, the client is:

A. Not at risk based on the boyfriend's current actions

B. In serious danger as it is likely that the boyfriend will engage in violence again in the future

C. Not at risk based on the boyfriend's remorse and commitment not to engage in violence again

D. At some risk that requires monitoring over time

120. Which of the following is the BEST definition of sublimation?

A. A maladaptive feeling or behavior that is unconsciously directed toward socially acceptable and adaptive channels

B. The ability to perceive things dichotomously—all good or all bad

C. Impulsive drives that are unconsciously constrained by the ego

D. The tendency of families to use preferred methods of interaction and communication patterns

121. When releasing information with the appropriate consent, a social worker should:

A. Send the entire file to ensure that all needed information is provided

B. Provide the least amount of information necessary to achieve the desired purpose

C. Give only records that contain the least sensitive information

D. Offer to summarize the material in order to protect the client's privacy

122. When a social worker is making observations in a setting in which he or she has minimal involvement or interaction with those being studied, the social worker is assuming which of the following roles?

A. Participant as observer

B. Observer as participant

C. Complete participant

D. Complete observer

123. During a first meeting with a client, which of the following will be LEAST effective in reducing resistance?

A. Acknowledging that it is often difficult to ask for help and receive services

B. Reviewing the frequency, length, and parameters of the services to be provided

C. Explaining confidentiality policies and their limits

D. Asking the client for assurance in cooperating with agency policies

124. Which of the following is TRUE about physical contact of a client by a social worker?

    A. It is strictly prohibited in all instances.
    B. It is allowed to occur as long as the client's informed consent is obtained.
    C. It is permitted if the contact is not sexual in nature.
    D. It is not allowed if there is a possibility of psychological harm to a client or it is sexual in nature.

125. Which of the following distinguishes between advocacy for micro, mezzo, and macro client systems?

    A. It involves working with different levels of client systems.
    B. It is based on different social work values.
    C. The aims of the intervention are vastly different.
    D. It requires unique skill sets and different educational degrees.

126. After determining that an ethical conflict exists, a social worker, engaged in ethical problem solving, should NEXT:

    A. Consult with a supervisor about the best course of action
    B. Suggest modifications in light of prioritized ethical values
    C. Weight the ethical standards in conflict in light of social work values
    D. Find out what has been done in the past to resolve similar issues

127. A 13-year-old client is staying home alone after school and is responsible for organizing her time. She is looking forward to high school next year and is selecting her classes so she can be a good candidate for college acceptance. This client is MOST likely in which of the following stages of cognitive development?

    A. Formal operations
    B. Concrete operations
    C. Sensorimotor
    D. Preoperational

128. A social worker notices that a client who has been very depressed in past weeks after being hospitalized for a suicide attempt appears to be much happier. The social worker should FIRST:

    A. Conduct a suicide risk assessment
    B. Complete a new biopsychosocial–spiritual–cultural assessment to reflect changes in affect
    C. Praise the client for the marked improvement
    D. Discuss the apparent changes with his or her supervisor

129. Acculturation is achieved by:

    A. Members of a minority cultural group adopting the practices and customs of a majority cultural group
    B. A "give and take approach" in which minority and majority cultural groups both change to facilitate interactions and achievement of common goals
    C. Both minority and majority cultural groups not altering their practices and customs, but trying to interact harmoniously
    D. Eliminating cultural differences between those in minority and majority cultural groups

130. A couple reports to a social worker that their parents are strongly opposed to them living together prior to marriage. They have been dating for many years and would like to move in together, but do not feel that they are ready to get married. The social worker should FIRST:

    A. Advise the couple to strongly consider the parents' beliefs prior to making any decision
    B. Ask the couple if they would like to bring the parents in to see the social worker to discuss this issue further
    C. Explore the impact that the parents' beliefs will have on the couple's decision
    D. Determine the reasons for the parents' opposition to living together prior to marriage

131. A social worker employed at a nursing home is informed by staff that an elderly client has become withdrawn and depressed. Her daughter, who is her legal guardian, has moved to another state and rarely sees her. The social worker believes that the client may benefit from counseling and would like to refer her for services that will be paid for by her insurance company. In order to appropriately make the referral, which of the following is required?

    A. The approval of the social worker's supervisor
    B. The consent of the daughter
    C. The assent of the client
    D. The consent of the daughter and the assent of the client

132. A social work administrator is concerned about the financial health of his agency. He is examining whether hiring an additional staff in an after-school program will generate enough funding to cover the cost of the staff, as well as bring in additional, much needed revenue. The social worker is engaging in a:

    A. Summative evaluation
    B. Task-achievement method
    C. Formative evaluation
    D. Cost-benefit analysis

133. A client states that she feels like hurting herself, but will not act on her urges so the social worker "should not worry." To most appropriately address the client's needs, the social worker should FIRST:

    A. Complete an assessment to determine the reason(s) for the depression
    B. Refer the client to a psychiatrist for an evaluation for antidepressants
    C. Assure the client of concern about her well-being in order to alleviate her anxieties
    D. Determine the client's suicide risk and protective factors

134. Which of the following is NOT a reason to seek collateral information related to client problems?

    A. Treatment records from prior providers may assist with discovering techniques and interventions that were effective and ineffective.
    B. The credibility and validity of the information currently gathered is questionable.
    C. There are gaps in information that the client is not able to provide about the length and severity of the problem.
    D. There could be payment and other service problems that should be known before formally accepting the client into services.

135. Which of the following is NOT an essential part of obtaining a client's informed consent?

    A. Requiring that all consent forms are stored in the client's file
    B. Informing the client of payment expected and consequences for nonpayment of fees
    C. Explaining what services will be provided, including risks and benefits to the client
    D. Ensuring the client understands service alternatives

136. Which is NOT an aim of community organization?

    A. Developing leadership skills of community members
    B. Increasing the ability of a community to solve its own problems in the future
    C. Effectively using outside expertise to strengthen the resource network available to solve future problems
    D. Strengthening cohesion among and participatory skills of community members

137. Which of the following is NOT a social work role?

    A. Rapport builder
    B. Case manager
    C. Catalyst
    D. Broker

138. A client complains that her 4-year-old son is not "potty trained" and would like a referral for a psychological evaluation because she is concerned about his development. A social worker should FIRST:

   A. Explain that many children are not "potty trained" by age 4
   B. Refer the child to a psychologist as soon as possible to alleviate the mother's concerns
   C. Ask the mother about his "potty training" and other developmental issues that are worrying her
   D. Work with the mother to develop a behavioral program to assist with "potty training."

139. Which of the following is NOT a basic or deficiency need?

   A. Security
   B. Esteem
   C. Physiological
   D. Self-actualization

140. Which of the following efforts represent a pre–post evaluation design?

   A. A social work administrator compares the test scores of students who completed one program with those who completed a similar program.
   B. A social work administrator compares the test scores of students before participation in the program with those taken after service completion.
   C. A social work administrator uses prior year test scores as benchmarks for successful student completion in the current year.
   D. A social work administrator collects test scores from a control group of students who do not participate in any programs to assist in achievement.

141. A client's mother is now receiving hospice and is confined to her bed as she is too weak to walk due to symptoms associated with her terminal cancer. The client says that her mother will be fine and her health will improve enough for her to be removed from hospice shortly. The client is MOST likely using the defense mechanism of:

   A. Repression
   B. Displacement
   C. Denial
   D. Conversion

142. A social worker receives a referral for a client who is in need of supportive counseling related to treatment for a medical condition about which the social worker knows very little. There are no other

service options available to the client. When treating the client, all of the following are required of the social worker to practice ethically EXCEPT:

A. The social worker should hold the appropriate license or certification.

B. The social worker should receive educational materials and training on issues related to having this medical condition.

C. The social worker should receive supervision or consultation focusing on the needs of clients with this health issue.

D. The social worker should ask the client's permission to contact his or her physician to get an updated status on the condition.

143. A client walks into a social worker's office speaking in a loud and hostile manner. It is BEST for a social worker to:

A. Get additional staff to assist with ensuring safety

B. Set limits for expression in order to de-escalate the situation

C. Listen to the client to understand what is causing him or her to be upset

D. Tell the client to calm down to facilitate more effective communication

144. What is the MOST important benefit of group work?

A. It is a cost-effective method of helping clients, allowing more individuals to be served.

B. It effectively addresses problems through mutual aid of peers who serve as the primary helping agent.

C. It can be used to treat diverse issues and problems, allowing wide applicability in practice.

D. It can be used in conjunction with individual therapy as an ancillary modality.

145. Which of the following is NOT associated with positive ego strength?

A. Being silent before replying

B. Exhibiting self-discipline and fighting addictive urges

C. Taking responsibility for actions

D. Getting overwhelmed by moods

146. According to the cycle of abuse, which of the following comes after a battering incident?

A. Equilibrium

B. Tension building

C. Honeymoon

D. Psychological trauma

147. Unconditional positive regard is BEST defined as:

    A. Using positive reinforcement techniques to increase adaptive behaviors
    B. Helping a client find the positives in every situation
    C. Allowing a client to define the boundaries of the therapeutic relationship
    D. Showing complete support and acceptance of a client regardless of what he or she says or does

148. In the precontemplation stage of change, a client is:

    A. Willing to look at the pros and cons of behavior change, but is not committed to working toward it
    B. Taking direct action toward making change
    C. Unaware, unable, and/or unwilling to change
    D. Experimenting with small changes, but still resistant

149. A social worker is reviewing the medical files of a client and notices that she has a diagnosis of arthrodesis. Using knowledge of basic medical terminology, the social worker identifies this condition is a fixation by fusion of the:

    A. Tendons
    B. Muscles
    C. Bones
    D. Joints

150. A client has been simultaneously diagnosed with a behavioral disorder as well as a health problem. These conditions are referred to as:

    A. Unaffiliated
    B. Comorbid
    C. Linked
    D. Disassociated

151. During an intake, a client reports that he has been drinking heavily for years. As a result of his alcohol abuse, he lost his job and his wife left him. He realizes that "things need to change" and he has not had a drink in the last 12 hours. In order to assist this client, the social worker should FIRST:

    A. Determine why he has decided to change now
    B. Identify natural supports that can assist in recovery
    C. Conduct a biopsychosocial–spiritual–cultural history to assist with designing interventions to support the client in his goal
    D. Refer the client to a substance abuse treatment agency

152. Which of the following is TRUE about spiritual development?

    A. Most people eventually develop blind faith in a spiritual being by the end of their lives.
    B. Individual spiritual development is stagnant throughout the life course.
    C. Most models explain spiritual development along a continuum moving from "egocentric" to "conformist" to "universal."
    D. Children start life with an integrated sense of self.

153. A social worker sees bruises on the body of a child in an after-school program. The child reports that they happened when he was "grabbed" by his father. The mother confirms that there was a fight between the child and his father, but reports that the father has gone out-of-state to work so there will be no contact between them for a while. In this situation, the social worker should:

    A. Speak to the mother about de-escalation strategies which can be used to diffuse similar situations in the future
    B. Attempt to contact the father to question him about the incident directly
    C. Ask the mother to inform the social worker when the father returns home so the situation can be monitored then
    D. Report the situation to the child protection agency

154. In the contemplation stage of change, which of the following is NOT the most effective way to respond to clients' resistance?

    A. Discussing the pros and cons of changing
    B. Designing a behavioral program to reward incremental steps toward change
    C. Identifying how change will assist clients in achieving their own goals
    D. Producing examples of change and clarifying what change is and is not

155. A husband tells a social worker that he is having problems with his wife because he would like to stay home to care for his new baby after his wife gives birth in about a month. He states that his wife has a good job and is better able to financially support the family. The wife tells the social worker that she is strongly opposed to this idea because she believes that a husband should be the "breadwinner" in a family. In order to be MOST effective, the social worker should focus on:

    A. Attitudinal differences that may exist with regard to gender roles
    B. Exposure to diverse child care arrangements
    C. Ability to work together and compromise on childrearing decisions
    D. Financial planning to make more child care options available to this couple

156. Which of the following is NOT found in a client's advance directive?

    A. Life-sustaining treatments desired by the client when he or she is seriously or terminally ill
    B. Description of how assets are to be distributed after a client passes away
    C. Name(s) of the person(s) able to make health care decisions for the client when he or she is unable to do so
    D. Medical services that a client does not want when he or she is not able to make such decisions in a medical crisis

157. Financial exploitation of older adults includes all of the following actions EXCEPT:

    A. Getting an older adult to sign a deed by using undue influence
    B. Obtaining a large sum of money from an older adult without paying it back
    C. Preventing an older adult from having access to his or her assets
    D. Cashing an older adult's checks without permission

158. Which of the following alone is NOT a strong correlate of violence toward others in adults?

    A. Gang involvement
    B. Drug and alcohol abuse
    C. Violent crime toward others in childhood
    D. Peers who are engaged in violent activity

159. A health screening reveals that a medication is contraindicated for a current client. This means that this medication must:

    A. Be taken exactly as prescribed to maintain good health
    B. Not be taken by the client as it may have serious consequences
    C. Undergo further evaluation to see if it is appropriate for use at this time
    D. Be prescribed in concert with other medications to adequately address the targeted health issue

160. Families in which incest has occurred are LIKELY to have:

    A. A proclivity to engage in atypical sexual practices
    B. Ego fusion between the mother and abused child(ren)
    C. Enmeshed family roles
    D. Liberal attitudes toward sexuality

161. A client tells a school social worker that she feels like a failure as she did not get a part in the school play. The client is very popular among her peers and has excellent grades. She is very active in many school

activities, but goes on and on about how she can do "nothing right." In response to the client's self-description, the social worker should FIRST:

A. Point out the other areas of her life in which she does well
B. Arrange for her to meet with the drama teacher to see what she can do to improve and increase her likelihood of being selected next time
C. Tell her that many students did not make the play
D. Explore why her identity appears to be defined by this incident

162. A family who is Hispanic and recently immigrated is in need of services to locate housing and employment. The parents only speak Spanish but their 16-year-old son is bilingual, speaking both Spanish and English. A social worker who receives the referral speaks English, but understands and speaks very little Spanish. In order to assist this family, the social worker should:

A. Provide assistance to the family to the extent possible given the social worker's limited Spanish fluency
B. Refer the family to another agency that has Spanish-speaking social workers
C. Obtain a qualified interpreter to assist with translation
D. Ask the son to translate because he is familiar with the family's needs and is able to assist immediately

163. Which statement BEST describes the relationship between biological factors and mental health?

A. Inherited genetic variations make some clients more susceptible to developing certain mental health disorders.
B. Mental health disorders result solely from environmental and social factors which have no biological basis.
C. Clients whose biological parents have certain mental health disorders will develop them as they are genetically passed from generation to generation.
D. Mental health disorders are linked to a specific chemical imbalance in the body which can be treated with medications.

164. A client is shown sketches of situations and asked to create or construct a story for each card given. Based on this description, the client is most likely being administered which of the following psychological tests?

A. Stanford–Binet Intelligence Scale
B. Minnesota Multiphasic Personality Inventory (MMPI)
C. Thematic Apperception Test (TAT)
D. Beck Depression Inventory

165. Which factor does NOT usually impact on group cohesion?

    A. Number of members in the group
    B. Diversity of group membership
    C. Agency setting in which group occurs
    D. Degree to which members are allowed to establish rules and goals of the group

166. Using a cognitive approach, assessment would focus on all of the following EXCEPT:

    A. Negative thought patterns that contribute to the problem
    B. Environmental reinforcers to problematic behavior
    C. Existing cognitive schemas related to the problem
    D. Beliefs that promote and inhibit change

167. A client receiving case management has been linked to all needed services and is in the process of terminating with a social worker. Suddenly, she learns that her father has been hospitalized. The social worker should:

    A. Assess whether termination is still appropriate at this time given this change in the client's life
    B. Terminate with the client because this is a different issue that may or may not require services
    C. Develop new goals for the client aimed at providing support related to this family crisis
    D. Make a referral to the hospital social worker

168. Which of the following is MOST critical in order for change to occur?

    A. A social worker and client must have a clear understanding of the rules that must be followed in service delivery.
    B. A social worker and client must acknowledge that they both have roles in fixing the problem.
    C. A social worker and client must realize that change is usually incremental.
    D. A social worker and client must use interaction in the helping relationship to understand why problems exist and how they can be addressed.

169. Which of the following is NOT typically a component of a client contract?

    A. Problem to be addressed and goals to be achieved
    B. Psychological and environmental factors that contributed to the problem
    C. Means used to monitor progress
    D. Client and social worker roles in the intervention

170. Which of the following is a distinguishing characteristic between an advance directive and a Physician Orders for Life-Sustaining Treatment (POLST)?

A. A POLST is not legally binding while an advance directive must be followed.

B. A POLST is a more current term for an advance directive and there are no differences between them.

C. A POLST contains medical orders, but an advance directive does not.

D. A POLST names a health care proxy, but an advance directive does not.

Practice Test

Answers

1. C

Social workers should refer clients to other professionals when the other professionals' specialized knowledge or expertise is needed to serve clients fully (A); when social workers believe that they are not being effective (B); and when social workers believe reasonable progress with clients is being made, but that additional service is required (D).

The belief by other professionals that their services may be more effective (C) is not proper justification for a referral.

Knowledge Area

Unit III—Interventions With Clients/Client Systems (Content Area); Use of Collaborative Relationships (Competency); Consultation Approaches (e.g., Referrals to Specialists) (KSA)

2. D

When social workers are creating intervention plans, it is essential that goals are written in observable and measurable terms. In this case vignette, the supervisor would judge it to be inadequate because it does not indicate the length of time that the child will be seated after being reminded or the time frame within which the objective is to be achieved—both critical elements of a measurable objective.

Knowledge Area

Unit III—Interventions With Clients/Client Systems (Content Area); Intervention Processes and Techniques (Competency); Methods to Develop and Evaluate Measurable Objectives for Client/Client System Intervention, Treatment, and/or Service Plans (KSA)

3. A

Social workers may only limit clients' rights to self-determination when, in the social workers' professional judgment, clients' actions or potential actions pose a serious, foreseeable, and imminent risk to themselves or others.

Knowledge Area

Unit IV—Professional Relationships, Values, and Ethics (Content Area); Professional Values and Ethical Issues (Competency); Client/Client System Competence and Self-Determination (e.g., Financial Decisions, Treatment Decisions, Emancipation, Age of Consent, Permanency Planning) (KSA)

4. A

All of the response choices are examples of partialization. However, the question was related to its use *during assessment*. As it is related to the delivery of service, A is not an assessment task, but is instead required during planning or intervention.

Knowledge Area

Unit II—Assessment (Content Area); Assessment Methods and Techniques (Competency); The Factors and Processes Used in Problem Formulation (KSA)

5. A

According to Erikson, older adults begin to slow down and contemplate their accomplishments. They assess whether they are satisfied with their life progression and become depressed or distraught if they are not. This stage is known as ego integrity versus despair.

Trust versus mistrust occurs in the first year of life as infants learn whether the world is a place where their needs can be met. Intimacy versus isolation happens in early adulthood, and autonomy versus shame and doubt is a stage from ages 1 to 3 when children begin to explore the world on their own, learning independence.

Knowledge Area

Unit I—Human Development, Diversity, and Behavior in the Environment (Content Area); Human Growth and Development (Competency); Theories of Human Development Throughout the Lifespan (e.g., Physical, Social, Emotional, Cognitive, Behavioral) (KSA)

6. C

The psychological consequences of abuse and neglect include isolation, fear, inability to trust, low self-esteem, anxiety, depression, and hopelessness. These difficulties can lead to relationship problems and the possibility of antisocial behavioral traits. Psychological abuse can, but does not always, happen at the same time (comorbid) with physical abuse. The most evident signs are the behavioral characteristics of victims.

Knowledge Area

Unit II—Assessment (Content Area); Concepts of Abuse and Neglect (Competency); Indicators and Dynamics of Abuse and Neglect Throughout the Lifespan (KSA)

7. D

Social exchange theory is based on the idea of totaling potential benefits and losses to determine behavior. A client will leave a battering relationship when the alternative is seen as better than the current situation (rewards outweigh costs).

Knowledge Area

Unit III—Interventions With Clients/Client Systems (Content Area); Intervention Processes and Techniques (Competency); The Impact of Domestic, Intimate Partner, and Other Violence on the Helping Relationship (KSA)

8. D

Human trafficking is not the same as human smuggling (D). "Trafficking" is based on exploitation and does not require movement across borders. "Smuggling" involves moving a person. Although human smuggling is very different from human trafficking, human smuggling can turn into trafficking if the smuggler uses force, fraud, or coercion to hold people against their will for the purposes of labor or sexual exploitation.

Sex trafficking exists, but it is not the only type of human trafficking, making A incorrect. Forced labor is another type of human trafficking. Both involve exploitation of people.

Human trafficking victims can be any age, race, gender, or nationality, and may come from any socioeconomic group. Therefore, B is incorrect.

Human trafficking exists in every country, including the United States, so C has to be eliminated.

Knowledge Area

Unit II—Assessment (Content Area); Concepts of Abuse and Neglect (Competency); The Indicators, Dynamics, and Impact of Exploitation Across the Lifespan (e.g., Financial, Immigration Status, Sexual Trafficking) (KSA)

9. B

Role complementarity happens when there is a coordination of roles in a dyad or group (i.e., individuals act as expected by others).

Role discomplementarity occurs when an individual acts differently than what is anticipated or is thought to be acceptable. Unclear expectations lead to role ambiguity and dysfunctional relationships or behavior. Thus, social workers aim to ensure that clients are aware of required actions and demands.

Knowledge Area

Unit I—Human Development, Diversity, and Behavior in the Environment (Content Area); Human Behavior in the Social Environment (Competency); Role Theories (KSA)

10. A

Social workers should take precautions to ensure and maintain confidentiality of information transmitted to other parties through the use of email, fax machines, telephones and telephone answering machines, and other electronic or computer technology.

   In this case vignette, the social worker's actions were unethical because all household members and others who listen to the message will be aware of confidential information—that is, the client's affiliation with the agency (A).

Knowledge Area

Unit IV—Professional Relationships, Values, and Ethics (Content Area); Confidentiality (Competency); Legal and/or Ethical Issues Regarding Confidentiality, Including Electronic Information Security (KSA)

11. A

Social work licensure establishes the rules and regulations for professional practice (B), allows those who have met these standards and who follow these rules to engage in social work (C), and investigates complaints by members of the public in order to decide whether violations of the regulations have occurred and whether social workers should continue to practice (D).

Knowledge Area

Unit IV—Professional Relationships, Values, and Ethics (Content Area); Professional Development and Use of Self (Competency); Professional Development Activities to Improve Practice and Maintain Current Professional Knowledge (e.g., In-Service Training, Licensing Requirements, Reviews of Literature, Workshops) (KSA)

12. C

The sensorimotor stage is first in Piaget's theory of cognitive development. It is characterized by primitive logic in manipulating objects (D), the onset of intentional actions (B), and imitative play (A). The ability to comprehend the difference between the past, present, and future (B) does not emerge, according to Piaget, until the preoperational stage, which begins at approximately age 2 and continues until about age 7.

Knowledge Area

Unit I—Human Development, Diversity, and Behavior in the Environment (Content Area); Human Growth and Development (Competency); Theories of Human Development Throughout the Lifespan (e.g., Physical, Social, Emotional, Cognitive, Behavioral) (KSA)

13. B

A formative evaluation *examines the processes* that are occurring in an attempt to determine which are promoting and/or inhibiting successful outcomes. Information gathered from a formative evaluation can help alter program provisions to increase efficiency and/or effectiveness. A summative evaluation is focused on *determining a program's effectiveness or outcomes*. A summative evaluation provides valuable data at a program's completion to determine whether it should be continued, modified, or eliminated.

Knowledge Area

Unit III—Interventions With Clients/Client Systems (Content Area); Intervention Processes and Techniques (Competency); Methods, Techniques, and Instruments Used to Evaluate Social Work Practice (KSA)

14. B

A subpoena and court order are not the same. When receiving a subpoena, a social worker should respond and claim privilege, but should not turn over records unless the court issues a subsequent order to do so (B). When a social worker gets a court order, he or she should try to limit its scope or request that the records be sealed.

Knowledge Area

Unit IV—Professional Relationships, Values, and Ethics (Content Area); Confidentiality (Competency); Legal and/or Ethical Issues Regarding Confidentiality, Including Electronic Information Security (KSA)

15. D

The social worker should intervene to let the client know that he is not alone as the social worker is available to assist (D). The client may feel isolated or alone because he has never met anyone with similar problems. It is important to acknowledge that each client's situation is unique, but a social worker must also instill hope by making it clear that others have made changes or overcome similar challenges.

Based on the client's use of the word "alone," there is no indication that he is at risk, so a risk assessment is not warranted (B). Exploring the client's feelings further (A) and receiving counseling (C) may be needed, but the case vignette does not provide enough information to indicate that the client is clinically depressed as opposed to having a typical response encountered with many clients who are experiencing a wide variety of problems.

Knowledge Area

Unit III—Interventions With Clients/Client Systems (Content Area); Intervention Processes and Techniques (Competency); The Principles and Techniques of Interviewing (e.g., Supporting, Clarifying, Focusing, Confronting, Validating, Feedback, Reflecting, Language Differences, Use of Interpreters, Redirecting) (KSA)

16. A

Although some social workers believe that disclosure of personal information about a narrow range of topics is appropriate, disclosure about other topics is much riskier and some topics are clearly inappropriate. The latter includes social workers' marital or relationship difficulties. The social worker should address the client's concern (A) without disclosing her emotional struggles during her own divorce (B and C). The social worker should seek supervision or consultation to address her emotional reaction, but should not refer the client to another agency (D) because the termination would be disruptive to treatment.

Knowledge Area

Unit IV—Professional Relationships, Values, and Ethics (Content Area); Professional Development and Use of Self (Competency); Self-Disclosure Principles and Applications (KSA)

17. C

Young children often throw temper tantrums in an attempt to communicate frustration. Toddlers and preschoolers do not have the self-regulation to deal with aggravation, so they may throw objects, cry, strike out, and/or scream. These are typical reactions and are not signs of greater psychological disturbance.

The other response choices (A, B, and D) are correct. Young children will understand what is said to them before they are able to articulate their feelings and desires. Play is an important activity for children because they learn socialization skills, are active physically, and learn to make connections between objects (how the world works). While there is a debate about the extent to which "nature versus nurture" impacts on development, there is agreement that both impact growth and functioning in life domains.

Knowledge Area

Unit I—Human Development, Diversity, and Behavior in the Environment (Content Area); Human Growth and Development (Competency); The Indicators of Normal and Abnormal Physical, Cognitive, Emotional, and Sexual Development Throughout the Lifespan (KSA)

18. D

Do Not Resuscitate (DNR) orders give clients the right to refuse any medical treatment, even life-sustaining treatments such as mechanical ventilation or even artificial hydration and nutrition (D). DNR orders do not mean that medical care cannot be given (C)—everything is done up to the point that a client is found to be in the active process of dying. They do not have to be done in conjunction with the appointment of a durable power of attorney (B). DNR orders concern the withdrawal or withholding of treatments that allow a disease or condition to progress on its natural course, whereas euthanasia actively seeks to end a client's life.

Knowledge Area

Unit IV—Professional Relationships, Values, and Ethics (Content Area); Professional Values and Ethical Issues (Competency); Legal and/or Ethical Issues Related to Death and Dying (KSA)

19. A

The client has expressed a desire to return to her home. Placement options should always be based on level of care in conjunction with client wishes. In order to respect her self-determination, the social worker should FIRST see if there are natural and other community supports available to assist (A) her to return home safely. If there are not, discharge may have to be delayed until they are available or can be created. Only when the client cannot return to her home safely should alternatives, such as assisted living, be explored.

Knowledge Area

Unit II—Assessment (Content Area); Assessment Methods and Techniques (Competency); Placement Options Based on Assessed Level of Care (KSA)

20. A

Even if the social worker knows a lot about the client's current situation, assessment is critical as it provides an opportunity for the social worker to determine the client's perception of his or her life circumstances. Assessment also allows the social worker to hear in the client's own words what help he or she believes is needed.

Knowledge Area

Unit II—Assessment (Content Area); Assessment Methods and Techniques (Competency); Methods of Involving Clients/Client Systems in Problem Identification (e.g., Gathering Collateral Information) (KSA)

21. D

The problem should always be considered within the person-in-environment or ecological perspective and using a strengths approach. It should not blame a client and/or client system for its existence.

There is nothing specified in the case vignette that indicates the onset of a psychiatric disorder or substance use issue. There is also no mention that these behaviors existed prior to the start of high school or that they are caused by a learning disability.

The social worker must initially view these problems as resulting from a new environment that involves demands and expectations. This teenager may be having difficulty with the autonomy and reduced structure that accompanies such a transition.

Knowledge Area

Unit II—Assessment (Content Area); Assessment Methods and Techniques (Competency); The Factors and Processes Used in Problem Formulation (KSA)

22. C

The use of "people first language" began in the disability self-advocacy community, but is now used universally. It is the belief that a person is not his or her disability; by referring to those with varying physical and cognitive abilities as "the disabled," society is dehumanizing them. Thus, sentence structure should be used that names the person first and the condition second in order to avoid perceived and subconscious dehumanization when discussing people with diagnoses, disabilities, or conditions.

Person first language would call for the use of "people with disabilities" rather than "disabled people" or "the disabled."

Knowledge Area

Unit I—Human Development, Diversity, and Behavior in the Environment (Content Area); Diversity, Social/Economic Justice, and Oppression (Competency); The Effects of Discrimination and Stereotypes on Behaviors, Attitudes, and Identity (KSA)

23. A

Social workers should inform clients, to the extent possible, about the nature of disclosed information and the potential consequences before the disclosure is made. This applies whether social workers disclose confidential information on the basis of a legal requirement or based on client consent.

In this case vignette, the social worker is mandated to provide the summaries, so client consent is not needed (B). In addition, the requirement cannot be waived (D). The MOST appropriate and ethical action would be to show the client the summaries prior to sending them (A) so the client is aware of the potential consequences. This practice is not subject to court oversight (C).

Knowledge Area

Unit IV—Professional Relationships, Values, and Ethics (Content Area); Confidentiality (Competency); Legal and/or Ethical Issues Regarding Confidentiality, Including Electronic Information Security (KSA)

24. A

Families strive *for* a sense of balance or homeostasis. When not found, rules or interactions may need to be adjusted in order to achieve or restore this balance. Equilibrium allows families to cope with the challenges that they encounter with the resources available within the family unit.

Knowledge Area

Unit I—Human Development, Diversity, and Behavior in the Environment (Content Area); Human Behavior in the Social Environment (Competency); Family Dynamics and Functioning and the Effects on Individuals, Families, Groups, Organizations, and Communities (KSA)

25. B

Negative entropy is desirable as it represents an open system in which there is an exchange of energy and resources. Conversely, entropy is used to describe a closed system in which energy is being used up and stagnation is occurring (C).

Homeostasis is a steady state in which balance is achieved (A) and systems theory indicates that an output (product) is a subsequent input in any system (D).

Knowledge Area

Unit I—Human Development, Diversity, and Behavior in the Environment (Content Area); Human Behavior in the Social Environment (Competency); Systems and Ecological Perspectives and Theories (KSA)

26. B

Social workers should not assume that clients are ready or have the skills needed to make changes in their lives. Clients may be oppositional, reactionary, noncompliant, and/or unmotivated. These attitudes or behaviors are often referred to as resistance. There are indicators that a social worker should take as evidence that a client may be resistant or not ready/able to fully participate in services. Some indicators include engaging in small talk with a social worker about irrelevant topics, false promising, and not keeping appointments.

Discussing current, as opposed to past, problems is NOT an indicator of a lack of readiness to participate in services—it is a desired behavior. Focusing on past issues can mean that a client is not ready to address the current ones.

Knowledge Area

Unit II—Assessment (Content Area); Assessment Methods and Techniques (Competency); The Indicators of Motivation, Resistance, and Readiness to Change (KSA)

27. A

The social worker must recognize the impact of illness or disability on all aspects of well-being, not just the physical restrictions. Systems theory is based on the concept that when one thing changes in a system, other aspects are affected. The student has experienced a change in physical functioning. This will likely impact on psychological and social well-being as the biopsychosocial functioning of an individual is interrelated. Performance in these domains will affect the spiritual and cultural aspects of one's life as well. A is the only response choice that acknowledges the biopsychosocial responses.

Knowledge Area

Unit II—Assessment (Content Area); Biopsychosocial History and Collateral Data (Competency); Biopsychosocial Responses to Illness and Disability (KSA)

28. B

Stereotypes serve to perpetuate myths and support the interests of a dominant group over those of a subordinate one. They maintain social hierarchies.

A perceived "positive" stereotype can functionally oppress a group. For example, when women are characterized as superior to men at childcare, this message is used to limit work opportunities and/or career advancement for women. Stereotypes are based on little (if any) factual information. The nature of stereotypes attached to particular groups do change with the shifting interests and concerns of a society.

Knowledge Area

Unit I—Human Development, Diversity, and Behavior in the Environment (Content Area); Diversity, Social/Economic Justice, and Oppression (Competency); The Effects of Discrimination and Stereotypes on Behaviors, Attitudes, and Identity (KSA)

29. A

Displacement is shifting thoughts, attitudes, or behaviors to a less threatening target. In this case vignette, the student cannot strike back at her abusive parents, so she is displaying displaced aggression toward other children.

Reaction formation is acting in a manner opposite of one's unconscious belief. Projection is attributing one's attitudes, wishes, feelings, and/ or urges to another; the attitudes, wishes, feelings, and/or urges are so threatening that they are removed from oneself and attributed to another. Incorporation is taking values, attitudes, expectations, and preferences of another into one's own identity.

Knowledge Area

Unit I—Human Development, Diversity, and Behavior in the Environment (Content Area); Human Behavior in the Social Environment (Competency); Psychological Defense Mechanisms and Their Effects on Behavior and Relationships (KSA)

30. B

Social workers are mandated reporters. Despite the supervisor's recommendation to "monitor" the situation instead of reporting, the social worker still must make a report based on the teenager's claims. It would not be appropriate to delay reporting to collect more information from the parents or see if subsequent allegations are made. In addition, the social worker should be forthcoming with her supervisor and the teenager about her actions and should not anonymously report after hours.

Knowledge Area

Unit IV—Professional Relationships, Values, and Ethics (Content Area); Professional Values and Ethical Issues (Competency); Legal and/or Ethical Issues Regarding Mandatory Reporting (e.g., Abuse, Threat of Harm, Impaired Professionals, etc.) (KSA)

31. C

John Bowlby suggested that children come into the world preprogrammed to form attachments with others because these attachments will help them to survive. This perspective views bonding within an *evolutionary* context in which a caregiver provides security and safety for a child.

An alternative perspective views bonding as a *learned behavior* that results from classical conditioning. It posits that a child develops an attachment over time with whoever feeds and cares for him or her because these actions reinforce contact with the caregiver.

Knowledge Area

Unit I—Human Development, Diversity, and Behavior in the Environment (Content Area); Human Growth and Development (Competency); The Principles of Attachment and Bonding (KSA)

32. A

The harm reduction model refers to any program, policy, or intervention that seeks to reduce or minimize the adverse health and social consequences associated with substance use *without requiring a client to discontinue use.* Needle exchange programs ensure that intravenous drug users have access to clean needles and syringes in order to reduce the passage of diseases caused by sharing "works." These programs may be available in concert with interventions aimed at motivating clients to stop using intravenous drugs, but this is not the focus of needle exchange programs.

Knowledge Area

Unit III—Interventions With Clients/Client Systems (Content Area); Intervention Processes and Techniques (Competency); Techniques for Harm Reduction for Self and Others (KSA)

33. D

Genograms are diagrams of family relationships that can help social workers and their clients visualize relationship conflicts, intergenerational patterns, and other important information used to better understand clients' current problems.

Histograms are bar graphs, flowcharts are diagrams that depict processes or workflows, and Venn diagrams show relationships between different sets of elements.

Knowledge Area

Unit III—Interventions With Clients/Client Systems (Content Area); Documentation (Competency); The Principles and Processes for Developing Formal Documents (e.g., Proposals, Letters, Brochures, Pamphlets, Reports, Evaluations) (KSA)

34. B

Hydrocodone is the most popular painkiller used to treat moderate to severe pain. Hydrocodone, a narcotic analgesic, relieves pain through the central nervous system. This drug can become habit-forming when used over an extended period of time.

Tardive dyskinesia (D) is a side effect of taking large doses of antipsychotic medications over a long period of time. It is characterized by involuntary movements, twitching, and so on.

Knowledge Area

Unit II—Assessment (Content Area); Assessment Methods and Techniques (Competency); Common Psychotropic and Non-Psychotropic Prescriptions and Over-the-Counter Medications and Their Side Effects (KSA)

35. C

Pansexuality is being attracted to others, regardless or independent of gender.

Knowledge Area

Unit I—Human Development, Diversity, and Behavior in the Environment (Content Area); Diversity, Social/Economic Justice, and Oppression (Competency); Sexual Orientation Concepts (KSA)

36. C

Child maltreatment is widespread with child neglect being the most common form of maltreatment. The most common victims of abuse and neglect are infants, toddlers, preschool children, and young adolescents. It is not uncommon for children to be the victim of more than one kind of maltreatment.

Knowledge Area

Unit II—Assessment (Content Area); Concepts of Abuse and Neglect (Competency); Indicators and Dynamics of Abuse and Neglect Throughout the Lifespan (KSA)

37. B

Social workers in fee-for-service settings may terminate services to clients who are not paying an overdue balance if the financial contractual arrangements have been made clear to a client, if a client does not pose an imminent danger to self or others, and if the clinical and other consequences of the current nonpayment have been addressed and discussed with a client.

There is no mention in the case vignette that the client poses any danger to self or others, and the client has been made aware of the payment policy and consequences, so termination should occur unless the outstanding balance is paid (B).

Knowledge Area

Unit IV—Professional Relationships, Values, and Ethics (Content Area); Professional Values and Ethical Issues (Competency); Legal and/or Ethical Issues Related to Termination (KSA)

38. A

In communication, there are two types of content, manifest and latent. Manifest content is the concrete words or terms contained in a communication while latent content is that which is not visible—the underlying meaning of words or terms.

The social worker in this case vignette is focused on the "tone" and underlying meaning of passages, which is the latent content (A).

Knowledge Area

Unit II—Assessment (Content Area); Assessment Methods and Techniques (Competency); Communication Theories and Styles (KSA)

39. D

While past sexual victimization can increase the likelihood of sexually aggressive behavior, most children who were sexually victimized never perpetrate against others (D).

The remaining answers are false because child sexual abuse crosses all socioeconomic, racial, ethnic, and other boundaries. Many acts of child sexual abuse leave no physical trace, and the vast majority of incidents occur with known perpetrators.

Knowledge Area

Unit II—Assessment (Content Area); Concepts of Abuse and Neglect (Competency); Indicators and Dynamics of Abuse and Neglect Throughout the Lifespan (KSA)

40. D

It is critical that social workers understand culture and its function in human behavior and society, recognize the strengths that exist in all cultures (B), and understand the nature of social diversity and oppression (C). However, these response choices do not directly address the cultural differences that exist between the social worker and the client. The social worker must acknowledge these differences and be aware of their impacts on the delivery of services (D) since the social worker will tend to use his or her own social, economic, and religious values as the norm. Insight is essential in this situation.

Knowledge Area

Unit IV—Professional Relationships, Values, and Ethics (Content Area); Professional Values and Ethical Issues (Competency); The Dynamics of Diversity in the Social Worker–Client/Client System Relationship (KSA)

41. D

Social workers should provide clients with reasonable access to their own records. Social workers should limit clients' access to their records, or portions of their records, only in exceptional circumstances when there is compelling evidence that such access would cause serious harm to clients, which is not the situation in this case vignette. In this case, the social worker should provide a copy of the record to the client (D).

Knowledge Area

Unit IV—Professional Relationships, Values, and Ethics (Content Area); Confidentiality (Competency); The Use of Client/Client System Records (KSA)

42. B

Social workers should not disclose confidential information to third-party payers, such as the foundation in this case vignette, unless clients have authorized such disclosure.

Knowledge Area

Unit IV—Professional Relationships, Values, and Ethics (Content Area); Confidentiality (Competency); Legal and/or Ethical Issues Regarding Confidentiality, Including Electronic Information Security (KSA)

43. D

Supplemental Security Income (SSI) is a benefit to low-income people who are 65 or older; to adults who are disabled or blind; and to children who are disabled or blind. The program is only for people who have very limited income and assets. It is for individuals who have not worked or not worked enough to qualify for Social Security Disability.

Unemployment insurance provides temporary financial assistance to unemployed workers who are unemployed through no fault of their own. This benefit is intended for those who are employed and lose their jobs due to reasons beyond their control.

Workers' compensation provides medical treatment, wage replacement, and permanent disability compensation to employees who suffer job-related injuries or illnesses, and death benefits to dependents of workers who have died as a result of their employment.

Social Security Disability Insurance (SSDI) is funded through payroll taxes and considered "insurance" because recipients have worked for a certain number of years and have made contributions toward the benefit. SSDI recipients must be younger than 65 and must have earned a sufficient number of "work credits."

Knowledge Area

Unit III—Interventions With Clients/Client Systems (Content Area); Use of Collaborative Relationships (Competency); The Effects of Policies,

Procedures, Regulations, and Legislation on Social Work Practice and Service Delivery (KSA)

44. B

When a social worker does not agree with a supervisor, he or she should speak to the supervisor directly (B). Conflicts can often be resolved through productive communication between the parties.

It is not appropriate to get colleagues involved in the disagreement (A), and the social worker should only contact the agency director (C) if the disagreement cannot be resolved and the directive would adversely affect clients. The social worker also should not comply with the directive without speaking to the supervisor (D) about his or her concerns.

Knowledge Area

Unit IV—Professional Relationships, Values, and Ethics (Content Area); Professional Development and Use of Self (Competency); The Supervisee's Role in Supervision (e.g., Identifying Learning Needs, Self-Assessment, Prioritizing, etc.) (KSA)

45. C

Transference refers to redirection of a client's feelings to a social worker (C). Transference is often manifested as an erotic attraction toward a social worker, but can be seen in many other forms such as rage, hatred, mistrust, parentification, extreme dependence, or even placing a social worker in an esteemed status.

Countertransference is redirection of a social worker's feelings toward a client (D).

Knowledge Area

Unit IV—Professional Relationships, Values, and Ethics (Content Area); Professional Development and Use of Self (Competency); The Impact of Transference and Countertransference in the Social Worker–Client/Client System Relationship (KSA)

46. B

Intradisciplinary teams are composed exclusively of social workers who may have different levels of training and skill within the profession. They can be useful in mentorship (A) and professional development (C). Members share the same professional orientation and values, which can facilitate consensus and cohesion within the group (D).

However, the ability to generate alternative solutions to problems, which can be associated with viewing problems from multiple professional perspectives, may be reduced, leading to groupthink (B).

Knowledge Area

Unit III—Interventions With Clients/Client Systems (Content Area); Use of Collaborative Relationships (Competency); The Process of Interdisciplinary and Intradisciplinary Team Collaboration (KSA)

47. D

Cultures are open, dynamic systems that undergo continuous change over time, making D not true.

It is crucial not to overgeneralize cultural information or stereotype groups in terms of fixed cultural traits (A). In the contemporary world, most individuals and groups are exposed to multiple cultures, which they use to fashion their own identities and make sense of experience (B). Culture refers to systems of knowledge, concepts, rules, and practices that are learned and transmitted across generations (C).

Knowledge Area

Unit I—Human Development, Diversity, and Behavior in the Environment (Content Area); Diversity, Social/Economic Justice, and Oppression (Competency); The Effect of Culture, Race, and Ethnicity on Behaviors, Attitudes, and Identity (KSA)

48. C

The social worker cannot recommend his sister (A) or her friends (D) to a supervisee because this would be a conflict of interest and place the supervisee in an awkward position, feeling compelled to hire based on the recommendations from his or her boss. Having the sister send in her résumé (B) is also not advisable because a conflict would exist if she were hired into a program indirectly overseen by her brother. The social worker should avoid any potential conflict of interest.

Helping the supervisee to locate other qualified candidates is the best response choice.

Knowledge Area

Unit IV—Professional Relationships, Values, and Ethics (Content Area); Professional Values and Ethical Issues (Competency); Ethical Issues Related to Dual Relationships (KSA)

49. C

As the urination is not caused by a medical problem, the social worker should FIRST conduct an assessment to determine the reasons for the behavior (C). The problem-solving process consists of the following steps: engagement, assessment, planning, intervention, evaluation, and termination. Since none of the response choices are engagement tasks, assessment is FIRST, followed by planning functions (A) and then interventions (B and D).

There is also no indication that the behavior began when he started school or is limited to the school setting. Thus, an assumption should not be made that it is tied to his feelings toward school.

Knowledge Area

Unit III—Interventions With Clients/Client Systems (Content Area); Intervention Processes and Techniques (Competency); Problem-Solving Models and Approaches (e.g., Brief, Solution-Focused Methods or Techniques) (KSA)

50. A

When clients are receiving services involuntarily, social workers should provide information about the nature (D) and extent (C) of services and about the extent of clients' right to refuse service (B).

A copy of the court order (A) is not required. However, a social worker should help the client obtain and understand the information in the court order if requested.

Knowledge Area

Unit III—Interventions With Clients/Client Systems (Content Area); Intervention Processes and Techniques (Competency); Methods to Engage and Work With Involuntary Clients/Client Systems (KSA)

51. D

A strengths-based approach is based on the assumption that a client has the ability to grow, change, and adapt, recognizing that there is always hope for change. A social worker with this focus looks at the skills that a client possesses, rather than his or her deficits. A social worker sees "the glass half full rather than half empty." He or she analyzes how a client's situation can be improved by capitalizing on the abilities that a client possesses, rather than focusing on the barriers that impede progress. The questioning of the social worker is a method to acknowledge one of the strengths of the client—help-seeking—despite the client's focus on problems.

Knowledge Area

Unit II—Assessment (Content Area); Assessment Methods and Techniques (Competency); Methods to Assess the Client's/Client System's Strengths, Resources, and Challenges (e.g., Individual, Family, Group, Organization, Community) (KSA)

52. D

There are advantages to using existing scales and instruments to evaluate practice. They are readily available for use (C). There are also considerable time and financial costs associated with developing new scales and instruments. Thus, using existing ones can be more efficient and less costly (B). In addition, existing scales and instruments may have undergone extensive testing, increasing their reliability and validity (A).

One major disadvantage is that existing scales and instruments may not have been tested cross-culturally in order to determine their appropriateness, reliability, and validity with diverse populations (D).

Knowledge Area

Unit III—Interventions With Clients/Client Systems (Content Area); Intervention Processes and Techniques (Competency); Techniques Used to Evaluate a Client's/Client System's Progress (KSA)

53. D

The selection and prioritization of service needs may be driven by many factors including client desires and motivation (A) and the results of the assessment process (B). Social workers should consider Maslow's hierarchy of needs when working with clients (C), prioritizing those related to addressing basic and safety needs.

Social workers should not limit recommendations to services that are familiar or provided by their employing agencies (D)—this would be a "cookie-cutter" or "one-size-fits-all" approach.

Knowledge Area

Unit III—Interventions With Clients/Client Systems (Content Area); Intervention Processes and Techniques (Competency); Theories and Methods of Advocacy for Policies, Services, and Resources to Meet Clients'/Client Systems' Needs (KSA)

54. C

Communication can be verbal and nonverbal. Silence is a form of communication and should be considered by a social worker when used by a client. The social worker should not change the topic (B) or assume that the silence is reflective of problems with her siblings (D). Although silence by a social worker can be an effective way to show acceptance of feelings (A), the social worker in this case vignette should probe for the reason for the silence (C) as a way of facilitating communication on issues related to the question.

Knowledge Area

Unit II—Assessment (Content Area); Assessment Methods and Techniques (Competency); Communication Theories and Styles (KSA)

55. A

Human development is the product of the interplay of biological, psychological, social, and spiritual functioning. Systems theory indicates that a change to any one area of a client's life will influence all others. Social workers must be aware of the relationships that exist between the life domains in order to provide effective services and meet a client's needs.

Knowledge Area

Unit I—Human Development, Diversity, and Behavior in the Environment (Content Area); Human Growth and Development (Competency); Theories of Human Development Throughout the Lifespan (e.g., Physical, Social, Emotional, Cognitive, Behavioral) (KSA)

56. A

Social workers focus on assisting clients to identify problems and areas of strength, as well as in increasing problem-solving strategies. It is essential that throughout the problem-solving process, social workers view clients as experts in their lives. Clients should be asked about what they would like to see changed in their lives and clients' definitions of problems should be accepted.

The social worker in this case vignette should not provide suggestions because the ideas must be generated from the client. There is no indication that the client is depressed. Although praising the client for coming to see the social worker is appropriate, it does not "assist the client" directly.

Knowledge Area

Unit II—Assessment (Content Area); Assessment Methods and Techniques (Competency); Methods of Involving Clients/Client Systems in Problem Identification (e.g., Gathering Collateral Information) (KSA)

57. C

The age of majority is when a client is recognized by law to be an adult, capable of managing his or her own affairs (A) and responsible for any legal obligations created by his or her actions (B).

A person who has reached the age of majority is bound by any contracts, deeds, or legal relationships, such as marriage, which he or she undertakes. Parental obligations typically end when a child reaches the age of majority (D).

In most states the age of majority is 18, but it may vary depending upon the nature of the activity in which the person is engaged. In a state, the age of majority for driving may be 16 while that for drinking alcoholic beverages is 21. Thus, it is NOT the same for every activity in every state (C).

Knowledge Area

Unit IV—Professional Relationships, Values, and Ethics (Content Area); Professional Values and Ethical Issues (Competency); Client/Client

System Competence and Self-Determination (e.g., Financial Decisions, Treatment Decisions, Emancipation, Age of Consent, Permanency Planning) (KSA)

58. D

Referent power is gained through charisma or associating with others who have power. Coercive power is obtained through control of punishment. Legitimate power comes from having legitimate authority. Reward power is obtained through control of rewards.

Knowledge Area

Unit III—Interventions With Clients/Client Systems (Content Area); Intervention Processes and Techniques (Competency); Community Organizing and Social Planning Methods (KSA)

59. D

The *DSM-5* was published in 2013 and is the current diagnostic framework used by social workers. It has many revisions in content and format from the *DSM-IV-TR*, which was used previously.

Knowledge Area

Unit II—Assessment (Content Area); Assessment Methods and Techniques (Competency); The Diagnostic and Statistical Manual of the American Psychiatric Association (KSA)

60. B

Dynamic risk factors can be improved by interventions such as change in living situation, treatment of psychiatric symptoms, abstaining from drug and alcohol use, access to weapons, and so on. Static risk factors cannot be altered (such as past offenses, history of violence, age) and, thus, should not be the target of interventions.

Knowledge Area

Unit II—Assessment (Content Area); Concepts of Abuse and Neglect (Competency); The Characteristics of Perpetrators of Abuse, Neglect, and Exploitation (KSA)

61. C

States were allowed to set their own benefit requirements under the Aid to Families with Dependent Children (AFDC) program, TANF's predecessor, which was created in 1935 as part of the Social Security Act. There were more restructured elements in TANF than those listed in A, B, and D.

Knowledge Area

Unit III—Interventions With Clients/Client Systems (Content Area); Use of Collaborative Relationships (Competency); The Effects of Policies, Procedures, Regulations, and Legislation on Social Work Practice and Service Delivery (KSA)

62. A

Empathy is conveyed through both verbal and nonverbal communication. Thus, the MOST effective technique for assisting a supervisee is one that can assess communication in both areas. Role playing allows the social worker to see if there is congruence between the supervisee's nonverbal actions and verbal messages. It also will allow the supervisee to practice empathic communication skills before having to use them with clients.

Knowledge Area

Unit III—Interventions With Clients/Client Systems (Content Area); Intervention Processes and Techniques (Competency); The Technique of Role Play (KSA)

63. C

The most important factor impacting on the effective treatment of clients from different racial or ethnic backgrounds is self-awareness about how these differences can impact on the problem-solving process. While ascertaining the comfort level of the client may be important, as is seeking supervision and consultation, they are not as essential as acknowledging and recognizing the impact of these differences so that they can be considered in service delivery.

A social worker should never make the decision for a client that he or she would be better served by a social work colleague of the same racial or ethnic background. There are more intragroup differences than intergroup differences among races and ethnicities. Thus, a social worker should not assume that the racial or ethnic differences between him or her and a client will be problematic.

Knowledge Area

Unit IV—Professional Relationships, Values, and Ethics (Content Area); Professional Values and Ethical Issues (Competency); The Dynamics of Diversity in the Social Worker–Client/Client System Relationship (KSA)

64. D

Role playing is a good way to assess and enhance clients' communication skills. Engaging in an active learning technique, such as role playing, will allow the client to practice asserting herself in a "safe" environment before doing so with her boss. This response choice is also BEST because it aims to enhance a skill that will be beneficial to the client not only in this situation, but in others in her life.

The problem is not that the client is not qualified or does not feel qualified, but instead that she is reluctant to engage in a needed conversation with her supervisor.

Knowledge Area

Unit III—Interventions With Clients/Client Systems (Content Area); Intervention Processes and Techniques (Competency); The Technique of Role Play (KSA)

65. B

Clients and others who use aggressive communication styles display a low tolerance for frustration, use humiliation, interrupt frequently, and use criticism or blame to attack others. They are usually not good listeners and may act in a condescending or superior manner.

Other communication styles include passive (avoiding expression of opinions/feelings, apologetic), passive-aggressive (acting passive, but sabotaging "behind-the-scenes"), and assertive (stating opinions/feelings and firmly advocating for position).

Knowledge Area

Unit II—Assessment (Content Area); Assessment Methods and Techniques (Competency); Communication Theories and Styles (KSA)

66. A

A social worker must work with the client to determine the reasons for his tiredness. As these symptoms may be caused by some underlying physical problem(s), the social worker should FIRST refer the client to a health care professional to determine if there is a medical etiology. Once it has been determined that the lethargy is not caused by a medical condition, the social worker should determine whether stress at work or other issues in the client's life are the reason for his trouble getting out of bed. Techniques to address the stress are interventions that may come later in the problem-solving process.

Knowledge Area

Unit II—Assessment (Content Area); Biopsychosocial History and Collateral Data (Competency); Biopsychosocial Factors Related to Mental Health (KSA)

67. B

The concept of environmental justice began as a movement in the 1980s due to the realization that a disproportionate number of polluting industries, power plants, and waste disposal areas were located near low-income or minority communities. The movement was established to ensure fair distribution of environmental burdens among all people regardless of their background. It is based in the belief that a person's health should not suffer because of the environment where he or she lives or works. While some of the other response choices (A, C, and D) are partially or entirely true, they are not the BEST definition of environmental justice.

Knowledge Area

Unit I—Human Development, Diversity, and Behavior in the Environment (Content Area); Diversity, Social/Economic Justice, and Oppression (Competency); Social and Economic Justice (KSA)

68. D

Gender conformity is distinct from one's sexual orientation. Those who are attracted to members of the same, opposite, or both sexes may be gender conforming or nonconforming. Gender nonconformity is defined as expressing oneself or engaging in behavior which does not fit with gender norms. Those who are gender nonconforming are often discriminated against because such nonconformity is not understood or accepted. Gender roles are usually strongly defined, and those who do not follow them are seen as aberrant. Public education is needed to dispel myths and stereotypes.

Knowledge Area

Unit I—Human Development, Diversity, and Behavior in the Environment (Content Area); Diversity, Social/Economic Justice, and Oppression (Competency); Gender and Gender Identity Concepts (KSA)

69. C

Maslow's hierarchy of needs indicates that physiological needs have to be addressed before other needs. A client's food and housing insecurity are related to basic services that are required FIRST for survival before addressing a client's relationship issues (social), self-esteem (esteem), and passion for writing (self-actualization).

Knowledge Area

Unit I—Human Development, Diversity, and Behavior in the Environment (Content Area); Human Growth and Development (Competency); Basic Human Needs (KSA)

70. D

Social workers should not discuss confidential information in any setting unless privacy can be ensured. Social workers should not discuss confidential information in public or semipublic areas such as hallways, waiting rooms, elevators, and restaurants.

Knowledge Area

Unit IV—Professional Relationships, Values, and Ethics (Content Area); Confidentiality (Competency); Legal and/or Ethical Issues Regarding Confidentiality, Including Electronic Information Security (KSA)

71. D

A behavioral approach is based on the belief that antecedents prompt certain indicators or behaviors.

It is essential that antecedents are identified and studied closely during assessment because altering or preventing them is the focus of intervention. During assessment, identification of triggers for psychosocial stress will help so that they can be reduced or eliminated.

Knowledge Area

Unit II—Assessment (Content Area); Biopsychosocial History and Collateral Data (Competency); The Indicators of Psychosocial Stress (KSA)

72. A

There is a myth that "color-blindness" is helpful to people of color by asserting that race does not matter. However, race does matter, because it affects opportunities, perceptions, income, and so on. "Color-blindness" comes from a lack of awareness of racial privilege and how race affects people of color and society as a whole. Thus, "color-blindness" creates a society that denies negative racial experiences, rejects cultural heritage, and invalidates unique perspectives based on race. In addition, when there are racial conflicts, "color-blindness" attributes them to individual shortcomings rather than examining the larger picture that involves cultural differences, stereotypes, and dominant values. Therefore, social workers must learn and train others to identify and interrupt "color-blind" ideology.

Knowledge Area

Unit I—Human Development, Diversity, and Behavior in the Environment (Content Area); Diversity, Social/Economic Justice, and Oppression (Competency); Systemic (Institutionalized) Discrimination (e.g., Racism, Sexism, Ageism) (KSA)

73. B

An emancipated minor can enter into a contract (C), sue others (D), make health care decisions (A), and so on. However, the emancipated minor still has to follow other laws and, thus, cannot get a driver's license or drink alcohol prior to the legal age to do so.

Knowledge Area

Unit IV—Professional Relationships, Values, and Ethics (Content Area); Professional Values and Ethical Issues (Competency); Client/Client System Competence and Self-Determination (e.g., Financial Decisions, Treatment Decisions, Emancipation, Age of Consent, Permanency Planning) (KSA)

74. C

Community organizing is based on the collective power of its residents to tackle problems of shared concern. There are several issues facing this community and it is critical that the social worker FIRST determine which of these problems, or other areas of concern, are most critical for residents. Social workers should not be making decisions about the focus of the intervention. As in micro practice, the social worker must immediately find out why the client has sought assistance. In this case vignette, the client is the community and the social worker must work with residents to prioritize concerns as part of the initial engagement process.

Knowledge Area

Unit III—Interventions With Clients/Client Systems (Content Area); Intervention Processes and Techniques (Competency); Community Organizing and Social Planning Methods (KSA)

75. A

Cannabis (marijuana) withdrawal occurs after a client stops using marijuana after having used it heavily for a long time. Both psychological and physical symptoms are likely to result. Psychological symptoms include anger, irritability, depressed mood, anxiety, nervousness, and so on. Physical symptoms include headache, stomach pains, sweating, fever, chills, and shakiness.

Cannabis (Marijuana) Withdrawal is a new diagnosis in the *DSM-5*. In order for the client to be diagnosed with Cannabis (Marijuana) Withdrawal, the symptoms must cause substantial problems at work, in social situations, or in other life areas, and cannot be explained by another physical or mental health condition.

Knowledge Area

Unit I—Human Development, Diversity, and Behavior in the Environment (Content Area); Human Behavior in the Social Environment (Competency); Addiction Theories and Concepts (KSA)

76. D

Confrontation (D) is calling attention to something. In the case vignette, the social worker is pointing out to the client that her actions are not consistent with her prior statements. Reflection (A) and validation (B) show empathic understanding of a client's problems. Interpretation (C) is pulling together patterns of behavior to get a new understanding.

Knowledge Area

Unit III—Interventions With Clients/Client Systems (Content Area); Intervention Processes and Techniques (Competency); The Principles and Techniques of Interviewing (e.g., Supporting, Clarifying, Focusing, Confronting, Validating, Feedback, Reflecting, Language Differences, Use of Interpreters, Redirecting) (KSA)

77. B

Undoing is performing an act to "undo" a previous unacceptable act. In this case vignette, the client buys his wife flowers and a ring to try to eradicate the fight that they had previously.

Symbolization is when a mental image is unconsciously represented by an object or another thought. Reaction formation is acting in a manner opposite of one's unconscious belief. Projective identification is what is commonly referred to as a "self-fulfilling prophecy" because it occurs when a person begins to identify with the impulses being projected on him or her and the person subsequently acts in a manner consistent with this projection.

Knowledge Area

Unit I—Human Development, Diversity, and Behavior in the Environment (Content Area); Human Behavior in the Social Environment (Competency); Psychological Defense Mechanisms and Their Effects on Behavior and Relationships (KSA)

78. B

Object permanence is the ability to realize that an object exists even if it is not seen, felt, or heard. It develops at about 8 to 12 months of age, within the sensorimotor stage of cognitive development, according to Piaget.

Knowledge Area

Unit I—Human Development, Diversity, and Behavior in the Environment (Content Area); Human Growth and Development (Competency); Theories of Human Development Throughout the Lifespan (e.g., Physical, Social, Emotional, Cognitive, Behavioral) (KSA)

79. A

Empowerment aims to ensure a sense of control over well-being and to instill hope that change is possible. A is the only response choice that enhances a client's skills with the goal that he or she will develop greater autonomy and ability to solve problems independently in the future.

Knowledge Area

Unit III—Interventions With Clients/Client Systems (Content Area); Intervention Processes and Techniques (Competency); Strengths-Based and Empowerment Strategies and Interventions (KSA)

80. B

Level of care determinations are based on identifying the needed service intensity along a continuum depending on clients' immediate needs. Clients enter services at a level appropriate to addressing their current problems and then step up to more intense treatment or down to less intense treatment as needed. Outpatient services are appropriate unless clients are at high risk. The goal is to serve clients in the least restrictive environments while ensuring health and safety.

Knowledge Area

Unit II—Assessment (Content Area); Assessment Methods and Techniques (Competency); Placement Options Based on Assessed Level of Care (KSA)

81. C

Mental status examinations are appraisals of the appearance, behavior, mental functioning, and overall demeanor of clients. These assessments are based on the observations and subjective judgments of social workers. Judgments about mental state should always consider the developmental levels of clients and age appropriateness of behaviors. Thus, mental status examinations are NOT objective.

Knowledge Area

Unit II—Assessment (Content Area); Biopsychosocial History and Collateral Data (Competency); The Components and Function of the Mental Status Examination (KSA)

82. D

Social work practice uses multiple modalities, including individual, family, and group therapy, to assist clients in resolving problems. A critical factor in deciding which is best is identifying the root cause of the problem. In this case vignette, the client is having problems in the family unit. Thus, arranging for her and her parents to come together to discuss the issues (D) is BEST. Treating her individually (A) or normalizing the situation (B) will not assist with resolving the family problems. The client response in quotation marks is typical of someone in this situation and there is no indication in the case vignette of suicide risk or dangerousness toward others, making a mental health screening (C) unnecessary.

Knowledge Area

Unit II—Assessment (Content Area); Assessment Methods and Techniques (Competency); The Factors and Processes Used in Problem Formulation (KSA)

83. B

Self-monitoring consists of a client systematically observing his or her own thoughts or behaviors. Most clients are not entirely aware of the extent to which they engage in various thoughts or behaviors. When clients are provided with the opportunity to observe their own thoughts or actions carefully, dramatic changes often occur. The reasons why self-monitoring results in changes are not completely understood. The information obtained through careful observation might provide important feedback. Self-monitoring may be effective because the act of observation itself may take on reinforcing or punishing properties.

In the case vignette, the client will better understand the problem by self-monitoring. She may gain insight into how often these thoughts are really occurring and when/why they emerge.

Knowledge Area

Unit III—Interventions With Clients/Client Systems (Content Area); Intervention Processes and Techniques (Competency); Client/Client System Self-Monitoring Techniques (KSA)

84. C

Group therapy can be very useful for those who are feeling lonely and isolated. Group members who have experienced similar losses will provide support during this period in the client's life and ideas about how to find new activities and feel comfortable when socializing.

Knowledge Area

Unit I—Human Development, Diversity, and Behavior in the Environment (Content Area); Human Behavior in the Social Environment (Competency); Theories of Group Development and Functioning (KSA)

85. B

Testing (B) is the role of the learning specialist or psychologist—not the social worker. As part of Individualized Education Plan (IEP) development, the social worker will complete the family history (A) and make observations about the child's relationships with other students and general participation in school (C). Parent/family participation is essential to the IEP process, and the social worker will help solicit this participation and ensure that parents/family members understand the process and outcomes (D).

Knowledge Area

Unit IV—Professional Relationships, Values, and Ethics (Content Area); Professional Development and Use of Self (Competency); The Social Worker's Role in the Problem-Solving Process (KSA)

86. A

The *DSM-5* has discarded the multiaxial system of diagnosis (formerly Axis I, Axis II, and Axis III) and combines the first three axes outlined in past editions of the *DSM* into one axis with all mental and other medical diagnoses.

It has replaced Axis IV with significant psychosocial and contextual features and dropped Axis V (Global Assessment of Functioning, known as GAF).

The *World Health Organization Disability Assessment Schedule 2.0 (WHODAS 2.0)* is added to "Section III, Emerging Measures and Models," under Assessment Measures.

Knowledge Area

Unit II—Assessment (Content Area); Assessment Methods and Techniques (Competency); The Diagnostic and Statistical Manual of the American Psychiatric Association (KSA)

87. B

Collectivist cultures emphasize family and group goals above individual needs or desires. Thus, traits that are helpful to working in groups are valued and those who engage in such behaviors are seen as being trustworthy, honest, and generous. Conversely, in individualist cultures, members are rewarded for being assertive and strong—characteristics that are helpful for competing. Capitalism is based on the belief that there should be few or no regulations that impede self-interest because the pursuit of one's self-interest, which is primary, simultaneously benefits the economic self-interest of others.

Knowledge Area

Unit I—Human Development, Diversity, and Behavior in the Environment (Content Area); Diversity, Social/Economic Justice, and Oppression (Competency); The Effect of Culture, Race, and Ethnicity on Behaviors, Attitudes, and Identity (KSA)

88. A

Flowcharts are easy-to-understand diagrams that show how the steps in *a process* fit together. Their simplicity makes them useful tools for communicating how processes work. There are many ways to measure the functioning and effectiveness of organizations. Usually, functioning is assessed as it relates to organizational structures, processes, and outcomes. The use of flowcharts indicates that the social worker is evaluating the agency's processes.

Knowledge Area

Unit II—Assessment (Content Area); Assessment Methods and Techniques (Competency); Techniques and Instruments Used to Assess Clients/Client Systems (KSA)

89. B

Social workers must be mindful of the ethical implications of self-disclosure. Self-disclosure can be an indicator of boundary issues that may lead to dual relationships (A). There are no clear guidelines regarding when social workers' self-disclosure to clients is appropriate, making self-disclosure in social work complex (C). Most practice situations can be addressed with little or no social worker self-disclosure (D).

However, when used skillfully and judiciously, self-disclosure can strengthen the therapeutic alliance and facilitate client trust, making B NOT true.

Knowledge Area

Unit IV—Professional Relationships, Values, and Ethics (Content Area); Professional Development and Use of Self (Competency); Self-Disclosure Principles and Applications (KSA)

90. A

Fibromyalgia is characterized by widespread pain, diffuse tenderness, and a number of other symptoms. Although fibromyalgia is often considered an arthritis-related condition, it does not cause inflammation or damage to the joints, muscles, or other tissues. Like arthritis, fibromyalgia can cause significant pain and fatigue, and it can interfere with a person's ability to carry on daily activities. It is considered a rheumatic condition, a medical condition that impairs the joints and/or soft tissues. Most of those diagnosed with fibromyalgia are women. The causes of fibromyalgia are unknown. Many people associate the development of fibromyalgia with physically or emotionally stressful or traumatic events or repetitive injuries. Others link it to an illness. For others, fibromyalgia seems to occur spontaneously.

Knowledge Area

Unit II—Assessment (Content Area); Biopsychosocial History and Collateral Data (Competency); Basic Medical Terminology (KSA)

91. A

An 8-year-old child may not have the cognitive and expressive verbal communication skills to adequately describe his or her feelings or thoughts. Thus, play therapy (A) that uses pictures, toys, puppets, dolls, and other objects is BEST used to assist in addressing the concerns in all steps of the problem-solving process.

The other techniques listed require insight and abstract thinking, which are not typical of an 8-year-old child, based on Piaget's work on cognitive development.

Knowledge Area

Unit III—Interventions With Clients/Client Systems (Content Area); Intervention Processes and Techniques (Competency); The Criteria Used in the Selection of Intervention/Treatment Modalities (e.g., Client/Client System Abilities, Culture, Life Stage) (KSA)

92. A

All of the response choices listed are possible neurologic symptoms. However, the question asked for *physical* issues. Confusion and delirium are changes in consciousness or mental signs of problems in neurologic functioning.

Knowledge Area

Unit II—Assessment (Content Area); Biopsychosocial History and Collateral Data (Competency); Basic Medical Terminology (KSA)

93. A

Substance Use Disorder in the *DSM-5* combines the *DSM-IV* categories of Substance Abuse and Substance Dependence into a single disorder measured on a continuum from mild to severe. Each specific substance (other than caffeine, which cannot be diagnosed as a Substance Use Disorder) is addressed as a separate use disorder (Alcohol Use Disorder, Stimulant Use Disorder, etc.). Drug craving is added as a criterion, and problems with law enforcement are eliminated because of cultural considerations that make this criterion difficult to apply. Gambling Disorder is the sole condition in a new category on behavioral addictions. Thus, all the response choices are false, except A.

Knowledge Area

Unit II—Assessment (Content Area); Assessment Methods and Techniques (Competency); The Diagnostic and Statistical Manual of the American Psychiatric Association (KSA)

94. B

All of the response choices are signs of abuse or neglect, but B is an emotional and psychological symptom. It is not physical.

Knowledge Area

Unit II—Assessment (Content Area); Concepts of Abuse and Neglect (Competency); Indicators and Dynamics of Abuse and Neglect Throughout the Lifespan (KSA)

95. A

According to the *NASW Code of Ethics*, social workers who are leaving an employment setting should inform clients of appropriate options for the continuation of services and of the benefits and risks of the options.

Knowledge Area

Unit IV—Professional Relationships, Values, and Ethics (Content Area); Professional Values and Ethical Issues (Competency); Legal and/or Ethical Issues Related to Termination (KSA)

96. C

A strengths approach views the client as the "expert" in his or her life circumstances. Although some of the response choices may be important for a social worker, such as collecting needed information from collateral sources (B) and ensuring confidentiality forms are signed (D), they are not directly linked to a strengths perspective. Asking the client about concerns is empowering and views the client as a partner in the assessment process. Suggesting coping strategies (A), while perhaps helpful, is not an assessment task.

Knowledge Area

Unit II—Assessment (Content Area); Assessment Methods and Techniques (Competency); Methods of Involving Clients/Client Systems in Problem Identification (e.g., Gathering Collateral Information) (KSA)

97. B

The core values include service, social justice, dignity and worth of the person, importance of human relationships, integrity, and competence.

Knowledge Area

Unit IV—Professional Relationships, Values, and Ethics (Content Area); Professional Values and Ethical Issues (Competency); Professional Values and Principles (e.g., Competence, Social Justice, Integrity, and Dignity and Worth of the Person) (KSA)

98. D

According to Erikson, industry versus inferiority takes place from age 6 to puberty. During this stage, children should initiate and complete projects, taking pride in their accomplishments. If they are not encouraged to do so or restricted in any way, children will feel inferior and lack confidence in their abilities.

Autonomy versus shame and doubt occurs between ages 1 and 3, followed by initiative versus guilt, which spans ages 3 to 6. Generativity versus stagnation is a psychosocial stage that is seen in middle adulthood, when individuals begin to view themselves as part of a larger society as opposed to being self-absorbed and preoccupied with their own well-being.

Knowledge Area

Unit I—Human Development, Diversity, and Behavior in the Environment (Content Area); Human Growth and Development (Competency); Theories of Human Development Throughout the Lifespan (e.g., Physical, Social, Emotional, Cognitive, Behavioral) (KSA)

99. B

The classic model of cultural, racial, and ethnic identity development refers to identity statuses rather than stages, because *"stages"* implies a linear progression of steps that may not occur for all. In *internalization and commitment*, the final status in the model, a client has developed a secure sense of identity and is comfortable socializing both within and outside the group he or she identifies with.

Identity development begins with a *pre-encounter* in which a client may not be consciously aware of his or her culture, race, or ethnicity and how it affects his or her life. In *encounter*, a client has an interaction that provokes thought about the role of culture, racial, and ethnic identification. After an encounter, there may be a period of *immersion–emersion*, followed by searching for information about cultural, racial, and ethnic differences and learning through interaction with others.

Knowledge Area

Unit I—Human Development, Diversity, and Behavior in the Environment (Content Area); Human Growth and Development (Competency); Theories of Racial, Ethnic, and Cultural Development Throughout the Lifespan (KSA)

100. D

A delusion is a false, fixed belief despite evidence to the contrary or believing something that is not true (D).

Some defense mechanisms, such as denial, ignore or fail to recognize the importance of key information, but defense mechanisms are much broader—such as engaging in action—than the definition provided in the question. Disorientation is confusion with regard to person, place, or time. Hallucinations are seeing, hearing, smelling, or feeling things that are not real or present.

Knowledge Area

Unit II—Assessment (Content Area); Biopsychosocial History and Collateral Data (Competency); The Indicators of Mental and Emotional Illness Throughout the Lifespan (KSA)

101. B

The PRIMARY purpose of social work supervision is to assure the delivery of the most effective and efficient client services. The supervisor achieves this aim by increasing a social worker's capacity to work more effectively, providing a work context conducive to productivity, and helping a social worker take satisfaction in his or her work.

Knowledge Area

Unit IV—Professional Relationships, Values, and Ethics (Content Area); Professional Development and Use of Self (Competency); The Supervisee's Role in Supervision (e.g., Identifying Learning Needs, Self-Assessment, Prioritizing, etc.) (KSA)

102. D

The *NASW Code of Ethics* states that social workers who believe that a social work colleague's impairment interferes with practice effectiveness and that the colleague has not taken adequate steps to address the impairment should take action through appropriate channels established by employers, agencies (A), National Association of Social Workers (NASW), licensing and regulatory bodies (B), and other professional organizations (C).

   The social worker should not provide services to the impaired colleague directly (D).

Knowledge Area

Unit IV—Professional Relationships, Values, and Ethics (Content Area); Professional Values and Ethical Issues (Competency); Legal and/or Ethical Issues Regarding Mandatory Reporting (e.g., Abuse, Threat of Harm, Impaired Professionals, etc.) (KSA)

103. C

Consultation in social work practice is done to assist agencies to solve specific problems that they identify (C). It is time-limited and agency leadership is not required to adopt a consultant's recommendations, making D and B incorrect. A consultant does not have formal authority within an agency (making A incorrect), so he or she cannot take official action on behalf of an agency—such as hiring or firing. However, consultants have a lot of informal authority as they are viewed as "experts" in their areas of practice, causing staff to frequently agree with their advice.

Knowledge Area

Unit III—Interventions With Clients/Client Systems (Content Area); Use of Collaborative Relationships (Competency); Consultation Approaches (e.g., Referrals to Specialists) (KSA)

104. C

Reaction formation is adopting attitudes, beliefs, and/or feelings contrary to what is actually believed unconsciously. It also may be acting differently than what would be expected given a client's unconscious views; for example, a client treats someone that he or she dislikes in an overly friendly manner.

Splitting is viewing people or things as all good or all bad. Substitution is replacing an unattainable goal, emotion, or object with a more realistic or acceptable one. Undoing is trying to erase a thought or feeling by doing something that is based on the opposite thought or feeling.

Knowledge Area

Unit I—Human Development, Diversity, and Behavior in the Environment (Content Area); Human Behavior in the Social Environment (Competency); Psychological Defense Mechanisms and Their Effects on Behavior and Relationships (KSA)

105. B

Delirium tremens (DTs) is a severe form of alcohol withdrawal with symptoms including hallucinations, rapid respiration, temperature abnormalities, and body tremors.

Knowledge Area

Unit I—Human Development, Diversity, and Behavior in the Environment (Content Area); Human Behavior in the Social Environment (Competency); Addiction Theories and Concepts (KSA)

106. D

Separation anxiety is a typical developmental stage associated with bonding that is seen in early childhood. In this case vignette, a social worker is asked to BEST *assist*, which means intervene. Two of the response choices, A and C, are assessment tasks and are not appropriate for other reasons. Separation anxiety will subside naturally as a child learns how to master his or her environment and learns that a caregiver will return even if out of sight for a period of time. Behavioral interventions or therapy for children experiencing separation anxiety are NOT warranted; they should be comforted and their parents should learn to cope with behaviors that children exhibit.

Knowledge Area

Unit I—Human Development, Diversity, and Behavior in the Environment (Content Area); Human Growth and Development (Competency); The Principles of Attachment and Bonding (KSA)

107. B

All of the response choices occur during the problem-solving process, but the completion of a biopsychosocial–spiritual–cultural assessment is done during assessment, the *second* step in the problem-solving process, while the rest are completed during engagement, the *first* step.

Knowledge Area

Unit III—Interventions With Clients/Client Systems (Content Area); Intervention Processes and Techniques (Competency); Problem-Solving Models and Approaches (e.g., Brief, Solution-Focused Methods or Techniques) (KSA)

108. C

When working with groups, a social worker should use the group as the major helping agent and not make decisions for the group. A social worker should only intervene when interactions or the communication pattern within a group is becoming fragmented or dysfunctional in some way. Thus, it is BEST for the social worker to encourage the client to discuss his feelings with the other group members (C). A does not use the group as the major helping agent, and B and D have the social worker engaging in actions that should be addressed by group members in this modality.

Knowledge Area

Unit I—Human Development, Diversity, and Behavior in the Environment (Content Area); Human Behavior in the Social Environment (Competency); Theories of Group Development and Functioning (KSA)

109. C

The social worker's documentation should include only information that is directly relevant to the delivery of services. Although there may be some justification for documenting that the client is having problems at home, since it is interfering with his school performance, there is no need to mention that he resides in a home with two same-gender parents.

Knowledge Area

Unit III—Interventions With Clients/Client Systems (Content Area); Documentation (Competency); The Principles of Case Recording, Documentation, and Management for Practice Records (KSA)

110. A

Homeostasis is the notion that families try to maintain their existing interaction patterns and functioning over time, even if dysfunctional. When there is a change in a family member's behavior, such as the husband's in this case vignette, all members are forced to adapt and change. This causes stress within the family system and subsequent conflict. A social worker must be aware that positive changes in a family member, such as becoming sober and seeking treatment for alcohol addiction, can disrupt the existing homeostasis, causing the family to need to learn new ways to communicate and interact with one another.

Knowledge Area

Unit I—Human Development, Diversity, and Behavior in the Environment (Content Area); Human Behavior in the Social Environment (Competency); Systems and Ecological Perspectives and Theories (KSA)

111. A

Spirituality should be included in all biopsychosocial–cultural assessments. In addition, if spirituality emerges as an issue related to a client problem, a more detailed spiritual history should be taken. All of the listed questions are usually asked when taking a spiritual history except attendance at religious services. Although "religious" and "spiritual" are used interchangeably by many, they are not the same. Religion is typically more formal or organized and it unites a group of people who share similar beliefs and who codify these beliefs into texts and rituals to facilitate deeper connections with their views. Someone may be spiritual, contemplating, and connecting with "something more," without being part of a larger religion.

Knowledge Area

Unit II—Assessment (Content Area); Biopsychosocial History and Collateral Data (Competency); The Components of a Biopsychosocial Assessment (KSA)

112. C

Paraphrasing restates what a client says in order to get a full understanding of the client's ideas and thoughts (C). Generalization (A) indicates that a client's behavior is typical of those in that situation to avoid feeling isolated or alone. Interpretation (B) is pulling together patterns of a client's behavior to get a new understanding. Clarification (D) is asking questions to ensure that a social worker has a correct and full understanding of a client's situation.

Knowledge Area

Unit III—Interventions With Clients/Client Systems (Content Area); Intervention Processes and Techniques (Competency); Verbal and Nonverbal Communication Techniques (KSA)

113. A

When conducting community assessments, it is essential for social workers to identify strengths or positive features (assets) of a community that can be leveraged to develop solutions to problems. Strengths can include organizations, people, partnerships, facilities, funding, policies, regulations, and/or culture.

Although recognizing challenges or problems is also part of a community assessment (B), there is not an assumption that problems *have to be addressed*. Community members must be the ones to determine if change has to occur and whether outside resources are desired and exist that can be helpful (C), as well as which strategies may work, based on past experience (D) and other factors.

Knowledge Area

Unit II—Assessment (Content Area); Assessment Methods and Techniques (Competency); Methods to Assess the Client's/Client System's Strengths, Resources, and Challenges (e.g., Individual, Family, Group, Organization, Community) (KSA)

114. A

A needs assessment is a systematic process for determining the magnitude of the problem. The social worker must fully understand transportation needs, such as geographic areas where it may be lacking, the types of transportation needed, cost barriers, and so on, before meeting with others inside (B) or outside (D) the agency with possible solutions. There are multiple methods for conducting needs assessments and completing one is the FIRST step in solving the problem (A).

The social worker is not ready to advocate on the client's behalf, making C inadvisable, as the full scope of the problem and viable solutions are unknown.

Knowledge Area

Unit III—Interventions With Clients/Client Systems (Content Area); Use of Collaborative Relationships (Competency); Methods to Assess the Availability of Community Resources (KSA)

115. C

In instances when social workers are not fluent in the languages spoken by their clients, qualified interpreters or translators should be used. Use of a qualified interpreter should not change the tone or content of the interaction. The social worker will want to stand near the interpreter so the client can see the nonverbal gestures of the social worker while listening to the interpreter (A). The social worker should also fully explain all concepts, not using slang or abbreviated terms (B). There is no need to speak louder or slower than usual, but clarity of speech is important so that the interpreter can understand what is being said (D).

The qualified interpreter is simply there to facilitate communication and should not be asked for or give opinions about the interaction or the client's situation (C).

Knowledge Area

Unit I—Human Development, Diversity, and Behavior in the Environment (Content Area); Diversity, Social/Economic Justice, and Oppression (Competency); The Principles of Culturally Competent Social Work Practice (KSA)

116. A

Burnout is often related to job environments and stresses attached to job requirements. It is a state of physical, emotional, psychological, and/or spiritual exhaustion. It can be manifested by cynicism or a lack of satisfaction in working with clients to resolve their problems.

Secondary trauma is the reaction to dealing with clients' situations. Secondary trauma results from engaging in empathic relationships with clients who have had traumatic experiences and witnessing their effects. The symptoms of secondary trauma mirror those experienced by the primary victim of trauma, including, but not limited to, insomnia, chronic irritability or angry outbursts, fatigue, difficulty concentrating, and/or avoidance.

Compassion fatigue is best defined as a syndrome consisting of a combination of the symptoms of secondary trauma and burnout.

The question states that the social worker is overwhelmed with paperwork—a job requirement. Thus, burnout is the MOST likely explanation/diagnosis.

Knowledge Area

Unit IV—Professional Relationships, Values, and Ethics (Content Area); Professional Development and Use of Self (Competency); Burnout, Secondary Trauma, and Compassion Fatigue (KSA)

117. D

Although connecting with other caregivers (A) and identifying family members who may assist (C) may be helpful, the social worker can be of MOST assistance by listening to the client's feelings about changes seen in her husband.

Caregiving comes with a multitude of psychosocial stressors due to the transitioning of roles and accompanying expectations. The client may feel worried, angry, resentful, guilty, tired, sad, anxious, and/or frustrated. These feelings are compounded when assistance is not appreciated by those being cared for. The social worker can provide help by listening, as well as assisting—if requested by the client—to sort out these feelings, find their roots, and reframe them into empowerment, opportunity, and choice.

Knowledge Area

Unit III—Interventions With Clients/Client Systems (Content Area); Indicators and Effects of Crisis and Change (Competency); The Impact of Caregiving on Families (KSA)

118. D

The social worker should not terminate services to pursue a social or sexual relationship with a client (B and C). The social worker should also not terminate services because the client raised the attraction (A). The social worker should appropriately address the situation by reconfirming professional boundaries (D).

Knowledge Area

Unit IV—Professional Relationships, Values, and Ethics (Content Area); Professional Values and Ethical Issues (Competency); Professional Boundaries in the Social Worker–Client/Client System Relationship (e.g., Power Differences, Conflicts of Interest, etc.) (KSA)

119. B

The cycle of abuse indicates that this may be the "honeymoon" phase that occurs after a battering incident. Just because there has not been any violence in the past year does not mean that the battering will not occur in the future. The "honeymoon" phase leads to "tension building" and then violence in the future.

It is likely that the boyfriend will engage in this behavior again without intervention. There is no mention in this case vignette that the boyfriend is receiving services. When abuse is present, traditional couples counseling is not advisable because treating both the client and her boyfriend together places the client at too much risk.

Knowledge Area

Unit III—Interventions With Clients/Client Systems (Content Area); Intervention Processes and Techniques (Competency); The Impact of Domestic, Intimate Partner, and Other Violence on the Helping Relationship (KSA)

120. A

Sublimation is a defense mechanism that channels unwanted dysfunctional feelings or behaviors into socially acceptable forms. It is both useful and constructive as it directs instinctual, unacceptable drives into productive activities. For example, a client with intense rage who pursues boxing instead of getting into street fights or engaging in other violent acts may be using sublimation.

Knowledge Area

Unit I—Human Development, Diversity, and Behavior in the Environment (Content Area); Human Behavior in the Social Environment (Competency); Psychological Defense Mechanisms and Their Effects on Behavior and Relationships (KSA)

121. B

Whenever releasing information, social workers should disclose the least amount of confidential information necessary to achieve the desired purpose; only information that is directly relevant to the purpose for which the disclosure is made should be revealed.

Knowledge Area

Unit IV—Professional Relationships, Values, and Ethics (Content Area); Confidentiality (Competency); Legal and/or Ethical Issues Regarding Confidentiality, Including Electronic Information Security (KSA)

122. B

All of the response choices are roles that social workers can take when making observations: complete participant (living the experience as a participant), participant as observer (interacting with those who are participating), observer as participant (limited relationship with others participating—primarily observer), or complete observer (removed from activity—observer only). Observation is a method used in scientific inquiry or other social work activities to collect data.

Knowledge Area

Unit III—Interventions With Clients/Client Systems (Content Area); Intervention Processes and Techniques (Competency); The Principles of Active Listening and Observation (KSA)

123. D

Resistance is often reduced by acknowledging the courage that it takes to seek help (A). Often a client is unclear about what to expect as part of services provision so explaining the parameters alleviates fear and anxiety (B). A client should also not be afraid to speak openly about his or her needs, so confidentiality policies should be reviewed (C).

Asking a client to commit to cooperating (D) may appear abrupt or threatening during a first meeting and is the LEAST effective technique in garnering a willingness to work together.

Knowledge Area

Unit II—Assessment (Content Area); Assessment Methods and Techniques (Competency); The Indicators of Motivation, Resistance, and Readiness to Change (KSA)

124. D

Setting clear, appropriate, and sensitive boundaries that govern physical contact are essential for professional practice. Social workers should *not* engage in physical contact with clients when there is a possibility of psychological harm to a client as a result of the contact (such as cradling or caressing clients).

Physical contact or other activities of a sexual nature with clients are clearly not allowable for social workers.

Knowledge Area

Unit IV—Professional Relationships, Values, and Ethics (Content Area); Professional Values and Ethical Issues (Competency); Professional Boundaries in the Social Worker–Client/Client System Relationship (e.g., Power Differences, Conflicts of Interest, etc.) (KSA)

125. A

There are different levels of social work practice—macro, mezzo, and micro. The macro level intervenes on a large scale, such as with communities. Micro social work, the most common type of practice, involves working directly with an individual or a family. The mezzo level falls right in between the macro and micro levels, and involves working with smaller groups and institutions.

All levels of practice are based on the same social work values, with the consistent goal of assisting in the acquisition of skills and resources to help others solve problems themselves. All levels of practice can be done with a social work degree, using core skills that can be applied to all levels of practice.

Knowledge Area

Unit I—Human Development, Diversity, and Behavior in the Environment (Content Area); Human Behavior in the Social Environment (Competency); Systems and Ecological Perspectives and Theories (KSA)

126. C

In order to resolve this conflict, ethical problem solving is needed. The essential steps in ethical problem solving include: (a) identifying ethical standards that are being compromised; (b) determining whether there is an ethical issue or dilemma; (c) *weighing ethical issues in light of key social work values and principles*; (d) suggesting modifications in light of the prioritized ethical values; (e) implementing modifications in light of prioritized ethical values; and (f) monitoring for new ethical issues or dilemmas.

Knowledge Area

Unit IV—Professional Relationships, Values, and Ethics (Content Area); Professional Values and Ethical Issues (Competency); Techniques to Identify and Resolve Ethical Dilemmas (KSA)

127. A

The formal operations stage of cognitive development is the last one according to Piaget. This stage, which begins at about age 11, is characterized by planning for the future, thinking hypothetically, and assuming adult roles.

The sensorimotor stage occurs in the first 2 years of life, the preoperational stage occurs between ages 2 and 7, and the concrete operations stage ends at about age 11. In the concrete operations stage, cause and effect relationships are understood and there is the beginning of abstract thought, but the level of abstraction is not as fully developed as it is in the formal operations stage.

Knowledge Area

Unit I—Human Development, Diversity, and Behavior in the Environment (Content Area); Human Growth and Development (Competency); Theories of Human Development Throughout the Lifespan (e.g., Physical, Social, Emotional, Cognitive, Behavioral) (KSA)

128. A

A client who has been depressed and suddenly appears happier may be at higher risk of committing suicide if the change in affect is attributable to a decision to act. A client is also at greater risk after being discharged from the hospital or after being started on antidepressants because he or she may now have the energy to implement a suicide plan. The question asks for the FIRST action that a social worker should take, which is the completion of a risk assessment to address safety concerns.

Knowledge Area

Unit III—Interventions With Clients/Client Systems (Content Area); Indicators and Effects of Crisis and Change (Competency); The Indicators and Risk Factors of the Client's/Client System's Danger to Self and Others (KSA)

129. B

Acculturation is a reciprocal process where both minority and majority cultural groups change in order to facilitate interaction and achieve common goals.

Members of a minority cultural group in a pluralistic society should never have to abandon their customs, traditions, or beliefs in order to conform. There is a responsibility by a majority cultural group to alter their dominant ways in order to ensure that those in the minority can be full participants, even with differences in practices or attitudes. Not acknowledging cultural differences leads to a lack of sensitivity and awareness and a failure to develop healthy cultural identities.

Knowledge Area

Unit I—Human Development, Diversity, and Behavior in the Environment (Content Area); Diversity, Social/Economic Justice, and Oppression (Competency); The Effect of Culture, Race, and Ethnicity on Behaviors, Attitudes, and Identity (KSA)

130. C

The social worker should FIRST determine the impact of the parents' beliefs on the couple's decision. Although some of the other response choices may be appropriate, they would occur later in the problem-solving process. An assessment should be completed after engaging with the couple. Central to the assessment is ascertaining the extent to which the parents' views are critical to or influence the couple's decisions.

Knowledge Area

Unit I—Human Development, Diversity, and Behavior in the Environment (Content Area); Diversity, Social/Economic Justice, and Oppression (Competency); The Effect of Culture, Race, and Ethnicity on Behaviors, Attitudes, and Identity (KSA)

131. D

In instances when clients lack the capacity to provide informed consent, social workers should protect clients' interests by seeking permission from appropriate third parties and obtaining assent in accordance with clients' level of understanding.

In the case vignette, the client is not her own legal guardian. Thus, the consent of the guardian and the willingness of the client to participate (her assent) are needed (D).

Knowledge Area

Unit IV—Professional Relationships, Values, and Ethics (Content Area); Confidentiality (Competency); The Principles and Processes of Obtaining Informed Consent (KSA)

132. D

A cost-benefit analysis determines the financial costs of operating a program as compared with the fiscal benefits. A cost-benefit ratio is generated to determine whether, and the extent to which, the costs exceed the benefits.

Knowledge Area

Unit III—Interventions With Clients/Client Systems (Content Area); Intervention Processes and Techniques (Competency); Methods, Techniques, and Instruments Used to Evaluate Social Work Practice (KSA)

133. D

In this case vignette, the social worker has not said or done anything to address the client's reports about hurting herself. It is essential that the social worker FIRST conduct a suicide risk assessment to determine if the self-report of the client—that she will not act—is supported. This assessment is based on identifying the risk and protective factors present. If there does not appear to be an imminent risk, the social worker can engage in other actions to address the client's underlying concerns, while continuing to monitor her suicidality.

Knowledge Area

Unit III—Interventions With Clients/Client Systems (Content Area); Indicators and Effects of Crisis and Change (Competency); The Indicators and Risk Factors of the Client's/Client System's Danger to Self and Others (KSA)

134. D

The use of collateral sources and information is not "a fishing expedition" to see what can be caught. Social workers can use collateral sources as informants, with clients' consent, to gather vital information from other professionals or agencies that may have treated clients in the past. Family members and friends may provide important information about the length or severity of issues or problems. The use of collateral information is also used when the credibility and validity of information obtained from a client or others are questionable.

Knowledge Area

Unit II—Assessment (Content Area); Assessment Methods and Techniques (Competency); Methods of Involving Clients/Client Systems in Problem Identification (e.g., Gathering Collateral Information) (KSA)

135. A

Prior to receiving services, clients must be informed of certain provisions and consent to them. These elements are often explicitly stated on a form which a client signs and dates. However, the requirement and storage of the form in a client's file is not a critical element to *obtaining* informed consent.

Informed consent includes, but is not limited to, explaining the services that will be provided (including any risks and benefits), alternative services available, payment expected and consequences for nonpayment of services, confidentiality policies and limits to confidentiality, and the procedures for revoking informed consent at any time.

Knowledge Area

Unit II—Assessment (Content Area); Assessment Methods and Techniques (Competency); Methods of Involving Clients/Client Systems in Problem Identification (e.g., Gathering Collateral Information) (KSA)

136. C

Community organization enhances participatory skills of members by working with and not for them and develops leadership, particularly the ability to conceptualize and act on problems. It strengthens communities so they can better deal independently with future problems. Community members have the capacity to resolve problems and should *not* need to rely on outside "experts" in the future to assist (C).

Knowledge Area

Unit III—Interventions With Clients/Client Systems (Content Area); Intervention Processes and Techniques (Competency); Community Organizing and Social Planning Methods (KSA)

137. A

All of the response choices are roles performed by social workers except rapport builder (A). Although establishing rapport is essential to engaging clients in the problem-solving process, it is not a role.

Roles consist of a set of rules or norms that function to guide behavior. Roles specify what goals should be pursued, what tasks must be accomplished, and how to behave in a given situation. Social work roles include, but are not limited to, resource allocator, advocate, educator, case manager, catalyst, and broker.

Knowledge Area

Unit IV—Professional Relationships, Values, and Ethics (Content Area); Professional Development and Use of Self (Competency); The Social Worker's Role in the Problem-Solving Process (KSA)

138. C

Based on the information provided, the client's development appears typical. Many children are not "potty trained" by age 4. There is also no information about how the client defines being "potty trained." He may be having accidents during the day or at night, with some bladder and bowel control. Her request to have a psychological evaluation results from her concerns "about his development." These concerns may involve issues in other areas of functioning. The social worker should FIRST find out the extent and scope of the perceived problem (as part of the assessment process) before deciding what actions or interventions are needed.

Knowledge Area

Unit I—Human Development, Diversity, and Behavior in the Environment (Content Area); Human Growth and Development (Competency); Theories of Human Development Throughout the Lifespan (e.g., Physical, Social, Emotional, Cognitive, Behavioral) (KSA)

139. D

According to Maslow, needs are divided into basic (or deficiency) needs, such as those related to physiological issues, security, socialization, and esteem, as well as growth needs such as self-actualization.

Knowledge Area

Unit I—Human Development, Diversity, and Behavior in the Environment (Content Area); Human Growth and Development (Competency); Basic Human Needs (KSA)

140. B

A pre–post design is when information collected before the onset of an intervention is compared with that collected after it is implemented. Only the correct answer contains these two comparisons.

Knowledge Area

Unit III—Interventions With Clients/Client Systems (Content Area); Intervention Processes and Techniques (Competency); Methods, Techniques, and Instruments Used to Evaluate Social Work Practice (KSA)

141. C

The client is using denial, the most common defense mechanism. She is failing to acknowledge the reality of her mother's prognosis. Repression is forcing thoughts into the unconscious (i.e., forgetting them). Displacement is shifting negative beliefs or negative impulses to less threatening targets. Conversion occurs when a repressed urge manifests itself in a disturbance of a bodily function.

Knowledge Area

Unit I—Human Development, Diversity, and Behavior in the Environment (Content Area); Human Behavior in the Social Environment

(Competency); Psychological Defense Mechanisms and Their Effects on Behavior and Relationships (KSA)

142. D

Social workers should represent themselves as competent only within the boundaries of their education, training, licensure and certification (A), consultation received, and/or supervised experience. When providing services in areas that are new to them or unfamiliar, social workers should engage in appropriate study and training (B), as well as receive consultation and supervision from people who are competent in these areas (C).

Getting an updated medical status (D) is not directly related to ethical practice in an area that is new to the social worker, which is the key issue in this case vignette.

Knowledge Area

Unit IV—Professional Relationships, Values, and Ethics (Content Area); Professional Development and Use of Self (Competency); Professional Development Activities to Improve Practice and Maintain Current Professional Knowledge (e.g., In-Service Training, Licensing Requirements, Reviews of Literature, Workshops) (KSA)

143. C

Social workers should understand how to communicate with clients who are upset and/or angry. Listening to a client who is expressing a lot of emotion shows acceptance of his or her feelings. There is nothing in the case vignette that states that this hostility or anger includes indicators of dangerousness to self or others.

Knowledge Area

Unit II—Assessment (Content Area); Assessment Methods and Techniques (Competency); Communication Theories and Styles (KSA)

144. B

Although all of the response choices may be true, the question asks for the most important *benefit*. Group work is effective or advantageous because it uses the reciprocal relationship between peers to evoke change. The members of the group serve in dual roles—as helpers and as those being helped, acting as a support system for one another. Participation in groups helps members realize that they are not alone and that others are experiencing similar struggles.

Knowledge Area

Unit I—Human Development, Diversity, and Behavior in the Environment (Content Area); Human Behavior in the Social Environment (Competency); Theories of Group Development and Functioning (KSA)

145. D

Ego strength is the ability of the ego to effectively deal with the demands of the id, the superego, and reality. It is a basis for resilience and helps maintain emotional stability by coping with internal and external stress.

Both B and C are indicators of positive ego strength while getting overwhelmed by moods (D) is associated with poor, not positive, ego strength. Being silent before replying (A) is not related to ego strength, the concept being tested in this question, making it an incorrect answer.

Knowledge Area

Unit II—Assessment (Content Area); Assessment Methods and Techniques (Competency); The Indicators of Client's/Client System's Strengths and Challenges (KSA)

146. C

The cycle of abuse begins with "tension building" which leads to "battering." After the abuse, there is a "honeymoon" phase in which the perpetrator shows remorse and says that it will not happen again. This period of contrition lasts until tension begins to emerge again and ultimately leads to another incident of violence.

Knowledge Area

Unit III—Interventions With Clients/Client Systems (Content Area); Intervention Processes and Techniques (Competency); The Impact of Domestic, Intimate Partner, and Other Violence on the Helping Relationship (KSA)

147. D

Unconditional positive regard refers to nonjudgmental acceptance and support of a client's traits and behaviors, regardless of what that client does or says (D). There are no conditions placed on this acceptance, and a social worker supports a client whether he or she is expressing "good" (adaptive) behaviors and emotions or "bad" (maladaptive) ones.

Knowledge Area

Unit III—Interventions With Clients/Client Systems (Content Area); Intervention Processes and Techniques (Competency); Verbal and Nonverbal Communication Techniques (KSA)

148. C

In precontemplation, a client is unaware, unable, and/or unwilling to change. In this stage, there is the greatest resistance and lack of motivation. It can be characterized by arguing, interrupting, denial, ignoring the problem, and/or avoiding talking or thinking about it. A client may not even show up for appointments or agree that change is needed.

Precontemplation is followed by contemplation (A), preparation (D), action (B), maintenance, and relapse.

Knowledge Area

Unit II—Assessment (Content Area); Assessment Methods and Techniques (Competency); Methods to Assess Motivation, Resistance, and Readiness to Change (KSA)

149. D

The musculoskeletal system includes the bones, muscles, and joints. Words used in medicine are comprised of one or more parts—the prefix, stem (root), and suffix. "Osteo" is a stem which means bone, "tendo" is a stem which means tendon, and "myo" is a stem which means muscle. The stem "arthro" means joint. The muscular system, together with the skeletal system, form the musculoskeletal system which is responsible for the movement of the human body.

Knowledge Area

Unit II—Assessment (Content Area); Biopsychosocial History and Collateral Data (Competency); Basic Medical Terminology (KSA)

150. B

Comorbid means existing with or at the same time. In this instance, the client has both a behavioral disorder and a medical/health problem. A and D indicate that the two conditions are not affiliated or associated, which is information that is not provided in the question. Similarly, there is no information that indicates that the conditions are linked or connected with one another (C).

Knowledge Area

Unit II—Assessment (Content Area); Biopsychosocial History and Collateral Data (Competency); The Indicators of Mental and Emotional Illness Throughout the Lifespan (KSA)

151. D

The client has been drinking heavily for years and has now reported stopping. He needs medical monitoring during withdrawal to ensure that it is done safely. This may include inpatient treatment. The setting in which the social worker is employed is unclear in the case vignette. Substance abuse treatment is specialized and will ensure that the client receives the proper level of care. Providing additional supportive services to the client may be helpful during his recovery, but he needs to undergo detoxification

FIRST, which is best handled by a substance abuse agency. The social worker should facilitate the referral by making the linkage with the client and ensuring that he receives immediate assessment and treatment.

Knowledge Area

Unit III—Interventions With Clients/Client Systems (Content Area); Use of Collaborative Relationships (Competency); Consultation Approaches (e.g., Referrals to Specialists) (KSA)

152. C

Most spiritual development models move from the "egocentric" (which is present in childhood) to "conformist" to "integration" or "universal." Individuals may move along the continuum during their life course or stay at the same point. The first stage is an unwillingness to accept a will greater than one's own. The second is blind faith in spiritual beings. After questioning and skepticism, there may be the development of a deeper understanding of good and evil and enjoying the mystery of existence. Although many individuals do have blind faith, it is usually not *developed* during the life course and is not specifically associated with spirituality in older adulthood.

Knowledge Area

Unit I—Human Development, Diversity, and Behavior in the Environment (Content Area); Human Growth and Development (Competency); Theories of Spiritual Development Throughout the Lifespan (KSA)

153. D

Social workers are mandatory reporters and must not delay in reporting or investigating such an incident themselves. All suspected abuse situations should be reported to the child protection agency immediately. The social worker should not delay due to the father's reported absence.

Knowledge Area

Unit IV—Professional Relationships, Values, and Ethics (Content Area); Professional Values and Ethical Issues (Competency); Legal and/or Ethical Issues Regarding Mandatory Reporting (e.g., Abuse, Threat of Harm, Impaired Professionals, etc.) (KSA)

154. B

In contemplation, a client is ambivalent or uncertain regarding behavior change; thus, his or her behaviors are unpredictable. In this stage, a client may be willing to look at pros and cons of behavior change, but is not committed to working toward it.

It is too premature to design a behavioral program to reward steps toward change. Small steps and direct action toward change do not occur till later in the process, when preparation and action occur, respectively.

Knowledge Area

Unit II—Assessment (Content Area); Assessment Methods and Techniques (Competency); Methods to Assess Motivation, Resistance, and Readiness to Change (KSA)

155. A

In this case vignette, the couple's problem seems to have arisen as a result of differences in beliefs about gender roles. The wife believes that the husband should work outside the home and be the primary financial supporter of the household. Conversely, the husband wants to be the one to stay home with their child. The problem-solving process should focus on assisting them to explore these differences in order to make a decision with regard to this dilemma.

Knowledge Area

Unit I—Human Development, Diversity, and Behavior in the Environment (Content Area); Diversity, Social/Economic Justice, and Oppression (Competency); Gender and Gender Identity Concepts (KSA)

156. B

An advance directive (also known as an advance health care directive) refers to a number of different documents (such as a living will) intended to convey a client's preferences about health care. Some advance health care directives appoint a person to make decisions on a client's behalf when the client is unable to do so, and some give specific instructions about what kind of and under what circumstances medical care is to be provided or withheld. It is not related to the distribution of assets once a client passes away, more commonly referred to as a will or property will (B).

Knowledge Area

Unit III—Interventions With Clients/Client Systems (Content Area); Use of Collaborative Relationships (Competency); The Effects of Policies, Procedures, Regulations, and Legislation on Social Work Practice and Service Delivery (KSA)

157. B

Financial exploitation of older adults can be devastating and is frequently traced to family members, trusted friends, and caregivers. It involves taking advantage or doing acts without the consent or knowledge of victims. Obtaining a large sum of money from an older adult can be abusive if the older adult is deceived or compromises his or her own well-being by the act. However, money given from one person to another does not always need to be repaid, so this behavior may not be exploitative if the older adult understood from the onset that it was a gift.

All the rest of the acts listed involve deceit or taking action without permission of the older adult.

Knowledge Area

Unit II—Assessment (Content Area); Concepts of Abuse and Neglect (Competency); The Indicators, Dynamics, and Impact of Exploitation Across the Lifespan (e.g., Financial, Immigration Status, Sexual Trafficking) (KSA)

158. B

The relationship between drug and alcohol use and violence is complex. Although abusers of certain substances may commit violent crimes, there are many clients who engage in drug and/or alcohol abuse who are not violent. Thus, those who commit violent acts are often drug or alcohol users, but those who are abusers of substances alone are not likely to be violent. Other crimes such as driving while impaired, theft, and so on, are linked to alcohol or drug abuse.

Knowledge Area

Unit III—Interventions With Clients/Client Systems (Content Area); Indicators and Effects of Crisis and Change (Competency); The Indicators of Traumatic Stress and Violence (KSA)

159. B

Contraindication means that the medication is not recommended or safe to use. If taken, the medication could have serious consequences.

Knowledge Area

Unit II—Assessment (Content Area); Assessment Methods and Techniques (Competency); Common Psychotropic and Non-Psychotropic Prescriptions and Over-the-Counter Medications and Their Side Effects (KSA)

160. C

In families in which incest has occurred, there is a lack of appropriate boundaries and enmeshment occurs (C). Although children who have been sexually abused may engage in sexual acting out or be promiscuous in attempts to fill voids caused by poor self-esteem or insecurity, there are not tendencies in these families to engage in atypical sexual practices (A) or relaxed attitudes toward sexuality (D). Ego fusion is not having a real sense of being a separate person, but is instead a poorly defined ego structure. Ego fusion between the mother and the abused child(ren) (B) is not likely to result from incest.

Knowledge Area

Unit II—Assessment (Content Area); Concepts of Abuse and Neglect (Competency); The Effects of Physical, Sexual, and Psychological Abuse on Individuals, Families, Groups, Organizations, and Communities (KSA)

161. D

The client appears to be defining herself by her inability to make the school play. The social worker should FIRST determine why this incident is so traumatic for her. There may be other issues that are related to this "failure." Exploration of the subject will allow the social worker to determine the explicit and implicit meaning of her comments.

Knowledge Area

Unit II—Assessment (Content Area); Assessment Methods and Techniques (Competency); Methods of Involving Clients/Client Systems in Problem Identification (e.g., Gathering Collateral Information) (KSA)

162. C

In instances when social workers are not fluent in the languages spoken by their clients, qualified interpreters or translators should be used. Using the son as a translator is not acceptable because the social worker has no ability to determine if communication is being relayed appropriately or distorted due to the son's impressions or interpretations of wording. The family should not be forced to go to another agency because social workers have the ethical mandate to provide culturally competent services, which includes using qualified interpreters. Without such translation, the social worker may miss important information conveyed by the family or fail to communicate effectively with them given the social worker's lack of Spanish fluency.

Knowledge Area

Unit I—Human Development, Diversity, and Behavior in the Environment (Content Area); Diversity, Social/Economic Justice, and Oppression (Competency); The Principles of Culturally Competent Social Work Practice (KSA)

163. A

Mental illnesses sometimes run in families, suggesting that clients who have family members with mental illnesses may be somewhat more likely to develop them. Susceptibility is passed on in families through genes. However, not all clients whose parents have mental health disorders will develop them. Many mental illnesses are linked to abnormalities in many genes rather than just one or a few and how these genes interact with the environment is unique for every person.

Knowledge Area

Unit II—Assessment (Content Area); Biopsychosocial History and Collateral Data (Competency); Biopsychosocial Factors Related to Mental Health (KSA)

164. C

The Thematic Apperception Test (TAT) contains cards with black and white sketches that are ambiguous. The client is asked to create or construct a story for each one. The TAT is used to understand motivational aspects of behavior and unusual themes or plots are considered.

Knowledge Area

Unit II—Assessment (Content Area); Assessment Methods and Techniques (Competency); Techniques and Instruments Used to Assess Clients/Client Systems (KSA)

165. C

Factors that impact on group cohesion include the stability and diversity of membership, the size of the group, and the degree to which group members are empowered to establish the rules and goals of the group. Groups in which membership changes frequently and those which contain diverse membership have a greater struggle for cohesion. Smaller groups, as opposed to larger ones, tend to be more unified. Lastly, groups that are able to make key decisions with regard to their functioning have greater investment by their membership and less fragmentation than those that do not have input into these policies.

The agency setting in which a group takes place does NOT usually impact on group cohesion.

Knowledge Area

Unit I—Human Development, Diversity, and Behavior in the Environment (Content Area); Human Behavior in the Social Environment (Competency); Theories of Group Development and Functioning (KSA)

166. B

All of the response choices are related to a cognitive approach EXCEPT examination of environmental reinforcers (B). This response choice would be part of a behavior management approach that examines what external factors reward problematic behavior, regardless of a client's beliefs or thoughts about changing it.

Knowledge Area

Unit II—Assessment (Content Area); Assessment Methods and Techniques (Competency); The Factors and Processes Used in Problem Formulation (KSA)

167. A

Assessment in social work is an ongoing process. Though the social worker was in the process of terminating with the client, she may now have new needs given a change in her life circumstances. The social worker should assess whether termination is still warranted at this time (A).

Knowledge Area

Unit III—Interventions With Clients/Client Systems (Content Area); Intervention Processes and Techniques (Competency); The Indicators of Client/Client System Readiness for Termination (KSA)

168. D

The core of the helping process is the relationship between a social worker and a client. The relationship between a social worker and a client is expressed through interaction in which a social worker and client gain insight on why problems exist and how they can be solved (D).

Understanding "the rules" or parameters under which services are delivered (A) is not directly related to making changes. Problems also should not be viewed as things needing to be "fixed" (B). Change is usually incremental (C), but such recognition does not increase the likelihood that it will occur.

Knowledge Area

Unit III—Interventions With Clients/Client Systems (Content Area); Intervention Processes and Techniques (Competency); The Principles and Techniques for Building and Maintaining a Helping Relationship (KSA)

169. B

The goals of intervention and the means used to achieve these goals are incorporated in a contractual agreement between a client and a social worker. The contract (also called an intervention or service plan) may be informal or written and specifies: the problem(s) to be worked on; the goals to reduce the problem(s); client and worker roles in the process; the interventions or techniques to be employed; the means of monitoring progress; stipulations for renegotiating the contract; and the time, place, fee, and frequency of meetings.

Psychological and environmental factors that contributed to the problem are part of the assessment—not the contract.

Knowledge Area

Unit III—Interventions With Clients/Client Systems (Content Area); Intervention Processes and Techniques (Competency); The Components of Intervention, Treatment, and Service Plans (KSA)

170. C

An advance directive is a legal document that allows patients to appoint a health care representative who will act in a client's best interest when the client can no longer make decisions on his or her own. Advanced directives are accepted nationally; however, not all states use Physician Orders for Life-Sustaining Treatment (POLST). The advanced directive is a document that contains the expressed desire of clients, but it does not have the same authority as a POLST since it is not signed by a physician. The POLST document is a physician's order that health care workers must follow. It is recommended that clients have both documents.

Knowledge Area

Unit III—Interventions With Clients/Client Systems (Content Area); Use of Collaborative Relationships (Competency); The Effects of Policies, Procedures, Regulations, and Legislation on Social Work Practice and Service Delivery (KSA)

Practice Test

Evaluation of Results

These tables assist in identifying the content areas and competencies needing further study. Within each of the competencies, there are specific KSAs that social workers should reference to assist with locating appropriate study resources. As there is tremendous overlap in the material that could be contained across the KSAs within a given competency, all KSAs for the competency should be reviewed to make sure of an adequate breadth of knowledge in the content area.

The results of this evaluation should be the basis of the development of a study plan. Social workers should get to a level of comfort with the material so that they can summarize relevant content, including key concepts and terms. Social workers do not need to be experts in all of the KSAs, but should understand their relevancy to social work practice. They should be able to describe how each of the KSAs specifically impact assessment, as well as decisions about client care.

	**Analysis of Bachelors Practice Test** Unit I: Human Development, Diversity, and Behavior in the Environment (25%)
Competency	**Question Numbers**	**Number of Questions**	**Number Correct**	**Percentage Correct**	**Area Requiring Further Study?**
1. Human Growth and Development	5, 12, 17, 31, 55, 69, 78, 98, 99, 106, 127, 138, 139, 152	14	__/14	__%	
2. Human Behavior in the Social Environment	9, 24, 25, 29, 75, 77, 84, 104, 105, 108, 110, 120, 125, 141, 144, 165	16	__/16	__%	
3. Diversity, Social/ Economic Justice, and Oppression	22, 28, 35, 47, 67, 68, 72, 87, 115, 129, 130, 155, 162	13	__/13	__%	

	Analysis of Bachelors Practice Test Unit II: Assessment (29%)				
Competency	**Question Numbers**	**Number of Questions**	**Number Correct**	**Percentage Correct**	**Area Requiring Further Study?**
4. Biopsychosocial History and Collateral Data	27, 66, 71, 81, 90, 92, 100, 111, 149, 150, 163	11	__/11	__%	
5. Assessment Methods and Techniques	4, 19, 20, 21, 26, 34, 38, 51, 54, 56, 59, 65, 80, 82, 86, 88, 93, 96, 113, 123, 134, 135, 143, 145, 148, 154, 159, 161, 164, 166	30	__/30	__%	
6. Concepts of Abuse and Neglect	6, 8, 36, 39, 60, 94, 157, 160	8	__/8	__%	

Analysis of Bachelors Practice Test Unit III: Intervention With Clients/Client Systems (26%)					
Competency	Question Numbers	Number of Questions	Number Correct	Percentage Correct	Area Requiring Further Study?
7. Indicators and Effects of Crisis and Change	117, 128, 133, 158	4	__/4	__%	
8. Intervention Processes and Techniques	2, 7, 13, 15, 32, 49, 50, 52, 53, 58, 62, 64, 74, 76, 79, 83, 91, 107, 112, 119, 122, 132, 136, 140, 146, 147, 167, 168, 169	29	__/29	__%	
9. Use of Collaborative Relationships	1, 43, 46, 61, 103, 114, 151, 156, 170	9	__/9	__%	
10. Documentation	33, 109	2	__/2	__%	

Analysis of Bachelors Practice Test
Unit IV: Professional Relationships, Values, and Ethics (20%)

Competency	Question Numbers	Number of Questions	Number Correct	Percentage Correct	Area Requiring Further Study?
11. Professional Values and Ethical Issues	3, 18, 30, 37, 40, 48, 57, 63, 73, 95, 97, 102, 118, 124, 126, 153	16	—/16	—%	
12. Confidentiality	10, 14, 23, 41, 42, 70, 121, 131	8	—/8	—%	
13. Professional Development and Use of Self	11, 16, 44, 45, 85, 89, 101, 116, 137, 142	10	—/10	—%	

Overall Results of Bachelors Diagnostic Practice Test				
	Content Area	**Number of Questions**	**Number Correct**	**Percentage Correct**
Unit I (25%)	Human Development, Diversity, and Behavior in the Environment	43	__/43	__%
Unit II (29%)	Assessment	49	__/49	__%
Unit III (26%)	Interventions With Clients/ Client Systems	44	__/44	__%
Unit IV (20%)	Professional Relationships, Values, and Ethics	34	__/34	__%
Overall Knowledge	ASWB® Bachelors Examination	170	__/170	__%

Index